The Presbyterians of Ulster
1680–1730

Irish Historical Monograph Series

ISSN 1740-1097

Series editors

Marie Thérèse Flanagan, Queen's University, Belfast
Eunan O'Halpin, Trinity College, Dublin
David Hayton, Queen's University, Belfast

Previous titles in this series

The Presbyterians of Ulster
1680–1730

Robert Whan

THE BOYDELL PRESS

First published 2013
The Boydell Press, Woodbridge

ISBN 978-1-84383-872-2

The Boydell Press is an imprint of Boydell & Brewer Ltd
PO Box 9, Woodbridge, Suffolk IP12 3DF, UK
and of Boydell & Brewer Inc.
668 Mt Hope Avenue, Rochester, NY 14620–2731, USA
website: www.boydellandbrewer.com

A CIP catalogue record for this title is available from the British Library

The publisher has no responsibility for the continued existence or accuracy of URLs for external or third-party internet websites referred to in this book, and does not guarantee that any content on such websites is, or will remain, accurate or appropriate.

Printed on acid-free paper

Typeset by Fakenham Prepress Solutions, Fakenham, Norfolk NR21 8NN

Contents

Illustrations

Illustration

Cover illustration: Plasterwork ceiling at Redhall, Ballycarry, depicting
gentlefolk, c.1730 (© Robert Whan. Photographed courtesy of John McClintock)

Figures

Acknowledgements

I am grateful to the Department of Education and Learning (Northern Ireland) for providing the funding that enabled much of the research for this book to be carried out. During that research and the course of writing I have incurred many further obligations. In particular, I would like to express my thanks to the series' editor, Professor David Hayton, for his support and encouragement throughout the process, and for reading drafts of the text. Useful feedback, comments, and suggestions were also received from Dr Toby Barnard (Hertford College, Oxford), and Dr Andrew Holmes and Dr John Bergin of Queen's University, Belfast. I am also indebted to the various libraries and record offices that allowed me to consult, and now cite and quote from, their collections. Most of these are listed in the bibliography but others not listed there, that I made use of, include the Area Local Studies Collection, Ballymena Central Library; the Carnegie Library, Ayr; the Institute of Historical Research, London; Local Studies, South Eastern Education and Library Board Headquarters, Ballynahinch and Downpatrick; and the National Portrait Gallery, London. Others who assisted with, or answered queries and questions relating to, aspects of the book that I would particularly like to thank include: Jennifer Dickson, librarian of the Presbyterian Historical Society of Ireland, her predecessors Alan McMillan and Bob Bonar, and successor, Valerie Adams; Donald Garvie of Union Theological College Library, Belfast; the Very Rev. Dr Godfrey Brown; Brenda Collins, Research Officer, Irish Linen Centre, Lisburn; the Dunleath family, Ballywalter; Julian Armstrong; Kate Morrill; Asuka Gamo of Glasgow University Library, Special Collections; Diarmuid Kennedy of Queen's University Library, Special Collections; the McClintock family, Ballycarry; Joe McLaughlin, Archivist and Rare Books Curator at the University of Ulster; Professor Laurence Brockliss of Oxford University; the Very Rev. William McMillan; Rev. Nigel Playfair of First (Non-Subscribing) Presbyterian Church, Rosemary Street, Belfast; Rev. Dr David Steers; and Professor M. A. Stewart. Finally, I would like to thank all those at Boydell Press that have been involved with seeing the book through to publication, which has been made possible by a grant from the Scouloudi Foundation in association with the Institute of Historical Research.

The publication of this book has been made possible by a grant from The Scouloudi Foundation in association with the Institute of Historical Research.

Abbreviations

Abp	Archbishop
Add. MS(S)	Additional Manuscript(s)
Agnew, *Belfast funeral register*	Jean Agnew (ed.), *Funeral register of the First Presbyterian Church of Belfast* (Belfast, 1995)
Agnew, *Merchant families*	Jean Agnew, *Belfast merchant families in the seventeenth century* (Dublin, 1996)
Antrim Pby Lib.	Antrim Presbytery Library, held at McClay Library, Queen's University, Belfast, Special Collections
Bailie, *Hist. of congns*	W. D. Bailie (ed.), *A history of congregations in the Presbyterian Church in Ireland 1610–1982* (Belfast, 1982)
Ballynahinch accounts	Ballynahinch Presbyterian Church account of collections and disbursements, 1704–34 (http://freepages.genealogy.rootsweb.ancestry.com/~rosdavies/ WORDS/BallynahinchPresbyDisburse.htm) (12 Jan. 2013)
Ballynahinch testimonials	Ballynahinch Presbyterian Church record of certificates and testimonials, 1715–34 (http://freepages.genealogy.rootsweb.ancestry.com/~rosdavies/ WORDS/BallynahinchPresbTestimonials.htm) (12 Jan. 2013)
Barkley, 'History of the eldership'	J. M. Barkley, 'A history of the ruling eldership in Irish Presbyterianism' (2 vols, M.A. thesis, QUB, 1952)
Barnard, *New anatomy*	Toby Barnard, *A new anatomy of Ireland: the Irish Protestants, 1649–1770* (London, 2003)
Benn, *Belfast*	George Benn, *A history of the town of Belfast* (London, 1877)
BL	British Library
Bp	Bishop
Bull. PHSI	*Bulletin of the Presbyterian Historical Society of Ireland*
corp. mins	corporation minutes
CSPD	*Calendar of State Papers, Domestic*
DIB	James McGuire and James Quinn (eds), *Dictionary of Irish Biography* (Cambridge, 2009) (The online version has been used throughout, and can be accessed at: http://dib.cambridge.org)
DNB	Leslie Stephen, Sidney Lee and Stephen Lee (eds), *Dictionary of national biography* (63 vols, London, 1885–1900)
GUA	Glasgow University Archive Services
GUL	Glasgow University Library
HIP	E. M. Johnston-Liik, *History of the Irish Parliament 1692–1800* (6 vols, Belfast, 2002)
HMC	Historical Manuscripts Commission
[Kirkpatrick], *Presby. loyalty*	[James Kirkpatrick], *An historical essay upon the loyalty of Presbyterians in Great-Britain and Ireland …* ([Belfast], 1713)

LHL	Linen Hall Library, Belfast
Lib.	Library
McConnell, *Fasti*	James McConnell, *Fasti of the Irish Presbyterian Church*, rev. S. G. McConnell, ed. F. J. Paul and David Stewart (Belfast, 1951)
MS(S)	Manuscript(s)
Munimenta alme Universitatis Glasguensis	*Munimenta alme Universitatis Glasguensis: records of the University of Glasgow* ... (4 vols, Glasgow, 1854)
NAI	National Archives of Ireland, Dublin
NAS	National Archives of Scotland, Edinburgh
n.d.	no date
NLI	National Library of Ireland, Dublin
NLS	National Library of Scotland, Edinburgh
ODNB	H. C. G. Matthew and B. H. Harrison (eds), *Oxford dictionary of national biography* (61 vols, Oxford, 2004) (The online version has been used throughout, and can be accessed at: http://www.oxforddnb.com)
Pby mins	Presbytery minutes
PHS	Presbyterian Historical Society, Belfast
PRONI	Public Record Office of Northern Ireland, Belfast
QUB	Queen's University, Belfast
RCPI	Royal College of Physicians of Ireland, Dublin
Reid, *Hist. of PCI*	J. S. Reid, *History of the Presbyterian Church in Ireland* (2nd ed., 3 vols, London, 1853), ed. W. D. Killen
RGSU	*Records of the General Synod of Ulster, from 1691 to 1820* (3 vols, Belfast, 1890–98)
sess. mins	session minutes
TCD	Trinity College, Dublin
UJA	*Ulster Journal of Archaeology*
UTC	Gamble Library, Union Theological College, Belfast
Witherow, *Hist. & lit. memls*	Thomas Witherow, *Historical and literary memorials of Presbyterianism in Ireland (1623–1800)* (2 vols, London, 1879–80)
Wod. Fol.	Wodrow Manuscripts Folio
Wod. Lett.	Wodrow Manuscripts Letters
Wodrow, *Analecta*	Robert Wodrow, *Analecta* ..., ed. M[atthew] L[eishman] (4 vols, Glasgow, 1842–3)
Wodrow, *Corresp.*	Robert Wodrow, *The correspondence of Rev. Robert Wodrow*, ed. Thomas McCrie (3 vols, Edinburgh, 1842–43)
Young, *Belfast town book*	R. M. Young (ed.), *The town book of the corporation of Belfast, 1613–1816* (Belfast, 1892)
Young, *Fighters of Derry*	W. R. Young, *Fighters of Derry* (London, 1932)
Young, *Historical notices of old Belfast*	R. M. Young, *Historical notices of old Belfast and its vicinity* (Belfast, 1896)

Editorial note

Unless otherwise stated, all dates are given in Old Style, although the year is taken to begin on 1 January, rather than 25 March, which in this period was still the formal convention. In quotations from contemporary sources, though, original spelling has been retained, capitalisation has been normalised and abbreviations, thorns and ampersands have been extended. Where more than one variant of a proper name exists, for example, Butle/Buttle, Mairs/Mears/Meres, McCartney/Macartney, etc., one has been chosen and used consistently throughout the book.

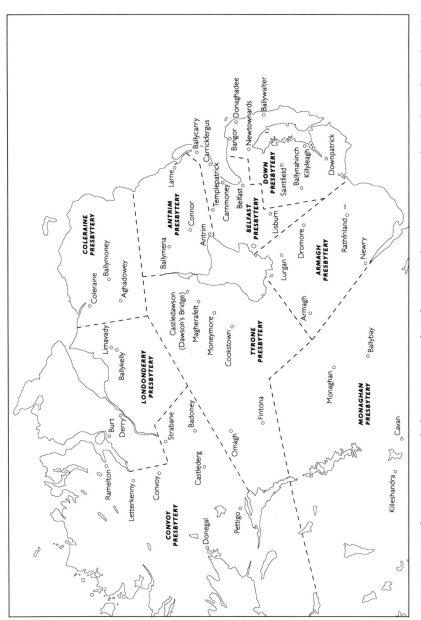

Map 1: Map showing principal places mentioned in the text and approximate presbytery boundaries (1704)

Introduction

Presbyterianism came to Ulster with the arrival of Scottish settlers in the seventeenth century. By 1700 Presbyterians formed more than half of Ulster's Protestants[1] and were the dominant confessional group in Counties Antrim and Down, as well as in certain parishes of Londonderry.[2] Despite this we know far less about the Presbyterian community than we do about the Anglican Protestants of Ireland. The social structure and material culture of Irish Protestants have been examined by Toby Barnard in his *New anatomy of Ireland* and *Making the grand figure*.[3] Barnard's work, however, focuses on Anglicans rather than the entire spectrum of Protestantism, and as he himself admits Ulster, particularly its Presbyterian society, is under-represented.[4] This book will correct this significant gap in Irish historiography by looking at the Presbyterian community in Ulster and the degree to which it provided an alternative Protestant society in Ireland.

To date, scholarly study of seventeenth- and eighteenth-century Ulster Presbyterianism has focused chiefly on the arrival of Presbyterianism in the early seventeenth century or the involvement of Presbyterians in the United Irish movement at the end of the eighteenth century.[5] In contrast, the period from 1680 to 1730, with the exception of denominational historians interested in the Subscription Controversy of 1719 to 1726, has been largely ignored by historians. Yet, it was a significant, and defining, period in Presbyterian history. For Finlay Holmes, 1690 marked the 'end of the beginning of Irish Presbyterian history' and both Raymond Gillespie and Richard Greaves have demonstrated how in the three decades after 1660 the Presbyterian church reached maturity and had become a sustainable and viable denomination.[6] The 1690s witnessed the last, and largest,

---

1   John Abernethy, *Scarce and valuable tracts and sermons* (London, 1751), p. 61; Liam Kennedy and Philip Ollerenshaw (eds), *Ulster since 1600: politics, economy and society* (Oxford, 2013), pp 70, 78.
2   'State of the dioceses of Down and Connor', 1693 (PRONI, Armagh Diocesan Records, DIO/4/5/3, no. 23); Bp King to Bp Nicolson, 1 Aug. 1718 (BL, Add. MS 6116, no. 88); George Hill, *An historical account of the MacDonnells of Antrim* (Belfast, 1873), pp 378, 380–2, 388.
3   Barnard, *New anatomy*; idem, *Making the grand figure: lives and possessions in Ireland, 1641–1770* (London, 2004).
4   Barnard, *New anatomy*, p. vii.
5   Key texts on the Plantation include: Raymond Gillespie, *Colonial Ulster: the settlement of east Ulster 1600–1641* (Cork, 1985); P. S. Robinson, *The Plantation of Ulster: British settlement in an Irish landscape 1600–1670* (Dublin, 1984; repr. Belfast, 1994); and Jonathan Bardon, *The Plantation of Ulster: the British colonisation of the north of Ireland in the seventeenth century* (Dublin, 2011). Important works on the role of Presbyterians in the United Irish movement are: A. T. Q. Stewart, *A deeper silence: the hidden origins of the United Irishmen* (Belfast, 1993); idem, *The narrow ground: aspects of Ulster 1609–1969* (Belfast, 1999); and I. R. McBride, *Scripture politics: Ulster Presbyterians and Irish radicalism in the late eighteenth century* (Oxford, 1998).
6   R. F. G. Holmes, *Our Irish Presbyterian heritage* ([Belfast], 1985), p. 55; Raymond Gillespie, 'The Presbyterian revolution in Ulster, 1660–1690' in W. J. Shiels and Diana Wood (eds), *The churches, Ireland and the Irish* (Oxford, 1989), pp 159–70; R. L. Greaves, *God's other children: Protestant Nonconformists and the emergence of denominational churches in Ireland, 1660–1700* (Stanford, 1997), pp 2–3, 382–3.

wave of Scottish immigration into Ulster, as Scots fled successive poor harvests and famine.[7] As Gillespie has written, 'the enduring legacy of seventeenth-century Ulster' and its 'distinctive Scottish tinge' was 'forged not in the first half of the [seventeenth] century but in the second'.[8] The flow of migrants from Scotland died away in the early 1700s and was replaced from 1718 by large-scale emigration from Ulster to the American colonies.[9] The end of our period also witnessed the church's first major doctrinal controversy over confessional subscription. This resulted in Ulster Presbyterianism being fractured along doctrinal and, to some extent, social lines.[10]

Historiography and sources

The first history of Presbyterians in Ulster was written in the seventeenth century itself.[11] It was not, however, until the middle of the nineteenth century that Presbyterian histories based on archival research began to appear. The first major historian was J. S. Reid, whose three-volume history, completed by W. D. Killen, remains the standard and most detailed study of the Irish Presbyterian church.[12] It provided a chronological history of the denomination and was able to use some sources that have since been lost. Its only drawback was that, like much of the general historical writing of the period, partisanship was occasionally displayed.

The focus of the study of Ulster Presbyterianism has moved from traditional ecclesiastical and institutional history towards a greater concentration on religious ideas and, more recently, popular belief and practice. Intellectual and theological developments have been well covered. Peter Brooke has demonstrated how the Presbyterians formed a distinct political and intellectual community in the north of Ireland.[13] Phil Kilroy considered the theological controversies between Presbyterians and Anglicans and studied the theological disputes of the period.[14] Church historians, too, have been interested in theological disputes, but have tended to focus on internal debates within Presbyterianism. For the early eighteenth

[7] Gillespie, 'Presbyterian revolution', p. 169; T. C. Smout, et al., 'Scottish emigration in the seventeenth and eighteenth centuries' in Nicholas Canny (ed.), *Europeans on the move: studies on European migration, 1500–1800* (Oxford, 1994), p. 85; William Macafee and Valerie Morgan, 'Population in Ulster, 1660–1760' in Peter Roebuck (ed.), *Plantation to Partition* (Belfast, 1981), pp 57–8.

[8] Raymond Gillespie, 'The world of Andrew Rowan: economy and society in Restoration Antrim' in Brenda Collins, et al., (eds), *Industry, trade and people in Ireland, 1650–1950* (Belfast, 2005), pp 10–11.

[9] R. J. Dickson, *Ulster emigration to Colonial America, 1718–1775* (London, 1966).

[10] Robert Allen, 'The principle of nonsubscription to creeds and confessions of faith as exemplified in Irish Presbyterian history' (2 vols, Ph.D. thesis, QUB, 1944), i; McBride, *Scripture politics*, p. 8.

[11] Patrick Adair, *A true narrative of the rise and progress of the Presbyterian Church in Ireland*, ed. W. D. Killen (Belfast, 1866). Although this was not published until 1866 it was written by Adair before his death which occurred c.1694.

[12] Reid, *Hist. of PCI*.

[13] Peter Brooke, *Ulster Presbyterianism: the historical perspective 1610–1970* (Dublin, 1987).

[14] Phil Kilroy, *Protestant Dissent and controversy in Ireland 1660–1714* (Cork, 1994), pp 171–203.

century this has meant the Subscription Controversy, which has been chronicled and written about by Robert Allen, William McMillan and Godfrey Brown.[15] The first historian to focus on Presbyterian worship was J. M. Barkley. During the 1950s and 1960s he wrote about the practice of the Lord's Supper in Presbyterian congregations and completed a study of the eldership, which involved much discussion of the relationship between the session and congregation and the practice of church discipline. In 1993 he published an article on Presbyterian marriage.[16] Barkley's consideration of Presbyterian worship, however, focused on public and corporate worship rather than 'popular' and private devotion and it has only been from the 1990s that historians such as Gillespie and Greaves for the late seventeenth and early eighteenth centuries, and Andrew Holmes for a later period, have considered private belief and practice.[17] A statistical study of Presbyterian discipline was completed by Roisín Browne in 1999.[18]

A clause added to an act of 1704 obliged everyone who held public office in Ireland to take communion in the established church. J. C. Beckett considered the relationship between Irish Presbyterians and the government during the period between the reign of James II and the repeal of this clause in 1780.[19] Much historiographical debate has centred on the sacramental test. Though the formulation and introduction of the test is largely agreed on,[20] historians have taken diverging

---

[15] Allen, 'Principle of nonsubscription'; William McMillan, 'The Subscription Controversy in Irish Presbyterianism from the Plantation of Ulster to the present day; with reference to political implications in the late eighteenth century' (2 vols, M.A. thesis, Univ. of Manchester, 1959); A. W. G. Brown, 'Irish Presbyterian theology in the early eighteenth century' (Ph.D. thesis, QUB, 1977); idem, 'A theological interpretation of the first Subscription Controversy (1719–1728)' in J. L. M. Haire, et al., *Challenge and conflict: essays in Irish Presbyterian history and doctrine* (Antrim, 1981), pp 28–45.

[16] J. M. Barkley, 'The evidence of old Irish session-books on the sacrament of the Lord's Supper', *Church Service Society Annual*, no. 22 (May 1952), pp 24–34; idem, *The eldership in Irish Presbyterianism* ([Belfast], 1963); idem, *A short history of the Presbyterian Church in Ireland* (Belfast, [1959]); idem, 'Marriage and the Presbyterian tradition', *Ulster Folklife*, xxxix (1993), pp 29–40.

[17] Raymond Gillespie, '"Into another intensity": prayer in Irish nonconformity, 1650–1700' in Kevin Herlihy (ed.), *The religion of Irish Dissent 1650–1800* (Blackrock, Co. Dublin, 1996), pp 31–47; Raymond Gillespie, *Devoted people: belief and religion in early modern Ireland* (Manchester, 1997); idem, '"A good and godly exercise": singing the Word in Irish Dissent, 1660–1701' in Kevin Herlihy (ed.), *Propagating the word of Irish Dissent 1650–1800* (Dublin, 1998), pp 24–45; Greaves, *God's other children*, pp 215–48; A. R. Holmes, *The shaping of Ulster Presbyterian belief and practice 1770–1840* (Oxford, 2006).

[18] R. M. Browne, 'Kirk and community: Ulster Presbyterian society, 1640–1740' (M.Phil. thesis, QUB, 1999). This is, to date, also the only work with a sustained attempt to consider the issue of gender and Ulster Presbyterianism during the late seventeenth and early eighteenth centuries. Gender is considered for the early seventeenth century in Mary O'Dowd, *A history of women in Ireland, 1500–1800* (Harlow, 2005), pp 169–74, 187–8, 249–50, and briefly for the late eighteenth and early nineteenth centuries in Holmes, *The shaping of Ulster Presbyterian belief*, pp 224–5, 296–303. Leanne Calvert, a Ph.D. student at QUB, is currently completing a thesis on Gender and the Ulster Presbyterian community, 1780–1844. Though there will not be a separate chapter on gender in this present work, where possible, throughout the body of the text specifically gender or female issues, and occupations, will be flagged up as appropriate.

[19] J. C. Beckett, *Protestant Dissent in Ireland 1687–1780* (London, 1948).

[20] Beckett, *Protestant Dissent*, pp 43–6; J. G. Simms, 'The making of a penal law (2 Anne, c. 6), 1703–4', *Irish Historical Studies*, xii (1960), pp 105–18.

views on the impact it had on Ulster Presbyterian political life.[21] Jean Agnew and David Hayton have undertaken a more precise analysis of its impact on Ulster corporations, but we still do not know its impact on the magistracy.[22]

Much of the research hitherto undertaken has dealt with the religious and intellectual, or aspects of the political, life of the Presbyterians and a social study of the Presbyterian community, in contrast, is lacking. Although John Nelson and Agnew have considered Belfast and its mercantile families[23] there is much that has yet to be done for Ulster as a whole. Patrick Griffin has made some attempt to look at late Stuart and early Hanoverian Presbyterian society in Ulster, but his approach and some of his conclusions are different from my own.[24]

This study has not been able to avail of a single collection of documentary evidence and it has been necessary to undertake a varied archival trail and piece together a range of disparate sources. There is the general problem of early modern records with their inevitable bias towards the upper social strata and the literate, as well as the particular defects of Irish sources as a result of the bombardment of the Irish Public Record Office in 1922. Although there were over 100 congregations only twelve session records, of varying quality, are known to exist which cover at least part of the period between 1680 and 1730, though, fortuitously, this is a greater survival rate than for the mid or late eighteenth century.[25] As well as congregational records I have made use of the records of the higher courts of the church which survive for six presbyteries, one sub-synod and the General Synod of Ulster.[26] In addition, there are diaries, autobiographies, manuscript and printed

---

[21] Beckett, *Protestant Dissent*, pp 143–4; S. J. Connolly, *Religion, law, and power: the making of Protestant Ireland 1660–1760* (Oxford, 1995), p. 163; Jonathan Bardon, *A history of Ulster* (new ed., Belfast, 2001), p. 173; T. C. Barnard, 'The government and Irish Dissent, 1704–1780' in Kevin Herlihy (ed.), *The politics of Irish Dissent 1650–1800* (Dublin, 1997), pp 9–27.

[22] Agnew, *Merchant families*, pp 76–104; D. W. Hayton, 'Exclusion, conformity, & parliamentary representation: the impact of the sacramental test on Irish Dissenting politics' in Kevin Herlihy (ed.), *The politics of Irish Dissent 1650–1800* (Dublin, 1997), pp 52–73.

[23] J. W. Nelson, 'The Belfast Presbyterians 1670–1830: an analysis of their political and social interests' (Ph.D. thesis, QUB, 1985); Agnew, *Merchant families*.

[24] Patrick Griffin, 'Defining the limits of Britishness: the "new" British history and the meaning of the Revolution Settlement in Ireland for Ulster's Presbyterians', *Journal of British Studies*, xxxix (2000), pp 263–87; idem, *The people with no name: Ireland's Ulster Scots, America's Scots Irish, and the creation of a British Atlantic world, 1689–1764* (Princeton, 2001), pp 9–97.

[25] Session records exist for Armagh, 1707–28; Aghadowey, 1702–61; Ballycarry, 1704–80; Burt, 1676–1719; Carnmoney, 1686–1748; Connor, 1693, 1699–1735; Dawson's Bridge, 1703–29; Drumbo, 1701–1734; Kirkdonald (Dundonald), 1678–1713; Larne and Kilwaughter, 1699–1701, 1720–69; Lisburn, 1688–1763; and Templepatrick, 1646–60, 1670, 1688–1743. Burt session minutes, which were until recently held at Union Theological College, Belfast, are currently missing and were unavailable during the time when research for this book was undertaken. For some idea of the material contained in the Burt minutes see K. M. Middleton, 'Religious revolution and social crisis in southwest Scotland and Ulster, 1687–1714' (Ph.D. thesis, TCD, 2010), which makes extensive use of them. The original Drumbo session minutes are currently lost, but extracts from them can be found in Barkley, 'History of the eldership', ii, 134–41; C. I. Reid, *The past revisited: a history of Drumbo Presbyterian Church* (Banbridge, 1992), pp 23–4, 26; and among the papers of Rev. David Stewart (PRONI, D1759/1/D/1). All that remains in the Armagh and Dundonald session books are essentially accounts, baptismal and marriage records.

[26] Presbytery records exist for the presbyteries of Antrim, 1654–8, 1671–75, 1683–91, 1697–1713;

sermons, religious tracts, official and private correspondence, petitions and political pamphlets, university records and the archives of professional bodies such as the Inns of Court and the Irish Royal College of Physicians.

Demographic and economic background

In a pre-census age there is no way of accurately measuring the population of Ulster in this period and historical demographers have reached different conclusions from the scanty documentation available.[27] Unlike the Irish Catholics, who were counted across the kingdom between 1731 and 1733, only occasional local surveys reveal the number of Presbyterians in select areas.[28] In 1672 the statistician William Petty estimated the population of Ireland to be around 1.1 million, of which 800,000 were Roman Catholics, 100,000 Anglicans, 100,000 Scottish Presbyterians and 100,000 non-Catholic Dissenters of other traditions.[29] These figures, which are suspiciously 'round', are no more reliable than any other early modern statistics and the number of Scottish families in Ireland is likely to have been exaggerated as a result of Anglican anxieties and paranoia. Jonathan Bardon has suggested that by 1714 there were about 200,000 Presbyterians in Ulster out of a total population of 600,000 in the province.[30] Rev. John Abernethy, the Presbyterian minister of Antrim and later Dublin, writing in the early 1730s, suggested that there were 216,000 Presbyterians in Ulster, though thousands had emigrated to America during the previous decade and a half.[31]

Within Ulster, the Presbyterian church was strongest in Counties Antrim, Down, Londonderry and east Donegal (the latter area known as the Laggan). It was also well represented in Armagh and Tyrone, and later in Monaghan. Presbyterianism was not restricted to Ulster but was also present in the rest of Ireland where it was much more thinly represented and confined largely to urban centres such as Dublin, Cork, Limerick, Sligo, Tipperary and Waterford. The Presbyterians in southern Ireland were more influenced by English than Scottish traditions and were not as tightly organised as the congregations in Ulster. Several

Laggan, 1672–1700; Route, 1701–06; Monaghan, 1702–12; Strabane, 1717–40; and Killyleagh, 1725–32. The only surviving sub-synod records are for Derry, 1706–36. Records of the General Synod, which survive for 1691–92, 1694, and continuously from 1697, have been published.

[27] Significant articles on the population of Ulster and Ireland are: L. M. Cullen, 'Population trends in eighteenth-century Ireland', *Economic and Social Review*, vi (1975), pp 149–65; Macafee & Morgan, 'Population in Ulster', pp 46–63; Stuart Daultrey, *et al.*, 'Eighteenth century Irish population: new perspectives from old sources', *Journal of Economic History*, xli (1981), pp 601–28; David Dickson, *et al.*, 'Hearth tax, household size and Irish population change 1672–1821', *Proceedings of the Royal Irish Academy*, lxxxii (1982), sect. C, pp 125–81.

[28] Lists of masters of families in Co. Tyrone, c.1692 (PRONI, Groves papers, T808/15118); religious census of Sir John Rawdon's estates, Moira, Co. Down, 1716 (Huntington Library, Hastings papers, HAM Box 75, folder 32); notes on the numbers of Protestants, Dissenters and Catholics, early 18th century (ibid., HAM Box 75, folder 36); lists of inhabitants according to their religion, 17th century (ibid., HAM Box 79, folder 9); list of householders in Cary barony, Co. Antrim, including their religious denomination, 1734 (PRONI, Groves papers, T808/14905).

[29] William Petty, *Sir William Petty's political survey of Ireland* (2nd ed., London, 1719), pp 8–9.

[30] Jonathan Bardon, *Belfast: an illustrated history* (Dundonald, 1982), p. 31.

[31] Abernethy, *Scarce & valuable tracts*, p. 61.

of the southern congregations had started as Independent or Congregational and had evolved into Presbyterian.[32] There were doctrinal differences between the northern and southern congregations. Communion was celebrated less frequently in Ulster and while the Dublin ministers were prepared to introduce hymns into worship services, the Ulster Presbyterians refused to sanction anything other than the use of the metrical psalms.[33] Presbyterians of English ancestry were also much more likely than their Scottish counterparts to conform, at least occasionally, to the established church.[34] Historians such as Kilroy, Gillespie and Greaves have made the distinctions between the English and Scottish Presbyterians in Ireland clearer than older histories which tended to look solely at one while largely ignoring the other, or else clump them together and treat them, inaccurately, as a single uniform group.[35] A union between congregations in Leinster and Munster in 1696 formed the 'Presbytery of Munster' and the Presbyterian ministers in Dublin joined with this presbytery to form the 'Southern Association'. The Synod of Ulster, however, began to set up congregations outside the geographical province of Ulster and so there were ministers and congregations outside Ulster that were connected to their brethren in the north. Barkley described the links between the Ulster and southern congregations as 'indeterminate and uncertain'.[36] The creation of new congregations outside Ulster, however, sometimes aroused the hostility of Anglicans, as was the case, for instance, at Drogheda in 1708 and Belturbet in 1712.[37]

The Presbyterian presence in Ulster was massively reinforced by immigration in the 1690s. Despite the establishment of Presbyterianism as the official church of Scotland in 1690, Scottish Presbyterians migrated into the north of Ireland in large numbers during the following decade. After the Williamite War refugees returned and landlords, with rentals in arrears, offered low rents and reduced entry fines to attract tenants on to their land. The numbers immigrating increased in the late 1690s as a result of poor harvests and famine conditions which occurred in Scotland from 1695 to 1698.[38] The migration to Ulster involved some people

---

[32] Wodrow, Analecta, i, 206; Finlay Holmes, The Presbyterian Church in Ireland: a popular history (Blackrock, Co. Dublin, 2000), pp 52–3.

[33] Joseph Boyse, Remarks on a late discourse of William Lord Bishop of Derry; concerning the inventions of men in the worship of God (Dublin, 1694), pp 135–6; Raymond Gillespie, 'Dissenters and Nonconformists, 1661–1700' in Kevin Herlihy (ed.), The Irish Dissenting tradition 1650–1750 (Blackrock, Co. Dublin, 1995), pp 24–6; idem, '"A good & godly exercise"', pp 24–45; A. W. G. Brown, The great Mr. Boyse: a study of the Reverend Joseph Boyse minister of Wood Street Church, Dublin 1683–1728 ([Belfast], 1988), pp 5, 7. When the minister of Francis St., Dublin, joined the General Synod of Ulster in 1704 it was recorded in the synod minutes, 'they now receive the sacrament [of communion] after our way of administration': RGSU, i, 77.

[34] List of the nobility and gentry of Ulster (Lambeth Palace Lib., Gibson papers, MS 1742, f. 56).

[35] Kilroy, Protestant Dissent, pp 15–29, 35–52; Greaves, God's other children, pp 160–2; Gillespie, 'Dissenters & Nonconformists', pp 18, 25–6.

[36] Barkley, Short history, p. 25.

[37] Reid, Hist. of PCI, iii, 55–7, 84–7; Dermot Foley, 'Presbyterianism in Drogheda, 1652–1827', Journal of the County Louth Archaeological and Historical Society, xxv (2002), pp 181–3; Eoin Magennis, 'Belturbet, Cahans and two Presbyterian revolutions in south Ulster, 1660–1770', Seanchas Ardmhacha: Journal of the Armagh Diocesan Historical Society, xxi–xxii (2007/8), pp 133, 139–42.

[38] Samuel Eyre to [Sir William Trumbull?], 12 May 1695 (HMC, Downshire MSS, i, pt 1, 468);

from England and a few from Wales, but the majority came from Scotland, particularly the Lowlands and the south-west.[39] Although a sizeable number of Highland Catholics settled in north County Antrim, most of the immigrants were Presbyterian.[40] Various estimates of the numbers involved in the immigration of the 1690s have been suggested, ranging from 40,000 to 80,000.[41] The increase in the number of Presbyterians in Ulster, as a result both of the new arrivals and natural increase, was reflected in the changing organisation of the church. Existing congregations were strengthened and new congregations formed. Between 1690 and 1711, 32 new congregations were established, 22 of them since 1700, and by 1720 another 17 had been set up.[42] The number of Presbyterian ministers connected to the Presbyterian church in Ulster rose from 86 in 1689 to over 130 in the early eighteenth century.[43] In 1697 the five presbyteries attached to the Synod of Ulster were increased to seven and split between two sub-synods. Five years later, in 1702, the congregations were again rearranged to make nine presbyteries and three sub-synods.[44]

By the 1690s Antrim and Down were already heavily settled and many of the newcomers who entered through the port of Derry settled in such areas as the Foyle Valley, other areas of Londonderry, and also Tyrone and parts of east Donegal, where previous settlements had been quite sparse.[45] County Monaghan witnessed a huge increase in the number of inhabitants of British origin in the seventy years

R. G. Gillespie (ed.), *Settlement and survival on an Ulster estate: the Brownlow leasebook 1667–1711* (Belfast, 1988), pp xviii, xxi–xxii, liv; William Macafee, 'The colonisation of the Maghera region of south Derry during the seventeenth and eighteenth centuries' in *Ulster Folklife*, xxiii (1977), pp 70, 76–8; idem & Morgan, 'Population in Ulster', pp 53, 56–8; Smout, *et al.*, 'Scottish emigration', p. 86; T. C. Smout, 'Famine and famine-relief in Scotland' in L. M. Cullen and T. C. Smout (eds), *Comparative aspects of Scottish and Irish economic and social history 1600–1900* (Edinburgh, [1977]), pp 23–4; B. A. Vann, ' "Space of time or distance of place": Presbyterian diffusion in south-western Scotland and Ulster, 1603–1690' (Ph.D. thesis, Univ. of Glasgow, 2006), pp 15, 51–52; K. J. Cullen, *Famine in Scotland: the 'ill years' of the 1690s* (Edinburgh, 2010).

[39] Alan Gailey, 'The Scots element in north Irish popular culture', *Ethnologia Europaea*, viii (1975), p. 3; W. H. Crawford, 'The social structure of Ulster in the eighteenth century' in L. M. Cullen and François Furet (eds), *Ireland and France 17th–20th centuries: towards a comparative study of rural history* (Paris, 1980), p. 120.

[40] John Richardson, *A short history of the attempts that have been made to convert the popish natives of Ireland, to the establish'd religion* (London, 1712), pp 101–2; James Duchal, *A sermon on occasion of the ... death of the late Reverend Mr. John Abernethy ...* (Dublin, 1741), p. 16.

[41] 'The Scots in Ireland, 1697' (Senate House Lib., Univ. of London, Chalmers papers, MS 30, ff 11–12); Bp Synge to Abp Wake, 22 Mar. 1715/16 (BL, Add. MS 6117, no. 19); Abp King to Abp Wake, 24 Mar. 1715[/16] (TCD, King papers, MS 2533/165); Bp Evans to Abp Wake, 30 Apr. 1717 (Christ Church, Oxford, Wake papers, xii: microfilm, Institute of Historical Research Library, London, XR.129/16); Smout, *et al.*, 'Scottish emigration', p. 88; Macafee, 'Colonisation of the Maghera region', p. 76; David Dickson, *New foundations: Ireland 1660–1800* (2nd ed., Dublin, 2000), p. 48.

[42] Beckett, *Protestant Dissent*, p. 109.

[43] W. H. Crawford, 'Economy and society in eighteenth century Ulster' (Ph.D. thesis, QUB, 1982), p. 23.

[44] *RGSU*, i, 23–4, 57–9.

[45] Finlay Holmes, 'The Scots' in Patrick Loughrey (ed.), *The people of Ireland* (Dublin, 1988), p. 103; Gillespie, *Settlement & survival*, p. xviii.

after 1660.[46] The only Presbyterian congregation to exist in any organised form in Counties Cavan and Monaghan before 1690 was at Killeshandra, but others followed at Monaghan town in 1697, Ballybay in 1698, Stonebridge in 1700, Breaky in 1703, Drum in 1704, Glennan in 1713, Bailieborough in 1714, and at Cootehill and Ballyjamesduff (Oldcastle) in 1721. Some of those who settled in Monaghan and Cavan were 'second-phase settlers'. Presbyterian farmers from the north-east, for instance, moved into the 'frontier' parish of Creggan which straddles the Armagh, Monaghan and Louth borders, and those who settled around Mullyash Mountain had come from Scotland to County Down before moving into County Monaghan.[47]

The late seventeenth and early eighteenth centuries were a time of significant mobility within Ulster. The survival of testimonials received by Presbyterian sessions allows some insight into internal migration. Testimonials were issued to anyone who left a congregation and were inspected before the holder could be admitted to another. From the names of the congregations from which they came or the name of the ministers supplying the testimonials it is possible to locate where the bearers came from. Of the 325 testimonials received by Ballynahinch congregation, in County Down, between 1715 and 1734, 142 were from single men, 127 from single women, 27 from couples and 19 from families.[48] The single travellers were probably moving to obtain work as labourers or servants. Similar data has been analysed for Carnmoney congregation by Bob Bonar.[49] In both cases most of the movement was short-distance, from an adjacent parish or within a radius of twenty or thirty miles, but occasionally some travelled much further. Scottish immigration declined by the second decade of the eighteenth century but did not cease completely. At Carnmoney testimonials were received from twenty-two individuals from Scotland and four Scottish families between 1708 and 1725, while at Ballynahinch ten testimonials were received from Scots between 1715 and 1734 and a further eight Scots were given poor relief between 1714 and 1726.[50] Scottish immigration declined as a result of improved conditions in Scotland, rising rents in Ulster and the growing appeal of America.[51]

By the second decade of the eighteenth century competition for land in Ulster

[46] K. A. Miller, Arnold Schrier, B. D. Boling and D. N. Doyle, *Irish immigrants in the land of Canaan: letters and memoirs from Colonial and Revolutionary America, 1675–1815* (Oxford, 2003), pp 666, 668–9.

[47] Thomas Hall, 'The history of Presbyterianism in east Cavan: and a small portion of Meath and Monaghan' (typescript in UTC), p. 67; John Donaldson, *The barony of Upper Fews in the county of Armagh* (1838; repr. Crossmaglen, 1993), pp 11, 13–14; L. T. Brown, 'The Presbyterians of Cavan and Monaghan: an immigrant community in south Ulster over three centuries' (2 vols, Ph.D. thesis, QUB, 1986), i, 57–60; J. B. A. Bell, *A history of Garmany's Grove Presbyterian Church* ([Newry], 1970), p. 11.

[48] Ballynahinch testimonials.

[49] R. H. Bonar, *Nigh on three and a half centuries: a history of Carnmoney Presbyterian Church* (Newtownabbey, 2004), pp 298–9, 318–19.

[50] Ibid., p. 299; Ballynahinch testimonials, 1715–34; Ballynahinch accounts, 2 Mar., 20 Apr., 11 & 25 May, 1 June, 20 July, 14 Sept. 1712, 19 Sept., 10 Oct. 1714, 18 Dec. 1718, 19 Mar. 1721, 13 Jan. 1723, 20 Feb. 1726.

[51] Macafee & Morgan, 'Population in Ulster', p. 59.

increased and as leases began to fall in landlords increased the rents. Poor harvests between 1716 and 1723 and again in 1727 and 1728 made it impossible for many to afford the increased rents. There was a temporary recession in the linen industry in 1718 and 1729 and, though economic reasons were in many cases probably more important, the religious difficulties experienced by the Presbyterians, who formed the majority of emigrants, may have motivated some to leave for the American colonies. In addition to the restrictions created by the test clause Presbyterians were obliged, at least formally, to pay tithes to the Church of Ireland, their marriages could be challenged in the ecclesiastical courts, and it was illegal for Presbyterians to maintain their own schools.[52] When Rev. James McGregor of Aghadowey preached his farewell sermon in 1718 he cited as reasons for his emigration his desire to 'avoid oppression and cruel bondage' and 'to have an opportunity of worshipping God, according to the dictates of conscience and the rules of his inspired Word'.[53] Though religious persecution was an additional factor, the peaks of emigration coincided with periods of food shortage and economic depression in 1718–20 and 1728–9. Another stimulus to emigration was given by information provided by emigrant letters and from propaganda issued by shipping owners and emigration agents.[54] In 1717 the Belfast Presbyterian printer James Blow published a pamphlet extolling the virtues of Carolina, in which the cheapness and availability of land was especially emphasised.[55] The assisted immigration provided by the indentured servant system made it possible for thousands to go who otherwise would not have been able.[56] The specific numbers of those who emigrated is unknown, but the

---

[52] The principal studies of the emigration of 1718–29 and its causes are: Dickson, *Ulster emigration*, pp 1–47; Audrey Lockhart, *Some aspects of emigration from Ireland to the North American colonies between 1660 and 1775* (New York, 1976); S. S. Warnock, 'Ulster emigration to Colonial America 1718–30; the formative years' (M.A. thesis, National University of Ireland, Galway, 1997). Graeme Kirkham, 'Ulster emigration to North America, 1680–1720' in H. T. Blethen and C. W. Wood (eds), *Ulster and North America: transatlantic perspectives on the Scotch-Irish* (Tuscaloosa, 1997), pp 76–117; Graeme Kirkham, 'The origins of mass emigration from Ireland' in Richard Kearney (ed.), *Migrations: the Irish at home and abroad* (Dublin, 1990), pp 81–90; Desmond McCourt, 'County Derry and New England: the Scotch Irish migration of 1718' in Gerard O'Brien (ed.), *Derry and Londonderry: history and society* (Dublin, 1999), pp 303–20; and Griffin, *People with no name*, pp 65–97. See also R. K. McMaster, *Scotch-Irish merchants in Colonial America* ([Belfast], 2009), pp 1–9, 27–30.
[53] E. L. Parker, *The history of Londonderry, comprising the towns of Derry and Londonderry, N. H.* (Boston, 1851), p. 34.
[54] James Kelly, 'Harvests and hardship: famine and scarcity in Ireland in the late 1720s', *Studia Hibernica*, no. 26 (1992), pp 83, 92; letter of James Murray to Rev. Baptist Boyd, 27 Oct. 1737 (PRONI, T1809/1); Hugh Boulter to the duke of Newcastle, 23 Nov. 1728 (Hugh Boulter, *Letters written by his excellency Hugh Boulter* (2 vols, Oxford, 1769–70), i, 260–61); 'Reports of the justices of the north west circuit on the emigration from the north of Ireland to America', 1729 (PRONI, Transcripts of State Papers relating to Ireland, T659/1, pp 75–6).
[55] *An historical description of Carolina north and south being an account of its discovery, settlement, and progress; its climate, soil, situation, productions, trade, and commerce* (Belfast, 1717).
[56] Hugh Boulter to the duke of Newcastle, 23 Nov. 1728 (Boulter, *Letters*, i, 261); McCourt, 'County Derry', p. 307. According to one New Hampshire merchant, the trade in Irish servants could render 'abbetter acct. than aney other imployment I can folow': Archibald Macphaedris to James & Robert Wilson, 28 Aug. 1718 (Baker Library, Harvard Univ., Macpheadris and Warner papers, MSS: 766, no. 2).

emigration of 1718–20 and 1728–30 was enough to concern government authorities not only in Britain and Ireland but also America.[57]

The late Stuart period was one of rapid economic change in Ulster. Whereas early in the seventeenth century exports had been based on pastoral farming, agricultural exports by the late seventeenth century had diversified into processed goods such as butter and barrelled beef. In the countryside domestic industry, particularly the production of linen cloth which was manufactured not only for domestic consumption but also, increasingly, for the market, offered people a subsidiary occupation.[58] The period, however, was not equally prosperous for all parts of Ulster and there were regional variations. Older port towns, such as Carrickfergus, were eclipsed by newer creations, such as Belfast, and some inland market towns established during the Plantation, like Lurgan, developed and prospered. The west of the province suffered from its distance from Belfast, the main Ulster port, and from the lack of economic stimulus from merchants seeking agricultural products for export. Though Derry was the second port in Ulster its merchants operated only as far as Strabane and did not have as much influence as their Belfast counterparts, who maintained a large hinterland including not only Lisburn and the Lagan Valley but also Dromore, Lurgan and Rathfriland.[59] In November 1704 Coleraine corporation complained to Queen Anne of a great decay in their trade and five years later Derry corporation found it necessary to buy wheat for the poor inhabitants of the city.[60]

Theological context

The late seventeenth and eighteenth centuries in Britain and Europe were a period of intellectual enquiry and theological turbulence. There was a growing tension between supporters of traditional orthodox Protestantism and those of a more liberal spirit. The latter were strongly suspected of unorthodoxy in relation to the doctrine of the Trinity, and even of harbouring the heresies of Arianism and Socinianism. Arianism represented Christ as a subordinate deity to God the Father and Socinianism denied both Christ's divinity and his pre-existence. Influenced by the scientific work of figures such as Newton, the period was marked by a new trust in reason, rather than revelation, as the only sufficient test of truth.[61] Key

---

[57] Warnock, 'Ulster Emigration', pp 67–84. For a summary of the differing views of historians on the number of emigrants from Ulster, see Patrick Fitzgerald and Brian Lambkin, *Migration in Irish history, 1607–2007* (Basingstoke, 2008), pp 123–4.

[58] Raymond Gillespie, *The transformation of the Irish economy 1550–1700* ([Dublin], 1991); idem, *Settlement & survival*, pp xiii, xxv–xxviii. W. H. Crawford, 'The Ulster Irish in the eighteenth century', *Ulster Folklife*, xxviii (1982), p. 28. Crawford has written extensively on the development of the linen industry in Ulster; see, for instance, his *The impact of the domestic linen industry in Ulster* (Belfast, 2005).

[59] Gillespie, *Settlement & survival*, pp xxiii, xxv, lx–lxiii.

[60] Coleraine corp. mins (PRONI, LA/25/2/AA/1A, pp 230–1); Derry corp. mins (ibid., LA/79/2/ AA/3A, p. 140).

[61] G. R. Cragg, *The church and the age of reason 1648–1789* (London, 1990); David Hempton, *The church in the long eighteenth century* (London, 2011), pp 107–27; H. T. Dickinson (ed.), *A companion to eighteenth-century Britain* (Oxford, 2006), pp 232–3, 266–7; McMillan, 'Subscription

individuals among the proponents of the new ideas in England were John Toland, Samuel Clarke and Benjamin Hoadly. Toland was born in County Donegal in 1676 and at the age of sixteen rejected his Catholic upbringing. Supported by Presbyterian sponsors who hoped he would become a minister, Toland attended Redcastle School in Londonderry and subsequently studied at the universities of Glasgow and Edinburgh. In 1695 he anonymously published his famous work *Christianity not mysterious*, in which he argued that no tenets of Christianity could be contrary to or above human reason, for if they were they would be unintelligible. Samuel Clarke, an Anglican cleric, published his sceptical *Scripture doctrine of the Trinity* in 1712, which was distinctly Arian. Benjamin Hoadly, who held three Anglican bishoprics in succession, denied the divine nature of his office and of the church itself and in his famous sermon of 1717, *The nature of the kingdom or church of Christ*, advocated private judgement over ecclesiastical authority.[62] Debates on the question of the Trinity occurred at Exeter among the Independents in 1718 and in the following year when the ministers of the three principal Protestant Dissenting denominations in London and the surrounding districts – Presbyterians, Independents and Baptists – met at Salters' Hall they split over subscription to Trinitarianism.[63] In Geneva subscription to human tests of faith was abolished in 1706 and the new ideas also had an impact in Scotland. In 1714 John Simson, professor of divinity at Glasgow, was tried before the General Assembly for teaching Arian and Pelagian errors, but only censured in 1717 for 'imprudent expressions'. In 1729 he was finally suspended from his teaching duties as a result of his views.[64]

Presbyterians in Ulster were not immune from these new ideas. In 1718 Francis Hutcheson, the philosopher, wrote from Dublin to a friend in Scotland, William Wright of Kilmarnock, about 'a perfect Hoadly mania among our younger ministers in the north' and stated that 'Dr Clarks book I'm sufficiently informed has made several unfixed in their old principles, if not intirely altered them'.[65] The Synod of Ulster in 1698, following the example of the Presbyterian Church of Scotland, enacted that 'young men, when licens'd to preach, be oblidged to subscribe the [Westminster] Confession of Faith, in all the articles thereof, as the confession of their faith'. This was not rigorously enforced at first but in 1705, in the wake of the trial and conviction of Thomas Emlyn, a Presbyterian minister in Dublin, for denying the divinity of Christ, the Synod of Ulster re-enacted the law of 1698 and extended it to cover any 'who are licens'd and have not subscrib'd' who were to 'be

Controversy', pp 62–5; John Spurr, *English Puritanism 1603–1689* (Basingstoke, 1998), p. 168; R. K. Webb, 'The emergence of rational Dissent' in Knud Haakonssen (ed.), *Enlightenment and religion: rational Dissent in eighteenth-century Britain* (Cambridge, 1996), pp 12–41.

62 *ODNB* (Toland, John), (Clarke, Samuel (1675–1729)), (Hoadly, Benjamin (1676–1761)).

63 Dickinson, *Companion to eighteenth-century Britain*, p. 244; McMillan, 'Subscription Controversy', pp 90–6; Cragg, *The church & reason*, p. 137. For an outline of the controversy in England, see Roger Thomas, 'The Non-Subscription Controversy among Dissenters in 1719: the Salters' Hall debate', *Journal of Ecclesiastical History*, iv (1953), pp 162–86.

64 *ODNB* (Simson, John); Anne Skoczylas, *Mr Simson's knotty case: divinity, politics, and due process in early eighteenth-century Scotland* (London, 2001).

65 'Francis Hutcheson to William Wright' quoted in letter from William Wright to Robert Wodrow, 27 Sept. 1718 (NLS, Wod. Lett. Qu., xx, f. 228).

oblig'd to subscribe before their being ordain'd'.[66] In 1705 Rev. John Abernethy of Antrim and Rev. James Kirkpatrick of Belfast formed what became the 'Belfast Society'. This was an association of ministers, licentiates, and a few laymen, who met periodically to listen to sermons, review books and discuss theological questions.[67] It helped sharpen the intellect of its members and it was from this group that the nucleus of the later Non-Subscribers, who refused to subscribe to the *Westminster Confession*, came. Between 1704 and the granting of the act of toleration in 1719 Irish Presbyterians were engaged in a discussion about the terms upon which to seek a legal toleration. Some thought that only total acceptance of the *Westminster Confession of Faith* would be satisfactory, while others were prepared to draw up an alternative formula of a briefer nature.[68]

The spark that lit the so-called Ulster Subscription Controversy was related to an issue of church order rather than theology. Abernethy was not satisfied when the General Synod decided in 1718 to move him from Antrim to Usher's Quay in Dublin. After spending only three months in Dublin he returned to Antrim in defiance of the synod's instruction. In December 1719 he preached a sermon before the Belfast Society which was a doctrinal justification for his act of disobedience. It was based on Romans 14:5 – 'Let every man be fully persuaded in his own mind' – and was published in spring 1720 under the title *Religious obedience based on personal persuasion*. Abernethy made a strong plea for the rights of individual conscience and insisted that Christian doctrines could not be imposed by ecclesiastical authority but could only be accepted by personal conviction.[69] His conflict was not so much with the substance of the *Westminster Confession*, but rather with the right of church courts to compel professions of belief.[70] A minority of ministers who were against subscription to man-made creeds supported Abernethy and a controversy that lasted from 1719 to 1726 was carried on with much bitterness not only in the church courts but also at public meetings, and in more than fifty publications, of various sizes, that were issued in connexion with the debates.[71] The ministers split into three groups: those willing to subscribe to the *Westminster Confession*, known as Subscribers; Non-Subscribers; and Moderates who sought a compromise between the other two groups. Eventually in 1725 a rearrangement of the presbyteries by the synod placed the non-subscribing ministers and their congregations into a separate presbytery, the Presbytery of Antrim, which in the following year was formally excluded from

[66] *RGSU*, i, 22, 30, 34, 73, 100.
[67] 'Circular letter of December 7 1720', *A narrative of the proceedings of seven General Synods* (Belfast, 1727), p. 20; Duchal, *Sermon on the death of Reverend John Abernethy*, pp 36–40.
[68] William Campbell, MS 'Sketches of the history of Presbyterians in Ireland' (1803), pp 173–4, 193–7 (PHS).
[69] *RGSU*, i, 458–64, 471, 476–7, 488–94, 506; John Abernethy, *Religious obedience founded on personal persuasion. A sermon preach'd at Belfast the 9th of December. 1719* (Belfast, 1720); M. A. Stewart, 'Abating bigotry and hot zeal' in Damian Smyth (ed.), *Francis Hutcheson*: suppt. to *Fortnight*, no. 308 (1992).
[70] Ian McBride, 'Ulster Presbyterians and the confessional state, c.1688–1733' in D. G. Boyce, Robert Eccleshall and Vincent Geoghegan (eds), *Political discourse in seventeenth- and eighteenth-century Ireland* (Basingstoke, 2001), p. 184.
[71] *A narrative of the seven General Synods*; Nelson, 'Belfast Presbyterians', pp 123, 128.

the Synod of Ulster.[72] With the exception of the Covenanters, who had existed in small numbers since the mid seventeenth century,[73] the Presbyterians in Ulster had until 1726 been united, but as a result of the Subscription Controversy two separate Presbyterian denominations were created in Ulster. Though the Non-Subscribers were orthodox with regard to the Trinity, with a few possible exceptions such as Rev. Samuel Haliday of First Belfast, their writings and sermons had a distinctive style and tone.[74] In particular they placed less emphasis on the traditional Calvinist doctrine of predestination. When Francis Hutcheson, who became associated with 'New Light' and moderate views, preached his first sermon as a probationer minister one of the members of the congregation complained to Hutcheson's orthodox father that the sermon was 'aboot a gude and benevolent God' instead of 'the gude, auld, comfortable doctrines of election, reprobation, original sin, and fa[i]th'.[75]

* * * * * * *

This book will construct a social profile of Ulster Presbyterianism, in a period characterised by social and economic change, and political conflict between Anglicans and Presbyterians. To date, the only social group among Presbyterians to have received attention from historians is, unsurprisingly, the ministry, and many congregational histories are essentially the history of their ministers. Ministers, however, were only one component of Presbyterian society and I will seek to correct the traditional historiography by considering who these other, numerically more significant but historiographically neglected, figures were and what they contributed to the religious and political life of the Presbyterian church in Ulster. Social groups to be considered are the ministers, gentry, merchants, legal and medical professionals, as well as servants, craftsmen and the Presbyterian poor. Early modern Irish society was a complex series of overlapping layers. It was not unusual for merchants or leading professionals, for instance, to be drawn from the gentry. I have tried to make distinctions where possible but some individuals inevitably fit simultaneously into more than one group.

I will explore how the Presbyterian community operated in Ulster and ask where power lay in Presbyterian society. In addition, I will examine what being a member

---

[72] RGSU, ii, 96, 104–5, 108–9. The ministers of the newly created Non-Subscribing Presbytery of Antrim in 1725 were: John Abernethy, Antrim; Michael Bruce, Holywood; Josias Clugston, Larne; Samuel Haliday, First Belfast; Samuel Harper, Moira; John Henderson, Duneane; James Kirkpatrick, Second Belfast; John Mears, Newtownards; Thomas Shaw, Ahoghill; William Taylor, Cairncastle; and Thomas Wilson, Ballyclare. Rev. John Elder of Aghadowey, Rev. Thomas Nevin of Downpatrick and Rev. Patrick Simpson of Dundalk joined the excluded Presbytery of Antrim in 1726. Rev. Alexander Colvill of Dromore joined the Presbytery of Antrim in 1730.

[73] For further information on the Covenanters and their early history see, Robert Allen, 'Scottish ecclesiastical influence upon Irish Presbyterianism from the Non-Subscription Controversy to the union of the synods' (M.A. thesis, QUB, 1940), pp 209–51; Adam Loughridge, The Covenanters in Ireland: a history of the Reformed Presbyterian Church in Ireland (Belfast, 1984); Greaves, God's other children, pp 205–14; and William Roulston, 'The origins of the Reformed Presbyterian Church of Ireland with some comments on its records', Familia, no. 24 (2008), pp 86–94.

[74] Brown, 'A theological interpretation of the Subscription Controversy', pp 37–8.

[75] James Stuart, Historical memoirs of the city of Armagh (Newry, 1819), pp 488–9.

of the Presbyterian community involved and how this may have varied according to social background. It will also be necessary to consider how the social and economic profile of Presbyterianism changed during the fifty years between 1680 and 1730. Finally, while many recognise and acknowledge the link between Scotland and Ulster much of what has been stated by historians in regard to it has been vague or speculative, and though some historians, notably L. M. Cullen and T. C. Smout, have explored the social and economic similarities and differences between the two countries,[76] research on the importance of the religious links has barely begun. Throughout the following chapters I will therefore examine connexions between Ulster and Scotland in all their various facets: familial, educational, commercial and religious.

It will never be possible to retrieve a full picture of Presbyterianism and Presbyterians in this period, as too many records are lost, but it would be a disservice not to try, and more can certainly be done than previous historians have been able to demonstrate. By the end it is hoped that a clearer and more composite picture of Ulster Presbyterian society will emerge.

---

[76] L. M. Cullen and T. C. Smout (eds), *Comparative aspects of Scottish and Irish economic and social history 1600–1900* (Edinburgh, [1977]).

1

Ministers

The ministry is undoubtedly the social group that has been best covered in the historiography of Ulster Presbyterianism. The ministers who served in the period 1640 to 1690 have been surveyed by Barry Vann, and those from 1690 to the end of the nineteenth century by Kevin Conway, while J. M. Barkley has provided a brief sociological description of the ministers in eighteenth-century Ireland, and K. D. Brown has concentrated on ministers who operated in the nineteenth century.[1] The purpose of this chapter is to construct a prosopographical and analytical portrait of the ministers who were active in the province of Ulster during the period 1680 to 1729.[2] As such, it will focus on the ministry as a whole rather than a few exceptional individuals. It will consider the ministers' origins in terms of geographical, social and academic background, as well as their role within the church, how they obtained and spent their income, and their status within the community. The intention is to produce an overview of the main characteristics and features of the Presbyterian ministry of Ulster in the period 1680–1729, and also to make progress towards obtaining answers to such vital questions as the precise connexion of Ulster Presbyterianism with Scotland and the degree to which the Presbyterian ministry had a corporate identity and role within late seventeenth- and early eighteenth-century Ulster society.

This analysis of the lives and careers of the ministers operating in Ulster Presbyterian congregations at this time actually covers a period of over a century and a half, since some of the ministers who were active in the decade before the Williamite War had been born during the reign of James I, while those ordained in the 1720s lived on well into the eighteenth century. I will also consider the impact on the church of the change in composition of the ministry, from the generation that had lived through the depositions of 1661 and the Scottish 'Killing Times' of the 1680s, to the new generation of younger ministers who replaced them in the

---

[1]   B. A. Vann, '"Space of time or distance of place": Presbyterian diffusion in south-western Scotland and Ulster, 1603–1690' (Ph.D. thesis, Univ. of Glasgow, 2006); idem, 'Presbyterian social ties and mobility in the Irish Sea culture area, 1610–1690', *Journal of Historical Sociology*, xviii (2005), pp 245–9; K. P. Conway, 'The Presbyterian ministry of Ulster in the eighteenth and nineteenth centuries' (Ph.D. thesis, QUB, 1997); J. M. Barkley, 'The Presbyterian minister in eighteenth-century Ireland' in J. L. M. Haire, *et al.*, *Challenge and conflict: essays in Irish Presbyterian history and doctrine* (Antrim, 1981), pp 48–50; K. D. Brown, 'Life after death? A preliminary survey of the Irish Presbyterian ministry in the nineteenth century', *Irish Economic and Social History*, xxii (1995), pp 49–63. Previously there was also W. M. Barbour, 'The ministry of the Presbyterian Church in Ireland' (Ph.D. thesis, QUB, 1965); and R. L. Greaves, *God's other children: Protestant Nonconformists and the emergence of denominational churches in Ireland, 1660–1700* (Stanford, 1997), pp 176–7, briefly considers the characteristics of the 169 ministers who served in Ireland from the Restoration to the mid-1690s.

[2]   The focus is on the province of Ulster rather than the area covered by the General Synod of Ulster (which had ministers in Dublin and the south and west of Ireland who were affiliated to it).

early decades of the eighteenth century. Data on the lives of ministers has been gathered chiefly from McConnell's *Fasti*, which provides skeletal biographies of most of them,[3] supplemented by material gleaned from other sources.[4] In total at least 303 ministers were employed by Presbyterian congregations in Ulster during the period 1680 to 1729, though the number of ministers operating at any one time increased as the number of Presbyterian congregations in Ulster grew. In 1689 Ireland had 86 Presbyterian ministers and 90 congregations, most of which were located in Ulster.[5] By 1725 almost 135 Presbyterian ministers were active in Ulster alone.[6]

I. Geographical and social background

The geographical origins of 265 (87%) of the 303 ministers who were active in the period can be identified, and are displayed in Figure 1. Overall the largest

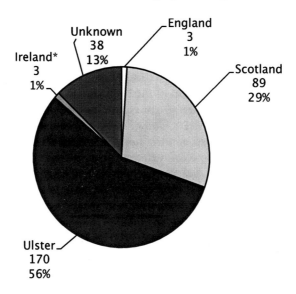

Figure 1   Geographical origins of the ministers who served in Ulster Presbyterian
congregations during the period 1680–1729
* = Province not specified.

[3]   McConnell, *Fasti*, pp 4–180. Not all the ministers active in Ulster during the period are included. For example, the *Fasti* does not contain any information on Rev. James Chrystie (minister of Badony, 1690–1708), Rev. Josias Clugston (minister of Larne and Kilwaughter, 1717–75), Rev. Thomas Harvey, jr (minister of Moville, 1715–47), or Rev. Francis Laird (Donoughmore, Co. Donegal, 1709–42).
[4]   Ministerial card index (PHS); Hew Scott, *Fasti Ecclesiae Scoticanae* (new ed., 7 vols, Edinburgh, 1915–28); Bailie, *Hist. of congns*; Witherow, *Hist. & lit. memls*; Aston Robertson, MS 'History of Irish Presbyterian congregations', c.1935 (QUB, Allen collection, MS 23, Box 1 – uncatalogued); ODNB; and various congregational histories.
[5]   Patrick Griffin, *The people with no name: Ireland's Ulster Scots, America's Scots Irish, and the creation of a British Atlantic world, 1689–1764* (Oxford, 2001), p. 21.
[6]   RGSU, ii, 82–4.

contingent was those born in Ulster. As Figure 1 shows 56% (170) were born in Ulster compared to 29% (89) born in Scotland.

Figure 1 deals with the period as a whole, but a closer look at the statistics (as shown in Table 1) shows that ministerial provision from Scotland declined in the period 1680–1729.

Table 1   Table showing the geographical origins of the ministers who served in Ulster Presbyterian congregations during the period 1680–1729

Decade ordained/ received:	1640– 1649	1650– 1659	1660– 1669	1670– 1679	1680– 1689	1690– 1699	1700– 1709	1710– 1719	1720– 1729
Ulster	1	2	1	7	9	32	45	44	29
Ireland*	–	–	–	–	1	1	–	1	–
Scotland	6	24	11	20	11	9	6	1	1
England	–	–	–	1	1	–	1	–	–
Unknown	–	1	1	3	3	9	8	8	5

* = Province not specified.

Before 1680 most Presbyterian ministers in Ulster were Scotsmen. During the decade beginning in 1680, however, Scotland and Ulster contributed ministers to the Presbyterian church in Ulster in almost equal numbers, and after the setting up of the General Synod of Ulster in 1690 the number of ministers from Scotland began a sharp downward trend. This decline can be explained not only by the expansion of the Presbyterian community in Ulster itself but also by the fact that, in the aftermath of the Revolution, the newly re-established Presbyterian Church of Scotland needed all available ministers, and probably more, to fill charges vacated by the Episcopalians, especially since many of the Presbyterian ministers ejected in the Restoration period there had died before 1690. Scotland was probably also appealing because life would have been easier for ministers in a country where Presbyterianism was the officially established church. Of course many of the Presbyterian ministers from Ulster had Scottish parents or grandparents. Evidence of this is provided by the descriptions of nationality contained in the matriculation and graduation albums of Edinburgh and Glasgow Universities, with many of the Ulster-born ministers educated there being designated as 'Scoto-Hibernus', that is, Ulster-Scots.[7]

England was never at any time important for recruitment to Presbyterian congregations in Ulster. In fact only three of the 303 ministers are known to

[7] A catalogue of the graduates in the Faculties of Arts, Divinity, and Law, of the University of Edinburgh, since its foundation (Edinburgh, 1858); Munimenta alme Universitatis Glasguensis, iii. Descriptions of nationality were more common in the Glasgow than the Edinburgh records, though, occasionally the same individual can be found with two different labels. In total 596 students of Irish origin studied at Glasgow, 1680–1730, i.e. 14.36% of the total new students entering Glasgow: A. D. G. Steers, '"New Light" thinking and non-subscription amongst Protestant Dissenters in England and Ireland in the early 18th century and their relationship with Glasgow University and Scotland' (Ph.D. thesis, Glasgow Univ., 2006), pp 289–93. The 596 students comprised 426 designated 'Scoto-Hibernus', 102 'Hibernus', 55 'Anglo-Hibernus', 7 'Hiberno-Scotus', 3 'Dubliniensis', 2 'Cambro-Hibernus' and 1 'Gallo-Hibernus'.

have originated from the English nonconformist community. They were Thomas Cobham, minister of Dundonald and Holywood; Thomas Jackson, a nephew of the Dublin minister Rev. Joseph Boyse, who was born in Leeds and served as minister of Downpatrick from 1700 to 1708; and Fulk White, minister of Broughshane (1687–1716). The Whites owned 'considerable property' in the West Riding of Yorkshire, but following their financial ruin as a result of their support of the Royalist cause during the English Civil War, Fulk, along with his brother (who later set up as a merchant in Belfast), emigrated to Ireland and settled in County Antrim around 1650.[8] A number of Huguenots also emigrated to Britain and Ireland, particularly after the Revocation of the Edict of Nantes in 1685, and Rev. Charles Lynd, who was minister of his native Fannet (Fanad) and Rathmullan, and later at Coleraine, was apparently descended from one of the French Protestant families who had taken refuge in Ireland.[9]

Within Ireland itself it was from the nine counties of Ulster that the majority of the 303 ministers were supplied and this is hardly surprising given that Presbyterians were concentrated in the province, particularly on the eastern side. Figure 2 shows the county origins of the Ulster-born ministers.

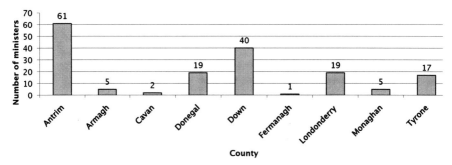

Figure 2   County origins of the ministers born in Ulster
(Chart does not include Rev. Samuel Hemphill (d. 1741), whose county origin (probably Monaghan or Cavan) is not known though he was a native of Ulster.)

Ministerial recruitment from within Ulster reflected the pattern of Scottish settlement over the course of the seventeenth century. From the time of the Plantation of Ulster Presbyterian settlement had been concentrated in the two eastern counties and it is therefore not at all unexpected to find that between them Counties Antrim and Down supplied 59% (101) of the ministers known to have been born in Ulster. From the early eighteenth century, Presbyterians were, however, moving westwards and 'Scots were displacing not only Catholics but also Anglicans from the more fertile lands in areas of previously English-dominated

---

8   Mortimer Durand, *The life of Field-Marshal Sir George White* (2 vols, Edinburgh, 1915), i, 2–4; 'Presbyterian Historical Society', *Irish Presbyterian*, xxii, no. 2 (1916), p. 27; Agnew, *Merchant families*, pp 250–1.
9   Reid, *Hist. of PCI*, iii, p. 132, n. 29.

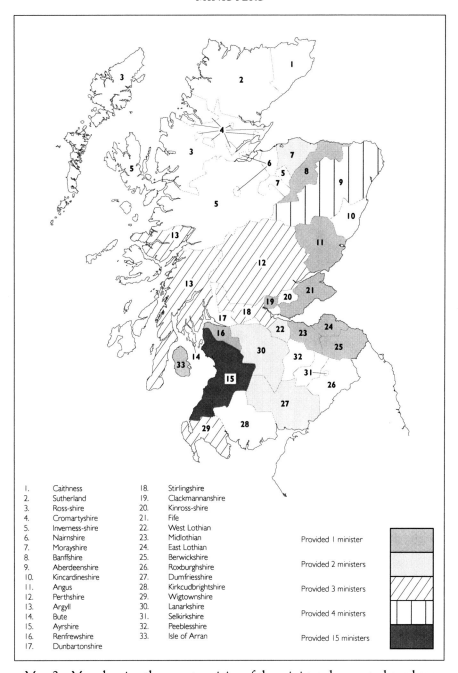

Map 2   Map showing the county origins of the ministers known to have been born in Scotland

1.	Caithness	18.	Stirlingshire
2.	Sutherland	19.	Clackmannanshire
3.	Ross-shire	20.	Kinross-shire
4.	Cromartyshire	21.	Fife
5.	Inverness-shire	22.	West Lothian
6.	Nairnshire	23.	Midlothian
7.	Morayshire	24.	East Lothian
8.	Banffshire	25.	Berwickshire
9.	Aberdeenshire	26.	Roxburghshire
10.	Kincardineshire	27.	Dumfriesshire
11.	Angus	28.	Kirkcudbrightshire
12.	Perthshire	29.	Wigtownshire
13.	Argyll	30.	Lanarkshire
14.	Bute	31.	Selkirkshire
15.	Ayrshire	32.	Peeblesshire
16.	Renfrewshire	33.	Isle of Arran
17.	Dunbartonshire		

Provided 1 minister

Provided 2 ministers

Provided 3 ministers

Provided 4 ministers

Provided 15 ministers

settlement such as Londonderry, Tyrone, and east Donegal'.[10] These three counties of Londonderry, Tyrone and Donegal each supplied around ten per cent of the ministers who came from Ulster. In contrast Presbyterianism had never developed as a strong force in Cavan and Fermanagh, and these counties were of little importance with regard to ministerial provision, with County Cavan supplying only two ministers and Fermanagh one.

Of the 88 ministers who are known to have been born in Scotland, the precise birthplace is known for just over half of them. As is shown in Map 2, the majority came from the south west of Scotland, particularly Ayrshire, which provided 15 of the 303 ministers.

The 303 ministers can be further characterised by their social background, which can be determined according to the occupation of their fathers. Unfortunately the sources are defective on this point and what can be found out gives no more than a vague picture. Of the 74 ministers whose social background is known, 62 were the sons of ministers, four came from gentry families, three were the sons of colonels, three the sons of merchants, one the son of a captain, and one the son of a farmer. Thus over a fifth of the ministers who served in an Ulster Presbyterian congregation during this period were 'sons of the manse'. It was not uncommon for sons to choose their father's trade or profession and this was by no means peculiar to the Presbyterian ministry, or indeed to the clerical profession.[11] In the late seventeenth and early eighteenth century over a third of all Lutheran clergymen in German territories were the sons of pastors and in the years between 1680 and 1740 the proportion in Sweden was between 40 and 45 per cent.[12] Of the 303 Presbyterian ministers under consideration as many as 39 had at least one brother who was a minister and 17 were the grandsons of ministers. In fact almost half (150) had at least one relation who was also a minister. A number of clerical dynasties were in existence or being formed in this period, including the Maclaines, Kennedys and, most famously, the Bruces.[13]

[10] S. J. Connolly, *Religion, law, and power: the making of Protestant Ireland 1660–1760* (Oxford, 1995), p. 170.

[11] Brown, 'Life after death?', p. 51; Jeremy Gregory, *Restoration, reformation and reform, 1660–1828: archbishops of Canterbury and their diocese* (Oxford, 2000), p. 76; Ian Whyte, 'Ministers and society in Scotland 1560–c1800' in Colin MacLean and Kenneth Veitch (eds), *Scottish life and society: religion* (Edinburgh, 2006), pp 434–6; Geoffrey Holmes, *Augustan England: professions, state and society, 1680–1730* (London, 1982), pp 107–8, 208; P. J. Corfield, *Power and the professions in Britain 1700–1850* (London, 1995), pp 228–9; Rosemary O'Day, *The professions in early modern England, 1450–1800: servants of the commonweal* (Harlow, 2000), p. 80.

[12] A. R. Holmes, 'The Protestant clergies in the European world' in S. J. Brown and Timothy Tackett (eds), *The Cambridge history of Christianity: iv: Enlightenment, reawakening and revolution 1660–1815* (Cambridge, 2006), pp 111–12.

[13] Rev. Archibald Maclaine, son of Rev. Alexander Maclaine of Kilmaglass, Argyllshire (1652–60), was minister of Markethill, County Armagh, 1700–34. He had four sons who were all ministers and his two daughters both married ministers. Rev. Gilbert Kennedy was minister of Dundonald and Holywood (1670–98), while his brother Rev. Thomas Kennedy was minister at Donoughmore (Carland), County Tyrone (1646–1716). Gilbert's son and grandson, both called Gilbert, were ministers and his daughter married Rev. William Tennant, founder of the famous Log College in America. Rev. Thomas Kennedy of Donoughmore had two sons, John and Thomas, who were both ministers and in this line the family were represented as ministers within

Sons of the manse were never in the majority, however, forming only a fifth of the total ministers active in the period. The Presbyterian ministry was a relatively open social group, in that men from outside the clerical profession could enter the service of the church. The fact that information on the social background of the majority of the ministers has not survived hints that their fathers may have been from lower down the social order. In this respect, the centrality of agriculture to the early modern Irish economy would suggest that many might have been from farming backgrounds. The costs of education need not have been a deterrent because presbyteries offered financial assistance to talented youths in penurious circumstances.[14]

II. Education and training

The Presbyterian church in Ulster placed much emphasis on maintaining an educated ministry. In September 1691 the Synod of Ulster enacted that candidates for the ministry be graduates.[15] The synod showed its willingness to enforce conformity to this act when in the following year it refused to ratify the call of Maghera congregation to John Thomb until he had first gone over to Scotland 'for lauriation'.[16] In 1702 it was further decreed that only those who had studied divinity for four years after their graduation could be entered on trials for the ministry.[17] As a result of these acts of 1691 and 1702 the Presbyterian church in Ulster had arguably one of the best educated ministries of any non-established church in the British Isles, or indeed in Europe.[18]

Education would have begun in local schools where reading, writing and possibly arithmetic were taught. Unfortunately very little is known about popular education in Ulster.[19] The Act of Uniformity of 1665 forbade schoolmasters from teaching unless they had obtained a licence from the Church of Ireland and the Presbyterians complained to Queen Anne that it was:

> ... a great grievance to us, that the education of our youth is extreamly discourag'd by our being depriv'd in many places of the liberty of entertaining common school-masters of our own persuasion ... And even many of those who teach only to read and write in country parishes are prohibited and prosecuted, to the great prejudice of children, and discouragement of parents, who are conscientiously concern'd for their education.[20]

the Presbyterian Church in Ireland until the second decade of the twentieth century when Rev. Gilbert Alexander Kennedy, the great-great-grandson of Rev. Thomas Kennedy of Donoughmore, died in 1916. For the Bruces see, Classon Porter, *The seven Bruces: Presbyterian ministers in Ireland in six successive generations* (Belfast, 1885).

14 See below, pp 27–8, 190–1.
15 *RGSU*, i, 6.
16 Ibid., i, 8.
17 Ibid., i, 57.
18 Holmes, 'Protestant clergies in Europe', p. 113.
19 J. R. R. Adams, *The printed word and the common man: popular culture in Ulster 1700–1900* (Belfast, 1987), p. 10.
20 17 & 18 Chas. II, c. 6 (*The statutes at large, passed in the parliaments held in Ireland* (20 vols, 1786–1804), iii, 143); *The present state of religion in Ireland* (London, [1712]), p. 27.

We do know, however, that at least some Presbyterian churches in Ulster did have schools attached to them in which prospective ministers as well as ordinary Presbyterians could receive a rudimentary level of education, although it would be impossible to suggest even an approximate number, since too many records have been lost.

Such Presbyterian schools operated under the watchful eye of the minister and elders. The session of Aghadowey, in County Londonderry, removed its teacher, Samuel McCullogh, in 1706 for maintaining heretical doctrines.[21] In 1673 it was brought to the attention of the archbishop of Armagh that there was a school in Strabane 'taught by a ffanatick person, which tends to the further perverting of the people'.[22] John Brown served as schoolmaster at the Presbyterian school at Kilwaughter, County Antrim, though it later seems that the minister, Rev. William Ogilvie, also acted as schoolmaster there.[23] In some cases congregations could have more than one school attached to them. These were placed throughout the bounds of the congregation so that one would be within easy reach of the children of all members. During congregational visitations by the Presbytery of Antrim one question asked (and indeed included in their list of rules and questions for visitation drawn up in 1707) was whether there were schools maintained in the parish and whether parents supported them by sending their children.[24] At a visitation at Cairncastle in July 1701 it was answered that the people did 'keep scholes in severall places of the parish' and in Ballyclare in 1706 they replied that 'ther[e] were schools'.[25] In some cases, though, the minister and elders of the congregation asked the presbytery to admonish some of the people for not taking enough care of their children's education. Such was the case at Donegore in 1709 when, from all they had heard, the presbytery 'found it proper to exhort that people to be more carefull in incouraging schoolmasters by puting their children to them and paying duely for their education by them'.[26] Nevertheless, some ministers in later life praised the efforts of their parents, and often their mother in particular, for encouraging them in their education.[27]

By law each Church of Ireland parish was supposed to contain a school run by the established Church and towards the end of the period under consideration a number of charity schools were also in existence. It is possible, though evidence has not survived, that some of the Presbyterian ministers received their early education in these establishments, or a school run by one of the municipal corporations.[28]

21 Aghadowey sess. mins, pp 49–50 (PHS).
22 James Buckley, 'The free schools of Ulster in 1673', UJA, ix (1903), p. 56.
23 'Extracts from the minutes of a manuscript dated 1700 and 1701' in Larne & Kilwaughter session book (PRONI, MIC1B/6A/1B, unpaginated section at end of MS); Barkley, 'History of the eldership', ii, 116–17, 120, 122.
24 Antrim Pby mins, 1697–1713 (PHS, pp 59, 77, 166, 168, 303, 306, 315, 331, 335–6, 458).
25 Ibid., pp 166, 303.
26 Ibid., p. 458.
27 Diary of Rev. John Cook, pp 3, 6 (PHS); Alexander Maclaine, A sermon occasioned by the death of the Reverend Mr. Robert Rainey (Belfast, 1736), p. 31.
28 The charity school erected by Sir John Rawdon at Moira, Co. Down, in 1716, for instance, catered for '24 children, (16 boys and 8 girls) half of whom are the children of Conformists, and the rest the children of Papists and Presbyterians'. The pupils, though, were, during their time at

The talented and promising among those who attended the schools run by the Presbyterian churches may have been given additional training by their minister. Francis Hutcheson's earlier years were spent under the tutelage of his grandfather, the Rev. Alexander Hutcheson of Saintfield, and the Rev. James Duchal, who was born, probably in Antrim, in 1697, was educated partly by the Rev. John Abernethy of Antrim.[29]

Presbyterians in Ulster also attempted to establish a number of 'academies' or 'grammar schools' to provide an intermediate level of education and prepare students for university and thus for training for the ministry. These academies offered a philosophical and classical education in Latin but were usually short-lived and tended to be single-teacher establishments. Rev. Thomas Gowan ran a private school at Connor when preaching there from 1666 to 1672. After his removal to Antrim in 1672 he set up an academy there. The church took Gowan's Antrim academy under its authority in 1674. There is some uncertainty, though, as to whether or not divinity was taught there. In June 1675 the Antrim 'Meeting' drew up an overture to the general committee that a divinity school be set in Antrim under the supervision of Mr Gowan and Mr Howe.[30] John Howe was then domestic chaplain to the Massereene family but within six months had returned to England, never to return, so if there ever was any divinity training at Antrim it was probably only for one term.[31] A gap in the surviving minutes of Antrim Presbytery from July 1675 to February 1683 (the year Gowan died) means we cannot be sure. Gowan was a renowned logician and Latinist and before his death published two works on logic: *Ars sciendi* (1681) and *Logica elenctica* (1683).[32] The former was dedicated to Massereene's son, Clotworthy Skeffington, and displays awareness of the traditional logic of Reformed scholastics such as Bartholomäus Keckermann (c.1572–1609) and Franciscus Burgersdicius (1590–1635), as well as the more recent continental philosophers, Johannes Clauberg (1622–1665) and the French Jansenist, Antoine Arnauld (1612–1694). As well as harmonising traditional and more recent philosophical approaches, it also provided guidance on hermeneutics, especially relevant to ministerial candidates.[33] Students who attended the academy at Antrim include Rev. Robert Henry, Rev. Francis Iredell and Rev. Robert Higginbotham.[34] In 1675 the ministers of Laggan Presbytery proposed that those who had completed their studies at Antrim should receive some public recognition 'in lieu and stead of

---

the school, obliged to 'attend the service of the Establish'd Church': [Edward Synge], *An account of the erection, government and number, of charity-schools in Ireland* (Dublin, 1717), p. 22.

[29] Francis Hutcheson, *A system of moral philosophy … to which is prefixed some account of the life, writings, and character of the author, by the Reverend William Leechman* (2 vols, Glasgow, 1755), i, p. i; Witherow, *Hist & lit. memls*, ii, 16.

[30] Antrim 'Meeting' mins (UTC, p. 174).

[31] *ODNB* (Gowan, Thomas).

[32] T[homas] G[owan], *Ars sciendi sive logica nova methodo disposita, et novis praeceptis aucta* (London, 1681); idem, *Logica elenctica, sive, summa controversiarum, quae circa materiam & praecepta logicae, agitari solent in qua etiam novae aliquot quaestiones tractantur* (Dublin, 1683).

[33] Witherow, *Hist. & lit. memls*, i, 54–5.

[34] McConnell, *Fasti*, pp 67–8, 105; William Campbell, MS 'Sketches of the history of Presbyterians in Ireland' (1803), p. 107 (PHS); Witherow, *Hist. & lit. memls*, i, 149; Herbert McLachlan, 'The Irish academies', *Transactions of the Unitarian Historical Society*, vi (1936), pp 92–4.

laureation' and David Stewart has suggested that since Francis Makemie, founder of the Presbyterian Church in America, was one of the few young men under the care of the Laggan Presbytery at that time, he might have also been one of the students taught by Gowan.[35]

Following Gowan's death the Presbytery of Antrim endeavoured to keep the school open, under Fulk White, but at a presbytery meeting on 5 January 1686 it was reported that 'Mr Fulk Whyte having no schollars come to him quits any hope of a philosophy school'.[36] White subsequently became minister of Broughshane and in 1709 the synod passed a resolution to pay him £10 a year to teach Hebrew.[37] Another academy existed in Newtownards and for a short time there was also one at Comber. A reference in the Ormond papers states that Andrew Ferguson was a schoolmaster at Comber in 1679, that John McBride was schoolmaster at Killyleagh and Robert Hamilton at Newtownards, while a philosophical school was also conducted at the latter by John Hutcheson.[38] John Hutcheson was the son of Rev. Alexander Hutcheson of Saintfield, and John himself subsequently became minister of Downpatrick in 1690 and later Armagh in 1697. There is a reference to this philosophy school in Kirkpatrick's *Presbyterian loyalty* which, after referring to Gowan's academy at Antrim, states that, 'Mr. John Hutchison, an ingenious man, and one not only of a very philosophical head, but of universal learning, taught philosophy for divers years at Newtown[ards] in the County of Down.'[39] The Newtownards school seems to have ended just before, or as a result of, the 'Glorious' Revolution, and John Binning's philosophical school at Comber can have been in existence no more than three years before the Revolution brought it too to an end. Binning was the son of Hugh Binning, regent and professor of philosophy at Glasgow University, 1646–53. John inherited his grandfather's estate of Dalvennan, in Ayrshire, in 1672, but following his involvement on the side of the Covenanters in the Battle of Bothwell Brig in 1679 the estate was forfeited, and John spent the rest of his life in an impoverished state, petitioning the Scottish General Assembly for relief on a number of occasions in the early eighteenth century.[40] Along with his mother, John was involved with the Cameronians and at their general meeting on 8 May 1683 it was resolved that 'Mr. John Binning should be desired to wait upon a school, for teaching some young men; and for his pains he was to have twenty-five pounds Scots per quarter … According to this resolution, Mr. Binning did teach Latin to some of these young men for some

---

[35] Laggan Pby mins, 1672–95 (UTC, p. 90); David Stewart, 'Irish Presbyterian seminaries', *The Witness*, 11 Mar. 1910. Among the lay students educated at Gowan's philosophical school in Antrim were John Magill, John Hawkins and Ralph Ryland, esq.: Testimonial of Mr John Leaske, n.d. (Bodleian Lib., MS Carte 221, f. 275).

[36] Antrim 'Meeting' mins (UTC, pp 207, 209).

[37] McConnell, *Fasti*, p. 83; *RGSU*, i, 212.

[38] David Maxwell to Dr John Coghill, 6 June 1679 (HMC, *Ormonde MSS*, n.s., v, 125).

[39] [Kirkpatrick], *Presby loyalty*, p. 505.

[40] Hugh Binning, *The works of the Rev. Hugh Binning* (Project Gutenberg EBook, 2008), pp 21–2, 100–3; extracts from a fee farm grant relating to the site of the meetinghouse and schools in Comber, 1686 (PRONI, Stewart papers, D1759/1/C/1, p. 63); Philip Crossle, 'Gordons in County Down: Rev. James Gordon, of Comber', *Banbridge Chronicle*, 12 Mar. 1913.

time.'[41] He appears to have come over to Ireland around 1687 and set up a school of philosophy at Comber, where his stepfather Rev. James Gordon had for a time been minister.[42] Archibald Pettigrew opened a school in Belfast in 1688 and in instructions given by a committee of the General Synod to a commissioner sent to represent them in London in 1711, there is mention of a 'Mr Stewart, who kept another school of philosophy at Templepatrick', who was prosecuted to excommunication, and also the general phrase that 'there are innumerable instances of hindering Dissenters from keeping grammar and reading schools'.[43] William Thompson, who later became minister of Ballybay, ran an academy in Augher for a few years, 'which soon took in sixty young gentlemen a considerable number of them he fitted for the colledge and the profits not only afforded him an independent support, in these times of calamnity but enabled him in three years to stock a tolerably large farm'.[44]

The philosophy school which was longest in existence was the Killyleagh Academy, which was conducted by Rev. James McAlpin from around 1697 until he returned to the clerical office in 1714.[45] We know more about the content of the teaching given at the philosophy school at Killyleagh than we do of its predecessors in Antrim and elsewhere. William Leechman, in his biography of the Ulster-born philosopher, Francis Hutcheson, tells us that at the Killyleagh Academy Hutcheson was taught the 'ordinary scholastic philosophy which was in vogue in those days'.[46] Descriptions of three notebooks belonging to students educated at the school, which were known about in the early twentieth century, offer us a further insight into the education that students received at Killyleagh.[47] The notebooks all consisted of exercises dictated and explained by McAlpin and written down by the students in Latin. The notebook (dated 1704) which belonged to John Henderson (later minister of Duneane and Grange) described McAlpin as 'a most learned man, and not lightly endowed with the riches of the goddess of wisdom'.[48] One of the books – that of John King (minister at Dromara, 1726–62) – has recently come to light. It contains 474 pages written in Latin, covering logic, metaphysics and ethics, and shows that the academic session at Killyleagh was from October to May.[49]

---

41 *Faithful contendings displayed: being an historical relation of the state and actings of the suffering remnant in the Church of Scotland* (Glasgow, 1780), p. 66.

42 Antrim 'Meeting' mins (UTC, pp 243, 277); Bailie, *Hist. of congns*, p. 326.

43 Antrim 'Meeting' mins (UTC, p. 277); Greaves, *God's other children*, p. 247; Witherow, *Hist. & lit. memls*, i, 153.

44 Thomson narrative (PRONI, MIC720/1, p. 11).

45 McLachlan, 'Irish academies', pp 94–5; David Steers, '"The very life-blood of nonconformity of education": the Killyleagh Philosophy School, County Down', *Familia*, no. 28 (2012), pp 61–79.

46 Francis Hutcheson, *A system of moral philosophy ... to which is prefixed some account of the life, writings, and character of the author, by the Reverend William Leechman* (2 vols, Glasgow, 1755), i, p. iii.

47 Alexander McCreery, *The Presbyterian ministers of Killileagh: a notice of their lives and times* (Belfast, 1875), pp 111–12; Aiken McClelland, *A short history of First Dromara Presbyterian Church* (Belfast, 1963), p. 12; David Stewart, 'Irish Presbyterian seminaries', *The Witness*, 18 Mar. 1910.

48 McCreery, *Presbyterian ministers of Killileagh*, p. 112.

49 Lecture notes of John King, 1710–13 (UTC); A. D. G. Steers, 'Killyleagh Philosophy School (c.1696–1714)', 'Dissenting academies online', Dr Williams's Centre for Dissenting Studies,

Besides Henderson and King, the only other two Presbyterian ministers known to have obtained their classical education at Killyleagh were Rev. Michael Bruce and Rev. Patrick Bruce.[50] However, the number must have been much greater than this, and probably was not limited to aspiring ministers. Certainly James Trail, from a lower gentry family, and a nephew of the minister of Killyleagh (Rev. James Bruce), is known to have attended McAlpin's academy.[51]

The established church attempted on a number of occasions to close down the academy at Killyleagh. In 1698 Rev. John McBride, minister of Belfast, was summoned before the Irish Lords Justices and questioned on whether or not divinity was taught at the academy. He told them that no divinity was taught there, and as to the philosophy 'it was no more than what was done in the reign of Charles II'.[52] That divinity was not taught at Killyleagh is confirmed by Rev. William Tisdall, vicar of Belfast, who in his *Conduct of the Dissenters*, attacked the Presbyterians by stating that

> The Dissenters of Ireland, in order to perpetuate their schism by a succession of planters and waterers (as they usually phrase their teachers) have erected a seminary in the north of Ireland, at a place called Killeleah, where students are taught their course of philosophy, and afterwards have been sent to be instructed in their divinity lectures, by the great professor Mr. Mc.Bride at Belfast.[53]

McBride did not deny this accusation in his reply to Tisdall's pamphlet, and, given also that McBride and Tisdall were both inhabitants of the same town, it would appear that there must have been truth in Tisdall's accusation.[54] McBride, as we have already seen, had served as a schoolmaster at Killyleagh around 1679 and while in Glasgow between 1705 and 1708 he declined a chair in divinity at the university.[55] Clearly, he possessed the capacity to teach students. James Trail, who lodged with McBride, wrote in his autobiography that McBride had 'a good many [young men] about him while I was in his family, that were students of divinity under his care' and a letter of 1704 mentions that one of McBride's students was Philip Mears.[56] Nor was it unknown for other Presbyterian ministers to teach divinity to ministerial candidates in Ulster. Rev. William Leggatt, Presbyterian minister at Dromore from 1675 to 1695, taught 'the course of divinity to six schollars (some whereof pretend

http://www.english.qmul.ac.uk/drwilliams/portal.html (12 Jan. 2013); idem, '"The very life-blood"', pp 70–5.

50 Bailie, *Hist. of congns*, p. 561.

51 Autobiography of James Trail (PRONI, D1460/1, opening 7). 'Several conformists', and other laymen, were also educated at the Killyleagh Academy: Witherow, *Hist. & lit. memls*, i, 153 (where Killyleagh has been incorrectly rendered 'Antrim').

52 Copy of petition from the B[ishop] of D[own] to the Lords Justices of Ireland, 1698 (PRONI, T525/12).

53 [Tisdall], *Conduct of the Dissenters*, p. 55.

54 Stewart, 'Irish Presbyterian seminaries', 18 Mar. 1910.

55 David Maxwell to Dr John Coghill, 6 June 1679 (HMC, *Ormonde MSS*, n.s., v, 125); ODNB (McBride, John (c.1650–1718)).

56 Autobiography of James Trail (PRONI, D1460/1, opening 5); extract of a letter from the north of Ireland, 19 Feb. 1704 (NLS, Scottish historic collections: miscellaneous letters and documents, MS 3740).

to be master of Arts) who lodging in the towne, come twice in the weeke to the said Mr Leggatt's house to be instructed, and to dispute in divinity'.[57]

After the closure of Killyleagh Academy the only other early eighteenth-century Presbyterian philosophical teaching for which any evidence survives is that of Rev. Charles Mastertown at Connor, and perhaps later in Belfast, where Mastertown became minister in 1723. One ministerial student known to have studied under him was Rev. Luke Ash, son of Captain Thomas Ash, one of the defending officers during the Siege of Derry. Rev. Ash's father was an Anglican, though his mother was a Presbyterian. According to an account written by his father, Luke after having 'read the Latin and Greek authors in Magherafelt', 'went to Connor, where he remained about two years under the care of Mr. Charles Mastertown at the study of philosophy: and in August 1723 he went to Belfast to learn the mathematicks, where he continued about six months'. After completing his education at Edinburgh University, from which he graduated as a Master of Arts, Luke became minister of the Presbyterian congregation at Sligo in 1732.[58]

Most ministers supplemented the education they obtained in the native academies by further study at university. At this time the only university in Ireland was Trinity College in Dublin. Although Trinity had among its first fellows two Presbyterians, in the seventeenth century it developed a strong Anglican ethos.[59] As a result Presbyterians in Ulster preferred to make the journey to one, or more, of the four universities in Scotland. Fortunately, the Scottish universities had the advantage of offering a high-quality education more cheaply than in Dublin or England. Universities were fee-paying institutions, though Glasgow in its fees took account of the ability of parents to pay. The *Records of the University of Glasgow* refer to charges being levied according to students' social standing and to the waiving of fees in cases of real poverty.[60] Irish presbyteries also gave financial support to some of the poorer students from Ulster[61] and in 1694 the Laggan Presbytery established

---

[57] Testimonial of Mr John Leask, n.d. (Bodleian Lib., MS Carte 221, f. 275).

[58] Thomas Witherow (ed.), *Two diaries of Derry in 1689* ... (Derry, 1888), pp xi, xvii–xviii; account and memorandum book of Bp Francis Hutchinson (PRONI, DIO/1/22/1, p. 178); Charles Mastertown to [Robert Wodrow], 10 Oct. 1728 (NLS, Wod. Lett. Qu., xxii, f. 157); J. W. Kernohan, *Rosemary Street Presbyterian Church Belfast: a record of the past 200 years* (Belfast, 1923), p. 22. Mastertown was minister at Connor from 1704–23 and Third Belfast, 1723–46.

[59] James Montgomery (minister at Castlereagh, 1701–10) was the only minister from the period under review who is known to have been educated at Trinity. Although Montgomery's mother was a Presbyterian, his father was Anglican and brought James up in the Anglican church. Interestingly, James's elder brother, Hans, was a minister in the Church of Ireland: William Montgomery, *The Montgomery manuscripts: (1603–1706)*, ed. George Hill (Belfast, 1869), pp 374–7; McConnell, *Fasti*, p. 118.

[60] D. B. Horn, *A short history of the University of Edinburgh: 1556–1889* (Edinburgh, 1967), p. 22; I. M. Bishop, 'The education of Ulster students at Glasgow University during the eighteenth century' (M.A. thesis, QUB, 1987), pp 12–13, 21–2, 50.

[61] Laggan Pby mins, 1672–95 (UTC, p. 18); Laggan Pby mins, 1690–1700 (PHS, pp 5, 7, 174–5); Route Pby mins (PHS, pp 15–16, 68, 136); Antrim Pby mins, 1697–1713 (PHS, pp 7, 13, 36, 73, 99, 114, 121, 124–5, 130, 144, 149, 152, 155, 242). Rev. Alexander McCracken of Lisburn wrote to Principal John Stirling of Glasgow University to introduce, and recommend for charity, Robert McKean, a poor Irish student: McCracken to Stirling, 26 Oct. 1720 (GUL, Stirling papers, MS Gen. 207, no. 122/2). Similarly Rev. John Stirling of Ballykelly wrote to his cousin, Principal John

a fund to assist students during their university course, from which some were granted £10 a year.[62] This was a considerable sum considering that one student at Edinburgh, Thomas Boston, calculated that his arts course from 1691 to 1694 cost him £10 14s 7²/₃d for the three years, though he added that he had lived 'meanly and perhaps more so than was needful or reasonable'.[63] Students could reduce their living costs by bringing provisions from home, and it was by no means uncommon for students travelling from Ireland in the eighteenth century to be seen walking with a bag of oatmeal from their hometown to Donaghadee and from Portpatrick to Glasgow or Edinburgh.[64] The Scottish General Assembly offered bursary assistance to those who knew the 'Irish tongue', especially as the Church of Scotland began to focus on church planting in the Highlands in the early eighteenth century, and it would appear that students destined for the Highlands could also avail of a shorter, and thus less expensive, divinity course.[65]

There seems to have been a relationship between certain individuals in the Scottish universities and particular ministers in Ulster, and a number of letters have survived which introduce Ulster students to John Stirling, principal of Glasgow University.[66] On 13 October 1701 Rev. John McBride wrote to Stirling, 'having recommended severall young men of this countrey to the care of such m[aste]rs as are proper to be their instructors in their capacities I hope due care will be taken of them; and if any should prove extravagant, which God forbid, I desire you may

Stirling, in 1725 to introduce William Calendar whose 'parents are in mean circumstances and therefor cannot doe much for him and wou'd be an act of charity to shew him all the favour you cane with respect to the college fees': Stirling to Stirling, 3 Jan. 1725 (GUL, Stirling papers, MS Gen. 207, no. 127).

[62] Laggan Pby mins, 1690–1700 (PHS, p. 61); Robert Allen, *The Presbyterian College Belfast 1853–1953* (Belfast, 1954), p. 11. For financial contributions, by a Kirk Session, towards the education of students, see Kirkdonald sess. mins (PHS, pp 55, 86).

[63] Horn, *Short history of the University of Edinburgh*, p. 22.

[64] Barkley, 'Presbyterian minister', p. 54.

[65] J. C. Whytock, 'The history and development of Scottish theological education and training, Kirk and Secession (c.1560–c.1850) (Ph.D. thesis, Univ. of Wales, 2001), p. 112. In 1716 the Scottish General Assembly sent a letter to the Scottish presbyteries 'desyring presbyteries to enqui[re] after, and give account of probationers, and also of students having the Irish language within their respective bounds': Glasgow Pby mins, 13 June, 1 Aug. 1716 (Mitchell Lib., Glasgow, CH2/171/9A, ff 27–8, 30).

[66] John McBride to John Stirling, 13 Oct. 1701 (GUL, Stirling papers, MS Gen 207, no. 114), introduces McBride's two sons who were sent 'to be under the care of Mr Jo[h]n Law', and Philip Mears and John McMinn, who were going to Glasgow 'to study divinity'; James Kirkpatrick to John Stirling, 13 Nov. 1704 (ibid., no. 118), introduces William Taylor and William Dick; Alexander McCracken to John Stirling, 26 Oct. 1720 (ibid., no. 122/2), introduces Robert McKoan; John Stirling to John Stirling, 3 Jan. 1725 (ibid., no. 127), introduces William Calendar; Samuel Hemphill to John Stirling, 16 Sept. 1725 (ibid., no. 128), introduces an unnamed 'near relation', who was bearer of the letter; Charles Mastertown to John Stirling, 24 Sept. 1725 (ibid., no. 129), introduces Mr James Stuart as a student of the university; Robert McBride to John Stirling, 7 Nov. 1726 (ibid., no. 130), introduces the bearer, William Orr, as a student; Charles Mastertown to John Stirling, 7 Nov. 1726 (ibid., no. 132), introduces 'Mr. Allexander', a divinity student. Principal Stirling had Ulster connexions as his uncle, Rev. Robert Stirling, was minister of Dervock, near Ballymoney, in Co. Antrim from c.1659–99, and his cousins were Rev. John Stirling, Ballykelly (1699–1752) and Rev. Thomas Stirling, Dervock (1703–18).

particularly let me kno that their friends may be able seasonablie to prevent the evils that may follow.'[67] Rev. James Kirkpatrick, then minister at Templepatrick, wrote to Stirling in November 1704 to introduce two students, William Taylor (son of Rev. William Taylor of Randalstown) and William Dick, who were that winter entering the *magistrand* (final year) class in Glasgow, having 'been educated in this place in a private philosophy school [probably Killyleagh]'. Kirkpatrick also added that 'I doubt not but both of 'em will be able to abide the tests of yor usuall examinations' and requested that Stirling keep him updated on the 'carriage of these two young men'.[68]

Further evidence of such a relationship between the philosophy schools in Ulster and Glasgow University, and of Glasgow's recognition of the Ulster schools, is suggested in the university's records, which state that on 29 November 1691:

> On application made by Samuel Ferguson and James Heron who had passed their tryalls in order to the ministry of the Gospell in the kingdome of Ireland where they had been privately educate in the late times in the study of philosophy ... and there being several certificates from ministers of credite and note in that kingdome of their behaviour, and that there was an agreement made by the Presbyterian ministers in the north of Ireland to admitt none unto the ministry but such as should be graduate Master of Arts in some university, and the faculty, judging that it would tend to the future good of this university and resort of students from Ireland, thought fit on their part and at the earnest desire of these ministers in the north of Ireland this day communicate unto them by letters to conferr the degrees of Master of Arts on the said Samuel Ferguson and James Heron, upon which the principal as vice-chancellor of the university therupon did accordingly.[69]

The conferring of degrees upon Ulstermen who had never attended the university was unusual and most attended the Scottish universities to undertake at least a short additional arts course before graduation.[70] At Edinburgh University it had become an increasing trend in the later seventeenth century to allow well-qualified and gifted students, who had already been taught at the superior grammar schools of Scotland, such as the one in Edinburgh itself, to enter straight into the second-year class.[71] Students educated in the Ulster philosophical schools may also have been able to avail of such a shorter course.

---

67 John McBride to John Stirling, 13 Oct. 1701 (GUL, Stirling papers, MS Gen 207, no. 114).

68 James Kirkpatrick to John Stirling, 13 Nov. 1704 (ibid., MS Gen 207, no. 118).

69 *Munimenta alme Universitatis Glasguensis*, ii, 362. See also Glasgow University Faculty meeting minutes, 1702–20 (GUA 26631), p. 59.

70 That it was unusual to confer degrees without attending a Scottish university is supported by the following reference in the Monaghan Pby mins: 'This day Mr Saml: McGachin ... produced his ticket from the Colledge of Glasgow which was read and approven, and also a letter was read from some of the masters of the colledge signifieing that there was something extraordinary in his case and that they would not deny the young man, but says that they will not make a president [sic] of it, to give young men their lauriation unless they spend some time in the university. The presbytery considering the said letter resolves for the future not to proceed with young men in tryalls, that hath not taken their degrees in some university': Monaghan Pby mins, 16 Apr. 1706 (PHS, pp 104–5).

71 Michael Lynch, 'The creation of a college' in R. D. Anderson, *et al.*, *The University of Edinburgh: an illustrated history* (Edinburgh, 2003), p. 31.

The majority (almost 60%) of the 303 ministers active in Ulster during the period 1680–1729 received their university education at Glasgow, the Scottish university closest to Ulster. After Glasgow, Edinburgh was the next most popular destination, with just over a fifth of the ministers studying there, and a further 26 studied at both Glasgow and Edinburgh. Of much less importance were the universities of Aberdeen and St Andrews, with seven and six ministers respectively. With the exception of the English-born Thomas Jackson, who attended both St Andrews and Edinburgh, and Robert Sinclair, whose birthplace is unknown, the other ministers who studied at St Andrews and Aberdeen were Scotsmen, and in the case of Rev. James Alexander, Rev. James Chrystie and Rev. Arthur Stratone, who had all studied at King's College, Aberdeen, Aberdeenshire was their native county. It is also possible to notice, with a few exceptions, the establishment of a tradition within particular families for a son to attend his father's *alma mater*. Interestingly a higher proportion of the students who studied at Edinburgh graduated with degrees than those who attended Glasgow, and those that attended both Glasgow and Edinburgh usually graduated from Edinburgh.

Three of the 303 ministers completed their education by studying on the continent: Robert McBride, Thomas Shaw and Samuel Haliday.[72] Robert McBride was the son of the Rev. John McBride of (First) Belfast and had attended Glasgow University before going to Leiden. A letter survives from him to Principal Stirling, in which the young McBride describes his attempts to purchase books for Stirling in Leiden. He added that he had completed his 'troublesome dispute', which he had dedicated to Stirling and the rest of the faculty in Glasgow, and though 'dreadfully threatned', was 'ataqued by none of these gentlemen but one, who was pleased to manage as modestly as possible as a man of his principle cou'd be expected to doe'.[73] In making his journey back from Holland Robert spent some time in London, where he was 'kindly entertain'd' by Hans Sloane,[74] the Ulster-born physician and virtuoso, before returning to Ulster where he become minister of Ballymoney congregation in 1716. Thomas Shaw was the youngest son of William Shaw, esq., of Bush, County Antrim, and he too after attending Leiden 'staid some time in the city of London, conversing there with men of learning and worth', before returning to Ulster where he was ordained as minister of Ahoghill in 1710.[75] Samuel Haliday was born probably in Omagh, County Tyrone, in 1685, where his father was the minister, and received his primary education in 'schools' in Ulster.[76] Like

---

[72] Esther Mijers, 'Irish students in the Netherlands, 1650–1750', *Archivium Hibernicum*, lix (2005), pp 66–78, lists nine Irish students attending the University of Leiden to study theology between 1698 and 1710. They were Robert Milling in 1698, Samuel Smith in 1699, Benjamin Smith in 1704, Samuel Haliday in 1705, Robert Milling in 1706, William Brown in 1708, John MacDowall in 1709, and William Brown and Thomas Shaw in 1710. It is also known that John Milling who was minister in Capel Street, Dublin (1702–5), received some of his education at Leiden as did Robert Craghead, minister of Capel Street, Dublin (1709–30): McConnell, *Fasti*, pp 94, 118.

[73] Robert McBride to John Stirling, 13 May 1710 (GUL, Stirling papers, MS Gen 207, no. 133).

[74] Robert McBride to Sloane, 30 June 1736 (BL, Sloane MS 4054, f. 263).

[75] James Duchal, 'Brief memoirs of the life and character of Mr. Thomas Shaw' in idem, *A sermon on occasion of the … death of the late Reverend Mr. John Abernethy* (Dublin, 1741), p. 20.

[76] James Duchal, 'Brief memoirs of the life and character of Mr. Samuel Haliday' in idem, *A sermon on death of Abernethy*, p. 30.

his father, Haliday attended Glasgow University, where he matriculated in 1701 and studied under John Loudon. He was subsequently admitted to Leiden on 19 November 1705, studying theology and philosophy.[77] On completion of his studies Haliday defended a thesis on Leviticus 24:11–16 before Leiden's divinity professor, Hermann Witsius, on 10 July 1706, and delivered another on Genesis 12:11–13, before Johannes à Marck. Both theses were published (in Latin) in 1706 by the Leiden publisher Abraham Elzevier, and a copy of the former is preserved in the Presbytery of Antrim Library.[78] Certainly up to this point Haliday seems to have shared his father's rigid Calvinism, and when he was licensed at Rotterdam in 1706 he subscribed the *Westminster Confession of Faith*.[79] He spent a further period travelling and studying in Switzerland, where he entered Basel University in the winter of 1706/7 to study theology, before travelling to the University of Lausanne, in the French-speaking part of Switzerland, which he entered in June 1708.[80] He chose to be ordained in Geneva (around 40 miles from Lausanne) in 1708 because 'the terms of church-communion there, are not narrowed by any human impositions'.[81] When he returned to Rotterdam his former professor, Mr. Miller, thought he had 'entirely changed'.[82]

According to Duchal, Haliday, while on the continent, 'conversed much with books, and laid a very considerable stock of valuable learning'.[83] Among the books in the Antrim Presbytery Library are Johannes Buxtorf's *Concordantiae Bibliorum Hebraicae*, John Pearson's exposition on the Apostles' Creed, and William Twisse's defence of predestinarianism against Jacobus Arminius, which all came from Haliday's library and may have been acquired by him in Leiden.[84] Studies on the

---

[77] *Munimenta alme Universitatis Glasguensis*, iii, 171; *Album studiosorum Academiae Lugduno Batavae MDLXXV–MDCCCLXXV* (The Hague, 1875), p. 789; Witherow, *Hist. & lit. memls*, i, 266–7; ODNB (Haliday, Samuel).

[78] *Disputatio philologico-theologica de facto hominis maledici & lege eâ occasione latâ. ad Lev. XXIV. 11–16. Quam auspice deo ter ppt. max. sub praesidio … D. Hermannu Witsii* (Leiden, 1706) (Antrim Pby Lib., B. 6. 1. 22). Another copy is held in Amsterdam Univ. Lib. which also has a copy of Haliday's second thesis, *Disputatio theologica de facto Abrahami, uxorem Saram pro sorore suahaberi volentis, ad Genes. XII. 11. 12. 13. Prima & altera.: qvam … praeside … Johanne à Marck* (Leiden, 1706).

[79] Samuel Haliday, *Reasons against the imposition of subscription to the Westminster-Confession of Faith* (Belfast, 1724), p. vi; ODNB (Haliday, Samuel); J. M. Barkley, 'Francis Hutcheson (1694–1746): professor of moral philosophy, University of Glasgow', *Bull. PHSI*, no. 14 (1985), p. 6, suggests it was the Belgic or Heideberg Catechism that Haliday signed but for the reasons outlined in David Steers, 'Samuel Haliday (1685–1739)', *Transactions of the Unitarian Historical Society*, xxii, no. 3 (2001), p. 277, Barkley's suggestion would appear to be incorrect. The reference in RGSU, i, 266–7, to Haliday being licensed by the Presbytery of Convoy must be a mistake on the part of the clerk.

[80] J. G. Wackernagel (ed.), *Die matrikel der Universität Basel* (5 vols, Basel, 1951–80), iv, 374.

[81] Haliday, *Reasons against the imposition of subscription*, p. iv.

[82] William Bruce, 'The progress of nonsubscription to creeds', *Christian Moderator*, i (1826), p. 273; ODNB (Haliday, Samuel).

[83] Duchal, 'Brief memoirs of Haliday', p. 30.

[84] *Johannes Buxtorfi Concordantiae Bibliorum Hebraicae* (Basel, 1632) (Antrim Pby Lib., B. 1. 6. 1.), which is inscribed 'Ex Libris Sam: Halidei Empt. Lugduni. Bat. 8ber 13 an. 1705 pret 9–15–0'; *Joannis Pearsonii … expositiox Symboli Apostolici, juxta editionem Anglicanam quitam, in linguam Latinam translata* (Frankfurt, 1691) (Antrim Pby Lib., B. 4. 3. 5.), which is inscribed 'Ex Libris

continent brought Haliday into contact with many of the leading theologians of Europe and during his travels Haliday assembled an album containing autographs and complimentary remarks from almost one hundred of Europe's leading Protestant theologians, including J. J. Hottinger, J. F. Ostervald, and Johannes Buxtorf. Such autograph books, known as *albi amicorum*, were popular among students from the Holy Roman Empire and the Low Countries. The entries in the *album amicorum* give an interesting summary of Haliday's movements on the continent with Utrecht, Leiden and Heidelberg visited in 1706, Lausanne, Basel, Bern and Zürich in 1707, and Neuchâtel, Geneva and Rotterdam in 1708.[85] When Haliday's references were taken up by the Synod of Ulster in 1721 they included testimonials from Leiden, Rotterdam, Basel and Geneva.[86]

Students usually entered the arts course in the Scottish universities between the ages of thirteen and fifteen. The academic session as stipulated by the parliamentary commission of 1690 was from 1 November to 30 June, though at Glasgow University the term continued to start earlier, on 10 October. Arts students had to meet a certain proficiency in Latin before their admission to the course,[87] and in this the education received by Ulstermen at the native academies must have proved useful. Until 1708 in Edinburgh, and 1727 in Glasgow, a single regent was responsible for teaching his group of students the entire arts course, which for the

---

Sam: Haliday Fily Lugduni'; and Guillielmus Twissus, *Vindiciae gratiae, potestatis ac providentiae Dei, hoc est, ad examen libelli Perkinsiani de praedestinationis modo & ordine, institutum à Jacobo Arminio, responsio scholastica, tribus libris absoluta* ... (Amsterdam, 1648) (Antrim Pby Lib., B. 5. 8. 11.), which is marked 'Ex Libris Sam. Haliday ... Lugduni Battavorium'.

[85] 'Album amicorum aangelegd door Samuel Haliday', 1706–8 (Leiden Univ. Library, AHM 8 (Olim Mus.7)).

[86] *RGSU*, ii, 9. In 1708 Haliday was appointed as chaplain to Colonel George Preston's Cameronian Regiment, serving in Marlborough's campaigns over the next four years. Haliday seems to have left active military service in 1712, but was retained on half-pay until as late as 1722. The choice of a regiment associated with traditional Calvinism and Covenanting beliefs is intriguing considering Haliday's later prominence among the Ulster Non-Subscribers. It suggests that at this stage of his career there was no suspicion surrounding his theological orthodoxy and his appointment may have been on the recommendation of William Carstairs. Haliday was accepted as a minister without charge by the General Synod of Ulster in 1712, but spent the next eight years active at the court in London as a kind of liaison figure between the Church of Scotland and Presbyterians in England and Ireland. He also accompanied Sir Hans Sloane's nephew, William, on a grand tour of Europe between 1715 and 1717, before becoming minister of First Belfast, in 1720, at the start of the Subscription Controversy: Charles Dalton, *George the First's army 1714–1727* (2 vols, London, 1910–12), i, 351–2; Haliday to Abp William King, 4 Nov. 1714, 20 Aug. 1715 (TCD, King papers, MSS 1995–2008/1541, /1705); Haliday to the duke of Montrose, 22 Sept. 1716 (NAS, GD220/5/1928/8); Haliday to Sir Hans Sloane, 13 Feb. 1715/16, 19 Mar. 1715/16, – Mar. 1715/16, 5 June 1716, 27 Jan. 1716/17 (BL, Sloane MS 4044, ff 132, 142, 147, 168, 261); William Sloane to Sir Hans Sloane, 29 Oct. 1716 (ibid., MS 4044, f. 233); Edmund Calamy to John Stirling, 15 Apr. 1718 (GUL, Stirling papers, MS Gen 207/85); A. D. G. Steers, 'Samuel Haliday (1685–1739): travelling scholar, court lobbyist, and non-subscribing divine' in Ruth Savage (ed.), *Philosophy and religion in Enlightenment Britain* (Oxford, 2012), pp 112–40. For abstracts of letters to, from and about Haliday contained in the correspondence of Jean-Alphonse Turrettini, see: Maria-Cristina Pitassi, *Inventaire critique de la correspondence de Jean-Alphonse Turrettini* (6 vols, Paris, 2009), ii, 354, 384, 393, 408, 423, 438, 448, 453, 459, 480, 768–9; iii, 29, 312, 348–9, 352, 450–1, 645–6, 692, 736.

[87] Bishop, 'Education of Ulster students at Glasgow', p. 45.

ordinary student usually lasted four years.[88] Students were taught Greek, some Latin, logic and the elements of arithmetic in the first two years, followed by ethics, metaphysics, more arithmetic and geometry in the third, and natural philosophy in the fourth.[89] Learning was through lectures (often called dictates), disputation, reading and memorisation.

Although much time would have been spent in study, with the student day beginning, for instance, in Edinburgh at 6 a.m. in summer and 7 a.m. in winter, there is nevertheless some evidence of student recreational activities. Students were given free time on Tuesday, Thursday and Saturday afternoons, and games such as archery, bowls, golf and handball were played. Playing cards and frequenting taverns and ale-houses were forbidden, and some students were reprimanded for breaking these regulations. Students were occasionally expelled for cases of indiscipline, including a number of Irish students.[90] Edward Baillie, who was minister of Drumbo, County Down, from 1699 to 1703, was among a group of students involved in a riot in 1693 and was imprisoned as a result in the tolbooth at Glasgow for a short while on the orders of the university principal. The riot had arisen when the principal had opposed the magistrand class' placing a knot of ribbons on their hats to distinguish themselves from the other classes. In 1722 John Smith, a Belfast divinity student, was expelled for attempting to resist the university authorities' encroachment of student rights in the choice of the rector.[91] On Sundays students and regents were expected to attend the Sunday morning and evening services in one of the local Presbyterian churches,[92] and each morning and evening there would also have been prayers by the students. A unique, if brief, insight into the devotional practices of the students at Glasgow is contained in the journal of James Trail who, when describing his experiences of lodging with Rev. McBride in Belfast, states that it was while there that he learnt to pray aloud, having the example of McBride's sons who were 'goeing and coming from Scotland' and 'had been used with their chamber fellows in the colledge [Glasgow] to pray together night about it being the custom there'.[93]

After graduation those intending to become ministers usually returned to university to study theology.[94] At Edinburgh the divinity professor from 1690 to 1701 was George Campbell. A description of the theology course under Campbell

[88] Nicholas Phillipson, 'Part II: the making of an enlightened university' in Anderson, et al., The University of Edinburgh, p. 61; Bishop, 'Education of Ulster students at Glasgow', pp 45–6.

[89] A. L. Brown and Michael Moss, The University of Glasgow: 1451–1996 (Edinburgh, 1996), p. 15; Lynch, 'The creation of a college', p. 29.

[90] A. T. Q. Stewart, A deeper silence: the hidden origins of the United Irishmen (Belfast, 1993), pp 82–4.

[91] Munimenta alme Universitatis Glasguensis, ii, 365–6; John Kerr, Scottish education school and university: from early times to 1908 (Cambridge, 1910), p. 123; Michael Brown, 'Francis Hutcheson and the Molesworth connection', Eighteenth-Century Ireland, xiv (1999), pp 65–6.

[92] Horn, Short history of the University of Edinburgh, p. 23.

[93] Autobiography of James Trail (PRONI, D1460/1, opening 5). McBride's eldest son, Robert, was minister of Ballymoney (1716–59), and another son, David, was a noted physician, chemist, and medical writer.

[94] For a list of Irish students of divinity at Glasgow, 1692–1727, see Steers, '"New Light" thinking', pp 297–300.

survives in a letter from George Lang (minister of Loughbrickland, 1701–41) to the Scottish historian, Robert Wodrow. Lang was the son of Rev. George Lang, minister of Newry, and had completed the arts course at Glasgow before coming to Edinburgh to study divinity. Lang stated that on Monday and Wednesday mornings Campbell usually gave a prelection, though occasionally the students had 'one of the morning exercises on the ministers of Lon[don]: compendised [and] read to us'. On Monday and Wednesday afternoons they studied Isaiah and considered an article or two of the *Confession of Faith*, in Latin, by way of exegesis. On Tuesday, the work of the strictly Calvinist Andreas Essenius (1618–77) was studied, as well as scripture doubts and reading of the Bible in its original languages. Seminars were offered by Campbell on Tuesday and Thursday afternoons for 'such as please' to have the Dutch theologian, 'Marchius explaind'. Essenius was again studied on Friday morning at 10 a.m., followed by Greek and Hebrew, and in the afternoon a lecture and homily. Study continued into Saturday when there were exegeses and Latin discourses on some topic or theme of theology.[95] Lang's account agrees with another of Campbell's students, Thomas Boston, who in his memoirs records that Campbell taught Leonardus Rüssenius' *Compendium* to a few of the new students in his private chamber, while 'publicly in the hall he taught Essenius's compend'.[96]

Campbell's successor, George Meldrum, was unable to compete with James Wodrow, the divinity professor at Glasgow, and for a time the number of divinity students attending Edinburgh declined.[97] The next divinity professor at Edinburgh was William Hamilton, who was appointed in 1709. Traditionally there has been some suspicion of Hamilton's orthodoxy, with J. S. Reid, for instance, describing him as a 'zealous moderate, who contrived to train up a race of heterodox ministers'.[98] It is true that a number of the early Scottish Moderates and some of the Ulster Non-Subscribers attended Edinburgh University, and one of Hamilton's students, James Oswald, in later life claimed that Campbell 'taught us moderation and a liberal manner of thinking upon all subjects'. Campbell is also known to have recommended to his students the reading of works written by English divines. This must, however, be set alongside the fact that Hamilton throughout the Subscription Controversy was the trusted friend of the Subscribers. It was the minister at Edinburgh, James Webster, who raised questions about the soundness of John Simson's doctrine and teaching at Glasgow and it is unlikely that Hamilton would have been given any peace had his teaching been unorthodox.[99]

Following Hamilton's death in 1732 James Smith was appointed as the new divinity professor at Edinburgh. An interesting notebook of jottings belonging to Samuel Boyce, a native of Lisnamuck, near Aghadowey, who was licensed by the Presbytery of Route in 1734, dates from this period. At the front of his notebook Boyce recorded books that were recommended as reading by the divinity professor

95 George Lang to Robert Wodrow, 10 Jan. 1698/9 (NLS, Wod. Lett. Qu., i, f. 68).
96 A. W. G. Brown, 'Irish Presbyterian theology in the early eighteenth century' (Ph.D. thesis, QUB, 1977), pp 424–5.
97 Ibid., pp 425–6.
98 Reid, *Hist. of PCI*, iii, 327.
99 Brown, 'Irish Presbyterian theology', pp 428–9, 432–3.

at Edinburgh. For chronology (that is, history) the German historian Johannes Carion's *Chronicon* was recommended, and on the subject of natural religion the work of Samuel Clarke, though it is unclear whether or not the latter was recommended as an example of error. Part of theological education involved looking at the tenets of the Christian faith, while also considering the weaknesses and inaccuracies of unorthodox teachings, so that students would be able to recognise and counter these. Boyce recorded that the professor had stated that, 'before we descend to the controversies among Ch[ristia]ns themselves it will be expedient to lay the foundat[io]n well of our Chr[istian] rel[igio]n and see w[ha]t the Deists have to say against it'. For this the professor recommended reading the Huguenot refugee and Irish dean Jacques Abbadie's *Vindication of the truth of Christian religion against all modern opposers*, Humphry Ditton's *Discourse concerning the resurrection of Jesus Christ*, and as the 'most satisfying answer to the grand Deist', Anthony Collins, he recommended that students read the work of Thomas Bullock.[100] Boyce's notebook also includes a list of 24 books that were bought by him in Belfast in 1731 for a total cost of £5 4s 9½d. The list included an Edinburgh *Confession of Faith*, William Sherlock on the Trinitarian controversy, Johannes Buxtorf (the elder)'s *Lexicon*, George Hakewill's *An apologie of the power and providence of God*, Peter King's *An enquiry into the constitution and worship of the primitive church*, a Hebrew grammar, William Burkitt's notes on the New Testament, John Spalding's *Synaxis sacra* (sermons preached at communions), Peter Martyr's *Common places*, Isaac Barrow's exposition on the creed, John Scott's *Christian life*, Thomas Forrester's *Rectius instruendum*, Ursinus's catechism, Calvin on the Pentateuch and Psalms, Benjamin Bennet's *Christian oratory*, Gilbert Burnet's *Exposition of the Thirty-Nine Articles of the Church of England*, and Wendelin's *Systems*.[101] This is interesting as it not only shows the reading material acquired by a ministerial student but also the variety of books that could be obtained in Belfast at this time.

At Glasgow the divinity professor from 1692 to 1707 was the thoroughly orthodox James Wodrow. Wodrow's methods of teaching were similar to Campbell's at Edinburgh, with the students engaged on Mondays in exercises and disputations and on Tuesdays lectures and homilies, which were criticized both by the professor and fellow students. On Wednesdays (except presbytery days) lectures were given by the professor in Latin and time was spent reading the scriptures in the original languages.[102] It could be argued that the Latin education received by students at university made them alien to lay culture and that there is a great difference between the sermon which students were required to deliver in Latin at university and the kind of popular sermon which they would later have to deliver to their congregations in English. Certainly it is true that in some surviving printed sermons there are lapses into foreign languages, though this may not have been the case when the sermons were originally delivered. Also in the early decades of the eighteenth century some regents and professors, such as Wodrow and Andrew Ross, were delivering some of their teaching in English. In addition, Wodrow spent

100 Petty cash book of Rev. Samuel Boyce, 1731–60 (PRONI, MIC139/1, p. 4).
101 Ibid., pp 5–7.
102 Robert Wodrow, *Life of James Wodrow, A.M.* (Edinburgh, 1828), pp 122–4.

Thursday afternoons lecturing on the English language in order to prepare students for preaching and often divided his students into smaller groups to write a 'skeleton', or plan, of a homily or sermon.

The remainder of Thursdays was spent on scripture doubts and religious controversies against Catholics, Lutherans, Arminians, Socinians, Anabaptists and 'other enemies of the truth'. On Friday the systematic theology of Wendelin's *Systema* was discussed and some of the older students were ordered to read the work of Calvinist theologians such as Francis Turretin, Antonious Walaeus and Gilbert Voetius, and Daniel Chamier (whose work dealt especially with 'the Roman controversy'), to see how they agreed or diverged from Wendelin. Others were ordered to read the work of Cardinal Robert Bellarmine, Faustus Socinus, Jacobus Arminius, Philipp van Limborch, and 'other adversaries of the received doctrine, that they might be ready to propose their strongest difficulties and objections'. Classes were abandoned on Wednesday morning when the Presbytery of Glasgow met and students were encouraged instead to sit in on the presbytery meetings to listen to the debates.[103] This would have been useful training for the aspiring ministers as it allowed them not only to learn the recognised procedures of debate, but the observation of cases of discipline being administered would have proved useful to their later role as moderator of the kirk session when they, along with the lay elders, would be responsible for overseeing the morals and behaviour of their congregations. On Saturdays, Wodrow encouraged his students to form praying societies and encouraged them to discuss pious and practical topics in these groups.[104]

Wodrow was succeeded by John Simson, who was investigated on a charge of Arminianism in 1714, and subsequently in 1726–7 on the charge of Arianism. Simson was suspended from his teaching duties in 1729 and remained as professor of divinity in name only for the last eleven years of his life.[105] Traditionally historians have regarded Simson as being responsible for spreading heterodox ideas among his students.[106] In his teaching Simson expounded the *Westminster Confession*, noting its differences from other reformed systems, and also allowed his students to discuss difficult scriptural passages and refute Christian writers from various denominations.[107] Though he may have allowed his students more latitude than earlier professors, such topics were common in divinity training as we have already seen. Also it is too simplistic to view the transference of ideas as a one-way traffic, especially in the intellectual context of the period when a more liberal theology was pervading England and parts of Europe. Allan Logan, minister of Culross, even suggested that Simson in some of his views 'followed … the Antrim non-declarers, and adopted their very terms' so that in some of his sentiments his 'eloquence and

103 Ibid., pp 124–7.
104 Ibid., pp 127–30; 'Cases answered by the societys of the students of divinity under Mr James Wodrow' (GUL, MS Gen 343); *ODNB* (Wodrow, James (1637–1707)).
105 Brown, 'Irish Presbyterian theology', p. 63. Arminianism rejects predestination, maintaining that God's grace is available to all and each individual's destiny is determined by their own free decision to resist or receive grace; Arianism is anti-Trinitarian, denying the divinity of Christ and maintaining that He is created by God the Father.
106 Reid, *Hist. of PCI*, iii, 159.
107 *ODNB* (Simson, John).

learning' was 'wholly Hybernian, and borrowed from the worst set of men in that kingdom'.[108]

As well as studying for the ministry at university each ministerial candidate was required to pass presbyterial trials before being licensed to preach. These tests, or trials as they were termed, were spread over several months. The General Committee in 1672 drew up a list of regulations regarding trials for licensing and ordination and these were reaffirmed in an overture approved in 1713, with the added clause that each candidate needed the approval of two-thirds of the ministers of the presbytery where he resided.[109] Candidates for licensing were expected to exhibit their skills by delivering a popular sermon, an exegesis (usually in Latin) upon a common head of divinity, and to give an exercise and addition. The 'exercise' involved giving a discussion of a particular passage of scripture before the presbytery; the 'addition' was where the ministerial candidate was given the opportunity to add to another's exercise by providing further comment, especially on the practical application of the biblical passage. They were also examined in their knowledge of the biblical languages. The testing of skills in Hebrew was usually limited to the Psalms, while the Greek test was open to any passage of the New Testament. In addition, knowledge of history and theology was examined when they were asked extempory questions and had to give a discourse to the presbytery members on an assigned period of church history, by presenting the main events, doctrinal developments, writings and personalities of a particular period. When these trials were satisfactorily approved and passed the student was licensed as a probationer for the ministry. A second set of trials had then to be undergone before he was ordained. In the intervening period the presbytery drew up preaching rotas for probationers, often in vacant congregations, and this helped to give them further experience before they were given sole charge of their own congregation. It also allowed them to earn some money as supply of vacant congregations was usually paid around ten shillings, though occasionally it was paid in kind, for example, in bottles of beer.[110]

Ordination, according to the regulations of 1672, was to be administered in secret,[111] but with the more settled period from the 1690s onwards it was something in which the whole congregation could participate. Before the service the planned ordination was intimated to the congregation several times (usually three) from the pulpit and a notice was fixed or proclaimed at the church door.[112] This practice was known as 'serving the edict' and allowed the congregation or, more specifically, the heads of its main families, to voice their consent or opposition to the ordination. In June 1702 the General Synod enacted that an ordination be celebrated as a fast day, both by the ministers involved in it and the congregation where the ceremony occurred.[113] This no doubt helped to heighten the sense of congregational

108 [Allan Logan], An enquiry into Professor Simson's sentiments on the doctrine of the Trinity, from his papers in the process against him (Edinburgh, 1729), p. 42.
109 Antrim 'Meeting' mins (UTC, pp 36–42); RGSU, i, 307.
110 Kirkdonald sess. mins (PHS, pp 62–4).
111 Antrim 'Meeting' mins (UTC, pp 36–42).
112 See, for instance, Killyleagh Pby mins (PRONI, Stewart papers, D1759/1/D/10, pp 11, 111–12); Barbour, 'Ministry of the Presbyterian Church', p. 98.
113 RGSU, i, 57.

participation and probably reinforced the Presbyterians' sense of being a distinctive community within Ulster.[114] The rite of ordination was itself a further aspect, in addition to their university education, differentiating Presbyterian clergy from laity. Francis Makemie, who was ordained by the Laggan Presbytery for America in 1682, wrote in 1694 that he 'received the imposition of hands, in that scriptural and orderly separation unto my holy and ministerial calling,' having given continuing 'satisfaction to godly, learned, and judicious, discerning men [the presbytery], of a work of grace and conversion wrought on my heart. ... not only was this required of me, but is expected of all ordained by presbyters'.[115]

III. Career patterns

The gap between licensing and ordination was usually two to three years but for some the gap between finishing university and licensing or between licensing and ordination could be significantly longer. Most of the ministers did not have any occupation before they entered the ministry, though we know that Andrew Ferguson, John McBride and John Hutcheson had been schoolmasters before they undertook charge of a congregation.[116] William Taylor, who became minister at Cairncastle in 1715, had previously been tutor to the Upton family at Templepatrick and John Thompson, who became minister of Macosquin in 1727, had previously been a captain in the army.[117] The gap between licensing and ordination lengthened for those ordained in the 1720s, probably because of the distractions created as a result of the Subscription Controversy and a desire on the part of the Subscribers to be more rigorous in testing candidates for theological orthodoxy. The average age of ordination for those ordained in 1700–9 was 25.6 years, but for those ordained in the 1720s the average age rose to almost 30 years. Similarly the gap between licensing and ordination rose from less than two years for those ordained before 1710 to 4.2 years for those ordained in the 1720s. Of the 303 ministers active in Ulster during the period, at least 57% were licentiates of Ulster presbyteries. Ten percent (31) were licensed by the Church of Scotland and two others in London. With regard to ordination, at least 83% (251) were ordained in Ulster, while only 6% were ordained in Scotland.

A key aspect of ministerial careers must be the number and duration of their pastorates. The majority of the 303 ministers led quite static lives, in the sense that they served in only one or two congregations. The following table shows the number of congregations that ministers served in.

---

[114] Greaves, *God's other children*, p. 183.

[115] Francis Makemie, *An answer to George Keith's libel. Against a catechism published by Francis Makemie* (Boston, 1694), p. 24.

[116] David Maxwell to Dr John Coghill, 6 June 1679 (HMC, *Ormonde MSS*, n.s., v, 125); [Kirkpatrick], *Presby. loyalty*, p. 505; McConnell, *Fasti*, pp 61, 64, 68.

[117] Classon Porter, 'Congregational memoirs. No. IV.–Cairncastle', *Christian Unitarian*, iv (1866), pp 224, 229; Bailie, *Hist. of congns*, p. 618.

Table 2   The number of congregations ministers active in Ulster in the period
1680–1729 served in during their entire career

Period ordained	Number of Pastorates					
	1	2	3	4	5	6
1640–1649	2	3	–	1	1	–
1650–1659	9	8	5	3	2	–
1660–1669	1	4	5	1	1	1
1670–1679	12	9	6	4	–	–
1680–1689	9	9	4	3	–	–
1690–1699	28	15	7	–	1	–
1700–1709	45	12	2	1	–	–
1710–1719	43	7	3	1	–	–
1720–1729	30	4	1	–	–	–
Total =	179	71	33	14	5	1

From this table it can be seen that almost 60% of the 303 ministers served in only one congregation, while a further 23% served in only two congregations. Those who served in five or more congregations formed less than 2% of the total number of ministers who were active during the period. There are a number of reasons why a minister might move from the congregation of his ordination. It may indicate something about the terms and conditions under which a minister found himself, or it may have been to minister at a church closer to his place of upbringing and family. Certain congregations may also have been viewed as more prestigious, for instance, if the congregation had a long history, a large and growing membership, or a higher remuneration. The table also shows that there was greater movement by those ministers ordained before 1690. This was probably because their careers coincided with more disturbed times, particularly during the Revolution, when many ministers fled to Scotland for safety and took up a charge there, thus inflating the number of congregations in which they had served.[118]

In total 71% (216) of the 303 ministers spent their entire career within Ulster. Just over a fifth (63) served in at least one Scottish church. An analysis of where in Scotland these ministers served reveals that the most popular area was within the bounds of the Synod of Glasgow and Ayr, followed by the Synod of Galloway, and the Synod of Lothian and Tweeddale. Smaller numbers served in the synods of Argyll, Dumfries, Perth and Stirling, Angus and Mearns, and Merse and Teviotdale. None spent any time as minister within the synods of Aberdeen; Ross, Sutherland and Caithness; or of Glenelg, Orkney and Shetland. Thirteen ministers who had been ordained after 1690 spent part of their career serving in at least one Irish

---

[118] Almost fifty Irish Presbyterian ministers took refuge in Scotland at the time of the Revolution, almost half of whom remained there in connexion with the established Church of Scotland: Reid, *Hist. of PCI*, ii, 395–6. At the meeting of the Synod of Galloway on 14 May 1689 there were seven ministers from Ireland in attendance: Synod of Galloway mins, 14 May 1689 (NAS, CH2/165/2, pp 1–2).

Presbyterian congregation outside Ulster. A further eight went to colonial America.[119] Thomas Gowan, jr, left Drumbo congregation in 1716 to become minister of the Scots Church in Leiden and Samuel Haliday, minister of First Belfast (1720–39), had previously been chaplain to the Scots Cameronian Regiment.[120]

IV. Libraries and continued study

A minister's education did not end when he was ordained. He was expected to continue adding to his knowledge through reading and private study. The General Synod in 1715 passed a resolution which recommended that ministers should:

> endeavour with the utmost industry to improve themselves in learning, particularly in the knowledg of the original languages, of the most celebrated controversies in divinity, of ecclesiastical history, and that they carefully read the most valuable practical treatises, both ancient and modern; and, because generally we have but few books, it will be expedient for supplying that want that they keep a correspondence among 'emselvs, and have frequent conferences on subjects of learning.[121]

A minister's preaching and doctrine, as well as his library, were usually examined during visitations. When the Presbytery of Antrim visited Templepatrick congregation in 1711 they inspected the library of the minister, Rev. William Livingston, and reported that he had 'a competent number of books for his assistance in study'.[122] The two members of Down Presbytery who inspected the library of Rev. William Biggar of Bangor in 1707 also reported that he had 'a good collection of useful and necessary books',[123] and there are other such references in the minutes of the presbyteries of Antrim, Down, Monaghan and Killyleagh.[124] Unfortunately presbytery minutes usually only record the relative size of a library, describing that

---

[119] Thomas Craghead (Donegal and Castlederg, 1698–1715) emigrated to America in 1715 along with his brother-in-law, William Holmes (Strabane, 1692–1714); Archibald Boyd (Maghera, 1703–16) emigrated to America some time after 1716; James McGregor (Aghadowey, 1701–18), Thomas Wilson (Killybegs and Inver, 1676–1689), James Woodside (Dunboe, 1678–1718) and Samuel Young (Magherally, 1703–18) all emigrated to America in 1718; and Matthew Clerk (Kilrea, 1697–1720) emigrated to America in 1729. For others the move to America was only temporary: William Trail (Lifford, 1673–82) was in Maryland, America, from 1684–90, and returned to Scotland at the Revolution; William Boyd (Macosquin, 1710–25) was in America from 1718–19; William Cornwall (Clogher, 1696–1718) was there from 1718–23; and Isaac Taylor (Ardstraw, 1718–29), was absent in New England from 1722–3.
[120] RGSU, i, 394–5; McConnell, Fasti, p. 103.
[121] RGSU, i, 383.
[122] Antrim Pby mins, 1697–1713 (PHS, p. 511).
[123] Down Pby mins (PHS, pp 32, 36).
[124] Antrim Pby mins, 1697–1713 (PHS, pp 306, 315, 331, 375); Down Pby mins (PHS, pp 71, 75–6, 84, 86, 88, 93, 96, 98–9, 102, 105, 108, 114, 129, 132, 141, 176, 179–80, 185–6, 225, 230, 251, 258, 275, 298, 307, 321–2, 353, 355, 357, 363); Monaghan Pby mins (PHS, p. 26); Killyleagh Pby mins (PRONI, Stewart papers, D1759/1/D/10, pp 21, 35, 51, 54, 59, 63).

of Stafford Pettigrew of Ballyeaston, for instance, as a 'small one',[125] and do not give an indication of the titles the libraries contained.

In 1709 the Presbytery of Antrim requested each of its ministers to compile a catalogue of their books. These catalogues were to be lodged with the clerk of the presbytery who would make them available to any minister within the presbytery. In this way every minister would be aware of the books that each other owned and a circulating library could operate, whereby ministers in the presbytery would be able to borrow books easily from other members. Unfortunately these catalogues, which would have been handwritten, have not survived and subsequent references in the presbytery minutes make it clear that some of the ministers were slow in compiling them.[126]

Occasionally we may gain some insight into the books owned by ministers through their wills. Rev. John Hutcheson left all his books and manuscripts to his son, Francis, while Rev. Thomas Fulton of Limavady left his to his nephew Archibald Ross, and another minister who died in 1725 left 'a small parcel of books' to his relatives.[127] Rev. Patrick Adair of Belfast specified that his wife and daughter were to be given 'a number of practicall books' and the other half was bequeathed to his son, William, who was minister of Ballyeaston and later Antrim.[128] Adair's successor at Belfast, Rev. John McBride, in his will dated 1718, left all his 'physick books' to his son Alexander.[129] Rev. James Bruce, minister of Killyleagh, who died in 1730, left his 'large house Bible, and two volumes of Poole's Annotations' to his eldest son, Michael, who was minister at Holywood, while the rest of his books were bequeathed to his other son, Patrick, minister at Drumbo.[130]

In 1715 the General Synod requested James Kirkpatrick, the minister of Second Belfast, to send to Holland for sixty copies of *Altare Damascenum*.[131] This book, written by the Scottish divine David Calderwood, had been first published in 1623. It considered the 'whole controversy between the English and Scottish churches as to government, discipline, and worship'.[132] There was a delay in obtaining the books and an express letter was sent to Scotland to enquire about them. When the books finally arrived some ministers were slow in paying for their copies and Kirkpatrick complained to the General Synod that he was therefore unable 'to pay off the said bill, but that it is still lying over his head bearing interest, and that ten or a dozen of 'em are yet unsold'.[133]

Ministers, in correspondence with their Scottish counterparts, would request news of the most recent publications and in turn send details of new works printed

[125] Antrim Pby mins, 1697–1713 (PHS, p. 306).

[126] Ibid., pp 455–6, 469, 474.

[127] Abstract will of Rev. John Hutcheson, 1728 (PRONI, Stewart papers, D1759/3/B/1, p. 38); will of Rev. Thomas Fultowne (Fulton) of Limavady, 1688 (PHS); 'Presbyterian Historical Society', *Irish Presbyterian* (Feb. 1909), p. 22.

[128] J. G. W. Erskine (ed.), 'The will of the Rev. Patrick Adair, Belfast', *Bull. PHSI*, xii (1993), pp 31–2.

[129] Benn, *Belfast*, p. 405, n. 2.

[130] Abstract will of Rev. James Bruce, 1725 (PRONI, Stewart papers, D1759/3/B/1, p. 12).

[131] RGSU, i, 371.

[132] Thomas McCrie (ed.), *Miscellaneous writings, chiefly historical* (Edinburgh, 1841), p. 78.

[133] RGSU, i, 371–2.

in Belfast, particularly during the time of the Subscription Controversy.[134] Students travelling to the Scottish universities were often given errands to purchase or deliver these publications.[135] Another example of ministers using their acquaintances to obtain books is John McBride, who, in 1700, wrote to Dr Hans Sloane in London to inquire about Sloane's *Philosophical Transactions* of the Royal Society in London that had been cited in a history of Orkney McBride had been reading.[136] Sloane did send McBride a copy of the work and in a letter of 1706 McBride wrote to Sloane, 'I have [for] some time opportunity to observe f[r]om the learned philosophicall transactions how diligent and successfull you are in the promoting of learning.'[137]

In 1705 a group of young ministers formed the Belfast Society. Its membership was composed of ministers, ministerial students, and interested laymen, who met monthly. The ministerial members took it in turns to preach, and also read portions of Scripture in Hebrew and Greek, and discussed theological and pastoral topics.[138] In addition, time was spent analysing and reviewing new books. Among the aims of the society was one that:

> considering the many disadvantages which arise from our being hamper'd in our education, from our low circumstances in the world, which cannot afford us competent libraries ... we consult of proper measures, for procuring the best intelligence about books, enter into concert for the buying of them, taking care that no two members purchase the same book (except where it is of constant use to all) by which means the whole reap the benefit of what each member possesseth. Every one communicates to the whole, what he has met with observable in the course of his private studies.[139]

Despite this useful aim the society became associated with New Light ministers and thus, in the eyes of the Subscribers, with unorthodoxy. In 1726 the Non-Subscribers

[134] Alexander McCracken to [Robert Wodrow], 1 Aug. 1703, 22 June & 8 Sept. 1709 (NLS, Wod. Lett. Qu., ii, ff 93, 123–4); George Lang to [same], 2 Nov. 1706 (ibid., iv, f. 82); Wodrow to McCracken, 24 Aug. 1709 (Wodrow, *Corresp.*, i, 31); William Hair to [Wodrow], 3 Nov. 1714 (N.L.S, Wod. Lett. Qu., xx, f. 195); Robert McBride to same, 8 Mar. 1714/15 (ibid., f. 210); Alexander McCracken to same, 23 June 1716, 2 Feb. 1716/17 (ibid., ff 216, 219); William Hair to same, 11 Nov. 1718 (ibid., f. 231); George Lang to same, 23 May, 4 Nov. 1721 (ibid., ff 246, 254); Gilbert Kennedy to same, 2 Feb. 1721/2 (ibid., f. 259); Robert McBride to same, 26 July 1722 (ibid., f. 283); Wodrow to William Livingston, 19 June 1723 (Wodrow, *Corresp.*, iii, 60); William McKnight to Wodrow, 26 July 1723 (NLS, Wod. Lett. Qu. xx, f. 314); Samuel Smith to [same], 24 June 1726 (ibid. xxii, f. 110); C[harles] M[astertown] to [same], 6 July 1726 (ibid., f. 117); Mr [Charles] M[astertown] to William McKnight, 28 July 1726 (ibid., f. 113); Robert McBride to Wodrow, 7 Nov. 1726 (ibid., f. 123); Charles Mastertown to [same], 18 Aug. 1727, 10 Oct. 1728 (ibid., ff. 141, 157); [William McKnight] to [same], [late 1728] (ibid., f. 159); Wodrow, *Analecta*, iii, 184.
[135] Robert McBride to Wodrow, 30 Nov. 1726 (NLS, Wod. Lett. Qu., xxii, f. 125).
[136] John McBride to Sloane, 30 Dec. 1700, 16 Jan. 1701/2 (BL, Sloane MS 4038, ff 117, 288–9).
[137] John McBride to Sloane, 28 Jan. 1705/6 (BL, Sloane MS 4040, f. 122).
[138] David Stewart, *History and principles of the Presbyterian Church in Ireland* (Belfast, 1907), p. 96.
[139] 'Circular letter of December 7 1720', *A narrative of the proceedings of seven General Synods of the northern Presbyterians in Ireland, with relation to their differences in judgment and practice, from the year 1720 to the year 1726* (Belfast, 1727), p. 20. See also Duchal, *Sermon on death of Abernethy*, pp 36–40.

were expelled from the General Synod, and formed themselves into a separate non-subscribing Presbytery of Antrim.

In 1765 the Presbytery of Antrim formed a library, in Belfast, for the use of the ministers and educated elite of the area. The library, which contains around 2,100 volumes, is now held in the McClay Library at Queen's University, Belfast.[140] Interestingly, a number of the books have the names of their past owners inscribed on them, and these include a number of Presbyterian ministers who were active in the early decades of the eighteenth century. Ownership of a book cannot be taken to mean that the recorded possessor had purchased the book himself or even that he had read it, but a number of points can nevertheless be suggested. Most of the books are in either English or Latin, with Greek and Hebrew and, to a lesser extent, Arabic and French. This shows that the ministers in Ulster were well educated and able to read in a number of languages and it was this fact which allowed students for the ministry who had been born in Ulster to continue their studies in some of the continental universities where teaching would have been in Latin. Most of the books were published in London and a significant number were written by Church of England authors such as Robert Sanderson, Francis Gastrell and John Williams, though particularly those who could be classified as being 'latitudinarian' in their views, such as Edward Stillingfleet, Thomas Taylor, Simon Patrick and Edward Reynolds. English Presbyterian authors are also represented, such as John Owen, and especially moderate Presbyterians, in the form of the works of William Bates, which was owned by John Henderson, and Edmund Calamy's *Abridgement of Mr Baxter's life and times*, which was owned by Josias Clugston. Surprisingly, books by Scottish authors are very scarce, though this may have been because those who formed the Presbytery of Antrim Library may have had some preference for books from the English nonconformist tradition. Gilbert Kennedy and Francis Laird, however, had Walter Steuart's *Collections and observations methodiz'd, concerning the worship, discipline and government of the Church of Scotland*, while the Covenanters were represented by Samuel Rutherford's *Disputatio scholastica de divina providentia* (which Samuel Haliday had owned), John Brown's *De causa Dei contra antisabbatarios* (belonging to John Rowatt), and *A large declaration concerning the late tumults in Scotland ... with a particular deduction of the seditious practices of the prime leaders of the Covenanters* (which the ultra-orthodox William Livingston owned).

Continental theology was well represented, with a significant number of the books being published in the Netherlands, and others in Switzerland, France and the German territories. There were books written by the Dutch theologians Johannes Cocceius, Johannes van der Waeyen, Johannes Leusden, Gisbertus Voetius and Gerardus Johannes Vossius, as well as Swiss theologians such as Francis Turretin, Jean-Frédéric Ostervald, and Johann Heinrich Hottinger, the French philosopher René Descartes, and the Polish-born grammarian, Victorinus Byther. Rev. John

---

[140] Antrim Pby Lib., B. 1–6, 8–10, B. 12. 6–10, B. 13–15. From the later minutes of Antrim Presbytery it is known that 235 volumes were donated from the library of Samuel Haliday by his grandson and 106 volumes also came from the library of William Laird, minister of Belfast 1747–80, who had clearly inherited some of them from his ministerial relatives: Antrim (Non-Subscribing) Pby mins (PRONI, T1053/1, pp 70, 166–7).

McBride owned a work of Johannes Sleidanus, the annalist of the Reformation, and works by Calvin were owned by McBride and John Kennedy. Almost all the books were theological, with religious controversy, apologetics, ecclesiastical history, doctrinal theology, biblical geography, biblical criticism and interpretation all present. Some of the ministers owned material that could be classified as classical or civil history and politics, and Robert McBride had the French satirist Trajano Boccalini's *Advertisements from Parnassus*. The ministers most likely began to acquire books during their student days and there are a number of lexicons and books on Hebrew and Greek grammar. The ministers probably supplemented those books with others bought during the course of their careers to aid them in their work and a number of different commentaries belonging to early eighteenth-century ministers are preserved in the Presbytery of Antrim Library. Josias Clugston owned the Anglican John Mayer's commentary on the prophetic books, George Lang possessed Johannes Piscator's Latin commentary on the New Testament and John McBride had John Owen's expositions on the epistle to the Hebrews.

Many of the books had been published for some time before they were acquired by the Ulster ministers, though a well-written theological text could have a long popularity, with divinity students in the early eighteenth century, for instance, spending some time on the works arising from the Arminian controversy and the Synod of Dort a hundred years earlier. With the exception of those owned by the Maclaines and John Mears, most of the books were representative of a conservative and orthodox theology. Rev. Archibald Maclaine of Banbridge was a member of the Belfast Society and a moderate subscriber.[141] He appears to have taken a keen interest in reading the works arising out of the English controversy over the nature of the Trinity and the Irish Subscription Controversy. He not only owned John Abernethy's *Seasonable advice*, but also a letter to Rev. William Tong and others on the differences among the English Dissenters on the Trinity, and the work of Hubert Stogden, an English Presbyterian minister of semi-Arian views who was considered heterodox. Archibald's brother, Thomas (minister of Monaghan), was also a moderate subscriber,[142] and one of his books was written by Samuel Chandler, an English Presbyterian minister who described himself as 'a moderate Calvinist', but whom others suspected of Arianism and Socinianism.[143] There were three ministers called John Mears who were active in this period but the books in the Presbytery of Antrim Library probably belonged to the one who was minister at Newtownards from 1720 to 1767. He had entered Glasgow University in 1710, and, after graduating in 1713, studied divinity under John Simson. During his student days Mears had doubts on the doctrine of the Trinity and corresponded with Rev. Gilbert Kennedy of Tullylish in order to help clear his views. During the Subscription Controversy he sided strongly with the Non-Subscribers.[144] Although

[141] McConnell, *Fasti*, p. 116.

[142] Ibid.

[143] *ODNB* (Chandler, Samuel). Thomas Maclaine also owned Nehemiah Donaldson, *A funeral sermon preach'd on occasion of the death of Thomas Edwards esq; of Castle-Gore in the County of Tyrone, who died April the 26th, 1721* (Dublin, [1726]), which is now held in the Morton Library, Richmond, U.S.A., and marked 'E Dono Authoris, Tho: Maclaine'.

[144] Gilbert Kennedy, *A defence of the principles and conduct of the reverend General Synod of Ulster.*

Mears, when he was in Dublin in 1719, had obtained Daniel Waterland's *Vindication of Christ's divinity*, which defended religious orthodoxy, he also owned William Whiston's heretical *Sermons and essays*, and Arthur Sykes's *Authority of the clergy and the liberties of the laity*, a work which maintained that the church could not lay down absolute standards of doctrine. It may be suggestive too, that Rev. Samuel Haliday, a leading figure among the Non-Subscribers, owned books by the Swiss theologian Jean-Frédéric Ostervald who was thought to have a leaning towards Socinianism and Arminianism, and whose *Traité contre l'impureté*, which Haliday owned, was a plea for a more ethical and less doctrinal type of Christianity. Haliday, however, also owned a number of traditional works such as John Pearson's exposition on the Apostles' Creed, Samuel Rutherford's work on the providence of God, William Twisse's defence of Calvinism and predestinarianism against Arminius, and Nicholas Arnold's attack on Valentinus Smalcius's Racovian Catechism, which Arnold regarded as 'the most subtle insinuation of the Socinian religion that was ever attempted'. These more traditional theological works may have been obtained by Haliday from his orthodox father.

Another means of analysing the reading habits of ministers is by way of subscription lists. An author would solicit subscriptions for a proposed work and when sufficient money had been raised would pay the printer who would then publish the book. Although subscription lists in Ireland are rare before the mid-1720s,[145] there are a few examples of Ulster Presbyterian ministers subscribing in order to obtain books. The first printing press was set up in Belfast by Patrick Neill in 1694. After Neill's death the business was taken over by Neill's brother-in-law, James Blow, and another printer, Robert Gardner, set up business in Belfast around 1713. The earliest known extant subscription list for a book published in Belfast is for Wetenhall Wilkes's *Essay on the existence of a God*, published by Gardner in 1730. In total 294 individuals subscribed for 483 copies of the book, and among the subscribers were more than ten Presbyterian ministers.[146] A further four ministers subscribed for a copy of the French divinity professor Louis Ellies du Pin's *New history of ecclesiastical writers*, published in Dublin by George Grierson in 1722,[147] and Rev. William Holmes and Rev. Francis Iredell were among the subscribers for Sir Isaac Newton's *Observations upon the prophecies of Daniel* which

Being an answer to a pamphlet published by the Reverend Mr. Samuel Haliday: containing his reasons against the imposition unto the Westminster Confession (Belfast, 1724), pp 9–11; Samuel Haliday, *A letter to the Reverend Mr. Gilbert Kennedy; occasion'd by some personal reflections, contain'd in his answer to Mr. Haliday's reasons against the imposition of subscription to the Westminster-Confession, or any such human tests of orthodoxy* (Belfast, 1725), pp 54–61; Wodrow, *Analecta*, ii, 251–2; Witherow, *Hist. & lit. memls*, ii, 27; ODNB (Mears, John).

145 F. J. G. Robinson and J. M. Robinson, *Irish book subscription lists, 1700–1850* (CD-ROM, [Great Britain]: Romulus Press Ltd, 2004).

146 Wetenhall Wilkes, *An essay on the existence of a God: particularly in answer to two atheistical letters of Mr. I___ T___ dated from Dublin, 1729* (Belfast, 1730), had among its subscribers the following Irish Presbyterian ministers: William Ambrose, James Cobham, James Creighton, James Fraser, John Hasty, William Holmes (of Urney), William Holmes (of Antrim), William Livingston, Charles Mastertown, James White and Timothy White. Other subscribers who may also have been Presbyterian ministers were William Cunningham, Robert Gordon and James Moor.

147 L. E. du Pin, *A new history of ecclesiastical writers*, ed. William Wotton (3rd ed., Dublin, 1722)

was printed in Dublin in 1733 by Samuel Powell.[148] Powell also printed Samuel Clarke's *One hundred and seventy three sermons*, which Rev. Alexander Colvill and Rev. Robert Higginbotham subscribed for.[149] Rev. John Abernethy and Rev. Robert Craghead subscribed for Burnet's *History of the Reformation of the Church of England*[150] and four Irish Presbyterian ministers appeared in the subscription list of William Starrat's *Doctrine of projectiles*.[151] But it was not only books in Belfast and Dublin for which Ulster Presbyterian ministers subscribed; nine Irish Presbyterian ministers subscribed for John Maxwell's translation of Richard Cumberland's *Treatise of the laws of nature*, which was published in London in 1727.[152]

Books were, therefore, more numerous and accessible among the Presbyterian clergy in Ulster than has been supposed, and could be obtained from a variety of sources both inside and outside Ireland. Finally, two Ulster Presbyterian ministers showed their support for student reading when they donated books to the library of the University of Glasgow. John McBride of First Belfast donated a copy of his *Sample of jet-black prelatick calumny* and James Kirkpatrick of Second Belfast donated a copy of his *Presbyterian loyalty* (both books sought to defend Presbyterians against Anglican attacks). In addition, McBride donated Sir James Ware's *Antiquities and history of Ireland* (1704) and John Colgan's two volumes on the Irish saints, *Acta sanctorum veteris et majoris Scotiae seu Hiberniae sanctorum insulae* (1645) and *Vitas et acts Divorum Patricii Columbae et Brigidae* (1647).[153]

V. Status and role

Ministers occupied the central role in Presbyterian worship. They were responsible for leading the services each Sunday, preaching, and administering the sacraments and ordinances. Sermons and prayers were extemporary, though ministers had still to spend time preparing them. A phrase used by Rev. Seth Drummond in his notebook is 'as the Lord helps me',[154] in other words, he did as much preparation as he could by making a plan for each sermon in his notebook, but on the actual

---

had 153 subscribers for 240 copies, including the following Irish Presbyterian ministers: John Abernethy, John Henderson, Robert Higginbotham and James Kirkpatrick.

[148] Isaac Newton, *Observations upon the prophecies of Daniel, and the Apocalypse of St. John* (Dublin, 1733). This work was published by Samuel Powell for George Risk, George Ewing and, an Ulster Presbyterian bookseller in Dublin, William Smith.

[149] Samuel Clarke, *One hundred and seventy three sermons on several subjects* (Dublin, 1734).

[150] Gilbert Burnet, *The history of the Reformation of the Church of England* (3 vols, Dublin, 1730–3). This was published by Aaron Rhames for Richard Gunne and the Ulster-born Dublin booksellers John Smith and William Bruce.

[151] William Starrat, *The doctrine of the projectiles demonstrated and apply'd to all the most useful problems in practical gunnery* (Dublin, 1733), had Richard Chapin (Choppin), Thomas Drennan, Victor Ferguson and Samuel Holliday (Haliday), among its 704 subscribers.

[152] The nine Irish Presbyterian ministerial subscribers to Richard Cumberland, *A treatise of the laws of nature ... made English ... by John Maxwell ...* (London, 1727) were John Abernethy, Richard Choppin, Alexander Colvill, Samuel Haliday, John Hasty, Robert Higginbotham, Archibald Maclaine, John Mears and Thomas Nevin.

[153] *Munimenta alme Universitatis Glasguensis*, iii, 448, 450.

[154] Notebook of Rev. Seth Drummond, 1705–7 (PHS).

occasion when it was delivered he relied on his memory and the inspiration of the Holy Spirit. The sermon was often discussed in Presbyterian homes after it was delivered and the congregation attached great importance to it. The reason why Antrim congregation refused to give a call to Neal Gray in 1690 was because they thought his voice was 'too low'.[155] Since the majority of the ministers served in two congregations or fewer they were in a good position to be able to judge what kind of sermon best suited the needs and intellect of their audience. Not all ministers, however, achieved this, and in 1697 the synod found it necessary to recommend 'that ministers and preachers use a sound form of words in preaching, abstaining from all romantick expressions and hard words, which the vulgar do not understand, as also from all sordid words and phrases'.[156] In 1715 the writer of 'An enquiry into the state of religion', which was published by the synod, complained further that lack of preparation in public prayers was evident in the 'indecent and indigested expressions, which are offensive and unedifying'.[157] The sermons that have survived, either in manuscript or print, show that the ministers relied heavily on the Bible, with many examples of scriptural language, quotations, allusion and references being used in the course of a single sermon. The Dublin minister Rev. Joseph Boyse stated that 'the non-conformist ministers in general, and particularly those in the north of Ireland never us'd to be sparing in the use of their concordances'.[158] The sermons also tended to be quite structured, and arranged into various points. This was probably in order to aid the preacher as he delivered them without notes.

A large proportion of a minister's week was taken up by pastoral care and visitation. The lives of ministers could be particularly hectic and demanding, and as they were constantly 'on call' their time was not their own. Summarising the contents of the diary of Rev. John Kennedy of Benburb, Constantia Maxwell wrote, 'Mr Kennedy was in the saddle for a great part of the day, and sometimes far into the night, in fair weather and foul, travelling far, baptizing, marrying, catechizing, visiting the sick and dying.'[159] Most ministers, despite the demands of the office, fulfilled their pastoral duties adequately and successfully and examples exist of faithful and hardworking ministers who had a genuine concern for their flock. Rev. John Abernethy, while minister at Antrim from 1703 to 1730, for instance,

> applied himself to his other congregational labours, ... viz. catechising, visiting families and the sick, as much as his necessary avocations would allow him, with care; always pointing them to the true ends of religion, and with good success; carrying it with tenderness and affection to his people; ready to serve everyone that needed, or could be the better for his assistance.[160]

---

155 Antrim 'Meeting' mins (UTC, p. 305).
156 *RGSU*, i, 25.
157 Ibid., i, 378.
158 Joseph Boyse, *The works of the reverend and learned Mr. Joseph Boyse, of Dublin* (2 vols, London, 1728), ii, 94.
159 Constantia Maxwell, *Country and town in Ireland under the Georges* (Dundalk, 1949), pp 351–2.
160 Duchal, *Sermon on death of Abernethy*, p. 16.

The minister, along with the elders of the congregation, formed the kirk session. Together they were responsible for overseeing and maintaining the moral standard of the community. Since ministers, as moderators of the session, were responsible for administering sessional discipline the ministers themselves had to lead suitable and exemplary lives in which they would be 'examples to the flock in holy life and good works'.[161] Despite the claim of Rev. Robert Craghead, of Derry, that 'no scandalous ministers are permitted to officiate with us, such as common swearers, profaners of Sabbaths, adulterers, drunkards, gaming and dancing until the Lord's Day',[162] there were a few instances when ministers failed to live the kind of life expected of them. Rev. Archibald Boyd of Maghera and Josiah Cornwall were both deposed for adultery, and in 1726 Rev. Robert Wirling of Killead was deposed for an unspecified offence. Robert Higginbotham of First Coleraine was rebuked before the synod in 1714 for refusing to fulfil his promise to marry Mrs Martha Woods, of Four-loan-ends in the parish of Belfast.[163] In 1701 the synod overtured 'that no minister joyn any party in marraige, till the partys be proclaim'd 3 severall Sabbaths' and the synod rigidly enforced this enactment,[164] with a number of ministers being temporarily suspended for celebrating marriages 'irregularly'.[165] In 1701 the synod was concerned that some ministers and their families were 'too gaudy and vain in their apparel, and some too sordid' and recommended it to the presbyteries to inquire into these cases and ensure that ministers 'study decency and gravity in their apparell and wiggs, avoid powderings, vain cravats, half shirts, and the like'.[166] In 1727 the synod further enacted that presbyteries were to censure any minister who attended stage plays.[167]

Ministers along with an elder from each congregation represented their church at the higher courts of presbytery and, after 1690, General Synod. These meetings kept the ministers abreast of developments and occurrences within the wider framework of the church. Such regular meetings also provided an opportunity for fellowship between the ministers. Presbyteries usually met every month and the synod met at least once a year. The attendance of ministers at these higher courts was one way in which the clergy were enabled to fashion and maintain their professional identity within Presbyterian society, and they offered the clergy an opportunity for sociability. Neighbouring ministers occasionally met up and together made the journey to presbytery or synod meeting. John Scott, a ministerial student from Donaghadee, recorded in his diary that on Tuesday 8 May 1705 he 'went to Ballywalter to the presbytery w[i]th Mr Hamilton [of Donaghadee], Mr. Bigger [of Bangor and moderator of the presbytery], Mr

---

[161] Robert Chambre, 'An explanation of the Shorter Catechisme of the Reverend Assembly of Divines' (1680) (MS in UTC), pp 369–70.
[162] Robert Craghead, An answer to a late book, intituled, a discourse concerning the inventions of men in the worship of God, by William, Lord Bishop of Derry (Edinburgh, 1694), p. 140.
[163] RGSU, i, 325, 327, 418; ii, 116, 140.
[164] RGSU, i, 53.
[165] J. M. Barkley, 'Marriage and the Presbyterian tradition', Ulster Folklife, xxxix (1993), p. 35.
[166] RGSU, i, 46.
[167] Ibid., ii, 120.

Boyd [of Maghera], and Hugo Ramsey [another ministerial student who became minister at Clough in 1707]'.[168]

Although the surviving minutes of presbyteries and synods are usually concerned with such issues as ministerial income, education and training of ministerial candidates, discipline, and other matters of church administration, there are a few references which make it clear that the meetings were not totally filled with formal business – the ministers also had a break during which they ate dinner together.[169] Scott records on 5 February 1706 that he 'went to Tonnochnive [Saintfield] to the presbytery and heard Mr Mairs on Pro[verbs]: 8: 32, after sermon we dined, and after din[n]er the presbytery was again constitute'.[170] The gathering of ministers at presbytery or synod gave them the opportunity to discuss practical issues connected with the ministerial office and even allowed them to discuss their reading or exchange books.[171] It is important not to exaggerate these events when it comes to considering the degree to which the Presbyterian clergy in Ulster had a corporate identity, because it must be borne in mind that, in contrast to the higher meetings of the established church which were composed solely of clerics, at both presbytery and synod elders as well as Presbyterian ministers could attend.[172] Also such gatherings could involve heated debates and exchange, as was the case especially during the years of the Subscription Controversy, which raged from 1719 to 1726. Nevertheless there was a fraternal spirit between the ministers, who often referred to themselves in the presbytery and synod minutes as 'brethren', and the absence of any hierarchy among the clergy in the Presbyterian church probably aided clerical cohesiveness.

Although there were no divisions between Presbyterian ministers created by hierarchy, distinctions did arise as a result of differences in the amount of income that ministers were able to secure and enjoy. The bulk of a minister's income was provided by his stipend. This was raised by bonds made by the head of each family in the congregation, who pledged a certain amount towards the minister's maintenance. Ministers usually received further payment in kind, in the form of corn, oats, turf, eggs or potatoes. Most congregations rented a farm and provided a house for their minister, and many also made arrangements to plough or sow the minister's farm.[173] The farm enabled the minister to keep cows to provide milk for his family and to keep a horse which would be useful in undertaking his pastoral duties and travelling to the higher courts of the church. Rev. John Kennedy's diary not only records ministerial duties but also mentions him planting hedges, carting manure, sowing and reaping his fields, attending local fairs and markets, buying cattle, and

---

168 Diary of John Scott in John Stevenson, *Two centuries of life in Down, 1600–1800* (Belfast, 1920), p. 157.
169 *RGSU*, i, 70; Monaghan Pby mins (PHS, p. 235); Antrim Pby mins, 1697–1713 (PHS, p. 44); Strabane Pby mins (UTC, pp 37, 42, 48, 84–5).
170 Stevenson, *Two centuries of life in Down*, p. 159.
171 Diary of John Kennedy, 15 June 1725 (PHS).
172 The role of elders in the presbyteries, initially, seems to have varied among the different meetings. Although elders were present at the Laggan Presbytery from 1672–81 it was not until October 1687 that they were present at the Antrim 'Meeting': Greaves, *God's other children*, p. 163.
173 Route Pby mins (PHS, pp 132, 154, 166, 252); Conway, 'The Presbyterian ministry', p. 200; Barkley, 'The Presbyterian minister', p. 49.

even slaughtering them.[174] In addition, ministers received further income from the royal bounty, or *regium donum*. This was first granted in 1672 at £600 a year, though it was discontinued for a time during the end of Charles II's reign and throughout James II's reign, before being reinstated and doubled in 1690. As a block grant it was equally divided, and in 1690 amounted to around £14 per minister. It was discontinued again briefly in 1714, but was revived under George I, who granted an additional £400 to the Synod of Ulster in 1718.[175]

Some ministers augmented their income with money gained from other employ-ments held simultaneously. Thomas Gowan, Fulk White, William Leggatt, and John McBride all taught students while ministering to their respective congrega-tions. Joseph Hemphill apparently kept a tan yard while minister of Pettigo and Termon,[176] and James Kirkpatrick in later life, when minister of Second Belfast, combined the work of a doctor with his clerical and pastoral duties, even publishing a medical treatise in 1739.[177] A number of the ministers were men of private means. Rev. Alexander Bruce of Donaghadee received the lands of Gartlet in patrimony from his father in 1670. In the following year Rev. Alexander Hutcheson purchased the townland of Drumalig (in the parish of Saintfield) from Viscount Clandeboye.[178] He left Drumalig to his son, Rev. John Hutcheson, of Armagh, who at the time of his death also held land in County Monaghan.[179] Other examples of private wealth include Rev. Thomas Milligan, minister at Keady, who obtained 80 acres of lands at Tullynamallogue and Iskey-meadow.[180] Rev. Victor Ferguson of Strabane was reputed to have possessed 'considerable private means' and bequeathed his house and farm at Carricklee to his ministerial successors in the congregation,[181] and Rev. Fulk White bought 180 acres of land upon which he built a house which he named White Hall. Fulk's eldest son, James, inherited the property and also succeeded his father as minister at Broughshane. By his marriage with Jane McCollum of Limnalary, James acquired considerable property on the north-east coast of Ireland which had been owned by his wife's nephew, Hugh McCollum.[182] Marriage also brought greater financial security to Francis Iredell, who married the daughter and co-heir of Arthur Macartney of Dublin in 1716, and Samuel Haliday's marriage

---

[174] Diary of John Kennedy, 1714–37 (PHS).

[175] C. E. Pike, 'The origin of the regium donum', *Transactions of the Royal Historical Society*, 3rd ser., iii (1909), p. 255; 'History of the regium donum', *McComb's Almanack* (1849), p. 71.

[176] M. L. Thompson, '*The meeting-house beside the big bush': a history of Pettigo Presbyterian Church* (Omagh, [2002]), p. 4; McConnell, *Fasti*, p. 104.

[177] Glasgow Univ. meeting minutes (Senate), 1730–49 (GUA 26631, pp 16–18); James Kirkpatrick, *An account of the success of Mrs. Stephens's medicines for the stone, in the case of James Kirkpatrick, doctor of divinity* (Belfast, 1739); ODNB (Kirkpatrick, James (c.1676–1743)).

[178] Scott, *Fasti*, i, 277; McConnell, *Fasti*, p. 41.

[179] Abstract will of Rev. Alexander Hutcheson, 1711 (PRONI, Stewart papers, D1759/3/B/1, p. 36).

[180] Bailie, *Hist. of congns*, p. 538.

[181] James Gibson and James Lumsden, *Two discourses delivered before the First Presbyterian Congregation, Strabane, on leaving their old and entering their new church, October, 1872* (Belfast, [1872]), p. 9.

[182] Durand, *Life of Field-Marshal Sir George White*, i, 2–4; 'Presbyterian Historical Society', *Irish Presbyterian*, xxii, no. 2 (1916), p. 27.

to the widow of Arthur Maxwell, esq., of Drumbeg, brought him 'considerable property'.[183] When Haliday died in 1739 he left £500 to his wife along with £200 *per annum* which she possessed as Maxwell's relict, and also various items of furniture and the leases of fields in the Shankill area of Belfast.[184]

From the wills of certain ministers we can gain some insight into their lifestyles and the type of goods they possessed. Rev. Gilbert Kennedy of Tullylish, for instance, in his will (which was dated 1745), left six silver spoons to his son, Dr James Kennedy.[185] Rev. John Hutcheson of Armagh, who died in 1729, left £100 to his wife Rachel, as well as a horse, two cows, and all meal, malt and wheat that was in the house at the time of his death. His daughter Rhoda received an annuity of £24, along with 'all the tea equipage'. To his son Hans he left six silver spoons from his old set; to his son Robert, six silver spoons from his new set; to his son Alexander, a large silver cup; to his son John, the silver server; and to his son Francis (the philosopher), a silver ladle, two salts, all his books and manuscripts, and the townland of Drumalig.[186] Rev. James Reid of Killinchy, County Down, who died in 1753, bequeathed to his wife, Isabel, the lease of his farm and house in Balloo, along with £150, his plate, furniture, horses, cows, sheep, and all meal, turf, corn and grain in the stockyard and growing. In addition to his books, his son, Thomas, also received his day clock, sword, pistols, 'hone' and razor; while, his daughter, Esther, was left 'the large trunk, looking-glass, and bed in the sleeping-room, commonly called the middle room, with proportion of bed-clothes, linen and woolen for it'.[187]

Richard Greaves has calculated that in the late 1680s the average income of the ministers in the Presbytery of Antrim was £25 15s per year, and that this rose to £33 9s 3d in the 1690s.[188] These figures need to be treated with caution as they deal only with the stipend that was pledged, not what was actually paid. Arrears were common and frequently presbyteries had to insist on the clearing of debts to a previous minister before they would ratify a call to a new one. We know that the stipend of Rev. John McBride of Belfast in 1708 was £160 Irish or £147 13s 10¼d sterling.[189] There were thus some wealthy men among the Presbyterian clergy, but others were living at subsistence level, or below. For instance, when Rev. William Gilchrist died he left a widow in very poor circumstances.[190] Towards the end of our period the General Synod attempted to put in place a system whereby wealthier congregations would contribute to help their poorer counterparts maintain a minister, but at times of scarcity some ministers still found themselves hard-pressed.[191]

---

183 McConnell, *Fasti*, pp 69, 103.
184 Benn, *Belfast*, p. 406, n. 1.
185 'Abstracts of wills', *Irish Ancestor*, ii, no. 2 (1970), p. 123.
186 Abstract will of Rev. John Hutcheson, 1728 (PRONI, Stewart papers, D1759/3/B/1, pp 38–9).
187 Abstract will of Rev. James Reid, 1749 (PRONI, Stewart papers, D1759/3/B/1, p. 83).
188 Greaves, *God's other children*, p. 193.
189 *DNB* (McBride, John (1651?–1718)).
190 McConnell, *Fasti*, p. 62.
191 J. L. McCracken, 'The ecclesiastical structure' in T. W. Moody and W. E. Vaughan (eds), *A new history of Ireland: iv: Eighteenth-century Ireland 1691–1800* (Oxford, 1986), p. 101; Griffin, *The people with no name*, pp 84–5.

As a result of the leading role that the clergy occupied in worship and also because of their education, training, and calling, Presbyterian ministers were usually respected within their own community and provided social leadership. When Rev. James McGregor emigrated to America in 1718 around 200 families accompanied him and similarly around 120 people from Garvagh went with their minister, James Woodside, when he sailed from Derry to America in the same year.[192] This could not have occurred without mutual respect and affection between minister and laity. The income that most Presbyterian ministers in Ulster received was such that, judged by the standards and income of those outside the Presbyterian community, they were edging towards the 'quality' in society. Toby Barnard argues that £40 was 'the threshold above which one could live politely'.[193] If we take Greaves's calculation that stipends averaged around £33 in the 1690s, together with what they received from the *regium donum*, and in kind, and the savings they made from having a house and farm provided for them, it must mean that, as Barnard argues, many non-conformist ministers in Ulster passed as 'pseudo-gentry' within their communities.[194] Rev. Thomas Nevin of Downpatrick appeared in a list of gentry compiled anonymously around 1725 and it was estimated that he enjoyed an annual wealth of at least £100.[195] As often one of the few members of the local community with a university education, Presbyterian ministers were at times asked by their congregation to give medical advice, or assistance in the making of wills.[196] They acted as mediators when disputes occurred within the Presbyterian 'community' and their position within society offered many opportunities for making and maintaining contacts with different social, economic and occupational groups. As Rev. James Duchal wrote, the Presbyterian minister had to be 'as the humours of the people direct; just as fit to live upon three-score pounds as three-hundred … travelling with the same humour among cottagers and labourers as among hall-houses and squires; bringing home a lodgment of fleas as happily as a good dinner and a glass of claret'.[197]

* * * * * * *

The clergy were one of the most recognisable and, arguably, one of the most important and influential groups within Ulster Presbyterian society. The lives and careers of the 303 ministers active in Ulster between 1680 and 1729 displayed both continuity and change. Scotland became less important as a pool for ministerial recruitment as the native Ulster Presbyterian population grew and, after 1690, Scottish ministers in Ulster were attracted to serving in the established Presbyterian church within their own country. In terms of their geographical origin, and where the ministers were licensed and ordained, the connexion with Scotland was not as

---

[192] Barkley, 'The Presbyterian minister', p. 69.
[193] Barnard, *New anatomy*, p. 113.
[194] Greaves, *God's other children*, p. 193; Barnard, *New Anatomy*, p. 113.
[195] List of the gentlemen of Co. Down and Co. Antrim, [c.1725] (Royal Irish Academy, Dublin, Upton papers, MS 24.K.19, no. 1).
[196] T. H. Mullin, 'Old customs and practices in the Irish Presbyterian church', *Bull. PHSI*, xxix (2004–5), p. 26; diary of John Kennedy, 23 Nov. 1723 (PHS, p. 5).
[197] 'Ministerial life in 1738', *Report of the Presbyterian Historical Society* (1912), p. 18.

important, except for education, as has sometimes been suggested. Across the period as a whole, less than a third of the ministers were born in Scotland, less than a tenth were licensed or ordained in Scotland, and four-fifths of the 303 ministers never served in churches outside Ireland. Many of the ministers, though, had Scottish parents or grandparents and despite local educational initiatives only rarely was education at the Scottish universities supplanted by education within Ulster alone. Even after the Subscription Controversy, both Subscribers and Non-Subscribers in Ulster sent their ministerial candidates to be educated at the same universities in Scotland. The Presbyterian ministers were accorded a certain respect and status within the Presbyterian community, sometimes out of proportion with their income, but rather as a result of their education, sense of calling, continued study and commitment to a particular way of life. Clergymen met at presbytery and synod and in other informal ways, such as at the Belfast Society, and the life of the church provided a context for clerical relationships to develop. This was probably aided by the relative geographical smallness of Ulster and the lack of social distinctions within the clerical group. The Presbyterian clergy's corporate identity, however, did not make them socially exclusive from the society in which they lived and worked and in the course of their work the Presbyterian ministry came into contact, and socialised, with many different types of people.

a) Rev. John McBride, minister of Clare
(1679–94) and (First) Belfast (1694–1718)

b) Rev. John Abernethy, minister of Antrim
(1703–30) and Wood Street, Dublin (1730–40)

c) Rev. Samuel Haliday, minister of First
Belfast (1720–39)

d) Rev. John Mears, minister of Newtownards
(1720–35), Clonmel (1735–40) and Wood
Street, Dublin (1740–67)

Figure 3   Portraits of Presbyterian ministers active in the early eighteenth century

2

Gentry

Over the last four decades a number of important studies have been written about the landed elites of England and Wales, at both national and regional levels,[1] and more recently historians have begun to consider the gentry in Ireland.[2] As yet, however, there has been no study of the Presbyterian gentry of Ulster. Presbyterian landowners in the province were not numerous, and numerically as a proportion of the Presbyterian population were almost insignificant. Nevertheless, as a result of the influence and prestige that their wealth and social status afforded them, and also because of the political power that it enabled them to exercise, the Presbyterian gentry are worthy of research. In this chapter I will examine the social, private and religious lives of the Ulster Presbyterian landed elite, their commitment to Presbyterianism, the importance of the Scottish connexion, and their role as landlords.

There was not always a clear distinction between the landed elite and the wealthiest and most successful of those engaged in trade and the professions. The upper branches of the medical and legal professions both received the majority of their recruits from gentry families.[3] Some of the gentry families dabbled in trade and apprenticed their younger sons to merchants.[4] Wealthy merchants often

[1]   G. E. Mingay, The gentry: the rise and fall of a ruling class (London, 1976); Peter Roebuck, Yorkshire baronets 1640–1760: families, estates, and fortunes (Oxford, 1980); Philip Jenkins, The making of a ruling class: the Glamorgan gentry 1640–1790 (Cambridge, 1983); Lawrence Stone and J. C. F. Stone, An open elite? England 1540–1880 (Oxford, 1984); Felicity Heal and Clive Holmes, The gentry in England and Wales, 1500–1700 (Basingstoke, 1994); N. A. R. Aubertin-Potter, 'Social mobility, marriage and kinship among some gentry and yeoman families of Wantage Hundred, c.1522–c.1670' (Ph.D. thesis, Oxford Brookes Univ., 1994); J. M. Rosenheim, The emergence of a ruling order: English landed society 1650–1750 (London, 1998).
[2]   K. J. Harvey, The Bellews of Mount Bellew: a Catholic gentry family in eighteenth-century Ireland (Dublin, 1998); D. M. Beaumont, 'The gentry of The King's and Queen's counties: Protestant landed society, 1690–1760' (2 vols, Ph.D. thesis, TCD, 1999); R. A. Richey, 'Landed society in mid-eighteenth century County Down' (Ph.D. thesis, QUB, 2000); Barnard, New anatomy, pp 21–80; idem, Making the grand figure: lives and possessions in Ireland, 1641–1770 (London, 2004); David Dickson, Old world colony: Cork and south Munster 1630–1830 (Cork, 2005), pp 61–112; A. P. W. Malcomson, The pursuit of the heiress: aristocratic marriage in Ireland 1740–1840 (Belfast, 2006).
[3]   See pp 127–8, 130, 142–3 below on gentry recruitment to the legal and medical professions.
[4]   Agnew, Merchant families, pp 41, 52; will of Arthur Upton, 1706 (NAI, Prerogative will book, 1706–8, MFGS 41/2, f. 28); Hamilton Maxwell to Agmondisham Vesey, 13 Jan. 1721/2, 3 Feb. 1721/2 (PRONI, Kirk papers, T2524/12–13); notes on families and places, Co. Down (ibid., Stewart papers, D1759/3/A/1, pp 42–5). It was not only Presbyterian gentlemen who were involved in trade or apprenticed their sons to merchants, see Toby Barnard, 'What became of Waring? The making of an Ulster squire?' in idem, Irish Protestant ascents and descents, 1641–1779 (Dublin, 2002), pp 235–65.

purchased land, such as William Crawford of Belfast who purchased Florida Manor, County Down, in 1692, and there were marriage alliances between the landed elite and leading mercantile families.[5] The distinction between the leading merchants and professionals, and the gentry, is therefore somewhat artificial. Nevertheless there were some merchants who did not purchase estates and who drew the largest proportion of their income from their mercantile activities, and I will not be concerned with such individuals in this chapter.[6] However, if they were merchants who had been recruited from a gentry background or were losing their interest in, and connexion to, trade, they will be considered here.

I. Numbers and geographical distribution

Contemporaries saw the Dissenters as being composed principally of men of the 'middling sort', merchants and craftsmen, and while this was an oversimplification of the social profile of Presbyterianism, it is true that few Dissenters were gentlemen.[7] Archbishop Hugh Boulter thought that the Irish Presbyterians were 'not proprietors of much land or wealth' and Henry Maxwell of Finnebrogue, near Downpatrick, an Anglican landlord from a clerical family, wrote in April 1716 to Viscount Molesworth, 'The body of our Dissenters consists of the middling and meaner sort of people, chiefly in the north and in the north not many of them are estated men compared with those of the established church.'[8] Shortly before, Bishop Edward Synge of Raphoe had written to the archbishop of Canterbury, William Wake:

> It is certain that the dissenting gentry are very few in this kingdom. In the province of Ulster (where the commonalty of that sort are most numerous) I cannot find by all accounts, that there are above fourty of them who pass in the rank of gentlemen; of which several have no real estates, and none of them (except about four) that are at all considerable. And in the other three provinces, their interest and their numbers are much smaller.[9]

It is impossible to quantify the Presbyterian gentry class exactly, though two gentry lists do survive for the end of the period, one at the Royal Irish Academy and the other at Lambeth Palace Library. While neither bears a date, the Academy list is a nineteenth-century copy of an original which from internal evidence can

---

[5] Copy of grant of the estate of Florida, Co. Down, 21 Apr. 1691 (PRONI, Gordon papers, D4204/A/2/1–4); partition of Florida Manor, 22 Apr. 1691 (ibid., D4204/A/3/1–2); re-partition of Florida Manor, 8 Sept. 1692 (ibid., D4204/A/7/1–3); Agnew, *Merchant families*, pp 46, 54–55, 219.
[6] See below, ch. 3, for a study of Presbyterian merchants.
[7] D. W. Hayton, 'Ireland and the English ministers, 1707–16' (D.Phil. thesis, Oxford Univ., 1975), p. 37.
[8] Abp Boulter to duke of Newcastle, 15 Jan. 1732 (PRONI, State papers, MIC223/166); Henry Maxwell to [Molesworth], 9 Apr. 1716 (PRONI, Transcripts of State Papers relating to Ireland, T448/1, p. 280).
[9] Abp Synge to Abp Wake, 3 Feb. 1715/16 (BL, Add. MS. 6117, no. 15).

be dated no earlier than 1725,[10] and the Lambeth list can from internal evidence be dated to around 1732 or 1733.[11] The Academy list gives the names of the 'nobility and gentry' of Counties Antrim and Down only, while the Lambeth list gives a breakdown of the leading figures in all nine counties of Ulster. Both give the denominational affiliation of the gentlemen and considered an estate worth £100 a year to be the minimum qualification to be considered a 'gentleman'. While some caution must be exercised in using these lists, and with the contemporary views quoted above, as they were 'prepared by opponents of Presbyterian relief, who were concerned to disparage the significance of the dissenting interest',[12] their detail is impressive, and does appear to be accurate when assessed against other available contemporary evidence. In June 1722 a petition was presented to the General Synod of Ulster, for moderation in the Subscription Controversy, in which the signatories described themselves as 'gentlemen of the Presbyterian persuasion'. Although the original is now lost, a full list of the 46 individuals who signed the petition was published in the *Irish Presbyterian*, many of them also being found in the Academy and Lambeth lists. [13]

[10] List of the gentlemen of Co. Down and Co. Antrim (Royal Irish Academy, Dublin, Upton papers, MS 24.K.19, no. 1). The dating to c.1725 is based on: (1) Omission of Clotworthy Upton, a leading Presbyterian layman. The Colonel Upton mentioned as a Co. Antrim Churchman must be his brother Colonel John Upton who succeeded to the Upton estates following Clotworthy's death on 6 June 1725; (2) Inclusion of Patrick Agnew of Kilwaughter, whose will was proved in 1725.

[11] List of the nobility and gentry of Ulster divided into Churchmen, Dissenters and Papists (Lambeth Palace Lib., Gibson papers, MS 1742, ff 49–56). The dating to c.1732/3 would fit in with the fact that it was at this time that there was an attempt to repeal the test and such numerical evidence of the low number of Presbyterian gentry would have been ammunition for high church Anglicans. Although there is no definite documentary evidence to prove it, the Lambeth list may have been drawn up by, or for, Marmaduke Coghill for the earl of Egmont. In 1733 Egmont informed Horatio Walpole 'that the Dissenters are not so considerable in proportion of numbers or estates in Ireland as given out, of which I would convince him [Walpole] by papers in my possession': *Egmont Diary* (HMC, London, 1920), i, 439; Coghill to Edward Southwell, jr, 23 Nov. 1733 (Marmaduke Coghill, *Letters of Marmaduke Coghill, 1722–1738*, ed. D. W. Hayton (Dublin, 2005), p. 143). Other reasons for the 1732/3 dating of the Lambeth list are: (1) Inclusion of Sir Henry Cairnes who succeeded to the baronetcy on the death of his brother Sir Alexander Cairnes on 30 Oct. 1732; (2) Comments after the list mention that there were only two Presbyterian M.P.s included – James Stevenson and Hugh Henry – therefore, the list must have been drawn up sometime between Sir Alexander's death on 30 Oct. 1732 and his brother Henry's election to succeed him as M.P. for Monaghan; (3) There is evidence that the list was drawn up and later amended, for example, for Co. Down it lists among the Anglican gentry Dr [Henry] Leslie, the archdeacon of Down, but his name is scored out, and written beside it 'now Peter Leslie'. Leslie died on 3 September 1733 and was succeeded by his son Peter.

[12] D. W. Hayton, 'Presbyterians and the confessional state: the sacramental test as an issue in Irish politics, 1704–1780', *Bull. PHSI*, xxvi (1997), p. 23.

[13] The full list of signatories to the 1722 petition is given in 'Presbyterian Historical Society: Presbyterian gentry', *Irish Presbyterian*, new ser., xiv, no. 5 (May 1908), p. 75. The places of residence appended to the names in the article, while mostly accurate, were not in the original document, which is now lost, but were added later by Rev. Classon Porter wherever he thought himself 'authorized either by actual knowledge or reasonable conjecture'. For the context in which the petition was presented to the synod in 1722, see *A narrative of the proceedings of seven General*

The following tables give a full breakdown of the information contained in the Academy and Lambeth lists.

Table 3   The gentry of Counties Antrim and Down, c.1725, as contained in a list held at the Royal Irish Academy, Dublin

	Churchmen	Dissenters	Roman Catholic(s)
Co. Antrim	63	18	2
Co. Down	86	24	1
TOTAL =	149	42*	3

* = Colonel Edward Brice is listed under both counties and therefore the total number of individuals is 41.

Table 4   The gentry of Ulster, c.1732/3, as contained in a list held at Lambeth Palace Library

	Churchmen	Presbyterian(s)	Quaker	Roman Catholic(s)
Co. Antrim	36	8	0	1
Co. Armagh	54	2	1	0
Co. Cavan	63	2	0	4
Co. Donegal	63	1	0	1
Co. Down	79	10	0	2
Co. Fermanagh	44	3	0	1
Co. Londonderry	34	1	0	0
Co. Monaghan	67	4	0	0
Co. Tyrone	50	8	0	0
TOTAL =	490	39	1	9

From these tables it is apparent that the Presbyterian gentry were concentrated mainly in the Counties of Antrim, Down and Tyrone. The signatories of the 1722 petition were also mainly located in Counties Antrim and Down. County Londonderry surprisingly had only one Presbyterian gentleman according to the Lambeth list. The wealthiest Presbyterians in Londonderry, however, were merchants rather than gentlemen, and operated in Coleraine and Derry city. The Presbyterian gentry located outside Ulster were few in number and once again the wealthiest southern Presbyterians were merchants, who were located in the cities of Cork and Dublin.[14] At the time of the passing of the test clause in 1704 there were only three Presbyterian justices of the peace outside Ulster – Sir Arthur Langford for County Meath, George Rogers for County Cork and Edward Rogers for County Wexford.[15]

Synods of the northern Presbyterians in Ireland, with relation to their differences in judgment and practice, from the year 1720 to the year 1726 (Belfast, 1727), pp 67–8.

[14] List of the nobility and gentry of Ulster, [c.1732/3] (Lambeth Palace Lib., Gibson papers, MS 1742, f. 56).

[15] 'The case of the sacramental test as it now stands in the act passed in Ireland for preventing the growth of popery', [c.1704–8] (Leicestershire, Leicester and Rutland Record Office, Finch MSS, DG7 IRE.9).

The Academy list names 41 Presbyterian gentlemen in Counties Antrim and Down, where Presbyterianism was strongest – 23 were located in County Down, 17 in County Antrim, and Colonel Edward Brice was named under both counties. If we combine the names contained in the Academy and Lambeth lists with the signatories of the 1722 petition we have a total of a hundred names. Some, however, drew their income from mercantile activities, and if they are excluded we are left with around 80 individuals who were, or had been, Presbyterian. In the early 1730s Rev. John Abernethy estimated that there were 60 Presbyterian gentlemen in Counties Antrim, Down and Tyrone who possessed estates worth from £200 to £1,400 *per annum*.[16]

Across the period 1680 to 1730 the Presbyterian gentry declined in number. The Lambeth list, compiled around eight years after the Academy list, shows a decline, so that by 1733 there were 39 Presbyterian gentlemen in Ulster as a whole, whereas eight years earlier there had been 41 in Counties Antrim and Down alone. Although some caution must accompany these figures, as 20 of the Presbyterians who appear in the Academy list are not mentioned in the later Lambeth list as either Presbyterians or Anglicans, the decline of gentry support for Presbyterianism is undeniable. In 1706 the General Synod appointed a group of 22 gentlemen to raise subscriptions for a new missionary fund, but when J. S. Reid reviewed 20 of the 22 names in the middle of the next century he noted that 'not a single representative of these families is now a member of the Presbyterian Church'.[17]

Welsh gentry families also declined from the late seventeenth century onwards, in part as a result of financial problems, but largely because of the tendency of families to die out in the male line.[18] The decline in the number of Presbyterian gentry families in Ulster was not due to biological failure but to defection from Presbyterianism to the Church of Ireland. At first glance, political and economic self-interest would appear to be an adequate explanation for the defection. In 1704 the Irish Parliament passed a test clause which required all who held 'offices under the crown' in Ireland to qualify themselves by taking communion according to the rites of the established church. While Presbyterians could still sit in parliament and vote in parliamentary elections where the franchise was not restricted to membership of a corporation, other civil and military offices, and traditional gentry professions such as the army, were closed to Dissenters, and as a result some Presbyterian gentry families bowed to the legal and social pressure and conformed, no doubt with varying degrees of sincerity, to the Church of Ireland.[19]

It is often hard to pinpoint the exact date at which conformity took place – there is no equivalent to the convert rolls which existed for Catholics. Often we are dependent on Presbyterians taking public offices to which the test applied, or their serving as churchwardens, to be able to assume that they were at least

---

[16] John Abernethy, 'Reasons for the repeal of the sacramental test. From the Dublin edition, 1733' in idem, *Scarce and valuable tracts and sermons, occasionally published, by the late reverend and learned John Abernethy, M.A.* (London, 1751), p. 61.

[17] *RGSU*, i, 115; Reid, *Hist. of PCI*, iii, 40–41.

[18] Jenkins, *Making of a ruling class*, p. 38–9.

[19] J. G. Simms, 'The making of a penal law (2 Anne, c. 6), 1703–4', *Irish Historical Studies*, xii (1960), pp 105–18; Barnard, *New anatomy*, pp 17–18.

occasional conformists.[20] It is apparent, nevertheless, that for the majority of those who conformed, conformity was not immediate in Ulster on the passing of the test. On 13 September 1704 Rev. Alexander McCracken of Lisburn wrote to Robert Wodrow, 'All the justices of peace that wer[e] Presbyterian have quit their commissions upon that of the sacramental test, and are now out.'[21] Those located in Dublin and the south of Ireland, though, were much more likely to conform. The remarks at the end of the Lambeth list state,

> There are some Dissenters in the county's of Tipperary, Cork and other countyes, and in the citties of Dublin and Cork, who have considerable fortunes, but most of the men of estate among them, who live in the country so far conform as to become justices of the peace, some have from thence conform'd entirely, and the apparent heirs of others are Churchmen.[22]

In the Academy list it is stated against two of the Dissenters that their eldest sons were Churchmen,[23] against three that their fathers had been Dissenters,[24] and against five Churchmen that they had once been Dissenters.[25] By 1732/3, when the Lambeth list was compiled, the eldest son of Arthur Graham of County Armagh had also become a Churchman. Usually younger Presbyterians were the more likely to conform. In 1710 McCracken wrote to Wodrow, 'When any of our young gentlemen take the test, they give quite up to us and think themselves obliged to allow and defend, not only that piece of conformity, but the whole, and so go off.'[26] It is often easier for younger people to shrug off their traditions, especially in a changing society. Older Presbyterians seem to have found it harder to break away from the Presbyterian church, while younger Presbyterians adapted more easily. A similar situation operated in England. A comparison of the figures of the Westminster parliaments of 1690 to 1715 exhibits a steady decline in the number of members with any claim to be included in the Dissenting interest. Hayton has suggested that part of the explanation may lie in the significant numbers of 'moderate' or occasionally conforming Presbyterians to be found in the early parliaments of William III's reign. With generational change, occasional conformity in due course often became outright conformity, and as veterans of the Commonwealth parliaments died (such as Sir Edward Harley) their descendants revealed themselves as members of the established church.[27] Even then the transformation from dissent

---

[20] When selected as churchwardens Presbyterians could, however, name deputies to serve in their place: Toby Barnard, 'The eighteenth-century parish' in Elizabeth FitzPatrick and Raymond Gillespie (eds), *The parish in medieval and early modern Ireland: community, territory and building* (Dublin, 2006), p. 301.

[21] Alexander McCracken to [Robert Wodrow], 13 Oct. 1704 (NLS, Wod. Lett. Qu., ii, f. 110).

[22] List of the nobility and gentry of Ulster, [c.1732/3] (Lambeth Palace Lib., MS 1742, f. 56).

[23] The two were Isaac Macartney and Mr [Alexander] McAulay.

[24] The three were William Johnston, John Huston and Captain Charles Brice.

[25] These individuals were Sir Robert Adair, Arthur Dobbs, Valentine Jones, Mr [George] Mathews of Springvale, and Mr [Edward] Bailey of Ringdufferin.

[26] Alexander McCracken to Robert Wodrow, 11 Nov. 1710 (NLS, Wod. Lett. Qu. ii, f. 154).

[27] D. W. Hayton, et al., *The history of parliament: the House of Commons 1690–1715* (5 vols, Cambridge, 2002), i, 314–15.

Figure 4   Portrait of Arthur Upton (1633–1706), of Castle Upton,
Templepatrick, painted late 17th century. He is wearing a dark coat, with a lace
neck-tie and long, brown-coloured wig.

to conformity was often a slow process. Robert Harley, earl of Oxford, retained many close friends and confidants among the Presbyterian clergy, while his younger brother Edward was a 'staunch Presbyterian', a patron of nonconformist education, and the author of a number of pious works of a Puritan character.[28]

It must be pointed out that often one branch of a family conformed earlier than the rest and that the Presbyterian gentry were in contact with members of the Church

---

[28] *ODNB* (Harley, Robert, 1st earl of Oxford (1661–1724)), (Harley, Edward (1664–1735)); Hayton, *History of parliament*, iv, 244, 277–8.

of Ireland through their social and public life. With such contacts and friendships already formed across the denominational divide the transition would have been much easier. James Stewart of Killymoon was a Presbyterian but his brother Henry conformed and was sheriff of Tyrone in 1711. When Henry died unmarried in 1717 he left money to the poor of the Church of Ireland at Derryloran and money to buy silver communion plate there, but his estate (which included lands in County Tyrone, and his interest in lands held from the archbishop of Armagh) was left to the Presbyterian second son of his elder brother, James Stewart.[29] Similarly, Arthur Upton who, 'had courage to assert his own principles and adhere to his persecution in the worst of times, in the face of the greatest opposition', had three sons – John, Thomas and Hercules – who conformed to the Church of Ireland while their elder brother, Clotworthy Upton, remained a firm and active Presbyterian.[30] Gentlemen often had sympathy for their social equals which, along with familial connexions, could transcend religious differences.

Others, after they had conformed, were still connected to nonconformity either personally or through their wives or parents. Colonel John Upton's wife, Mary, was described by Rev. William Livingston as a 'staunch Presbyterian'. Livingston also recorded that though John Upton was 'of the established church', as a result of his being 'in the army since he was very young', when he succeeded to the family estate at Castle Upton, in Templepatrick, in 1725, he declared openly 'that he hath a fixed principle of moderation, that he is resolved to serve the interests of his country, of the Protestant religion, and to do what is in his power for the protection, peace, and liberty of Dissenters, as any of his predecessors have done before him'. To this Livingston added that John was 'extremely civil' to him and allowed Livingston to perform worship in the Upton household. While John attended the service in the Church of Ireland in the morning, he attended the Presbyterian service in the Templepatrick meetinghouse 'every Sabbath afternoon'.[31]

Decades later, some of those who conformed were still mindful of their Presbyterian origins. In the 1780s Clotworthy Upton, first Viscount Templetown, and James Stewart of Killymoon supported the efforts of the Synod of Ulster to have the state grant towards the payment of the Presbyterian ministers (known as the *regium donum*) increased, and Stewart not only supported the act that repealed the test clause but also proposed the act that declared marriages by Presbyterian ministers to be valid.[32] The transformation from Presbyterianism to Anglicanism was usually a slow process rather than an event and tended to be by a drift rather

[29] Will of Henry Stewart, 14 Feb. 1714 (PRONI, LPC/944).
[30] [Edward Kimber], *The new peerage* (3rd ed., 3 vols, London, 1784), iii, 355; [William Livingston] to [Robert Wodrow], 3 Sept. 1725 (NLS, Wod. Lett. Qu., xxi, f. 182); *HIP*, vi, 453–7; list of high sheriffs of counties in Ireland (PRONI, D302/1, p. 5). *HIP*, vi, 455–6 incorrectly ascribes to John Upton, a conformist, various activities on behalf of the Presbyterians and the General Synod. Instead these were the actions of his elder brother, Clotworthy. Johnston-Liik's mistake probably arises from the fact that both brothers were called 'Colonel' Upton.
[31] [William Livingston] to [Robert Wodrow], 3 Sept. 1725 (NLS, Wod. Lett. Qu., xxi, f. 182).
[32] 'Lobbying in the Irish parliament, 1783. [From the Rev. Wm. Campbell's *Journal*]', *Report of the Presbyterian Historical Society* (1912), pp 7–16; Ian McBride, 'Presbyterians in the penal era', *Bull. PHSI*, xxvii (1998–2000) p. 19; *HIP*, vi, 340; W. J. H. McKee, *Aspects of Presbyterianism in Cookstown* (Belfast, 1995), pp 6–7.

than an entire abandonment of Presbyterianism. It was not always necessarily the recently conformed Presbyterian gentry who tried to keep a 'foot in both religious camps' as they sought to retain their influence over their Presbyterian tenants; the Presbyterian church also tried to keep what influence it could with those who had conformed. Ballycarry session in 1718, in making proposals to end differences in the congregation because of disputes concerning seating arrangements, stated in their minute book, 'We hope this will be ane obligation on Mr Dobbes when he sees their is as much care taken to accomodate his tenants as any others, thoe we be under the unhappinesse of his being now of a different communion.'[33]

II. Wealth and ranks

Though small in number, the Presbyterian gentry were not homogeneous and there were gradations in wealth and status. A striking feature of the Academy and Lambeth lists is the absence of peers among the ranks of Presbyterian landholders. While it is true that when these lists were compiled there were no Presbyterian aristocrats in Ireland, there had been members of the aristocracy who had supported, or sympathised with, Presbyterianism in the seventeenth century. James Hamilton (c.1560–1644), first Viscount Clandeboye, and Hugh Montgomery, first earl of Mount-Alexander, who played a leading role in the development of Scottish settlement in east Ulster in the opening decades of the seventeenth century, were both Presbyterian. Hugh Montgomery (1651–1717), second earl of Mount-Alexander, though a member of the Church of Ireland, was associated with the Dissenting interest and in Queen Anne's reign acted as an intermediary between the Irish government and the Ulster Presbyterians.[34] James Hamilton, second Viscount Clandeboye and first earl of Clanbrassil, though by his education 'inclined … to be Episcopal … was therein very moderate … and was in his practice Presbyterian'.[35] After Clanbrassil's death, his wife Alice employed Patrick Peacock, a Presbyterian minister from Scotland, as her household chaplain at Killyleagh, and Peacock was reputedly connected to the Hamilton family through marriage.[36] The Massereene family of County Antrim leaned towards English Presbyterianism and employed a succession of Presbyterian chaplains at Antrim Castle including John Howe and Elias Travers.[37] The Presbytery of Antrim sought the opinion of the

---

[33] Ballycarry sess. mins, 30 Oct. 1718 (PRONI, CR3/31/1).

[34] *DIB* (Montgomery, Hugh (1651–1717)).

[35] T. K. Lowry (ed.), *The Hamilton manuscripts* … (Belfast, [1867]), p. 71.

[36] Alexander McCreery, *The Presbyterian ministers of Killileagh: a notice of their lives and times* (Belfast, 1875), p. 101.

[37] Edmund Calamy, *Memoirs of the late Revd. Mr. John Howe* (London, 1724), pp 50–1, 53–4, 58; [Joseph Boyse], 'A sermon on the occasion of the death of the Reverend Mr. Elias Travers. (Who dy'd May 5th, 1705) Preach'd at the meeting-house in Cook-Street, May 17th' in idem, *The works of the reverend and learned Mr. Joseph Boyse* (2 vols, London, 1728), i, 430; earl of Arran to Ormond, 14 & 18 Aug. 1683 (HMC, *Ormonde MSS*, n.s., vii, 104–5, 109); W. S. Smith, 'Sir John Skeffington, Second Lord Massereene', *Report of PHS* (1911), pp 9–10; J. T. Carson, 'John Howe: chaplain to Lord Massereene at Antrim Castle, 1671–1677', *Bull. PHSI*, no. 7 (1977), pp 11, 13–14; *DIB* (Skeffington, Sir John (1632–95)).

Massereene family on the siting of a meetinghouse for the people of Grange and Duneane in the 1680s and in 1712 Massereene wrote to the General Synod to have Rev. John Abernethy continued as minister of Antrim.[38]

When in Dublin in the late seventeenth century the Massereenes and a number of other aristocrats including Lady Cole of the Enniskillen family, Viscountess Loftus of Ely (who was a niece of the Presbyterian M.P. Sir Arthur Langford), Catherine, countess of Granard, and Letitia Hicks, countess of Donegall, frequented the city's Presbyterian meetinghouses.[39] The countess of Donegall employed Joseph Boyse and Thomas Emlyn as her domestic chaplains and the third earl of Donegall, though an Anglican, was on book-lending terms with the Presbyterian minister of Belfast, Rev. John McBride. When McBride refused to take the oath of abjuration in 1704 Donegall offered to stand surety for him 'to the value of his estate'.[40] Three of the Presbyterian families among the landed elite of Ulster bore the lesser title of baronet. Sir Hercules Langford of Kilmackevett (that is, Crumlin), County Antrim, and Summerhill, County Meath, was made a baronet in 1667, and was succeeded in the title by his sons, Arthur and Henry. Robert Adair, landlord of Ballymena, was knighted by King William in 1690 for services at the Battle of the Boyne, and Sir Alexander Cairnes was created a baronet of both England and Ireland in 1708.[41]

Unfortunately estate records are lacking for the Presbyterian gentry families, with only occasional rentals and estate surveys surviving. Knowledge of the income of the families often depends on chance references and estimates, which may not necessarily be accurate. A list of the Protestants who fled from Ireland at the time of the 'Glorious' Revolution gives the estimated yearly value of their estates and includes a number of Presbyterian gentlemen, the leading figures of whom were Arthur Upton of Templepatrick (£800), Robert Adair of Ballymena (£800), William Shaw of Ganaway, County Down (£700) and James Ross of Portavo, County Down (£600).[42] The Academy and Lambeth lists both give estimates of the yearly income of the landed Dissenters and a well-informed Dublin official assessed and detailed in a list, in late 1713, the annual income of 80% of the 300 members of the Irish House of Commons.[43] From these sources we learn that while the majority of the Presbyterian gentry were worth less than £400 a year, others were much more

<hr/>

38 Antrim 'Meeting' mins (UTC, pp 260, 262); *RGSU*, i, 252, 279, 283.

39 C. H. Irwin, *A history of Presbyterianism in Dublin and the south and west of Ireland* (London, 1890), pp 266, 317, 322; Robert Craghead, *A funeral sermon on ... the death of ... Catherine, countess dowager of Granard* (Dublin, 1714); Phil Kilroy, *Protestant Dissent and controversy in Ireland 1660–1714* (Cork, 1994), pp 40, 55. Though himself a conformist, Sir Arthur Forbes, earl of Granard, defended the political loyalty of the Ulster Presbyterians and was instrumental in achieving the *regium donum* grant in 1672: [Kirkpatrick], *Presby. loyalty*, pp 525–6.

40 Thomas Emlyn, *The works of Mr. Thomas Emlyn* (3 vols, London, 1746), i, pp vii–xi; [Kirkpatrick], *Presby. loyalty*, p. 474.

41 G. E. C[okayne], *Complete baronetage* (5 vols, Exeter, 1900–06), iv, 204; v, 7; *HIP*, iii, 56. The Langfords were moderate Presbyterians. During the 1680s Sir Arthur Langford attended not only the morning and evening services in the Church of Ireland but also those conducted by his Presbyterian chaplain, Mr Tate, after the parish service: Edward Synge to Bp Dopping, 5 Aug. 1683 (Armagh Public Lib., Dopping papers, P001498149, i, no. 36).

42 Benn, *Belfast*, pp 737–9.

43 Printed list of members of the Irish parliament, [late 1713] (PRONI, T3411/1).

Figure 5   Portrait of Sir Henry Cairnes (1673–1743) of Monaghan, Donaghmore, Co. Donegal, and London, painted in the Kneller School

substantial. According to the Lambeth list Robert Blackwood of Ballyleidy, County Down, was worth £1,400 *per annum*; James Ross of Portavo, James Stevenson of Killyleagh and William Stewart of Killymoon were each worth £1,000 *per annum*; Sir Henry Cairnes of Monaghan, £950 *per annum*; John Hamilton of Dunnamanagh, County Tyrone, £800 *per annum*; and Archibald Edmonstone of Redhall, Ballycarry, and Arthur Graham of County Armagh, £700 *per annum*.[44]

In 1713 the annual income of Clotworthy Upton of Castle Upton, Templepatrick, was estimated at £1,200 and his brother Thomas's at £200.[45] Around 1698 the

44   List of the nobility and gentry of Ulster, [c.1732/3] (Lambeth Palace Lib., MS 1742, ff 49–56).
45   Printed list of members of the Irish parliament, [late 1713] (PRONI, T3411/1).

County Antrim lands of their father Arthur Upton included the 'freehold' estate of Templepatrick, which had a rental of £377 11s 11d, and a leasehold estate from the earl of Donegall worth £463 *per annum*. At the same time Upton held lands in County Londonderry, with a rental of £364, made up from freeholds, bishop's lands, and lands held from the Irish Society.[46] The freehold, or fee simple, part of Stewart of Killymoon's landholdings included the eighteen townlands, or manor of Clananize (or Clananeese), which extended to 4,040 statute acres around 1730, with a rental of £434. The bulk of the Stewart estate however was church land leased from the primate.[47] A rental of William Conyngham of Springhill from 1683 to 1684 includes lands in Counties Armagh, Londonderry and Tyrone. Conyngham usually collected his own rents in County Londonderry, which amounted to £100, while the rents in County Tyrone (£102) were collected by Tirlagh Mulhollan and those in County Armagh (£94) by Walter Dawson.[48] These examples illustrate how complicated was the structure of landholding in early modern Ireland and that gentlemen of all ranks often held a varied collection of lands that could include freeholds, mortgaged lands, lands in trust and leases ranging from fee farm, lives renewable, lives or shorter periods.

Rent from land was the principal source of gentry wealth, but some Presbyterian gentry earned in addition income derived from other sources. Some were agents for other greater or absentee landlords. Captain William Dobbin of Moneyglass was agent for the County Antrim estates of the Hollow Sword Blade Company of London.[49] The Donaldsons were agents for the earls of Antrim, John Henderson was one of several agents employed in the 1690s by the fifth earl of Abercorn, and William Conyngham of Springhill managed lands for the Drapers' Company and was ranger of the Irish Society's woods.[50] Others obtained revenue from their commercial and professional activities. Hugh Kennedy of Cultra was a successful physician in Belfast and David Cairnes of Knockmany, County Tyrone, was a barrister.[51] The Cairnes brothers – William, Alexander and Henry – whose principal estate was in Monaghan, were bankers in London and Dublin. Their business included activities

46 Rental drawn up at the time of an Upton-Stewart of Killymoon marriage, c.1698 (NLI, Stewart papers, MS 8734/2); *HIP*, vi, 454.
47 Survey of Clananize, [c.1730] (NLI, Stewart papers, MS 8734/1); maps of lands in the Cookstown area belonging to the primate of Armagh and held by William Stewart of Killymoon (PRONI, D1/1/A–C); *HIP*, vi, 354.
48 [Edward MacLysaght],'Doneraile papers: interim report', *Analecta Hibernica*, no. 15 (1944), pp 357–8.
49 Agnew, *Merchant families*, p. 21.
50 Antrim Pby mins, 1697–1713 (PHS, p. 162); Isaac Macartney to William Cairnes, 28 May 1705, 3 June 1706 (PRONI, D501/1, pp 117, 318); W. J. Roulston, *Restoration Strabane, 1660–1714: economy and society in provincial Ireland* (Dublin, 2007), pp 27, 34; George Shaw's deposition taken at Antrim, 20 Feb. 1702 (PRONI, O'Neill papers, D1470/3/5); queries to be answered by William Conyngham about the deposition, 16 Mar. 1702 (ibid., D1470/3/6); James Garvey's deposition, 20 Mar. 1702 (ibid., D1470/3/7); account of William Conyngham's management of the Moneymore proportion, 1690–5, 1702/3, 1710 (ibid., D1470/3/16); Mr [William] Conyngham's accounts of the rents of the Drapers' proportion (ibid., D1470/6/1); Massereene to Sir Robert Clayton, 27 May 1696 (PRONI, Castletown papers, T2825/B/7/7).
51 See pp 128–9, 132, 135, 150–1, below, for further information on Kennedy and Cairnes.

such as providing maritime insurance and transferring rents.[52] Henry Cairnes was also a director of the East India Company.[53] While in London, Sir Alexander kept himself informed of all aspects of estate business through correspondence with staff and relatives in Ireland, principally his brother-in-law, Captain John Henderson of Donoughmore and Strabane, and his steward, A. Wrightson.[54] Sir Alexander's wealth was estimated by one source in 1713 at £2,000 *per annum*, and around the same time John Toland thought Sir Alexander was 'worth 3,000*l*. a year in land, besides his stock as a merchant'.[55] Though he lost heavily in the South Sea Bubble, Sir Alexander died a very wealthy man with estates in Counties Tipperary, Kilkenny and Wexford, as well as the Monaghan estate, and until around 1725 he maintained a house and business premises at Blackheath in London.[56] Another member of the Presbyterian gentry involved in banking was Hugh Henry, M.P. for the borough of Antrim from 1727 to 1743. Henry was the son of Rev. Robert Henry, Presbyterian minister of Carrickfergus and later Capel Street, Dublin, who was clerk of the Presbytery of Antrim (1674–92) and clerk of the General Synod of Ulster (1690–2). About 1710 Hugh established a banking business in Dublin, *Hugh Henry and Co.*, with Ephraim Dawson and William Lenox, which after the collapse of Burton's bank in 1733 was the sole government money-exchanger. Hugh Henry's wealth was estimated at £1,000 in 1713, and after the banking partnership was dissolved in 1737, he took up residence on his newly acquired estate at Straffan, County Kildare, while also continuing to maintain his lands in County Antrim.[57]

III. Origins, lineage and inheritance

Most of the Presbyterian gentry families were, unsurprisingly, of Scottish origin, though there were notable exceptions, such as the Dalways of Bellahill, near Carrickfergus, and the Uptons of Castle Upton in Templepatrick, both descended from Devonshire men who had come over to Ireland in the army of the earl of Essex in the late sixteenth century. The Langfords of County Antrim and Summerhill, County Meath, were also of English origin.[58] The Perry family of County Tyrone

---

[52] David Butle letter book (PRONI, D1449/13/1); Isaac Macartney letter book (ibid., D501/1); C. M. Tenison, 'The old Dublin bankers', *Journal of the Cork Historical and Archaeological Society*, iii (1894), pp 120–1; Agnew, *Merchant families*, pp 174–5, 186.

[53] *HIP*, iii, 359.

[54] Letters to the Cairnes family, mostly to Sir Alexander Cairnes, about the affairs of his Co. Monaghan estate (PRONI, Rossmore papers, T2929/2/1–48).

[55] Printed list of members of the Irish parliament, [late 1713] (PRONI, T3411/1); John Toland to [the earl of Oxford], [c.1712] (HMC, *Portland MSS*, v, 259).

[56] 'A memoir and history of the duchess of Marlborough' by M[ary Cairnes], Lady Blayney (BL, Blenheim papers, Add. MS 61466, f. 185); E. M. Richardson, *Long forgotten days (Leading to Waterloo)* (London, 1928), p. 245; H. C. Lawlor, *A history of the family of Cairnes or Cairns and its connections* (London, 1906), pp 86–7; *HIP*, iii, 357–8. In 1710 Sir Alexander paid £18,600 for lands formerly part of the Ormond estate: T. P. Power, *Land, politics and society in eighteenth-century Tipperary* (Oxford, 1993), p. 80.

[57] Tenison, 'Old Dublin bankers', pp 194–5; *HIP*, iv, 409–10.

[58] Sir Bernard Burke, *A genealogical and heraldic dictionary of the landed gentry of Great Britain and*

was of Welsh descent. James Perry obtained a fee farm lease of the lands of Moyloughmore from Sir Audley Mervyn in 1662. His son Captain Samuel Perry originally worshipped at Omagh Presbyterian Church, but was later a founding member of a Presbyterian congregation at Termon McGurk (later Clogherney), near Beragh, County Tyrone, on whose behalf he appeared as a commissioner at the Presbytery of Strabane.[59] Although the Agnews of Kilwaughter Castle had been established in Antrim long before the Plantation,[60] the ancestors of most of the Presbyterian gentry families of this period, including the Hamiltons of Killyleagh Castle,[61] the Cairnes of County Tyrone, and also of Monaghan,[62] the Springhill Conynghams,[63] the Stewarts of Killymoon,[64] the Shaws of Ganaway, County Down, Bush and Ballygally Castle, County Antrim,[65] and the Blackwoods of Ballyleidy in County Down, had emigrated to Ulster from Scotland (particularly from south-west Scotland) in the first two decades of the seventeenth century.[66] Others had come later. The grandfather of James Trail of Killyleagh had been a lieutenant-colonel in the Commonwealth army and been granted lands at Drumnaconnor and Raleagh, in County Down, in satisfaction of his claims for pay, and the townland of Rademon, in the parish of Kilmore, also in County Down, was passed to Lieutenant Walter Johnston in payment of what had been due to him.[67] The Kennedys of Cultra too were from a noted Scottish family, and the first of the family to settle in Ulster, Dr Hugh Kennedy, had come from Ayrshire in 1668. Opportunely Hugh's arrival in Ulster coincided with the disposal of parts of the Clanbrassil estate and in 1671 the Kennedy family purchased the north Down coastline from Ballycultra to Ballyrobert, and built Cultra House, which served the family for over a century.[68]

Some families continued to maintain estates on both sides of the North Channel. Sir Robert Adair of Ballymena was also laird of Kinhilt in Wigtownshire until the family's Scottish lands were sold to the earl of Stair in 1716, and the Edmonstones of Redhall, near Carrickfergus, had Scottish estates at Duntreath, in Stirlingshire,

---

Ireland (4th ed., London, 1863), p. 333; Young, *Fighters of Derry*, p. 38; Agnew, *Merchant families*, p. 49. William Livingston wrote to Robert Wodrow, on 3 Sept. 1725, following Clotworthy Upton's death, that 'He [Upton] loved that nation [Scotland] more than ever knew in any Englishman' (NLS, Wod. Lett. Qu., xxi, f. 182).

[59] A. H. Culyner (comp.), 'Notes on the Smith family of Northern Ireland, England and Canada; the Perry family of Tyrone and Fermanagh; the Robinsons of Tyrone and St. Louis, Missouri, Seskinore and Moyloughmore' (PRONI, D3000/72/1, p. 11); Strabane Pby mins (UTC, pp 18–19, 38–9, 103, 105, 123, 134–5); M. L. Thompson, *'The meeting-house beside the big bush': a history of Pettigo Presbyterian Church* (Omagh, [2000]), p. 4.

[60] Young, *Fighters of Derry*, p. 213.

[61] Burke, *Genealogical & heraldic dictionary of the landed gentry* (1863), pp 636–7.

[62] Young, *Fighters of Derry*, p. 102.

[63] Ibid., p. 70.

[64] Burke, *Genealogical & heraldic dictionary of the landed gentry* (1863), pp 1435–6.

[65] Young, *Fighters of Derry*, pp 44–5; J. W. Kernohan, 'Historic Ulster homes: castles and builders: Ballygally and the Shaws: Macartneys of Lissanoure', *Belfast Telegraph*, 27 Oct. 1919.

[66] William Maguire, 'The Blackwoods of Ballyleidy' in Ulster Architectural Historical Society, *Clandeboye* ([Belfast, 1985]), p. 35.

[67] Notes on families and places, Co. Down (PRONI, Stewart papers, D1759/3/A/1, p. 55); David Stewart, *The story of Kilmore Presbyterian Church* (Belfast, 1932), pp 17–19.

[68] Con Auld, *Holywood Co. Down: then and now* (Holywood, 2002), pp 32–3.

while the Agnews of Lochnaw, Wigtownshire, had lands in Kilwaughter, County Antrim, until around 1708.[69] Before his death, which occurred near Derry in 1689, Archibald Edmonstone requested that he be buried in Strathblane church, Stirlingshire, and his wishes were observed.[70] Others, while they no longer had lands in Scotland, had family there, whom they sometimes remembered in their wills. Arthur Maxwell, of Drumbeg, in County Down, who died in 1720, left £20 to the son of George Maxwell, laird of Dalswinton, near Dumfries, and David Kennedy of Cultra in his will of 1697 mentioned not only his younger brother Dr Hugh Kennedy of Cultra but also his eldest brother, John Kennedy, an apothecary in Edinburgh.[71] William Hamilton of Killyleagh Castle was a writer to the signet in Edinburgh, and is believed to have been the author of the *The Hamilton manuscripts*. If he was, it suggests both an interest in his family's Scottish background and pride in the history of the family as it developed in Ireland.[72] Nevertheless over time the link of immigrants to Scotland could decline. During several generations it was customary from time to time for the heads of families in Ireland and Scotland who were descended from Hans Hamilton, vicar of Dunlop, to each subscribe a small sum for the repair of their ancestors' tomb in Scotland, but it would appear that by 1704 funds were no longer forthcoming from the Irish branch of the Hamilton family.[73]

Lineage, and particularly the maintenance of the family surname down through generations, was important to gentry families. This is evident from the 'name and arms clauses' that appeared not only in Irish Presbyterian gentry wills but also in other gentry and aristocratic wills throughout the British Isles, from the late seventeenth century onwards.[74] This was a clause by which the beneficiary of a will was required to change his surname to that of the testator as a condition of receiving the estate. When William Conyngham of Springhill, County Londonderry, died in 1721 he was succeeded by his nephew, George Butle, who assumed the additional name of Conyngham. Sir Arthur Langford of Summerhill, County Meath, who

69 'The Adairs of Ballymena', *McComb's Almanack* (1866), p. 73; Frances Craig, 'The Adair family: the proprietors of the estates of Ballymena from 1626 to 1688' (Clough, [1991], ch. 3 (typescript in N.E. Area Local Studies Collection, Ballymena Central Library); *HIP*, iii, 56; Archibald Edmonstone, *Genealogical account of the family of Edmonstone of Duntreath* (Edinburgh, 1875); Agnew Irish estate papers, 1636–1712 (NAS, Agnew of Lochnaw papers, GD/154/505–34). During their absence in Ireland the Scottish lands of the lairds of Duntreath were managed by the Edmonstones of Spittal or Brioch.
70 Edmonstone, *Genealogical account of the family of Edmonstone of Duntreath*, p. 52.
71 Will of Arthur Maxwell, 1720 (PRONI, D1769/60/2/3); abstract will of David Kennedy, 1697 (ibid., Stewart papers, D1759/3/A/1, p. 7).
72 Raymond Gillespie, 'The social world of County Down in the seventeenth century' in L. J. Proudfoot and William Nolan (eds), *Down: history and society* (Dublin, 1997), p. 143; Lowry, *Hamilton manuscripts*, p. viii; George Hamilton, A *history of the House of Hamilton* (Edinburgh, 1933), p. 987.
73 Lowry, *Hamilton manuscripts*, pp 3–4.
74 Will of Arthur Maxwell, 1720 (PRONI, D1769/60/2/3); will of William Conyngham of Springhill, 1721 (ibid., Lenox-Conyngham papers, D1449/1/33); Lawlor, *History of the Cairnes*, p. 113; P. B. Eustace (ed.), *Registry of Deeds Dublin: abstracts of wills*, i: *1708–1745* (Dublin, 1956), pp 90, 264; Stone & Stone, *An open elite?*, pp 127, 139; Eileen Spring, *Law, land, and family: aristocratic inheritance in England, 1300 to 1800* (London, 1993), pp 95–6.

died unmarried in 1716, left his Antrim estates to his brother Henry Langford, but also added in the will that in default of issue male to Henry Langford then it was to go to Henry's daughter, 'provided always that such daughter or daughters and the heiresses of their bodys to whom the said estate shall come take on them the sirname of Langford'.[75] Full surname and arms change was always much more likely to be accepted when a man of inferior status and income, rather than one of a more illustrious name, was concerned.[76] Archibald Edmonstone of Duntreath and Redhall realised this and in the disposition of his estates he stipulated that 'in case any of such heirs-female shall … happen to be married to a peer' then the Edmonstone estates were to go to the second son of such marriage and 'shall only be capable to succeed who, and everyone of them, shall from that time forward assume the sirname of Edmonstone, and bear the arms of the family of Duntreath'.[77]

A sense of continuity was stressed after death by the existence of family tombs and burying plots in particular churches which had become associated with a gentry family over a number of years. John Shaw of Ballygally, County Antrim, requested that he 'be interred among the bodys of my ancestours in my burrying place in the church of Carncastle' and similar instructions appear in the wills of other members of the Presbyterian gentry.[78] Burials in such tombs could be a bitterly defended privilege. Controversy arose in Bangor around 1740 when the Ross family of Portavo were denied burial rights at the family's traditional burying ground in the churchyard of Bangor Abbey. Incensed at this, James Ross and his relative Robert Blackwood of Ballyleidy mobilised their Presbyterian tenants in order to frustrate the efforts of Rev. James Clewlow, rector of Bangor, to obtain money from the parish vestry to carry out repairs to the church bells and steeple.[79]

Sometimes the defence of a gentleman's honour could lead to a resort to arms. Duelling was criticised by some on both religious and secular grounds. James Trail of Killyleagh condemned this 'false notion of honnour' which 'prevails among gentlemen' and in 1744 the General Synod of Ulster felt compelled to rebuke one of its ministers, Rev. William Armstrong of Donagheady, County Tyrone, for his 'scandalous' conduct for 'having challenged, or accepted a challenge to a duell and going to the place of combat, armed with sword and pistol'.[80] Although Ulster produced the least number of recorded duels out of the four Irish provinces,[81] there are two examples of members of the Presbyterian gentry being involved in duels. In 1690 a disagreement, reputedly over the escape of a Catholic priest, led to a duel between Bernard Ward and his cousin Jocelyn Hamilton, half-brother of the

[75] Will of Arthur Langford, 1715 (PRONI, T168/1).
[76] Stone & Stone, An open elite?, p. 130.
[77] Disposition and tailzie, by Archibald Edmonstone of Duntreath, to Archibald Edmonstone, his eldest son ([Edinburgh, 1769]), p. 3.
[78] Will of John Shaw, 1691 (PRONI, Nicholson papers, T828/22); will of Henry Dalway, 1720 (ibid., Castle Stewart papers, D1618/8/14); will of Henry McCulloch, 1728 (NLI, Prerogative will book, 1728–9, MFGS 41/4, ff 165–7); will of Hugh Henry, 1743 (PRONI, LPC/1302).
[79] James Clewlow to Michael Ward, 19 Feb. 1738/9, 20 Nov. 1740, 2 Mar. 1740[/41], 10 Oct. 1741 (PRONI, Ward papers, D2092/1/5, pp 33, 72, 88, 98).
[80] Autobiography of James Trail (PRONI, D1460/1, opening 27); RGSU, ii, 307; James Kelly, 'That damn'd thing called honour': duelling in Ireland 1570–1860 (Cork, 1995), pp 43, 49, 63.
[81] Kelly, That damn'd thing called honour, p. 63.

Presbyterian M.P. James Hamilton of Tollymore, County Down. Both duellists were killed. Captain John Cairnes, the only son of David Cairnes of Knockmany, County Tyrone, was also killed in a duel at Newcastle-upon-Tyne in 1719.[82]

IV. Family life, marriage and education

It was the practice for the majority of the gentry families to marry partners from within their own social class and from within Ulster, if not their own county. However, because of the small number of Presbyterian gentry families the choice of partners in Ulster was limited and it was not unknown for marriages to occur with leading mercantile families or across the denominational divide. Although John Shaw of Ballytweedy, County Antrim, married the sister of Lieutenant-Colonel Sir Andrew Agnew, baronet of Lochnaw,[83] the few who obtained marriage partners from Scotland tended to be those with lands there. Archibald Edmonstone of Redhall, Ballycarry, and laird of Duntreath, married first Anne, daughter of Henry Erskine, Lord Cardross, and secondly, in 1716, Anne, daughter of John Campbell of Mamore, Scotland, the son of the earl of Argyll.[84] Similarly, those who had English spouses were usually those with connexions or business there, such as the London bankers, Sir Alexander and Henry Cairnes. Sir Alexander Cairnes married Elizabeth, sister of Sir Nathaniel Gould, one of the directors of the Bank of England, while his brother Henry Cairnes married Frances, daughter of Sir Nathaniel's brother John, another bank director.[85] As a result of the intermarriage between the Presbyterian gentry families in Ulster during the seventeenth century, by the early eighteenth century there was a dense network of relationship. The marriages of Arthur Upton's children, for instance, created links with a number of other Presbyterian families located throughout Ulster including the Brices of Belfast, Conynghams of Springhill, Kennedys of Cultra, Shaws of Ballygally, Stewarts of Killymoon, and with the Lenoxes, a mercantile family based at Derry and later also at Belfast.[86]

The head of the family directed much attention to finding and negotiating suitable matches for his children, but the wider family network also took an interest,

[82] James Hamilton [of Bangor] to [James Hamilton of Tollymore], Oct. 1690 (NLI, Stevenson papers, MS 1702, p. 47); E. G. S. Reilly, *Historical anecdotes of the families of the Boleynes, Careys, Mordaunts, Hamiltons, and Jocelyns, arranged as an elucidation of the genealogical chart at Tollymore Park* (rev. ed., Newry, 1839), p. 140; James O'Laverty, *An historical account of the Diocese of Down and Connor, ancient and modern* (5 vols, Dublin, 1878–95), i, 313; Kelly, *That damn'd thing called honour*, p. 35; Lawlor, *History of the Cairnes*, pp 168, 174, n. 1; [John Mitchelburne], *Ireland preserved; or, the Siege of Londonderry and Battle of Aughrim*, ed. John Graham (Dublin, 1841), p. 316. Hamilton of Tollymore is designated as a Presbyterian in W. D. Killen, *The ecclesiastical history of Ireland: from the earliest period to the present times* (2 vols, London, 1875), ii, 182, n. 1.
[83] Will of John Shaw, 11 Jan. 1728/9 (NLI, Prerogative will book, 1726–8, MFGS 41/2, f. 187); Shaw research (PHS, Genealogies, 3).
[84] Edmonstone, *Genealogical account of the family of Edmonstone*, pp 52–3.
[85] Sir Alexander Cairnes to Thomas Wotton, 11 Feb. 1726 (BL, Wotton papers, Add. MS 24120, ff 174–5).
[86] W. H. Upton, *Upton family records: being genealogical collections for an Upton family history* (London, 1893), p. 13.

particularly in the marriage of the heir.[87] Parents sought to control marriages and the wills that survive from the period often stated that the children were not to receive their portion unless they married with the consent of their mother or the guardians named in the will.[88] Once a marriage was made, the parents and wider kin, who had been heavily involved in its construction, played less of a role, though frequently parents provided accommodation for the young couple in the early years of marriage.[89] Though most heads of gentry families married, in order to preserve the family name and estate, there were exceptions. Sir Arthur Langford and his brothers Theophilus and Henry all died unmarried, and the family estates were eventually inherited by the son of their sister Mary, who had married Sir John Rowley of Castleroe.[90]

Lawrence Stone has suggested that before the eighteenth century marital relations were distant, that marriages were arranged for economic reasons rather than love, and that this changed in the early eighteenth century when 'affective' family relations developed. He also suggested that, as a result of high levels of child mortality, relationships between parents and children were distant too.[91] Any attempt to study the quality of the relationship between husbands and wives, and their attitude to their children, is problematic because of the scantiness of the extant evidence. Much of the surviving information about marriage comes from the legal settlements that accompanied them, and it is much harder to uncover the emotional side. There are examples of happy marital relations. James Trail of Killyleagh came from a confessionally mixed family. He was born the son of a Presbyterian in 1690, but after the death of his father two years later, his mother brought him up in the Church of Ireland.[92] His uncles included James Clewlow, rector of Killyleagh, and two Presbyterian ministers, Rev. James Bruce of Killyleagh and Rev. John Hutcheson of Downpatrick.[93] When he was 17 Trail chose to join the Presbyterian church, the main motive being the 'great esteem' he had for a certain young lady, Mary Hamilton of Killyleagh Castle, who was a Presbyterian. Trail went to Cultra to see Mary, where she was visiting the Kennedys, and 'let her know' that his 'affections' were 'very far engaged to her'. He then 'acquainted her friends of his design and desire' and, after overcoming some disagreement between the two parties concerning the marriage settlement, James Trail and Mary were married in the dining room of Killyleagh Castle.[94] In his journal, later in life, Trail wrote,

---

[87] John Henderson to Sir Alexander Cairnes, 1 Sept. 1712 (PRONI, Rossmore papers, T2929/2/13); William Bruce to James Trail, 14 Apr. 1739 (ibid., Bruce papers, T3041/1/B/48).

[88] Will of Robert Dalway, 1699 (PRONI, Castle Stewart papers, D1618/8/5); abstract will of John Boyd, 1701 (ibid., Stewart papers, D1759/3/B/1, p. 9); will of Hugh Henry, 1743 (PRONI, LPC/1302).

[89] Heal & Holmes, *Gentry in England and Wales*, pp 68–9; autobiography of James Trail (PRONI, D1460/1, opening 12).

[90] G. E. C., *Complete baronetage*, iv, 204; *HIP*, v, 56–7.

[91] Lawrence Stone, *The family, sex and marriage in England 1500–1800* (London, 1977).

[92] Autobiography of James Trail (PRONI, D1460/1, opening 1).

[93] A short account of the Trail family of Blebe, Scotland, and their descendants (ibid., T273/1).

[94] Autobiography of James Trail (ibid., D1460/1, openings 9–11); Killyleagh Presbyterian Church marriage register, 23 Mar. 1710 (ibid., MIC1P/53/1, p. 8); a short account of the Trail family of Blebe, Scotland, and their descendants (ibid., T273/1).

(a) Oil painting of William Conyngham (d. 1721), builder of Springhill, Co. Londonderry, painted in the last seventeenth century. He has a dark-brown coloured wig and is wearing a red gown over a white shirt, with a long lace cravat.

(b) Oil painting of Ann Upton (1664–c.1744), daughter of Colonel Arthur Upton, painted c.1690s, wearing a low-cut blue shift and a gold/brown cloak draped over her left shoulder. Ann married William Conyngham in 1680.

Figure 6   Portraits of William Conyngham and his wife Ann Conyngham (née Upton)

'She [that is, his wife] is a most desierable companion, a woman of an excellent natural temper, and the desire of my eyes … I can never sufficiently testifie my gratitude to God that provided a companion for me soe agreeable in all respects.'[95] Testators too often expressed the feelings which had sustained their family relations, with Arthur Maxwell of Drumbeg, William Conyngham of Springhill, and others referring to their 'dear and loving wife'.[96] Adjectives such as 'dear' and 'loving' were more frequently used for spouses than for describing relations with children. At the time of Arthur Upton's marriage with Dorothy, daughter of Michael Beresford, the settlement drawn up to accompany the marriage compelled Upton to leave his wife a jointure of £100. However, when he drew up his will in 1706, Upton, on account 'of the great love and respect' he had for his 'dear wife', ordered that the jointure be increased to £150 *per annum*.[97]

There are, however, also examples of marital breakdown. Sir Robert Adair of Ballymena married four times, and his third marriage came to an end when his

---

95 Autobiography of James Trail (PRONI, D1460/1, opening 17).
96 Will of Arthur Maxwell, 1720 (ibid., D1769/60/2/3); will of William Conyngham, 1721 (ibid., Lenox-Conyngham papers, D1449/1/33); will of Robert Dalway, 1699 (ibid., Castle Stewart papers, D1618/8/5); will of Patrick Agnew, 1724 (ibid., LPC/1034); will of Hugh Henry, 1743 (ibid., LPC/1302).
97 Will of Arthur Upton, 1706 (NAI, Prerogative will book, 1706–8, MFGS 41/2, f. 28).

wife, Ann McAuley, left him.[98] Mary Cairnes, the only surviving child of Sir Alexander Cairnes, was married first to Cadwallader, seventh Lord Blayney, and it was a particularly unhappy marriage.[99] In later life she described the relationship to her cousin, Mrs Lavington: 'He had an agreeable outside, but there was a terrible inside. I endured all sorts of indignity for several years, even frequent blows', and was thankful that she had had no children to such a man. Eventually she decided to move back to her father's home at Monaghan.[100] When Sir Alexander wrote his will in 1732 all his estates and property were left 'to his only surviving child Mary, Lady Blaney, absolutely, and entirely free from the control of her husband Lord Blaney'.[101] In the event, Lord Blayney died only a few months after his father-in-law, and Mary remarried, this time a relative, Colonel John Murray, whom she described as 'the choice of my reason as well as my heart' and on this occasion her 'expectations were fully satisfied' and she had children very soon, which gave her 'great pleasure', as she 'loved the father'.[102]

Gentry women played an important role in supervising the upbringing of children, but husbands also took an interest. The evidence that survives, in contrast to Stone's theory, would suggest that parents were interested in the development and education of their children and had hopes and fears about their future.[103] The death of a child was naturally a cause of great upset to both parents. In 1726 when Colonel Edward Brice's two-year-old daughter died, his brother-in-law, Arthur Dobbs of Castle Dobbs, wrote to Michael Ward, 'my dear Brice has lost his hopefull girle for which he and my sister greaves excessively'.[104] The character of relationships depended much on the personalities and outlook of those involved and, then, as now, some husbands and wives were more loving than others and some parent-child relationships closer than others.

Running an estate was not necessarily always the exclusive responsibility of the male members of gentry families. Many a gentleman made his wife the executrix of his will which would suggest familiarity with her husband's affairs.[105] Absences of the proprietor at parliament or on other business, together with illness or premature death, meant that estate and other affairs were often temporarily or permanently in the hands of wives, daughters or widows.[106] Probably, however, only a minority of widows had unrestricted control over their former husband's assets, unless the marriage had been childless, and most widows enjoyed only limited possession as life tenants, usually of a third of the estate. Remarriage could also lead to a considerable

[98] Craig, 'The Adair family', ch. 3.
[99] Richardson, Long forgotten days, pp 244–6; Malcomson, Pursuit of the heiress, pp 59–60, 113–14; Jane Falloon, Throttle full open: a life of Lady Bailey, Irish aviatrix (Dublin, 1999), p. 194.
[100] Richardson, Long forgotten days, pp 244–5.
[101] Lawlor, History of the Cairnes, p. 87.
[102] Richardson, Long forgotten days, p. 246; Malcomson, Pursuit of the heiress, pp 60, 113–15.
[103] Autobiography of James Trail (PRONI, D1460/1).
[104] Arthur Dobbs to Michael Ward, 20 Feb. 1725/6 (ibid., Ward papers, D2092/1/2, p. 85).
[105] Eustace, Registry of Deeds, i, 115, 264; abstract will of John Boyd, 2 July 1701 (PRONI, Stewart papers, D1759/3/B/1, p. 9); will of Arthur Graham, 11 Apr. 1732 (ibid., Bryson collection, D4006/3); will of Hugh Henry, 1743 (ibid., LPC/1302).
[106] Mingay, The gentry, p. 89; Reilly, Historical anecdotes, p. 76; Robert Jocelyn, earl of Roden, Tollymore: the story of an Irish demesne (Belfast, 2005), pp 18–19.

decline in living standards unless the new husband had a similar level of wealth. In cases where legacies were reduced or made void on a widow's remarriage, the testator was mainly interested in protecting his children and keeping the estate intact, rather than punishing his wife.[107]

The overriding evidence from the small number of wills, copies, or abstracts of wills to survive is that in terms of smaller legacies and bequests testators concentrated on their partners, children and close kin, that is brothers and sisters. However, elderly or temporarily homeless relatives from the extended family were often offered assistance or accommodation by the head of the family.[108] Servants too were integral to the gentry household and there are fleeting references to them in wills and other sources.[109] David Kennedy of Cultra in 1697 left a miserable annuity of £1 to his housekeeper, a widow called Agnes Creighton, while Henry Dalway in 1720 bequeathed his 'gray coat trim'd with gold' to his 'old servant James Brae'.[110] Others were much more generous. Sir Arthur Langford, of Summerhill, who died unmarried, bequeathed £200 to Thomas Granger and £100 each to two other servants.[111] One of the most detailed sources on servants is the cash book for the Blackwoods of Ballyleidy, County Down, covering 1720–39. The Blackwoods employed not only a butler and housekeeper, but also grooms, kitchenmaids, general and farm servants, brewer, gardeners and a series of coachmen. They also engaged a number of individuals for a few days or half days as need arose. For all these there is a recording of the wages paid along with details of livery provided, if applicable.[112]

Most gentry families employed domestic tutors to educate the children, and sometimes the tutor also acted as chaplain to the family.[113] The curriculum varied according to the knowledge of the master, but probably included religious instruction, the classics, and for the older and more able children, Latin.[114] William Taylor, later Presbyterian minister at Cairncastle, was in his early life tutor to the Upton family of Castle Upton, and while instructing the children he met his future wife, Mary Latimer, another member of the same household.[115] In the late seven-

[107] Peter Earle, *The making of the English middle class: business, society and family life in London, 1660–1730* (London, 1989), p. 321.

[108] Autobiography of James Trail (PRONI, D1460/1, openings 36–7).

[109] For instance, will of Robert Dalway, 1699 (PRONI, Castle Stewart papers, D1618/8/5); autobiography of James Trail (PRONI, D1460/1, openings 4, 15, 28); Craghead, *Funeral sermon on the death of Catherine, countess dowager of Granard*, p. 23.

[110] Abstract will of David Kennedy, 1697 (PRONI, Stewart papers, D1759/3/A/1, p. 7); will of Henry Dalway, 1720 (ibid., Castle Stewart papers, D1618/8/14).

[111] Will of Sir Arthur Langford, 1715 (PRONI, T168/1). See below, ch. 5, for more information on servants.

[112] Blackwood cash book, 1720–39 (PRONI, Dufferin and Ava papers, D1071/A/B/2/1).

[113] The Blackwoods of Ballyleidy employed Rev. Robert MacKewan (minister of Newtownards Non-Subscribing Presbyterian Church), as tutor to their sons in the late 1730s: Blackwood cash book, 1720–39 (ibid.).

[114] Raymond Gillespie, '"Into another intensity": prayer in Irish Nonconformity, 1650–1700' in Kevin Herlihy (ed.), *The religion of Irish Dissent 1650–1800* (Blackrock, Co. Dublin, 1996), p. 37.

[115] Classon Porter, 'Congregational memoirs: no. IV – Cairncastle', *Christian Unitarian*, iv (1866), 224, 229; Alexander Gordon, *Historic memorials of the Remonstrant Presbyterian Congregation of Templepatrick* (Belfast, 1899), p. 37.

teenth century a Mr May and Patrick Plunkett, who taught in the congregational school at Cairncastle, acted as tutors to the Shaw family of Ballygally. Around 1740 the same family employed David Manson as tutor to their children. Manson, who became famous as a teacher in Belfast later in the eighteenth century, was of the opinion that children learned best in a friendly atmosphere. He emphasised the importance of play and enjoyment in education, encouraged achievement by reward, and denounced harsh discipline and corporal punishment.[116] Parents thought that children derived not only intellectual, but also moral, benefits from being tutored at home.[117] In the 1730s James Trail of Killyleagh and his cousin Rev. Michael Bruce clubbed together to give their sons private education, with the instruction alternating every six months between the two households.[118] Trail believed this scheme to be advantageous as the 'children are freer from evel habits then they would have been in a publick scool' and he was 'shure they are much freer from vice' than he was at their age.[119] For a time the tutor was a Mr McCormick, though Bruce expressed concerns that McCormick did not follow his employers' directions on discipline. Although 'some allowances I'm sensible are to be made for a master who is apt to be provok'd by the boys follies and idleness', Bruce wrote to Trail; 'on the other hand great care should be taken that they are not harshly dealt with which may make them hate their books, and perhaps prejudice their health'.[120] McCormick may subsequently have been tutor to the Johnston family of Rademon as one of the witnesses to the will of Hugh Johnston of Rademon, dated November 1737, was 'William McCormick, schoolmaster, Rademon'.[121] James Trail, born in 1690, was himself at the age of eight sent to the Latin school at Killyleagh where he continued for five years. In 1715 he spent nine months in Belfast in a school taught by a Mr Collinwood, while he lodged with Rev. John McBride, and at the same time was also attending a French master. When he returned to Killyleagh Trail spent three months at the philosophical academy run there by Rev. James McAlpin, before going to Dublin where he was taught in a school run by a clergyman called Mr Scot.[122]

Although evidence is scant it would appear that most of the Presbyterian gentry in the late seventeenth and early eighteenth centuries were educated locally rather than at the public schools of England. Only a small number of Presbyterians were

---

[116] Classon Porter, *Congregational memoirs of the Old Presbyterian Congregation of Larne and Kilwaughter*, ed. and updated by R. H. McIlwrath and J. W. Nelson ([Larne, 1975]), p. 52; Belfastiensis, 'David Manson, schoolmaster', *UJA*, vii (1901), pp 158–9; J. J. Marshall, 'David Manson, schoolmaster in Belfast', *UJA*, xiv (1908), pp 59–61, 66.

[117] M. A. Henry, 'The making of elite culture' in H. T. Dickinson (ed.), *A companion to eighteenth-century Britain* (Oxford, 2002), p. 316.

[118] Autobiography of James Trail (PRONI, D1460/1, opening 40); Michael Bruce to James Trail, 10 & 17 Apr. 1735 (NLI, Bruce papers, MS 20,867).

[119] Autobiography of James Trail (PRONI, D1460/1, opening 40).

[120] Michael Bruce to James Trail, 10 Apr. 1735 (NLI, Bruce papers, MS 20,867).

[121] Abstract will of Hugh Johnston, 20 Nov. 1737 (PRONI, Stewart papers, D1759/3/B/1, p. 96).

[122] Autobiography of James Trail (PRONI, D1460/1, openings 3–8). 'Mr Collinwood' was probably Peirce Collingwood, schoolmaster of the Free School of Belfast, who received an annual salary of £40 from the Donegall family: Donegall rents and payments, 1706–15 (PRONI, Maguire papers D4512/4/4).

educated at Trinity College, Dublin, which had an Anglican ethos, but among those were Alexander and Henry Dalway, who entered in 1687 and 1692 respectively, and Sir Arthur Langford, who entered in 1670.[123] Attendance at Oxford and Cambridge was rarer than at Trinity. One of those educated at Cambridge was Randal Brice, son of the Lisburn M.P. of the same name. Randal entered Trinity College, Cambridge, in 1707, at the age of sixteen, and subsequently attended both the Middle and Inner Temple.[124] There was a slightly larger, though still modest, attendance of Presbyterian gentry at Glasgow University, with some families, such as the Uptons and Blackwoods, attending even after they had conformed.[125] John, later Sir John, Blackwood of Ballyleidy attended Francis Hutcheson's Dublin Academy and transferred to Glasgow University when Hutcheson took up a post there, and at Glasgow Blackwood produced a Master's thesis on civil government.[126] Thomas Shaw, the youngest son of William Shaw of Bush, County Antrim, passed through the divinity hall of one of the Scottish universities before finishing his theological education at the University of Leiden, and was ordained as Presbyterian minister of Ahoghill in 1710.[127] Thomas Cairnes, son of William Cairnes of Killyfaddy, received his doctorate in medicine from the University of Utrecht in 1705.[128]

Sons of some of the leading figures of the Presbyterian gentry, and occasionally those of the wealthiest Presbyterian merchants, finished their education with a Grand Tour of Europe.[129] A Mr McConchy, who had been taught by Rev. Charles Mastertown of Belfast, was tutor to one of the Stewarts of Killymoon, and in 1728 accompanied his pupil to the University of Edinburgh and then on foreign travel.[130] Daniel Mussenden of Belfast and Larchfield, near Annahilt, reckoned that his heir's stay in the Low Countries in the early 1740s, which lasted twenty-seven months, cost almost £960.[131] In 1738 William Bruce, son of Rev. James Bruce of Killyleagh, became tutor to the children of Hugh Henry. Henry's two eldest sons, Robert and Joseph, both undertook extensive Grand Tours, and when Hugh Henry wrote his will in 1743 he mentioned the 'great confidence' he had in Bruce and the 'care' he

123 G. D. Burtchaell and T. U. Sadleir (eds), *Alumni Dublinenses* (new ed., Dublin, 1935), pp 207, 481.

124 H. A. C. Sturgess (comp.), *Register of admissions to The Honorable Society of the Middle Temple* (3 vols, London, 1949), i, 266; *HIP*, iii, 263. See pp 127–8, 130 for further information on Presbyterian gentry attendance at the English Inns of Court.

125 *Munimenta alme Universitatis Glasguensis*, iii, 162, 167, 234; W. I. Addison, *The matriculation albums of the University of Glasgow from 1728 to 1858* (Glasgow, 1913), p. 10.

126 M. A. Stewart, 'Abating bigotry and hot zeal' in Damian Smyth (ed.), *Francis Hutcheson*: suppt. to *Fortnight*, no. 308 (1992), p. 5.

127 James Duchal, 'Brief memoirs of the life and character of the Reverend Mr. Thomas Shaw' in idem, *A sermon on occasion of the much lamented death of the late Reverend Mr. John Abernethy* (Dublin, 1741), p. 20; McConnell, *Fasti*, p. 120.

128 R. W. Innes Smith, *English-speaking students of medicine at the University of Leyden* (Edinburgh, 1932), p. 39; Esther Mijers, 'Irish students in the Netherlands, 1650–1750', *Archivium Hibernicum*, lix (2005), p. 70; Lawlor, *History of the Cairnes*, p. 111; Thomas Cairnes, *Disputatio medica inauguralis de pleuritide et peripneumonia* (Utrecht, 1705).

129 Stone & Stone, *An open elite?*, p. 245; Barnard, *Making the grand figure*, pp 323–5; Robert Black's travel journals, 1727–8 (PRONI, Black papers, T1073/2–3).

130 Charles Mastertown to [Robert Wodrow], 10 Oct. 1728 (NLS, Wod. Lett. Qu., xxii, f. 157).

131 Barnard, *Making the grand figure*, p. 313.

expected Bruce would take of his 'children and their education'. Hugh left £100 to be paid annually to Bruce provided Bruce took 'care of such of' his 'younger children as shall want him', and left £150 *per annum* for the 'maintenance and education' of his second son, Joseph, until he turned eighteen, and for the three years after the amount was increased to £200 *per annum*.[132]

V. As landlords and 'improvers'

Much of the contemporary material relating to the Presbyterian gentry's role as landlords has not survived, but from what remains some general observations can be made. Most of the Presbyterian gentry managed their estates personally but some, particularly those with larger estates or lands in various locations, employed one or more stewards to collect the rents and supervise the lands.[133] Receivers' fees, usually six pence per pound of rent, were included in most leases of the period. If rents were not paid when due the landowner or his representatives could enter the lands and seize goods to the value of what was owed. Distraint, however, was an expensive undertaking, and could be counter-productive as, left without their cattle or other goods, tenants might not be able to pay their rents and the land would go to waste. In most cases landlords appear to have been considerate and were willing to abate rents in periods of economic difficulty or in cases of individual hardship.[134] Edward Brice, by his will, bequeathed a year's rent to every one of his poor tenants, and Sir Arthur Langford was also said to be a 'kind and indulgent landlord'.[135]

An exception occurred in 1690 when an attempt by landlords in the Six Mile Water area of County Antrim to collect their rents resulted in riots. The Presbytery of Antrim, as a result of the disruptions and dislocations created by the Williamite War, declared on 26 November 1689 that 'if rents and tyths be exacted w[i]thout moderation the country will unavoidably be broken so as they can't live'.[136] When Lord Donegall, the chief landlord, and those who held in fee under him, such as Benjamin Adair of Leighinmohr and Arthur Upton of Templepatrick, distrained

---

[132] William Bruce to James Trail, 15 Nov. 1737 (PRONI, Bruce papers, T3041/1/B/39); A. T. Q. Stewart, *A deeper silence: the hidden origins of the United Irishmen* (Belfast, 1993), p. 117; W. B. Armstrong, *The Bruces of Airth*, p. 129; T. D. Hincks, 'Notices of William Bruce, and of his contemporaries and friends, Hutcheson, Abernethy, Duchal, and others', *Christian Teacher*, new ser., v (1843), pp 73, 81; will of Hugh Henry, 1743 (PRONI, LPC/1302); [Gabriel Cornwall], *An essay on the character of the late Mr. William Bruce. In a letter to a friend* (Dublin, 1755), pp 14–15.
[133] 'Antiquities of Car[n]money and Templepatrick', *McComb's Almanack* (1881), p. 88; [MacLysaght], 'Doneraile papers', pp 357–8.
[134] W. H. Crawford, 'The influence of the landlord in eighteenth century Ulster' in L. M. Cullen and T. C. Smout, *Comparative aspects of Scottish and Irish economic and social history, 1600–1900* (Edinburgh, 1977), p. 196; will of Henry Dalway, 1720 (PRONI, Castle Stewart papers, D1618/8/4).
[135] 'The Rev. Edward Brice and his descendants', *McComb's Almanack* (1859), p. 68; will of Sir Arthur Langford, 1715 (PRONI, T168/1); Joseph Boyse, *A funeral sermon on the occasion of the death of the late Sir Arth. Langford, Bar. Preach'd at Woodstreet, Dublin, April the 8th, 1716* (London, 1717), p. 24.
[136] Antrim 'Meeting' mins (UTC, p. 288).

for the rents due to them, their tenants resisted and argued 'that the landlord cou'd not justly crave any rent where the tenant was not kept in peaceable possession, which every body knows they were not that year, having very little but their lives left, that the enemy cou'd take from them'.[137] Lord Donegall sent men to assist Benjamin Adair, but one was wounded by a pitchfork and the cattle that had been seized were rescued by the tenants. The next day, Donegall came out himself, along with Captain William Shaw of Ballygally, Captain William Shaw of Bush, Mr John Crawford of Ballysavage, Mr Robert Crawford of Holestone, and a company of foot. When the tenants opposed the driving of the cattle, the troops were ordered to fire, and though none of the tenants were harmed, opposition ended. Soon after the event some attempted to present the riots as a Presbyterian outbreak against the members of the established church, but Adair, the Crawfords, Shaws and Upton were all members of the Presbyterian gentry and the incident illustrates that the Presbyterian gentry and Anglican landed elite could unite when their common interests were threatened.[138]

The late seventeenth and eighteenth centuries were characterised by a 'cult of improvement'. Improvement, however, is not easily defined, as it could take many forms and could be economic, cultural, political, religious or intellectual in nature.[139] The Dublin Society was established in 1731 to act as a forum for those seeking the latest ideas on how to stimulate farming and industry in Ireland. Thomas Upton was among the foundation members and Hugh Henry a member of the Society from 1738 until his death in 1743.[140] It is usually thought that Anglicans principally promoted improvement: those interested in developing the linen industry included such members of the established church as Arthur Brownlow, Sir George and Sir Arthur Rawdon, and Samuel and William Waring.[141] Although the Linen Board, established in 1711 to encourage the expansion of the industry in Ireland, had only Anglican trustees, Presbyterian landowners helped to stimulate linen manufacture by initiatives on their own lands. Sir Robert Adair of Ballymena built a weir across the Braid River at Ballygarvey, on the eastern border of his estate, cutting a mill race that brought water through Ballymena and drove four water mills. One of these mills was situated at Leighinmohr, where Benjamin Adair, or his son Thomas

---

137 [Kirkpatrick], Presby. loyalty, p. 416.
138 [William Tisdall], The conduct of the Dissenters of Ireland, with respect both to church and state (Dublin, 1712), pp 15–16; [Kirkpatrick], Presby. loyalty, pp 415–19.
139 Toby Barnard, Improving Ireland? Projectors, prophets and profiteers 1641–1786 (Dublin, 2008); Beaumont, 'The gentry of The King's & Queen's counties', i, 120–1.
140 Dublin Society mins (NLI, P 3053, pp 2, 7, 16); James Meenan and Desmond Clarke, 'The RDS 1731–1981' in idem (eds), The Royal Dublin Society, 1731–1981 (Dublin, 1981), p. 1.
141 R. G. Gillespie (ed.), Settlement and survival on an Ulster estate: the Brownlow leasebook 1667–1711 (Belfast, 1988), pp xxxvi–xxxviii; W. H. Crawford, The impact of the domestic linen industry in Ulster (Belfast, 2005), pp 13, 62, 72, 112; Barnard, Improving Ireland?, pp 85–6; D. W. Hayton, 'Thomas Prior, Sir John Rawdon, third baronet, and the mentality and ideology of "improvement": a question of upbringing' in Raymond Gillespie and R. F. Foster (eds), Irish provincial cultures in the long eighteenth-century: making the middle sort: essays for Toby Barnard (Dublin, 2012), pp 113–14.

Benjamin, had a bleach green. These Adairs claimed to be a branch of the Adair family of Ballymena.[142]

When a farmer had woven his cloth he generally disposed it in the brown, unfinished state, as beetling and finishing were an expensive business, which limited the creation of the larger concerns to those with capital. In 1725 James Hamilton Maxwell applied to the Linen Board for financial support in establishing a bleach green at Drumbeg, County Down. The board granted £40 *per annum* over a three-year period to pay the wages of an experienced bleacher who was brought over from Holland, who was in turn to instruct three apprentices. After the three years of financial assistance had ended Maxwell was obliged to continue the Dutch style of bleaching, at his own expense, for a further seven years. Maxwell is credited with introducing, in the late 1720s, the first water-powered beetling machine in Ulster and in about 1747 is supposed to have built the first scutch mill in County Down.[143] Captain John Henderson who had lands at Strabane, County Tyrone, and Donoughmore, County Donegal, was also involved in the linen industry, and between 1706 and 1708 received grants totalling £180 from the Linen Board.[144] Henderson was a brother-in-law of the Cairnes brothers of County Monaghan, who were themselves involved in the early development of the linen industry in County Monaghan.[145]

The Linen Board distributed flaxseed to encourage the linen industry and Hamilton Maxwell was active in seeking to avail of this for this tenants.[146] In 1722 he wrote to his brother-in-law, Agmondisham Vesey, the son of the archbishop of Tuam,

> I presume you are now soun to distrebute the Kings flaxseed to the cunterey. I most [sic] again put you in mind to favor me with your intrist in procuring for me what quantety you think proper for to be distrebuted to the poor people in this place which I ashuor you will be an act of charety, for it is the cheef thing they have heer about to live by.

[142] H. C. Lawlor, 'Rise of the linen merchants in the eighteenth century', *Irish and International Fibres and Fabrics Journal*, vii, no. 8 (1941), p. 11; Craig, 'The Adair family', ch. 3. See also Robert Adair to John Reilly, 1741 (PRONI, Adair papers, D929/HA12/F4/1/15).

[143] *Precedents and abstracts from the journals of the Trustees of the Linen and Hempen Manufactures of Ireland, to the twenty-fifth of March, M, DCC, XXXVII* (Dublin, 1784), p. 76; Hugh McCall, *Ireland and her staple manufactures* (2nd ed., Belfast, 1865), p. 58; Lawlor, 'Rise of the linen merchants in the eighteenth century', *Irish & International Fibres & Fabrics Journal*, viii, no. 3 (1942), p. 68. Hamilton Maxwell appeared at the General Synod as a commissioner on behalf of Drumbo congregation in 1730: RGSU, ii, 154.

[144] John Henderson to William Cairnes, 8 Dec. 1705 (PRONI, Rossmore papers, T2929/2/6); A. Wrightson to Sir Alexander Cairnes, 14 Mar. 1711/12 (ibid., T2929/2/11); John Henderson to Sir Alexander Cairnes, 15 Mar. 1711/12 (ibid., T2929/2/12); Roulston, *Restoration Strabane*, p. 34.

[145] A. Wrightson to Sir Alexander Cairnes, 14 Mar. 1711/12 (PRONI, Rossmore papers, T2929/2/11); John Henderson to Sir Alexander Cairnes, 15 Mar. 1711/12 (ibid., T2929/2/12); Archdeacon Cranston and Mr Lucas, 'Co. Monaghan', 1738/9, in 'Topographical and statistical returns from various respondents sent to Walter Harris and the Physico-Historical Society of Ireland' (Armagh Public Library, P001498343); Crawford, *The impact of the domestic linen industry*, p. 63; Roulston, *Restoration Strabane*, p. 34; Lawlor, *History of the Cairnes*, p. 100.

[146] *Precedents & abstracts from the journals of the Trustees of the Linen & Hempen Manufactures of Ireland*, p. 103; Hamilton Maxwell to Agmondisham Vesey, 13 Jan. 1721/2, 21 July 1722, 9 Oct. 1723 (PRONI, Kirk papers, T2524/12, /16, /19).

Maxwell offered to pay the expense of delivery and promised not to 'sow on[e] peck of it but devide it among the poor of the perish'.[147] By helping his tenants, Maxwell was able to ensure they would be able to pay their rents, and many 'improvement' schemes were carried out not only for practical but also economic and possibly selfish reasons. These examples of Presbyterian involvement in the linen industry show that it was not necessary to be a member of parliament, or of the Dublin Society, to engage in improvement, and although some Presbyterians such as James Hamilton of Tollymore were involved in legislative initiatives to support the linen industry,[148] a larger number of the Presbyterian gentry worked to promote it locally.

Other forms of agricultural improvement undertaken by Presbyterian gentlemen included wetland reclamation and enclosure. In 1723 James Stevenson of Killyleagh spent money on 'ditching and other improvements' in his demesne lands and in the early 1740s Hugh Henry not only enclosed his 115-acre demesne at Straffan, County Kildare, but enclosed five fields (an area of about 60 acres), for his cottiers to graze their cattle and have their homes.[149] Sometimes improvement was carried out by the tenants themselves, though landlords stimulated such activity by the terms of leases granted and other incentives offered to tenants.[150] In order to establish the boundaries of their holdings, to see where to cut ditches, to determine the acreage and quality of their lands, and the rent that they should charge, they increasingly employed land surveyors,[151] and Presbyterian landlords were no exception. Edward Brice had 21 acres surveyed in 1725; John Sloane was employed to carry out surveys by both John Blackwood of Ballyleidy and James Ross of Portavo; William Stewart of Killymoon had surveys carried out in 1731 and 1736; and Hugh Henry had his demesne lands at Straffan surveyed by James Jerrett in the early 1740s.[152]

Landlords were also heavily involved in infrastructural improvements. They invested capital in road improvements, the construction of bridges, and the purchase of patents for holding fairs and markets. Such markets helped to develop the economy of a town. In order to set up a market landlords had to apply for (or sue out) a royal patent in Dublin, and although this involved initial expense plus the annual payment of quit-rent, the landlord was able to make money from the tolls

---

[147] Hamilton Maxwell to Agmondisham Vesey, 13 Jan. 1721/2 (PRONI, Kirk papers, T2524/12).

[148] Richard Holt to Hamilton of Tollymore, 29 Feb. 1695/6 (PRONI, Roden papers, MIC147/8/132); *The journals of the House of Commons, of the kingdom of Ireland* (3rd ed., Dublin, 1763–82), ii: 1662–1698, pp 657, 685, 729.

[149] *ODNB* (Forbes, Arthur, 1st earl of Granard); 'an account of several payments paid for the use of James Stevenson', 11 May 1723 (PRONI, Dufferin and Ava papers, D1071/B/B/7/1); will of Hugh Henry, 1743 (PRONI, LPC/1302).

[150] [Sir Alexander Cairnes] to Charles Campbell, 29 Jan. 1716[/17], 2 Feb. 1716[/17?] (PRONI, Rossmore papers, T2929/2/21–22); lease of Hugh Edwards, Castle Gore, to Thomas Sproule, Golan, Co. Tyrone, 1732 (PRONI, Ferguson papers, D1453/8).

[151] Gillespie, *Settlement & survival*, p. xxviii.

[152] Survey of eight parks of Captain [Edward] Brice, 13 Oct. 1725 (NLI, Brice papers, MS 21,961); Maguire, 'The Blackwoods of Ballyleidy', pp 34, 42, n. 2; Peter Carr, *Portavo: an Irish townland and its peoples: part one: earliest times to 1844* (Belfast, 2003), pp 104–5; survey of Clananize, [c.1730] (NLI, Stewart papers, MS 8734/1); Stewart of Killymoon surveys, 1731 & 1736 (PRONI, D2–3); will of Hugh Henry, 1743 (ibid., LPC/1302).

and customs that arose out of the markets connected with his land.[153] In 1680 Hugh Hamill took out patents for fairs and markets at Ballindrait and Dunfanaghy in County Donegal and Castlederg in County Tyrone, and George Butle Conyngham of Springhill was granted fairs at Coagh.[154]

Rev. Joseph Boyse, the Presbyterian minister of Dublin, preached Sir Arthur Langford's funeral sermon in 1716, having been acquainted with Langford for 'upwards of thirty years'. According to Boyse, Langford 'divided his time between the innocent improvements of his seat in the country and his books'.[155] Many other gentry figures had a similar interest in this more aspirational form of improvement which involved development of country estates and conspicuous display. Occasionally the books that they owned would suggest some interest in this area. Sir Alexander Cairnes, who added to the family castle at Monaghan in 1725,[156] was a subscriber to Richard Bradley's A philosophical account of the works of nature, which contains an account of the state of contemporary gardening and information on how to improve barren ground.[157] John Donaldson and Archibald Edmonstone were both among the subscribers for John Laurence's A new system of agriculture, which James Trail may also have owned, and Henry Dalway of Bellahill possessed a copy of Sir Henry Wotton's The elements of architecture.[158]

A prolonged period of domestic peace after the 'Glorious' Revolution allowed landowners to develop the surroundings of their homes and the term 'improved' was often used by eighteenth-century topographers in the description of country houses and their demesnes.[159] William Conyngham, who for a number of years after the Siege of Derry held the post of 'overseer of the woods and forests of Ulster' under the Irish Society, improved his home at Springhill by adding beech trees and planting a 'new cherry garden'.[160] In 1721 James Hamilton Maxwell of Drum House had the carpenters in and hoped in the summer to avail of advice from his brother-in-law Agmondisham Vesey on further improvements to the house, which Maxwell had recently inherited from his uncle.[161] Such work helped the local economy by providing work for local masons, carpenters, and other skilled craftsmen.[162] William

---

[153] W. H. Crawford, 'The creation and evolution of small towns in Ulster in the seventeenth and eighteenth centuries' in Peter Borsay and L. J. Proudfoot (ed.), Provincial towns in early modern England and Ireland: change, convergence and divergence (Oxford, 2002), pp 107–8.

[154] Roulston, Restoration Strabane, p. 37; translation of grant of fairs and markets at Coagh, Co. Tyrone, to George Conyngham, 1725 (PRONI, Lenox-Conyngham papers, D1449/1/40).

[155] Boyse, A funeral sermon on the death of the late Sir Arth. Langford, pp 22, 24.

[156] Lawlor, History of the Cairnes, pp 97, 99.

[157] Richard Bradley, A philosophical account of the works of nature (London, 1721).

[158] John Laurence, A new system of agriculture. Being a complete body of husbandry and gardening (Dublin, 1727); 'a catalogue of the books of James Trail taken 21 Feb. 1731/32' in autobiography of James Trail (PRONI, D1460/1); Sir Henry Wotton (ed.), The elements of architecture (London, 1624) (Antrim Pby Lib., B. 12. 7. 21).

[159] Dean William Henry's topographical description of the coast of Co. Antrim and north Down, c.1740 (PRONI, T2521/3/5, pp 13, 15); [Charles Smith & Walter Harris], The antient and present state of the county of Down (Dublin, 1744), pp 41, 48, 68, 71, 76, 84.

[160] Mina Lenox-Conyngham, An old Ulster house: Springhill and the people who lived in it (Belfast, 2005), pp 10, 21.

[161] Hamilton Maxwell to Agmondisham Vesey, 15 July 1721 (PRONI, Kirk papers, T2524/5).

[162] The Blackwoods, for instance, engaged glaziers and nailers: Blackwood cash book, 1720–39

Cairnes and Sir Alexander Cairnes in Monaghan spent much time not only planting trees, but also making parks and stocking them with deer.[163] The ability to remove such large tracts from regular cultivation proclaimed their wealth and standing in the community. At Larchfield, near Lisburn, Daniel Mussenden planted around six acres with 8,000 assorted trees arranged in the shape of an octagon and was so pleased with the results that he resolved to henceforth devote himself to 'farming and improvement' as 'a very pleasant and useful study'.[164]

VI. Interests, expenditure and sociability

It has been stated that the religious beliefs of the Presbyterians made them more austere and ascetic than their Anglican counterparts.[165] The evidence, however, would seem to suggest that apart from their denominational differences the lifestyle of the Presbyterian and Anglican gentry in Ulster was not radically different. Individual personality and preferences were often the most important determinant, and religious ideology rarely acted as the sole variable in determining social behaviour, being more likely to be of importance when combined with other external circumstances. All gentlemen, irrespective of their religion, were under some obligation to build, act and dress in a style appropriate to their status.[166] Although Sir Arthur Langford supposedly lived unpretentiously in order that he might have more to give away to charitable and pious causes,[167] others enjoyed a more opulent lifestyle. Arthur Maxwell was described as 'a very rich man' who 'loved the things of the world too much',[168] which suggests both visible wealth and a luxurious lifestyle. Maxwell's hangings,[169] and the striking plasterwork ceilings preserved in two rooms at Redhall,[170] could easily have been found in the home of an Anglican gentry family, while Anglicans, such as William Waring and Arthur Brownlow, who left instructions for a frugal funeral,[171] were not always extravagant in their lifestyle and social behaviour.

Wills occasionally offer some insight into gentry possessions and the interior of gentry homes. Robert Dalway of Bellahill bequeathed various items to family relatives including his 'little cabinet', a 'well furnished bed', his 'silver inkhorn' and two 'big' desks.[172] His son Henry, whose will was dated 1720, mentioned 'fire arms', a

(PRONI, Dufferin and Ava papers, D1071/A/B/2/1, pp 6–7).

[163] John Henderson to William Cairnes, 8 Dec. 1705 (PRONI, Rossmore papers, T2929/2/6); Alexander Montgomery to William Cairnes, 8 Feb. 1705/6 (ibid., T2929/2/8); John Henderson to Sir Alexander Cairnes, 15 Mar. 1711/12 (ibid., T2929/2/12); Young, *Historical notices of old Belfast*, p. 160.
[164] Barnard, *Making the grand figure*, pp 195–6, 236.
[165] Ibid., p. 115.
[166] Heal & Holmes, *The gentry in England & Wales*, p. 146.
[167] Boyse, *A funeral sermon on the occasion of the death of the late Sir Arth. Langford*, pp 24–5.
[168] Autobiography of James Trail (PRONI, D1460/1, opening 28).
[169] Will of Arthur Maxwell, 1720 (ibid., D1769/60/2/3).
[170] C. E. B. Brett, *Buildings of County Antrim* (Belfast, 1996), pp 70, 76.
[171] Benn, *Belfast*, p. 250; Gillespie, *Settlement & survival*, p. 163.
[172] Will of Robert Dalway, 1699 (PRONI, Castle Stewart papers, D1618/8/5).

'cane with a gold head', 'silver hilted sword', 'diamond locket', 'sett of silver castors', 'silver tankard' and 'tortoiseshell snuff box'.[173] Margaret Stewart of Killymoon left her grandson a 'gold watch' and a 'cane with the gold head'.[174] There is also evidence that some families had goods which were maintained as family heirlooms. A gold watch and diamond ring, given to Margaret Upton in 1660 when she married James Shaw of Ballygally, were kept in the Shaw family, and handed down to the eldest daughter of the family from generation to generation.[175] Robert Dalway in his will left instructions that his 'rubie sett in gold', his 'gold chain and big gold thumb ring', along with his 'big brewing pot' and his 'big brass pott' were to be maintained as heirlooms.[176] Members of the gentry distinguished themselves from the generality by their diet. High-status foodstuffs in the eighteenth century included tea, coffee, chocolate, sugar and exotic fruit. In 1718 Archibald Edmonstone obtained an Indian tea table, six green-tea cups and six bohea-tea cups and dishes for £5 8s, and Lady Granard was a noted coffee drinker.[177] The Blackwood cash book of 1720–39 contains inventories of plate, china, glasses, linen and 'kitchen furniture', listing items entrusted to the housekeeper and butler. There were, for instance, wine glasses, 'flowred water glases', china plates, ivory knives and forks, two coffee pots, a tea kettle, napkins, cravats, tablecloths and sheets. Interestingly, a distinction was made between the tablecloths and sheets for the family and those for the servants.[178]

Some of the gentry were patrons of art and commissioned portraits of themselves or members of their family which they used to adorn their homes. When Jane Pottinger died in 1721 her furniture was assessed as being 'once valewable but ... not soe now' and included beds, two 'loucking glasses', chairs, trunks, and some pictures.[179] Hugh Henry was a particularly noted patron of art and his home at Straffan was famous for the family's collection of paintings.[180] In 1705 the Belfast merchant Isaac Macartney mentioned two pictures ordered by William Stewart of Killymoon, and the Upton family of Castle Upton in the later eighteenth century owned valuable pictures, some of which were by the Florentine painters Andrea del Sarto and Leonardo da Vinci.[181] William Conyngham of Springhill had his portrait painted in oils, reputedly by Sir Peter Lely, as did Sir John Skeffington, second Viscount Massereene, and other members of the Massereene family.[182] Mary Beale, the first noted female professional painter in England, painted a portrait

[173] Will of Henry Dalway, 1720 (ibid., D1618/8/14).

[174] Will of Margaret Stewart, 1727 (NLI, Prerogative will book, 1726–8, MFGS 41/2, ff 273–4).

[175] Classon Porter, 'Ballygally Castle', ed. F. G. Bigger, in *UJA*, vii (1901), p. 74.

[176] Will of Robert Dalway, 1699 (PRONI, Castle Stewart papers, D1618/8/5).

[177] Captain Edmonstone's account, 1719 (PRONI, Castle Stewart papers, D1618/8/8); John Forbes, *Memoirs of the earls of Granard*, ed. George Arthur Hastings [Forbes] (London, 1868), pp 10–11.

[178] Blackwood cash book, 1720–39 (PRONI, Dufferin and Ava papers, D1071/A/B/2/1).

[179] Hamilton Maxwell to Agmondisham Vesey, 11 Nov. 1721 (PRONI, Kirk papers, T2524/8).

[180] [Richard Twiss], *A tour in Ireland in 1775* (London, 1776), pp 24–5.

[181] Isaac Macartney to [Sir Alexander and Henry] Cairnes, 13 Jan. 1704/5 (PRONI, D501/1, p. 37); J. W. Kernohan, 'Some Ulster castles: historical sketch of Upton', *Belfast Telegraph*, 29 Oct. 1919.

[182] Lenox-Conyngham, *An old Ulster house: Springhill*, p. 19; Massereene to Sir Richard Newdegate, 6 Aug. 1679, 27 Apr. 1682, 8 Nov. 1683, 23 Apr. 1684, 24 Nov. 1686 (Warwickshire County

of William Cairnes, and others, such as Cairnes' brothers and his cousin David Cairnes of Knockmany, were painted by Sir Godfrey Kneller or other artists of the Kneller school.[183] Such portraits were sometimes given to family members as gifts and helped to keep ancestors and lineage constantly in view. In 1720 Henry Dalway bequeathed his portrait to his aunt.[184] Mary Upton married Sir Hercules Langford, of Summerhill, and the pictures in the entrance hall at Summerhill included one of her father, Captain Henry Upton, and her brother, Arthur Upton.[185] Other members of the Presbyterian gentry were involved in collecting. George Mathews, a Presbyterian who later conformed, was a captain in the Royal Navy. Mathews travelled to many countries and brought back to his home at Springvale, County Down, a hoard of unusual curios, including ancient coins, Egyptian hieroglyphics and mummies.[186] Edward Brice leased lands at Kilroot from the bishop of Down and Connor and at Kilroot House had a 'garden in which is a shell house made beautiful by a great variety of shells from all parts of the world and put together with a paste inferior to none in the kingdom'.[187]

Only occasionally are we able to uncover the books that the Presbyterian gentry were purchasing and reading. Patrick Agnew of Kilwaughter bequeathed his books to his eldest son, William.[188] Robert Dalway bequeathed all his Hebrew, Greek and Latin books to his sons, Alexander and Henry, and requested that his English books be divided among his wife and two daughters.[189] When Henry Dalway wrote his will he desired that his books might be sold and the money raised be spent on purchasing communion cups for Carrickfergus Presbyterian Church.[190] Six books of Dalway provenance are now contained in the Presbytery of Antrim Library.[191] The Dalways' neighbour and relative, Archibald Edmonstone, who was head of the family from 1689 until his death in 1768, left his 'religious and history' books to the Presbyterian minister of Ballycarry, and in the Presbytery of Antrim Library there is a copy of William Turner's *A compleat history of the remarkable providences*, which

Record Office, Newdegate MSS, CR/136B/281, /284–6, /288); Toby Barnard, 'Art, architecture, artefacts and ascendancy', *Bullán*, i, no. 2 (1994), p. 23.

183 Lawlor, *History of the Cairnes*, pp 83–7, 158–9.

184 Will of Henry Dalway, 1720 (PRONI, Castle Stewart papers, D1618/8/14).

185 *The Georgian Society records of eighteenth century domestic architecture and decoration in Dublin: introduction by Desmond Guinness* (Shannon, 1969), pp 55–6. The interior of the entrance hall at Summerhill was destroyed by a fire c.1800.

186 List of the gentlemen of Co. Down and Co. Antrim, [c.1725] (Royal Irish Academy, Dublin, Upton papers, MS 24.K.19, no. 1); [Smith & Harris], *Antient & present state of Down*, p. 68.

187 Dean William Henry's topographical description of the coast of Co. Antrim and north Down, c.1740 (PRONI, T2521/3/5, p. 17).

188 Will of Patrick Agnew, 1724 (ibid., LPC/1034).

189 Will of Robert Dalway, 1699 (ibid., Castle Stewart papers, D1618/8/5).

190 Will of Henry Dalway, 1720 (ibid., D1618/8/14).

191 Samuel Clarke, *A survey of the Bible: or, an analytical account of the Holy Scriptures* (London, 1693) (Antrim Pby Lib., B. 3. 5. 3.); Paolo Sarpi, *A treatise of matters beneficiary* (London, 1680) (ibid., B. 3. 7. 17.); René Descartes, *Renati Des-Cartes principia philosophiae* (Amsterdam, 1692) (ibid., B. 5. 5. 2.); Richard Brown, *Prosodia pharmacopoeorum: or, the apothecary's prosody* (London, 1685) (ibid., B. 6. 10. 11); Sir Henry Wotton (ed.), *The elements of architecture* (London, 1624) (ibid., B. 12. 7. 21.); and Thomas de Laune, *A plea for Non-conformists: shewing the true state of their case* (London, 1719) (ibid., B. 14. 3. 22.).

belonged to Edmonstone and in which there is a bookplate bearing the Edmonstone coat of arms.[192] Clotworthy Upton owned Charles Owen's *Plain-dealing, or separation without schism, and schism without separation*, obtained a copy of Robert Wodrow's *History* from Scotland and, along with his younger brother, Thomas Upton, Robert Dalway and Archibald Edmonstone, was a subscriber to the Dublin edition of Gilbert Burnet's *History of his own time*, which was published in 1724.[193] Clotworthy Upton occasionally lent books, including this work by Burnet, to the Presbyterian minister of Templepatrick, Rev. William Livingston.[194]

Gentry women, too, if they were educated were able to engage in reading.[195] Elizabeth Cairnes, wife of Sir Alexander Cairnes, requested her friend, Sarah, duchess of Marlborough, to send her Buckingham's *Works*, and she may have been the owner of Matthew Henry's *An exposition of the historical books of the Old Testament*, now in the Antrim Presbytery Library, which is marked 'E Cairnes'.[196] Lady Cairnes employed the Frenchman Louis de Guernier, who came over from Paris to England in 1708, to execute a bookplate.[197] Her copy of Abraham Ortelius' *Theatrum orbis terrarium* (London, 1606), which contained 161 engraved maps, some heightened with gold, is now held in the W. G. Arader III Gallery, New York. It is bound in late seventeenth-century English black goatskin, tooled in gilt, and both covers, which have a triple border, enclose the owner's name, and are further ornamented with urns and flower heads.[198]

Very few library lists survive from the period, though one exception is that of James Trail of Killyleagh, who in 1732 compiled a list of books in his possession along with the price he had paid for them or value he placed on those he had received as gifts.[199] The library consisted of almost 90 titles, of which the largest sector could be classified as religious works, including two English-language bibles (one valued at 14s; the other at 2s), Watts's *Translation of the Psalms*, *The worship and discipline of the Church of Scotland*, and Calvin's *Institutes*, as well as Lancelot Andrewes's *Sermons on prayer*, Thomas Hooker's *Unbelievers preparing for Christ*, and works of

---

[192] Classon Porter, 'Congregational memoirs – Ballycarry (or Broadisland) congregation' in *Christian Unitarian*, ii (1864), p. 160; William Turner, *A compleat history of the most remarkable providences, both of judgment and mercy, which have hapned in this present age* (London, 1697) (Antrim Pby Lib., B. 6. 7. 2.).

[193] Charles Owen, *Plain-dealing: or separation without schism, and schism without separation. Exemplify'd in the case of Protestant-Dissenters and Church-men* (London, 1715) (Antrim Pby Lib., B. 5. 3. 14.); William McKnight to Robert Wodrow, 26 July 1723 (NLS, Wod. Lett. Qu. xx, f. 314); William Livingston to Robert Wodrow, 22 Apr. 1724 (ibid., Wod. Lett. Qu. xxi, ff 144–5); Gilbert Burnet, *Bishop Burnet's history of his own time* (Dublin, 1724), vol. i.

[194] William Livingston to Robert Wodrow, 22 Apr. 1724 (NLS, Wod. Lett. Qu. xxi, ff 144–5); [Alexander Gordon], 'Congregational memoirs – Templepatrick', *The Disciple*, ii (1882), p. 267.

[195] James Cobham, *Preparation for death describ'd in a sermon occasion'd by the death of Mrs. Anna-Helena Edmonstone* (Belfast, 1711), p. 22.

[196] E[lizabeth] Cairnes to Sarah, duchess of Marlborough, 31 Mar. [1725?] (BL, Blenheim papers, Add. MS 61466, f. 133); Matthew Henry, *An exposition of the historical books of the Old Testament* (London, 1708) (Antrim Pby Lib., B. 8. 6. 7.).

[197] Walter Hamilton, *Dated book-plates (Ex Libris) with a treatise on their origin and development* (London, 1895), p. 39; W. J. Hardy, *Book-plates* (2nd ed., London, 1897), pp 73–4.

[198] Information kindly supplied by W. Graham Arader III Gallery, New York.

[199] 'Catalogue of books of James Trail' in autobiography of James Trail (PRONI, D1460/1).

the Covenanting divine, James Durham. Among the works on classical and ancient history were the French historian Charles Rollin's *Ancient history* and Basil Kennet's *Antiquities of Rome*. While the majority of the authors were English, and as many Anglican as Presbyterian, there were some Irish Presbyterian works including James Kirkpatrick's *Historical essay on the loyalty of the Presbyterians*, Robert Craghead's *Walking with God*, Joseph Boyse's *Discourses on the four last things*, five copies of Rev. James Reid of Killinchy's *Formal Christians*, as well as the works of James Trail's cousin, Francis Hutcheson, philosophy professor at Glasgow University. Another of James Trail's cousins was the Dublin bookseller William Bruce, and some of the books may have been acquired through this acquaintance. Trail also owned the works of William Molyneux and John Locke, and *The Independent Whig*, a political tract that was anticlerical as well as 'republican'. Some interest in foreign travel was suggested with the presence of Justus Zinterling's *Itinerarium Galliae* and in European affairs with Laurence Echard's *Gazetteer*, which provided a geographical index of the cities, bishoprics and forts of Europe, and capitalised on the interest aroused by the European wars that were in progress at the time, such as the War of the Spanish Succession.[200] Henry Dalway left his 'large sett of mapps of the world' to his cousin Archibald Edmonstone and his 'other mapps of Flanders' to Colonel Robert Dalway.[201]

While inventories such as Trail's list of books help us to gain an insight into the extent of gentry libraries, they cannot tell us whether the books were read or that the owner agreed with the opinion of the authors. However, interspersed among farming accounts in Trail's autobiography are notes made by him on the books of the Bible, which exhibit familiarity not only with the Bible but also with the works of Moses Maimonides, St Basil, Josephus, Bishop William Lloyd, Jean-Frédéric Ostervald, Dr John Pearson and Dr Daniel Whitby.[202] Correspondence can occasionally shed light on reading habits, and from Trail's correspondence we learn that he obtained a work by Ostervald from his cousin Rev. Michael Bruce, and that another of his cousins, Rev. Patrick Bruce, sought to read Trail's copy of Simon Patrick's *Paraphrase*. While staying with his brother-in-law, James Read, Inspector of the Barracks of Ireland, Trail read Richard Baxter's *Practical works*, with which he 'was much delighted' and he recorded in his autobiography that he used two discourses by Bishop Burnet of Salisbury to instruct his family.[203] Subscription lists may also indicate definite interest in a particular book and members of the Presbyterian gentry and Presbyterian gentlemen who conformed are found among those who subscribed for books during this period.[204] A number of books that

---

[200] *ODNB* (Echard, Laurence).

[201] Will of Henry Dalway, 1720 (PRONI, Castle Stewart papers, D1618/8/14).

[202] 'The substance of the several books of the Old and New Testaments in their order with some observations on the authors of them' in autobiography of James Trail (PRONI, D1460/1).

[203] Michael Bruce to James Trail, [1731/32] (NLI, Bruce papers, MS 20,867); Patrick Bruce to James Trail, 23 Dec. 1731 (ibid., MS 20,868); autobiography of James Trail (PRONI, D1460/1, openings 30, 44).

[204] Some examples include: Sir Alexander Cairnes subscribed for *The lucubrations of Isaac Bickerstaff, esq* (2 vols, London, 1713); Mr. Cairnes Henderson, son of Captain John Henderson and nephew of Sir Alexander Cairnes, subscribed for Sir Isaac Newton, *The chronology of ancient*

belonged to William Conyngham, the builder of Springhill, are still preserved in the library there, which bear not only his signature but also marginal notes made by him. Such marginalia would suggest that Conyngham was jotting down his thoughts as he read the texts.[205] Most of the titles which bear Conyngham's name are religious, including *Jus divinum ministerii evangelicii: or, the divine right of the gospel ministry* (London, 1654) and Richard Baxter's *A treatise of episcopacy* (London, 1681), which Conygham obtained when in London shortly after the Siege of Derry. Other books at Springhill belonged to family relatives including a French and English dictionary, which belonged to Conyngham's brother Richard, and a copy of Richard Baxter's *The life of faith* (London, 1670), which is inscribed by William Conyngham's mother-in-law, Dorothy Upton.[206]

As with other gentry families a common occurrence at gentry homes was the visit of friends and relatives.[207] During the visits the family and their visitors shared meals and were able to socialise with one another in other ways. Billiards and chess were played by some of the Presbyterian gentry.[208] While in England Mary Cairnes, daughter of Sir Alexander Cairnes, was taught dancing along with the granddaughters of the duke of Marlborough and was involved in amateur theatricals for the duke and duchess of Marlborough and their friends. A description of one of the dramas performed, entitled 'All for love', is extant and the prologue for it was written for the occasion by Bishop Benjamin Hoadly.[209] In Ireland the highlight of the social season was the 'parliament winter', which occurred every second year when the lord lieutenant was in residence at Dublin, and usually lasted for about six months. During this time members of parliament and others who could afford it took up residence in either their Dublin townhouses or in one of the city's lodgings, and attended the weekly balls and drawing room night at the castle.[210] Prolonged

kingdoms amended. To which is prefix'd, a short chronicle from the first memory of things in Europe, to the conquest of Persia by Alexander the Great (Dublin, 1728); Robert Donaldson, esq., and Mr. Valentine Jones were subscribers for John Gay, *Poems on several occasions* (Dublin, 1729); Robert Adair, esq., John Donnellon (Donaldson), esq. and Colonel Dolloway (Dalway) were among the subscribers to Aeschines, *The orations of Aeschines and Demosthenes, concerning the crown. Translated into English from Greek, and illustrated with notes historical, geographical, and critical. By Thomas Dawson* (Dublin, 1732); and Colonel Robert Dalway and Robert Ross, esq., jr., subscribed for [Captain Downes], *All vows kept: A comedy: as it is acted at the Theatre-Royal in Smock-Alley* (Dublin, 1733).

[205] Lenox-Conyngham, *An old Ulster house: Springhill*, p. 10; Mark Purcell, *The big house library in Ireland: books in Ulster country houses* (Swindon, 2011), pp 45–6.

[206] Purcell, *The big house library*, pp 43–8.

[207] Michael Bruce to James Trail, 13 Nov. 1730 (PRONI, Bruce papers, T3041/1/A/5); Carr, *Portavo*, p. 101.

[208] Autobiography of James Trail (PRONI, D1460/1, opening 6); H. M. B. Reid, *The divinity professors in the University of Glasgow 1640–1903* (Glasgow 1923), p. 200. There was also a billiard room at Castle Gore, Co. Tyrone, the home of the Edwards family: Lawlor, *A history of the Cairnes*, p. 176.

[209] Lady [Mary] Blayney to General Cunningham, 24 Oct. 1777, (BL, Blenheim papers, Add. MS 61466, f. 179); 'All for love', n.d. (ibid., f. 176); William Coxe, *Memoirs of the duke of Marlborough, with his original correspondence* (2nd ed., 6 vols, London, 1820), iii, 416–19.

[210] Tighernan Mooney and Fiona White, 'The gentry's winter season' in David Dickson (ed.), *The gorgeous mask: Dublin, 1700–1850* (Dublin, 1987), pp 1–2; J. L. McCracken, 'Social structure &

stay in Dublin, though, was not always welcomed. Elizabeth Cairnes, who had been used to the entertainments available in London and England, wrote from Dublin in 1724 to the duchess of Marlborough, 'bad as Monaghan [the Cairnes' seat] is I begin to wish my self there out of hurry dirt and noise, that we have now here. And evin what are cald diversions are so litle refin here that one finds very litle miss of them when out of the way.' She added, however, that 'our court keeps very gay and obliging my litle family'.[211] Those who could afford it travelled to England, principally to Bath, but also to Buxton, Epsom Wells and Tunbridge Wells to avail of hydrotherapy in order to treat various ailments, and to engage in the opportunities for sociability that existed in such spa towns. Ireland had its own alternatives and there were spas situated close to Dublin, as well as at Wexford, Kilkenny and Limerick.[212] Alexander Dalway, of Bellahill, wrote from Dublin to his cousin Richard Dobbs in May 1694 to tell him that he hoped to see Dobbs at Harry's Well before the end of August. Dalway added that his mother and sister planned to spend part of the summer at either the Wexford waters or Kirkdonnell (that is, Dundonald) Well in County Down.[213]

Hunting and shooting were popular outdoor pastimes for the male members of the gentry. As a result of an act of 1698 only those with at least £40 *per annum* from freehold land, or £1,000 personal estate, were allowed to hunt game, and this, along with the requisite associated costs, limited it to the 'quality'.[214] Maintenance of a huntsman, 24 hounds and two horses was estimated at £40 *per annum* in 1714.[215] Among the subscribers to William Starrat's *The doctrine of projectiles demonstrated and apply'd to all the most useful problems in practical gunnery*, which was published at Dublin in 1733, were George and James Gledstanes, William Hamilton of Dunnamanagh, John Henderson and his son Cairnes Henderson, Robert Ross, and the conformist Valentine Jones, who was originally a Presbyterian. Hunting was popular among the landowning classes not only as a form of recreation, but as a source of meat, and as a means for gentlemen to flaunt their manliness. Clotworthy Upton's Irish wolf dogs are credited with killing the last wolf in Ulster in 1692.[216] As the wolf became extinct in Ireland, the gentry focused their attention on the hunting of deer, hares, and later foxes, and there are examples of Presbyterian

social life' in T. W. Moody and W. E. Vaughan (eds), *A new history of Ireland: iv: Eighteenth-century Ireland 1691–1800* (Oxford, 1986), p. 49.
[211] E[lizabeth] Cairnes to Sarah, duchess of Marlborough, 8 Dec. 1724 (BL, Blenheim papers, Add. MS 61466, f. 126).
[212] J. A. Sharpe, *Early modern England: a social history 1550–1760* (2nd ed., London, 1997), p. 81; T. C. Barnard, 'The cultures of eighteenth-century Irish towns' in Peter Borsay and L. J. Proudfoot (eds), *Provincial towns in early modern England and Ireland: change, convergence and divergence* (Oxford, 2002), pp 199–200.
[213] Alexander Dalway to Richard Dobbs, 19 May 1694 (PRONI, Dobbs papers, D162/10).
[214] 10 Will. III, c. 8 (*The statutes at large, passed in the parliaments held in Ireland* (20 vols, 1786–1804), iii, 487–96); Barnard, *New anatomy*, p. 59.
[215] Arthur Stringer, *The experienced huntsman*, ed. James Fairley (Belfast, 1714; repr. 1977), p. 140.
[216] J. Crompton, *A compendious system of chronology* (Belfast, 1823), p. 135; John Marshall to F. G. Bigger, 6 May 1904 (Belfast Central Library, Bigger Collection, MA 121 (1)); 'Upton's wolves' (ibid., Bigger collection, H88). There is also a copy of the latter in PHS.

gentlemen involved in these different types of hunting.[217] Organised horse races took place at various locations in Ulster including Downpatrick and the Maze, near Hillsborough, both in County Down, and another was organised by Belturbet corporation in County Cavan. Prizes normally took the form of silver plate or money.[218] The second Viscount Massereene and his eldest son were noted patrons of the turf and were interested in the breeding of horses.[219] Major Hugh Montgomery, a Presbyterian who held a bishop's lease in Maghera, was also a noted horse-breeder.[220] In 1710 Massereene wrote to Joshua Dawson, enclosing a list of subscribers for a plate to be run at Donegore, County Antrim, and among the subscribers were Massereene (£40) and Clotworthy Upton (£5).[221] Keeping and breeding horses was an expensive business, with costs involved in purchasing, feeding, stabling and the employment of staff. From the mid-1740s the Ross family of Portavo experienced financial difficulties. At the same time Portavo had stabling for 50 horses, and part of the reason for the family's financial difficulties has been attributed to Captain James Ross, head of the family from the late 1720s, who was 'intemperate, lived well, and was "rather too fond of horses for his own good"'.[222]

As well as hunts, gentlemen also met together at the assizes and at funerals.[223] Funerals were a last opportunity for displaying one's wealth and status. Though many of the gentry asked for 'decent' funerals 'without pomp',[224] they were nevertheless often costly affairs. David Crawford of Belfast and Florida Manor, County Down, stipulated that not more than £80 was to be expended on his funeral, while William Conyngham of Springhill placed a limit of £50 on his funeral, and in the case of Jane Pottinger who died in 1721, though Hamilton Maxwell assessed her funeral as 'decent and creditable and at as little expense as posable', it cost £50 – an amount which was more than most of the Presbyterian ministers earned in a single

---

[217] Tom Fulton, 'A brief history of hunting in Ireland' in Claude Costecalde and Jack Gallagher (eds), *Hunting in Ireland: a noble tradition* ([Holywood, Co. Down], 2004), p. 20; autobiography of James Trail (PRONI, D1460/1, opening 72); Dean William Henry's topographical description of the coast of Co. Antrim and north Down, c.1740 (PRONI, T2521/3/5, p. 10).

[218] *Belfast News-Letter*, 1 June 1739; [Smith & Harris], *Antient & present state of Down*, pp 35–6, 95–6; articles and rules for the race of Belturbet, n.d. (Cavan County Archives Service, Belturbet corp. mins, 1657–c.1730, BC/1, p. 325); Blackwood cash book, 1720–39 (PRONI, Dufferin and Ava papers, D1071/A/B/2/1), p. 4; McCracken, 'Social structure & social life', p. 47; Barnard, *Making the grand figure*, pp 228–9.

[219] Massereene to Sir Richard Newdegate, 8 Nov. 1683, 23 Apr. 1684, 20 Feb. 1687/8 (Warwickshire County Record Office, Newdegate MSS, CR/136B/285–6, /289; *DIB* (Skeffington, Sir John (1632–95)); John McLeane to Sir James Agnew, 27 Nov. 1700 (NAS, Agnew papers, GD154/677/2).

[220] Bailie, *Hist. of congns*, p. 619; 'Notes by Rev. David Stewart' in Antrim 'Meeting' mins, 1671–91 (PRONI, Stewart papers, D1759/1/A/3, p. 259); Viscount Dungannon to Sir George Rawdon, 18 Dec. 1666 (Edward Berwick (ed.), *The Rawdon papers* (London, 1819), p. 222).

[221] 'Horse-racing in Antrim in 1710', *UJA*, vii (1901), p. 158.

[222] Carr, *Portavo*, pp 108, 112–13.

[223] Diary of Rev. John Kennedy, 15, 17–22 Nov. 1727 (PHS, pp 136–7); autobiography of James Trail (PRONI, D1460/1, opening 28); Beaumont, 'The gentry of The King's & Queen's counties', i, p. 52.

[224] Will of Penelope Brice, 1707 (NLI, Prerogative will book, 1706–8, MFGS 41/2, f. 109); will of Robert Dalway, 1699 (PRONI, Castle Stewart papers, D1618/8/5); will of Sir Arthur Langford, 1715 (PRONI, T168/1); will of Henry Dalway, 1720 (ibid., Castle Stewart papers, D1618/8/14); will of Hugh Henry, 1743 (PRONI, LPC/1302).

year.[225] Letters were usually written to inform other members of the Presbyterian gentry of the death that had occurred and to invite them to the funeral.[226] Scarves and other items were distributed to the mourners, and cloaks for the mourners and palls to drape over the corpse were hired, often from Belfast Presbyterian Church.[227]

VII. Religious life

The leading figures, or wealthiest members, among the gentry often employed a chaplain and the domestic chapel formed the focus for household worship. The Uptons are known to have had chaplains at Castle Upton during the seventeenth century and Patrick Peacock was the chaplain at Killyleagh Castle before the Revolution. The chaplains of the Uptons, and the Langfords at Summerhill, also acted as tutors to children within the household.[228] According to Rev. Joseph Boyse, Sir Arthur Langford was 'strict and constant in keeping up the exercise of family religion, and thought it not beneath his character to officiate himself, when ministers were not present'.[229] For lesser gentry figures, like James Trail, the responsibility of overseeing family worship devolved upon the head of the household. After he set up his own household Trail began observing evening prayers in his home at Killyleagh and later added morning prayers, along with the daily singing of a psalm and reading from the Bible.[230]

Certain members of the gentry are noted in the surviving source material as regularly attending worship and also the sacraments and ordinances of the Presbyterian church, as well as being diligent in their private devotions.[231] In 1726 Arthur Dobbs, a member of the established church, wrote in a letter to Michael Ward that he had written to his brother-in-law Edward Brice 'but being sacrament day as they call it he could not answer my letter'.[232] James Trail in his autobiography recorded the times he took communion and his serious preparation for it.[233] Some Presbyterians prepared for communion by making and renewing personal covenants. Such covenants, which were committed to paper, were not restricted

[225] Will of David Crawford, 1733 (PRONI, Gordon papers, D4204/B/2/1); will of William Conyngham of Springhill, 1721 (ibid., Lenox-Conyngham papers, D1449/1/33); Hamilton Maxwell to Agmondisham Vesey, 11 Nov. 1721 (ibid., Kirk papers, T2524/8); Agnew, *Belfast funeral register*, pp 24, 49. See above, p. 51, for more information on ministerial income.

[226] Autobiography of James Trail (PRONI, D1460/1, opening 28).

[227] Diary of Rev. John Kennedy, 15, 17–18 Nov. 1727, 16 & 19 Mar. 1727/8 (PHS, pp 135–6, 146); Agnew, *Belfast funeral register*.

[228] McCreery, *The Presbyterian ministers of Killileagh*, p. 101; Raymond Gillespie, *Devoted people: belief and religion in early modern Ireland* (Manchester, 1997), p. 12.

[229] Boyse, *A funeral sermon on the death of Sir Arth. Langford*, p. 23.

[230] Autobiography of James Trail (PRONI, D1460/1, openings 13–15).

[231] Cobham, *Preparation for death describ'd in a sermon occasion'd by the death of Anna-Helena Edmonstone*, pp 22–3; William Livingston, *The blessings of a long life well spent and happily concluded: a sermon preach'd at Temple-Patrick Feb. 20th. 1720/21 on the occasion of the death of Mrs. Dorothy Upton* (Belfast, 1721), pp 26–7; Craghead, *Funeral sermon on the death of Catherine, countess dowager of Granard*, pp 26–7.

[232] Arthur Dobbs to Michael Ward, 20 Feb. 1725/6 (PRONI, Ward papers, D2092/1/2/1, p. 85).

[233] Autobiography of James Trail (PRONI, D1460/1, openings 22, 25–6).

to the communion season, and were sometimes written and renewed at the start of each new year.[234] Alexander Cairnes, whom Swift described as 'a scrupulous puppy' and a 'shuffling scoundrel', made such a covenant in 1688, which begun, 'O most dreadful God, for the passion of thy son, I beseech thee, accept of thy poor prodigal son, prostrating himself at thy door. I have fallen from thee, by my own iniquity, and am by nature, a son of death, and a thousand-fold more the childe of hell by my wicked practices.'[235] Raymond Gillespie has written that 'The idea of providence, God at work in the world, was the fundamental building block of the religious response of the laity in early modern Ireland.'[236] Trail in his diary records the special providences that had secured himself and others known to him from a variety of disasters, including a providential rescue from a kitchen fire.[237] The reason Trail gave for writing his autobiography was 'to observe and record how I have or shall perform the duetys of piety and devotion ... I owe to God ... [and] also the various dispensations of Gods providence towards me, my family, friends, neighbours, or that are remarkable in his Church on Earth or in his government of the world'.[238]

Trail developed a number of friendships with the purpose of encouraging and motivating each other in their spiritual life. In 1716 his cousin Rev. Michael Bruce, the minister of Holywood, wrote to Trail, 'My wife and I long very much to see you and to have some of that profitable conversation wherewith I have been entertained by you which has made me in some measure experience the usefulness and necessity of that scripture precept that we should exhort one another daily least we be burdened through the devil fullness of sin',[239] and a number of similar letters were exchanged between the two with the purpose of encouraging and sustaining each other in their religious lives.[240] In addition, Trail used to converse 'freely together [with his cousin, Patrick Bruce, later minister of Drumbo, and Mr John Brown of Killyleagh] on religious subjects and communicate to each other the troubles and difficulties we had to strugle with in a religious course of life and to encourage and endeavour to support each other under them'. Trail added that he 'had much comfort in there [sic] conversation and often found our friendship of great use to me'.[241]

In the closing years of the seventeenth and the opening years of the eighteenth century religious societies flourished in England and were followed by the Societies for the Reformation of Manners, with which they had a close association. While the religious societies tended to focus on promoting virtue among their own members, the Societies for the Reformation of Manners sought to convict

---

[234] Ibid., openings 25, 31–32; diary of Rev. John Kennedy (PHS, p. 25); A. R. Holmes, *The shaping of Ulster Presbyterian belief and practice 1770–1840* (Oxford, 2006), pp 176–7.

[235] [Mitchelburne], *Ireland preserved*, pp 393–6; Jonathan Swift, *Journal to Stella*, ed. Harold Williams (2 vols, Oxford, 1948), i, 301, 310.

[236] Gillespie, *Devoted people*, p. 57.

[237] Autobiography of James Trail (PRONI, D1460/1).

[238] Ibid., opening 1.

[239] Michael Bruce to James Trail (NLI, Bruce papers, MS 20,867).

[240] Same to same, 27 Feb. 1716/17, 16 Sept. 1721 (PRONI, Bruce papers, T3041/1/A1–3).

[241] Autobiography of James Trail (PRONI, D1460/1, opening 18).

and punish evil-doers.[242] From the mid-1690s similar religious societies were also present in Dublin, and later at Drogheda, Kilkenny and Maynooth. Presbyterians and Anglicans were both involved in the Dublin religious societies, and a number of Presbyterian ministers preached sermons to them.[243] The societies may have had an impact on, or influenced, the formation of the Belfast Society in 1705, which provided an opportunity for ministers and lay members of the Presbyterian church to meet together for discussion and fellowship.[244] James Trail and his cousin, Patrick Bruce, were among those who attended the Belfast Society. Returning from a meeting of the Belfast Society in 1714 Bruce proposed to Trail:

> That we should join to gether in forming a society of private Christians in Killilagh to promote our knowledge in divine things in which we should use al Christian freedom with one another, soe as to repro[v]e what we observed crimanal in each others conduct, to encourage each other in the practise of religion and to comfort and support one another as there might be occasion.[245]

The society was duly formed at Killyleagh, with Trail, Patrick Bruce and John Brown (an excise officer), as its first members. They kept the day of the first meeting as a fast day and the meeting commenced with Bruce giving 'a short but substantial discourse, concerning the nature, usefulnes, and encouragements to begin such a society, from the word of God and the practise of Christians. He then sang a part of a Psalm sutable to the occasion and prayed for a blessing on our society.' They were soon joined by three elders from the Presbyterian church at Killyleagh and two other 'private Christians'.[246] Patrick Bruce's brother William, the Dublin bookseller, was also for a time a member of the Killyleagh Society.[247] After Patrick Bruce's call to be minister of Drumbo in 1717 the Society at Killyleagh lost much of its impetus but continued to exist, as Trail describes it, 'very droopingly'.[248]

---

[242] D. W. R. Bahlman, *The moral revolution of 1688* (New Haven, 1957); Brown, 'Irish Presbyterian theology', pp 290, 551; M. R. Hunt, *The middling sort: commerce, gender, and the family in England, 1680–1780* (London, 1996), pp 101–17; David Hayton, 'Moral reform and country politics in the late seventeenth-century House of Commons', *Past & Present*, no. 128 (1990), pp 51–57.

[243] Diary of Rev. John Cook, pp 9–10 (PHS); Boyse, *Works* (1728), i, 363–71; Nathaniel Weld, *A sermon before the Societies for the Reformation of Manners in Dublin, preached in New-Row, April 26th 1698* (Dublin, 1698); Thomas Emlyn, *A sermon preach'd before the Societies for Reformation of Manners in Dublin, October the 4th, 1698* (Dublin, 1698); Alexander Sinclare, *A sermon preach'd before the Societies for Reformation of Manners in Dublin, April the 11th, 1699* (Dublin, 1699); Francis Iredell, *A sermon preached before the Societies for the Reformation of Manners in Dublin, April 22 1701* (Dublin, 1701); T. C. Barnard, 'Reforming Irish manners: the religious societies in Dublin during the 1690's', *Historical Journal*, xxxv (1992), pp 805–38. A religious society for young men was formed at Cork Presbyterian meetinghouse in 1717: Cork (Princes Street) Presbyterian 'vestry' mins, Aug. 1717 (Cork City and County Archives, U87/1, p. 1).

[244] 'Circular letter of December 7 1720', *A narrative of the proceedings of the seven General Synods*, p. 20. See also appendix to Duchal's *Sermon on death of Abernethy*, pp 36–40.

[245] Autobiography of James Trail (PRONI, D1460/1, openings 22–3).

[246] Ibid., opening 23.

[247] Ibid., opening 41; Mary Pollard, *A dictionary of members of the Dublin book trade 1550–1800: based on the records of the Guild of St Luke the Evangelist, Dublin* (London, 2000), pp 60–1.

[248] Autobiography of James Trail (PRONI, D1460/1, opening 24).

Presbyterian gentry were generous benefactors to their church in life and death. Charity was seen as both a religious and a social duty and many members of the Presbyterian gentry left money to the poor of their local parishes, usually not exceeding £10,[249] though some were substantially more generous.[250] Others left bequests of money or mourning rings to their ministers or contributed towards the purchase of church plate.[251] John Shaw of Ballyganaway, in Donaghadee, County Down, bequeathed £100 to the poor of the Presbyterian congregation of Carnmoney, where his friend Andrew Crawford was minister. Shaw also left a small legacy for Crawford's son, who later became minister at Crumlin, and another £100 for keeping the roof of the church at Carnmoney in repair. Before his death Shaw presented Carnmoney congregation with a set of six silver communion cups, on which were engraved the Shaw arms and motto.[252] Such gifts were another form of gentry display and the engraving of armorials kept the locally powerful in the remembrance of those who handled the church plate. Edward Brice similarly gave a set of six silver communion cups, with a Dublin hallmark of 1680, to the congregation of Ballycarry, where his grandfather had been the first minister, and the silver baptismal bowl at Ballycarry bears the Edmonstone coat of arms, and the inscription, 'The gift of Archibald Edmonstone.'[253]

Arthur Maxwell, an elder in Drumbo Presbyterian Church, was a particularly generous benefactor to the Presbyterian church throughout Ireland. He left £1,300 to a number of trustees, the interest of which was to be applied to aid newly-formed Presbyterian congregations in Ulster in the support of their ministers, with any surplus to assist in educating poor students for the Presbyterian ministry.[254] In the will Maxwell referred to Rev. James Kirkpatrick, Rev. James Cobham and Rev. Michael Bruce as 'friends', and he left £7 to his own minister, Rev. Patrick Bruce, and £5 each to Rev. John Malcolm, Rev. Andrew Crawford, Rev. James Cobham and Rev. James Stewart. In addition, he left instruction that a mourning ring to the value of 20s be given to seven Presbyterian ministers, as well as Rev. Patrick Bruce's wife. Patrick Bruce himself also received £3 per year as stipend for Maxwell's two seats in Drumbo meetinghouse, 'so long as he preaches to that congregation'.

---

[249] Abstract will of David Kennedy, 1692 (PRONI, Stewart papers, D1759/3/A/1, p. 7); will of John Blackwood, 1698 (NLI, D. 19,724); Ballycarry sess. mins, 13 Apr., 8 May & 10 June 1712 (PRONI, CR3/31/1); will of Henry Dalway, 1720 (ibid., Castle Stewart papers, D1618/8/14); will of Arthur Graham, 1732 (ibid., Bryson collection, D4006/3); will of Ann Conyngham, 1744 (ibid., Lenox-Conyngham papers, D1449/1/59A).

[250] Will of William Cairnes, 1707 (NLI, Prerogative will book, 1706–8, MFGS 41/2, f. 117); will of Arthur Maxwell, 1720 (PRONI, D1769/60/2/3); will of Hugh Henry, 1743 (PRONI, LPC/1302); Porter, 'Congregational memoirs – Ballycarry', Christian Unitarian, ii (1864), p. 194.

[251] Will of Henry Dalway, 1720 (PRONI, Castle Stewart papers, D1618/8/14); will of Arthur Graham, 1732 (ibid., Bryson collection, D4006/3); Porter, 'Congregational Memoirs – Ballycarry', pp 160–1.

[252] Memorandum about a legacy from Mr [John] Shaw for money to be distributed to the poor of Carnmoney, 27 Apr. 1716 (PRONI, Carnmoney Presbyterian Church poor list, 1716–84, MIC1P/37/6/4); R. H. Bonar, Nigh on three and a half centuries: a history of Carnmoney Presbyterian Church (Carnmoney, 2004), pp 27, 302–3.

[253] Porter, 'Congregational memoirs – Ballycarry', pp 194, 226–7; Bailie, Hist. of congns, p. 57.

[254] RGSU, i, 106, 141, 190, 218, 247, 449, 483; will of Arthur Maxwell, 1720 (PRONI, D1769/60/2/3); Reid, Hist. of PCI, iii, 40.

A bequest of £24 was left to the poor of Drumbo and £6 to the poor of Dunmurry, Maxwell adding that,

> Whereas I have before left twenty four pounds sterling to the poor of the congregation of Drumbo and six pounds to the poor of the congregation of Dunmurry my meaning is to the poor of the Presbyterian congregation of Drumboe and to the poor of the Presbyterian congregation of Dunmurry and not otherwise.[255]

In 1706 the Synod of Ulster established a missionary fund to support new congregations in the south and west of Ireland. The 22 gentlemen nominated in the several presbyteries to solicit subscriptions and collect money for the fund, with a few exceptions who were wealthy merchants, reads like a 'Who's Who' of the Presbyterian gentry of Ulster.[256] Four years later, in 1710, the southern ministers founded another fund to support southern congregations, which is usually referred to as the 'General Fund'. Among the original contributors and trustees were Sir Arthur Langford, who gave £500, and Hugh Henry who contributed £100. Sir Arthur Langford left a further legacy of £3,000 to the General Fund, besides £1,500 for the use of the ministers of Wood Street Presbyterian Church, Dublin, and their successors, and his sister Susannah Langford, who died in 1726, bequeathed £700 to the General Fund.[257]

The Presbyterian gentry were also instrumental in granting leases to Presbyterian churches and were generous to the church's building projects, especially the establishment of new congregations.[258] The leases were often granted at a peppercorn rent, if demanded, as the lease for the new meetinghouse at Templepatrick was granted, for instance, in 1693 by Arthur and Clotworthy Upton, and Captain William Shaw of Bush gave the land and a lease for the congregation of Larne and Kilwaughter in 1699.[259] After a dispute between the Church of Ireland rector and the Presbyterians at Cookstown in 1701 Mrs Margaret Stewart, eldest daughter of

---

[255] Will of Arthur Maxwell, 1720 (PRONI, D1769/60/2/3).

[256] *RGSU*, i, 115.

[257] William Frazer, 'A history of the General (Presbyterian) Fund for the south and west of Ireland. Instituted in 1710. Restored to its original uses in 1852' (typescript in PHS, dated Nov. 1862), pp 2–4; Irwin, *History of Presbyterianism in Dublin & the south*, pp 33–5, 316–17; Reid, *Hist. of PCI*, iii, 62–3; will of Sir Arthur Langford, 1715 (PRONI, T168/1); *DIB* (Langford, Sir Arthur); will of Susannah Langford, 8 Nov. 1726 (National Archives, Kew, London, Prerogative Court of Canterbury will registers, PROB 11/612).

[258] [Alexander Gordon], 'Rademon congregation: historical sketch', *The Disciple*, iii (1883), pp 137–8; Edward Synge to Bp Anthony Dopping, 14 May, 5 Aug. 1683, with draft letter of Dopping to Mr Tate, 12 July 1683 (Armagh Public Lib., Dopping papers, P001498149, i, nos 35–6); Swift to Sir Arthur Langford, 30 Oct. 1714 (Jonathan Swift, *The correspondence of Jonathan Swift, D.D.*, ed. David Woolley (4 vols, 1999–2007), ii, 92–3); will of Sir Arthur Langford, 1715 (PRONI, T168/1); James Gourley (comp.), MS History of Killinchy Presbyterian Church, (1874), p. 72 (ibid., CR3/5/1); H. A. Boyd, 'The parish of Finvoy: Diocese of Connor: beside the shining Bann', *Ballymena Observer*, 12 Oct. & 2 Nov. 1945; John Donaldson, *The barony of Upper Fews in the county of Armagh* (1838; repr. Crossmaglen, 1993), pp 11–12; L. T. Brown, 'The Presbyterians of Cavan and Monaghan: an immigrant community in south Ulster over three centuries' (Ph.D. thesis, QUB, 1986), pp 86–9; Aston Robinson, 'Glennan' in MS History of the congregations of the Presbyterian Church in Ireland (QUB, Allen collection, MS 23 (Box 1)).

[259] Lease of the new meetinghouse of Templepatrick, 5 Feb. 1693 (PRONI, CR4/12/C/1); 'A chapter in early congregational history', *Report of Presbyterian Historical Society* (1910), p. 7.

John Shaw of Ballygally and wife of William Stewart of Killymoon, County Tyrone, possibly at her own expense, provided a site for a new Presbyterian meetinghouse to be built on the Killymoon estate.[260]

Another way in which the gentry helped to promote the Presbyterian cause in this period was by their patronage of Presbyterian education. The Hamiltons and Stevensons of Killyleagh gave their encouragement to the philosophical academy that was run at Killyleagh by Rev. James McAlpin, who later married into the Hamilton family. In a formal agreement drawn up in 1697 the Hamiltons and Captain Hans Stevenson, as a result of their 'good liking for learning', agreed to provide McAlpin with a dwelling house free of charge, along with grazing for a cow, a meadow for hay, and 200 loads of turf per year for firing for McAlpin and his family. The Killyleagh Academy continued in existence until 1714 when McAlpin resumed the clerical office.[261] William Cairnes of Monaghan and Dublin, in his will of 1707, left £24 *per annum* for the establishment and annual support of a 'mathematicall school intended to be erected and settled at Monaghan'.[262]

Some of the gentry were elected as members of the kirk session in the church that they attended. James Trail was an elder at Killyleagh and later at Ballynahinch,[263] John Blackwood at Bangor,[264] Arthur Maxwell at Drumbo,[265] and Clotworthy Upton at Templepatrick.[266] Captain John Henderson was also an elder,[267] and in the Presbytery of Antrim there were Patrick Agnew,[268] Henry McCulloch,[269] John Shaw[270] and Captain William Shaw of Bush.[271] In the surviving church records representatives from at least 32 Presbyterian gentry families appear either as elders or commissioners for their congregation, though interestingly they were more often commissioners than ruling elders.[272] Gentry presence at the church courts

---

[260] McKee, *Aspects of Presbyterianism in Cookstown*, pp 5–6.

[261] Lowry, *Hamilton manuscripts*, pp 151–2; Stewart, 'Abating bigotry', p. 5.

[262] Will of William Cairnes, 1707 (NAI, Prerogative will book, 1706–8, MFGS 41/2, f. 117).

[263] Autobiography of James Trail (PRONI, D1460/1, opening 25); *RGSU*, i, 412, 451, 482; ii, 2, 34, 77.

[264] Down Pby mins (PHS, pp 31, 115, 145, 150, 232, 255, 332, 365). His son, Robert Blackwood, was a commissioner from Bangor to the General Synod in 1730: *RGSU*, ii, 152.

[265] *RGSU*, i, 106, 141, 190, 218, 247, 449, 483.

[266] Templepatrick sess. mins (PRONI, CR4/12/B/1, pp 250, 254, 278, 280, 284, 291, 292, 295, 302–3); *RGSU*, i, 218, 248, 289, 385, 449, 482, 513; ibid., ii, 1, 27, 42; Antrim Pby mins, 1697–1713 (PHS, pp 513, 534, 551).

[267] *RGSU*, ii, 2, 23, 41, 67, 101, 113, 122, 127, 139, 148, 159; Sub-synod of Derry mins (PHS, pp 205, 242, 253, 266, 279, 287, 295, 333).

[268] *RGSU*, ii, 1; Larne & Kilwaughter sess. mins (PRONI, MIC1B/6A/1B, pp 136, 144).

[269] Antrim Pby mins, 1697–1713 (PHS, p. 396).

[270] *RGSU*, i, 449, 513; ii, 22, 42, 53–4, 62, 64.

[271] Ibid., i, 141, 346, 413; Antrim Pby mins, 1697–1713 (PHS, pp 343, 378, 393, 524, 534).

[272] *RGSU*, i–ii; Antrim 'Meeting' mins, 1671–91 (PRONI, Stewart papers, D1759/1/A/2); Antrim Pby mins, 1697–1713 (PHS); Strabane Pby mins, 1717–40 (UTC); Killyleagh Pby mins (PRONI, Stewart papers, D1759/1/D/10). The 32 families represented were Adair of Ballymena, Agnew of Kilwaughter, Blackwood of Ballyleidy, Boyd of Glastry and Downpatrick, Cairnes of Co. Tyrone, Conyngham of Springhill, Crawford of Belfast and Florida Manor, Dalway of Bellahill, Dobbin of Duneane and Moneyglass, Donaldson of Glenarm, Edmonstone of Redhall, Fairies (or Ferrys) of Co. Monaghan, Hamilton of Dunnamanagh, Hamilton of Killyleagh, Henderson of Strabane and Donoughmore, Hunter of Co. Down, Jackson of Co. Antrim, Johnston of Knappagh, Johnston

declined after 1720 as the number of gentry families itself declined, but there were still gentry participants even after that date. At the General Synod Patrick Agnew, an occasional conformer, appeared in 1721, John Blackwood in 1731 and 1748, Captain John Henderson in 1731, Henry McCulloch in 1732, 1733 and 1737, James Trail in 1721, and Clotworthy Upton in 1721, 1722 and 1723; Thomas Boyd of Glastry appeared at Killyleagh Presbytery in 1725 and his son, David, appeared there in 1727.[273] Choosing to send gentry figures to the higher courts was probably not just out of deference but also because of pragmatism, as such men would have been likely to carry more weight and been better at articulating the interests and concerns of their congregations. Gentry were often part of the commissions sent to presbytery and synod, for instance, when it was necessary to supplicate for supplies during a vacancy, or when issues of finance and stipend were concerned.

The presbytery itself often appealed to Presbyterian landlords when tenants were deficient in keeping their pledges towards ministerial stipend, hoping that the landlord would assist in the recovery of the deficiencies.[274] Presbyterian landlords, such as the Agnews of Kilwaughter, Blairs of Blairmount, Shaws of Ballygally and others, bound their tenants in their leases to pay a portion of their rent 'in the shape, and under the name, of stipend to the Protestant dissenting minister of the parish'.[275] Even in cases where the landlord was not an elder he could be asked to be present at session meetings to give advice with regard to difficult cases. In 1723 the presence of Colonel Edmonstone and Robert Dalway was requested by the session of Ballycarry when the case of Jane Colvil, who had died suddenly, was being discussed. There was a rumour circulating that the alleged father by whom she had previously had a child had given her a powder which had caused not only her miscarriage but her death as well. After witnesses had been heard the two landlords and the session concluded that the matter was one for the civil courts and once it had been dealt with there then the scandal part could be considered by the session.[276]

In 1694 a Letterkenny man accused his minister of causing 'some of meaner cappacity in the world to give publick satticefaction, while others of greater substance he took pryvate satticefaction of' and nine years later another Donegal man declared 'no justice has been done me but injustice because I am a poor man'.[277]

of Co. Monaghan, Kennedy of Cultra, Kyle of Ballybeen, McCulloch of Co. Antrim, Maxwell of Drumbeg, Maxwell of Rhubane, Perry of Co. Tyrone, Potter of Killinchy, Shaw of Ballygally, Shaw of Bush, Stevenson of Killyleagh, Trail of Killyleagh, Upton of Castle Upton, and Waddall of Co. Monaghan.

273 RGSU, ii, 1–2, 22, 34, 42, 159, 164, 176, 183, 229, 335; Killyleagh Pby mins (PRONI, Stewart papers, D1759/1/D/10, pp 1, 32a).

274 Antrim 'Meeting' mins (UTC, pp 261, 264, 277–8, 293); Gordon, 'Congregational memoirs – Templepatrick', Disciple, ii, 10; Antrim Pby mins, 1697–1713 (PHS, pp 82, 88, 136, 506–7); Ballycarry sess. mins, 30 Oct. 1718 (PRONI, CR3/31/1); RGSU, i, 528; D. H. Akenson, God's peoples: covenant and land in South Africa, Israel, and Ulster (Ithaca, 1992), p. 127.

275 Porter, 'Congregational memoirs: Cairncastle', p. 264; idem, Congregational memoirs of the Old Presbyterian Congregation of Larne & Kilwaughter, p. 50.

276 Ballycarry sess. mins, 30 Jan. 1723 (PRONI, CR3/31/1).

277 Laggan Pby mins, 1690–1700 (PHS, pp 55–6); Patrick Griffin, 'Defining the limits of Britishness: The "new" British history and the meaning of the Revolution Settlement in Ireland for Ulster's Presbyterians', Journal of British Studies, xxxix (2000), p. 280.

While in the majority of cases we have no reason to suspect that social status influenced the execution of church discipline, one noteworthy exception is preserved in the session minutes of Templepatrick. Clotworthy Upton was M.P. for County Antrim from 1703 to 1725, and was described by Bishop John Evans of Meath as 'the chief lay dissenter in Ireland'.[278] When Margaret Fisher had an illegitimate child to Clotworthy's brother, Thomas, the session of Templepatrick was unsure how to proceed and consulted Clotworthy, who advised them that she should be publicly disciplined as normal but that 'she be not interrogat to whom she brought forth her child'. The session complied.[279]

* * * * * * *

The number of Presbyterian gentry families in Ulster was never large – probably never above 80 at any time during the period, and they were always dwarfed by the much larger number of Anglicans. Most were descended from immigrants who had arrived in Ulster from Scotland, particularly south-west Scotland, in the early decades of the seventeenth century. Within Ulster their geographical spread was uneven with Counties Antrim and Down, on the east of the province, having the largest settlement, although there was also a significant number in County Tyrone. Most of the gentry took their religious life and practice seriously, and were often important as benefactors to the Presbyterian church, granting land and leases for church buildings, and in some cases encouraging Presbyterian education. Although the number of gentry families declined during the period, conformity was not immediate on the passing of the sacramental test clause in 1704, and the drift to conformity was a slow process. Even then outward conformity might not mean the severance of all ties with Dissent.

---

[278] Bp Evans quoted in *ODNB* (Upton, Clotworthy).
[279] Templepatrick sess. mins (PRONI, CR4/12/B/1, pp 232, 258).

3

Merchants and Commerce

The aim of this chapter is to depict the Presbyterian urban elite of late seventeenth- and early eighteenth-century Ulster. When Presbyterian gentry families conformed to the Church of Ireland, merchants (along with professional men) were the obvious candidates to fill the vacuum in social leadership. Toby Barnard has suggested that there was not always a clear distinction between the landed elite and those operating at the higher levels of trade in Ireland.[1] I will therefore consider the connexions between the merchants and the gentry and the distinctions and similarities between the two groups. Merchants, at least until the enactment of the sacramental test in 1704, were eligible and active in municipal and local government and it will be necessary to consider the issue of conformity and whether they conformed to the established church in order to fulfil civic ambitions. As with the gentry in England, the historiography is more extensive for English merchants than their Irish counterparts, though some important work has been completed. In addition to Barnard's work, David Dickson has written about trade and merchants in Cork and Munster, and Patrick Fagan about Catholic merchants in Dublin.[2] With regard to Ulster, Belfast merchants (the best referenced in the sources)[3] have been the subject of intense research by Jean Agnew, and William Roulston has given some insight into the lives of merchants based in Strabane during the late seventeenth century.[4] In contrast, very little has been written about merchants in other Ulster towns and so I will include Presbyterians from Coleraine, Derry, Dromore and Newry, at least so far as the surviving source material will allow. The merchants' careers and working lives, in terms of entry, trading methods and business contacts, income and status in the community, the part religion played in their lives and the role they themselves played in the government of the Presbyterian church will all be explored.

During this period 'merchant' was a term that was used to describe both small-scale retailers and those engaged in international trade. A total of 255 of the individuals in the Belfast freemen's roll of 1636 to 1682 were classed as 'merchants'

---

1   Toby Barnard, 'What became of Waring: the making of an Ulster squire' in idem, *Irish Protestant ascents and descents, 1641–1779* (Dublin, 2002), pp 235–65.
2   Barnard, *New anatomy*, pp 256–63; David Dickson, *Old world colony: Cork and south Munster 1630–1830* (Cork, 2005), pp 113–69; Patrick Fagan, *Catholics in a Protestant country: trades and professions in eighteenth-century Dublin* (Dublin, 1998), pp 159–73.
3   Out-letter book of 'Black' George Macartney, 1679–81 (PRONI, MIC19/2); out-letter book of Isaac Macartney, 1704–6 (PRONI, Lenox-Conyngham papers, D501/1); out-letter book of David Butle, 1696–1703 (ibid., D1449/13/1). 'Black' George Macartney was originally a member of the Church of Ireland, but became a Presbyterian a few years before his death: [Kirkpatrick], *Presby. loyalty*, p. 436.
4   Agnew, *Merchant families*; W. J. Roulston, *Restoration Strabane, 1660–1714: economy and society in provincial Ireland* (Dublin, 2007), pp 38, 40–6.

and 72 of the deaths listed in the funeral register of the Belfast Presbyterian congregation between 1712 and 1736 are also so described.[5] The majority of these individuals, however, were shopkeepers, who serviced the needs of their town and its immediate vicinity. The merchants to be considered in this chapter are the leading figures operating at the time who were involved in trade outside the province of Ulster and, in particular, trade overseas. Agnew has estimated that at no time in the seventeenth century were there more than 50 Belfast merchants engaged in overseas trade,[6] and this number is unlikely to have been exceeded in any of the other Ulster towns, including Derry.

I. Origins, setting up in trade and the importance of connexions

Most of the Presbyterian merchant families in Ulster had settled there during the course of the seventeenth century. As with the Presbyterian ministers and gentry, the merchant families came predominately from Scotland, particularly south-west Scotland. Among the mercantile families that entered Belfast during the 1630s were the Clugstons (from Wigtown) and the Doakes (who probably originated in Ayr), along with the Lockharts.[7] They were joined in the 1650s and 1660s by the Andersons from Glasgow, the Biggers, who probably came from Irvine, the Eccles from Ayrshire and the Smith family.[8] The Lenoxes of Derry and Belfast, the Haltridges of Dromore and Newry, and the Galts of Coleraine were also of Scottish origin.[9] Some of the later immigrants were from a more dispersed Scottish origin: for instance, the Pottingers, who were active in trade at Belfast from the 1660s, came from Orkney.[10]

Merchants began their careers as apprentices to existing merchants from whom they learnt their trade. They normally became apprentices in their early teens, probably after being educated in a Presbyterian congregational school or one of the other educational establishments then in existence. Alexander Stewart, who was born at Ballylawn, near Moville in County Donegal, served his apprenticeship in the office of the Belfast merchant Isaac Macartney, after having studied previously at the Free School in Derry.[11] The concern of merchants for the education of their children is sometimes referred to in their wills. John Galt, a Presbyterian merchant in Coleraine, left instruction that his children were to be 'handsomely educated and maintained' until the girls were 18 and the boys 21.[12] Apprentices lived in the home

---

[5] Young, Belfast town book, pp 246–86; Benn, Belfast, p. 585.
[6] Agnew, Merchant families, p. xvii.
[7] Ibid., pp 10–11, 218, 221.
[8] Ibid., pp 10–11, 209–10, 223, 245; Raymond Gillespie and S. A. Royle (eds), Belfast: part I, to 1840: Irish historic towns atlas (Dublin, 2003), p. 2.
[9] Agnew, Merchant families, pp 231, 253, 255.
[10] Ibid., pp 11, 241.
[11] Indenture of apprenticeship between Daniel Mussenden and Robert Rainey, 1738 (PRONI, Mussenden papers, D354/400B); [Thomas Witherow], 'The Londonderry family', Irish Presbyterian, new ser., xi, no. 2 (Feb. 1905), p. 29.
[12] Will of John Galt, 1715 (PRONI, Maxwell Given papers, D2096/1/15D).

Figure 7   Portrait of Alexander Stewart (1700–81) of Belfast (and later Mount
Stewart, near Newtownards, Co. Down). He was an elder in First Belfast
Presbyterian Church and father of Robert, first Marquess of Londonderry.
Alexander is wearing a red coat and a cravat over a gold-embroidered jacket.

of their masters, whom they served, usually for a term of seven years. The father of
the young apprentice paid a sum, called a premium, to the master in return for the
training, experience, bed and board to be given to his son. The size of the premium
depended on the standing and experience of the master, as well as the social standing
and background of the apprentice. Some leading merchants, such as Hugh Eccles
or 'Black' George Macartney, both of Belfast, could obtain premiums of at least

£200.[13] Arthur Upton of Castle Upton, County Antrim, a leading figure among the Presbyterian gentry, spent £100 'breeding' his seventh, but fourth surviving, son Hercules to 'the calling of a merchant' and left him a further £400 as capital to purchase stock or land. Although Hercules eventually joined the army instead, this nevertheless shows the possible size of a premium at this time.[14] It also illustrates that merchants could be recruited from the younger sons of gentry families, which was common in the late seventeenth and early eighteenth centuries.[15]

After completing his apprenticeship the young merchant was able to become a freeman if he resided in a corporate town.[16] Some spent a number of years working with their master after they had completed their apprenticeship, in order to earn sufficient capital to set up independently or in partnership with one or two others. Capital was usually obtained from family members or at marriage through the dowry brought by the merchant's wife. Intermarriage between mercantile families was common, and the connexions brought by such marriages were often useful in furthering a merchant's career. As was the case elsewhere, friends and relatives were important, acting as partners in cargoes or ships, providing apprenticeships for sons, marriage partners, and ultimately acting as executors or overseers after death.[17] John Galt of Coleraine, in his will, named six executors, including his sons-in-law Alderman James Lenox of Derry and John Rainey of Belfast, along with John Thompson, a merchant in Coleraine, and Patrick Smith of Belfast. Among the six overseers named were another son-in-law, John Chalmers of Belfast, and John Paterson, a merchant in Coleraine.[18]

Many of the merchants in particular towns were related to one or more of the other merchants operating in the same location. Agnew, in her study of 32 of the families operating in Belfast, was only able to find four unrelated to the others by blood or marriage. Merchants tended to marry those of their own social class and often those of the same religious denomination.[19] As a result of the limited number of eligible partners in their home towns many looked to neighbouring towns for marriage partners. This had been occurring throughout the seventeenth century and by the early eighteenth century there was a complicated network of close-knit interconnexions between many of the merchants that operated throughout Ulster.

Increasingly by the early eighteenth century merchants had relatives who had settled outside Ulster, not only in Ireland but also in Britain, in Europe, or elsewhere.[20] The sons of the Belfast merchant John Black included Charles of Cadiz and London, Robert, who was consul at Cadiz, and John who settled at

---

[13] Agnew, *Merchant families*, p. 41.

[14] Will of Arthur Upton, 1706 (NAI, Prerogative will book, 1706–8, MFGS 41/2, f. 28); W. H. Upton, *Upton family records: being genealogical collections for an Upton family history* (London, 1893), pp 110–11.

[15] Agnew, *Merchant families*, pp 41, 51–2, 55.

[16] Derry corp. mins (PRONI, LA/79/2/AA/2, pp 51, 66).

[17] M. R. Hunt, *The middling sort: commerce, gender, and the family in England, 1680–1780* (London, 1996), pp 22–3; Agnew, *Merchant families*, pp 27–35.

[18] Will of John Galt, 1715 (PRONI, D2096/1/15D).

[19] Agnew, *Merchant families*, p. 29; Roulston, *Restoration Strabane*, p. 43.

[20] Agnew, *Merchant families*, pp 185–6, 188–9, 231–2.

Figure 8   Portrait of James Lenox (1652–1723), merchant, shipowner, alderman and M.P. of Derry City, painted c.1700. He is wearing a red robe and white stock, and has a long, curled, brown wig.

Bordeaux in 1699.[21] Robert Cowan, son of the Derry merchant and alderman John Cowan, entered the service of the East India Company before 1720 and was governor of Bombay from 1729 to 1734.[22] William Moore, a Belfast merchant and shipowner, was probably related to Robert and William Moore of Barbados, with whom the Belfast merchants David Butle and Isaac Macartney both corresponded.[23] Robert Lenox started his career as a merchant in Derry but after the Williamite

21 John Black to Lord Lamont, 19 Aug. 1723 (PRONI, Black papers, D4457/28); Black family tree (ibid., D4457/363).
22 [Witherow], 'Londonderry family', p. 29; papers of Sir Robert Cowan, 1704–35 (PRONI, Londonderry papers, D654/B/1).
23 David Butle to William Moore, 10 Jan. 1697/8 (PRONI, D1449/13/1, p. 53); Isaac Macartney

War moved to Belfast. His brother James remained in Derry. Robert Lenox married, as his second wife, Ann Conyngham (Cunningham), a sister of the Liverpool merchant, John Cunningham. The marriages of James Lenox's daughters, Sarah and Mary, extended the family's English connexions, as Sarah married a Mr Pope, merchant of Bristol, and Mary married her cousin, James Hillhouse of Bristol. These family links proved useful to the trading activities of the merchants who remained in Ulster, with John Cunningham and James Hillhouse both acting as factors for a number of Belfast merchant families in the early eighteenth century.[24]

II. Trading activities

The Ulster Presbyterian merchants, like their counterparts from the established church, did not specialise in the trading of any particular commodity and engaged in trade with a number of different locations. As a result of the agricultural nature of the Irish economy Ulster merchants were primarily involved in the provisions trade. Belfast was the most important of the Ulster ports in terms of the volume of its trade. It was the fourth port in Ireland, after Dublin, Cork and Waterford, and by 1715 had overtaken the latter.[25] The second port in Ulster was Derry, but in the 1680s its exports were only a quarter of those of Belfast.[26] In 1683 the Belfast merchants exported 33,880 cwt. of butter, 12,445 hides, 7,017 barrels of corn and 4,610 barrels of beef to a variety of locations in England, Scotland, the American colonies, France and Flanders, Holland, Spain and the Mediterranean, and the Baltic region.[27] William Sacheverell, when visiting Belfast in 1688, noted 'the quantity of butter and beef which it sends into foreign parts, are [sic] almost incredible: I have seen the barrels pil'd up in the very streets'.[28] Belfast merchants obtained these commodities from their rural hinterland, with agents in some of the smaller local towns, such as Lisburn, and in the 1720s Alexander Stewart of Belfast regularly obtained butter from Daniel Nevin 'of this town butter-buyer'.[29] At certain

to William Moore, 18 Jan. 1704/5 (ibid., D501/1, p. 43). William Moore of Barbados was also the brother-in-law of the Belfast merchant James Arbuckle, as the latter letter shows.

[24] 'Articles of marriage between James Hilhouse and Mary Lenox', 24 May 1718 (PRONI, Lenox-Conyngham papers, T3161/1/9); David Butle letter book (ibid., D1449/13/1); Isaac Macartney letter book (ibid., D501/1); Agnew, *Merchant families*, pp 231–2.

[25] Benn, *Belfast*, p. 327; Richard Dobbs, *An essay on the trade and improvement of Ireland* (Dublin, 1729), pp 15–16; George Story, *A true and impartial history of the most material occurrences in the kingdom of Ireland during the two last years* (2nd ed., London, 1693), p. 38.

[26] Raymond Gillespie (ed.), *Settlement and survival on an Ulster estate: the Brownlow leasebook 1667–1711*, p. xxv.

[27] Benn, *Belfast*, pp 317–18.

[28] William Sacheverell, *An account of the Isle of Man, its inhabitants, language, soil, remarkable curiosities, the succession of its kings and bishops, down to the present time* (London, 1702), p. 125.

[29] Isaac Macartney to Nathaniel Hornby, 1 Nov. 1704 (PRONI, D501/1, p. 5); same to Thomas Thompson, 30 June 1705 (ibid., pp 131–2); same to John Knox, 13 Nov. 1705 (ibid., p. 226); *CSPD, 1679–80*, pp 282–3, 298, 396; W. H. Crawford, 'Economy and society in eighteenth century Ulster' (Ph.D. thesis, QUB, 1982), p. 107; Raymond Gillespie, 'Small towns in early modern Ireland' in Peter Clark (ed.), *Small towns in early modern Europe* (Cambridge, 1995), p. 164; expense ledgers of Alexander Stewart, 1725–32 (PRONI, Londonderry papers, D654/B/2/156–7).

times the demand for provisions exceeded the supply available locally and in 1679 'Black' George Macartney obtained beef, butter and hides from Ballyshannon, in County Donegal, and butter from Derry.[30] These were brought by coastal shipping as it was cheaper and easier to transport large quantities of goods by water than by land.

In the early 1680s France provided the most important market for beef and butter exports, followed by Spain.[31] Although provisions were still exported to France in the early eighteenth century (often via Scotland),[32] the amount involved had declined as a result of the high tariffs that the French government placed on imports of beef towards the end of the 1680s.[33] Spain, however, remained an important customer for butter and there was competition among the Belfast merchants to be the first to arrive there with it each summer.[34] As a result of the closeness of Ulster and Scotland there was trade between the two countries, but the volume was not as large as might be supposed. This was because merchants in the two countries tended to export the same products and were therefore in competition for similar markets.[35] An exception to this was the import of coal into Ulster, often from Glasgow, though coal was also obtained from England, principally from Whitehaven.[36] Large quantities of grain were also traded across the North Channel during times of scarcity. Grain was exported from Ulster to Scotland during the late 1690s, when there was famine in Scotland, and in 1729 Scottish grain was imported into Derry and the north-west region during a time of scarcity in Ulster.[37]

Grain was also exported from Ulster to the American colonies and the West Indies, and in Europe the most important market for corn was Scandinavia, from which tar and deals were imported.[38] Ulster is often thought to have been denuded

---

[30] 'Black' George Macartney to John Delap, 2 Aug., 16, 24 & 30 Sept. 1679 (PRONI, MIC19/2, pp 70–1, 101–2, 104–5, 112); same to Edmund Harrison, 2 Aug. 1679 (ibid., pp 71–2); same to Sir Joshua Allen, 13 & 16 Aug. 1679 (ibid., pp 78–80).

[31] Agnew, Merchant families, p. 109; Raymond Gillespie, Early Belfast: the origins and growth of an Ulster town to 1750 (Belfast, 2007), p. 115.

[32] Isaac Macartney to Daniel Hays, 30 Oct. 1704 (PRONI, D501/1, p. 4); same to William Sloane, 11 Nov. 1704 (ibid., pp 9–10); same to Alexander Carstaires, 27 Nov. 1704 (ibid., p. 19).

[33] L. M. Cullen, Anglo-Irish trade 1660–1800 (Manchester, 1968), pp 18–19.

[34] 'Black' George Macartney to Francis de Muhar, 24 May 1679 (PRONI, MIC19/2, pp 47–8); Agnew, Merchant families, p. 109.

[35] The best studies of trade between Scotland and Ireland are T. C. Smout, Scottish trade on the eve of Union 1660-1707 (Edinburgh, 1963) and L. E. Cochran, Scottish trade with Ireland in the eighteenth century (Edinburgh, 1985).

[36] Port Glasgow customs book: exports, 1680–81 (NAS, E72/19/2), 1681–82 (ibid., E72/19/6), 1690 (ibid., E72/19/19); Isaac Macartney to Robert Stewart, 24 June 1706 (PRONI, D501/1, pp 328–9); Cochran, Scottish trade with Ireland, pp 24–38; J. V. Beckett, Coal and tobacco: the Lowthers and the economic development of West Cumberland, 1660–1760 (Cambridge, 1981), pp 6–7, 39–41, 46, 62, 97–9. Over half of the ships entering Belfast in the mid-1680s were carrying coal: Belfast customs register, 1682–87 (PRONI, HAR/1/G/1/13/1).

[37] [Charles Smith & Walter Harris], The antient and present state of the county of Down (Dublin, 1744), p. 65; Cochran, Scottish trade with Ireland, pp 99, 101, 103; Crawford, 'Economy & society', p. 26; David Butle to John Graham, 14 Sept. 1696 (PRONI, D1449/13/1, p. 41); Londonderry corp. mins (PRONI, LA/79/2/AA/4, p. 163).

[38] 'Black' George Macartney to John Delap, 2 & 5 June 1680 (PRONI, MIC19/2, pp 205, 209); Isaac Macartney to John Innis, 16 Nov. 1704 (PRONI, D501/1, pp 12–13); same to Edward

of trees by the early eighteenth century, with acts passed by the Irish parliament to encourage planting.[39] In 1704 Isaac Macartney informed William Sloane that timber was 'very scarce in Ireland'. Isaac Macartney, however, exported 12,000 staves to Bristol in 1705 and asked his correspondent there, William Galbraith, if he could sell a further 100,000 staves the following year. It is likely that Macartney had contracted to take the timber of a landed gentleman who was trying to liquidate some of his assets in order to clear off his debts.[40] Coleraine was an important port for the export of timber from the early seventeenth century through to 1710, or even 1720, with the Presbyterian merchant Robert Thompson being involved. The timber was cut in the woods around the north-west shore of Lough Neagh and floated down the River Bann to Coleraine where Thompson stored it in his wood yard until it was exported, often to Scotland, or sold to supply the north Antrim fisheries.[41]

The Coleraine merchants were involved in the trade of fish.[42] The Bann fisheries were let to a number of Presbyterian merchants and gentlemen in the late seventeenth and early eighteenth century. Lord Massereene became the tenant in 1683 for seven years. The Massereene papers, however, suggest that the fisheries were unprofitable. From 1700 to 1707 James Lenox of Derry leased the fisheries at £1,400 *per annum* and built a new fish house at Cranagh. The fisheries were then leased to Sir Alexander Cairnes, a member of the Ulster Presbyterian gentry and a banker in London, who leased them for 14 years from 1707 at £1,600 *per annum*.[43] The yields of fish fluctuated, but were often disappointing, with the result that demand exceeded supply and orders could not be fulfilled by the Ulster merchants. In 1680 'Black' George Macartney was unable to obtain 100 tons of salmon for a London client as the catch was poor.[44] The Belfast merchants also obtained fish from Ballyshannon and

---

Brice, 21 Feb. 1704/5 (ibid., pp 54-5); same to Andrew Skeen, 18 Dec. 1704 (ibid., pp 28-9); same to David Christy, 27 Apr. 1705 (ibid., p. 94); same to William Galbraith, 9 July 1705 (ibid., pp 140-1); Belfast customs register, 1682-87, and newspaper cutting on 'Trade of Belfast', 1715 (PRONI, HAR/1/G/1/13/1, pp 16-19, 24-5, 54-5, 60-1, 98-9, 152-5, 158-9).

[39] J. F. Durand, 'The history of forestry in Ireland' in E. C. Nelson & Aidan Brady (eds), *Irish gardening and horticulture* (Dublin, 1979), p. 206.

[40] Isaac Macartney to William Sloane, 11 Nov. 1704 (PRONI, D501/1, pp 9-10); same to William Galbraith, 9 July 1705 (ibid., pp 140-1); Agnew, *Merchant families*, p. 107.

[41] A short account of the history of the Coleraine port, 1610-1716 (PRONI, Maxwell Given papers, D2096/1/72); an account of timber shipped in the ports of Belfast and Coleraine, c.1695 (PRONI, T1075/6, p. 59); T. H. Mullin, *Coleraine in Georgian times* (Belfast, 1977), p. 195.

[42] 'Black' George Macartney to Daniel Arthur, 22 July 1679 (PRONI, MIC19/2, p. 68); same to Sir Joshua Allen, 9 & 16 Aug. 1679 (ibid., pp 73-4, 79-80); same to William Squire, 11 & 23 June 1680 (ibid., pp 210, 215); David Butle to Robert Thompson, 19 Feb. 1697[/8] (PRONI, D1449/13/1, p. 54); Isaac Macartney to John Galt, 26 May 1705 (ibid., D501/1, p. 115); same to René St Fleurant, 16 & 21 July 1705 (ibid., pp 144, 147).

[43] William Conolly to James Lenox, 1 Mar. 1711[/12] (PRONI, Lenox-Conyngham papers, T3161/1/8); Joshua Draper to the Saddlers' Company, 25 May 1720 (ibid., Salters' Company records, D4108/1/14C); Mullin, *Coleraine in Georgian times*, pp 195-6.

[44] 'Black' George Macartney to Daniel Arthur, 23 June, 6 & 13 July 1680 (PRONI, MIC19/2, pp 215-16, 218-19, 225); same to Sir Joshua Allen, 17 & 23 July, 3 & 11 Aug. 1680 (ibid., pp 228-30,

Carlingford, as well as Scotland, which they used to supply both the West Indies and the local market.[45]

Some manufactured goods were exported by Ulster merchants, but the quantities remained small, at least until the export of linen became more important in the eighteenth century.[46] In 1703 and 1704 Samuel Smith, a merchant of Belfast, sent not only butter and cheese but also cloth to Sir James Agnew, of Lochnaw Castle, Wigtownshire. Among the consignments were 20 yards of Carrick ratteen, 20 yards of coarser ratteen, 15 dozen 'new fashon'd buttons', and eight ounces of mohair, as well as 12 yards of 'light coler drugat'. Smith supplied clothes to a number of Scottish gentlemen and was confident that, though 'as fashonable as in Edinbrough', the clothes made in Belfast would be much cheaper than those available in the Scottish capital.[47] Export figures for Belfast in 1683 show that frieze, drapery, hats and stockings were all exported, principally to England and the American colonies. Linen was also exported in 1683, with 235 pieces going to England, 76 to the American colonies, 18 to Spain and the Mediterranean, and 12 to Scotland: in total about 17,000 yards.[48] Linen cloth, though present in small quantities beforehand, did not become important as an export commodity until legislative changes. In 1696 the English parliament removed the duty on Irish linen imported into England and following another act Irish merchants were able to export linen directly to the American colonies after 28 June 1705. In anticipation of the new opportunity that this second piece of legislation would bring, Isaac Macartney wrote to John Buck, his correspondent at Bideford, north Devon, to enquire if Buck wanted to be involved with him in the export of linen from Belfast to Virginia or the West Indies. Macartney informed Buck:

> Now when the parliament of England is pleased to lett poore Ireland export directly linnen to the English plantation for which trade this is the only fitt port in the kingdom of Ireland, the north of Ireland being the chiefe part for the linnen manufactory there being very little made elsewhere in the kingdom, if you incline to be concerned in that trade either for the West Indies or Virginia the months of June, July, August and September is the only season for buying the same.[49]

Macartney stressed to his correspondents that linen was always cheaper in Belfast than in Dublin.[50]

236, 240); same to William Squire, 23 July 1680 (ibid., pp 231–2); Agnew, *Merchant families*, p. 106.
[45] 'Black' George Macartney to John Delap, 9 Aug. & 16 Sept. 1679, 14 Dec. 1680 (MIC19/2, pp 74, 101–2, 310–11); same to Daniel Arthur, 26 Aug. 1679 (ibid., p. 88); Isaac Macartney to William Stanus, 3 Oct. & 17 Nov. 1705 (PRONI, D501/1, pp 198, 228).
[46] J. C. Beckett, 'The seventeenth century' in idem and R. E. Glasscock, *Belfast: the origin and growth of an industrial city* (London, 1967), p. 34; Benn, *Belfast*, pp 317–18; Agnew, *Merchant families*, pp 107–8.
[47] Samuel Smith to Sir James Agnew, 12 Aug. 1704 (NAS, Agnew papers, GD154/677/1). Druggett was a wool, or partly wool, fabric used for clothing.
[48] Benn, *Belfast*, pp 317–18.
[49] Isaac Macartney to John Buck, 12 Mar. 1704/5 (PRONI, D501/1, p. 68).
[50] Isaac Macartney to George Tyrer, 9 Oct. 1705 (ibid., p. 202); same to Richard Warrall, 25 Feb. 1705/6 (ibid., p. 274).

Trade with the West Indies was dominated by the import of sugar, which was sold to the sugar refiners of Belfast in its semi-processed state.[51] The most important import from North America was tobacco, and 360,413 lbs were brought into Belfast in 1683.[52] Roll and leaf tobacco were both sold at Belfast and there were a number of tobacco spinners located in the town in the early eighteenth century.[53] Salt was another important import. It was used especially in the preparation of the beef, hides and fish that the Ulster merchants exported. The salt was obtained from France, Spain, Portugal and England.[54] English, Spanish and Portuguese salt was preferred by the Ulster merchants 'because it not only preserves the beef well but it likewise keeps it cleaner and makes it look good'.[55] Luxury foodstuffs, such as fruit, wines and brandy, were imported from France and Spain. The fruits imported included currants, figs, oranges and lemons. Vinegar and spices such as nutmeg were also imported.[56]

As a port Belfast boomed in the late seventeenth century.[57] In 1693 George Story described Belfast as a 'very large town, and the greatest for trade in the north of Ireland' and William Sacheverell mistakenly thought it was 'the second town in Ireland'.[58] As Belfast prospered, other Ulster ports such as Carrickfergus, Coleraine and Donaghadee declined. For centuries Carrickfergus had been the principal port in County Antrim but by 1688 Sacheverell described the town 'as very ancient ... but of little trade and ruinous'.[59] Richard Dobbs attributed the decline of Carrickfergus to the move of the customs house from Carrickfergus to Belfast, but other important factors must be that Belfast was closer to the important markets on the English mainland, and to Dublin.[60] During the course of the seventeenth century a change occurred in the nature of the commodities exported from Ireland. In the early seventeenth century the exports were mainly unprocessed

---

[51] Belfast customs register, 1682–87 (PRONI, HAR/1/G/1/13/1, pp 20–1, 60–1, 110–11, 158–61); David Butle to William Moore, 10 Jan. 1697/8 (PRONI, D1449/13/1, p. 53); Isaac Macartney to William Smith, 9 June 1705 (ibid., D501/1, pp 121–3).

[52] Belfast customs register, 1682–87 (PRONI, HAR/1/G/1/13/1, pp 20–1, 50–3, 56–7, 96–7, 100–3, 130–1, 134–5, 152–3, 158–9); T. M. Truxes, *Irish-American trade, 1660–1783* (Cambridge, 1988), p. 21; Benn, *Belfast*, p. 319.

[53] Isaac Macartney to John Buck, 12 Mar. 1704/5 (PRONI, D501/1, p. 68); Gillespie, *Early Belfast*, p. 116; Agnew, *Belfast funeral register*, pp 23, 30.

[54] Belfast customs register, 1682–87 (PRONI, HAR/1/G/1/13/1, pp 14–15, 20–1, 30–3, 46–7, 66–7, 106–7, 112–13, 158–9); Benn, *Belfast*, p. 319; Agnew, *Merchant families*, p. 108.

[55] Isaac Macartney to Patrick Harper, 18 Sept. 1706 (PRONI, D501/1, pp 358–9).

[56] Belfast customs register, 1682–87, and newspaper cutting on 'Trade of Belfast', 1715 (PRONI, HAR/1/G/1/13/1, pp 4–5, 12–13, 20–1, 32–7, 54–5, 74–7, 88–9, 106–7, 116–9, 122–5, 142–3, 158–9); Agnew, *Merchant families*, pp 108, 112, 114–15. A cookery book belonging to Margaret McBride, wife of the minister of First Belfast Presbyterian Church, included recipes that made use of such imported foodstuffs as 'appricocks', 'orranges', 'leimonds', 'currains', walnuts, dates, quinces, almonds and 'jaculat' [chocolate]': R. M. Young, 'A Belfast cookery book of Queen Anne's time', *UJA*, 2nd ser., ix (1898), pp 114–21.

[57] Gillespie, *Early Belfast*, p. 128.

[58] Story, *Impartial history*, p. 38; Sacheverell, *Account of the Isle of Man*, p. 125. See also 'The Scots in Ireland, 1697' (Senate House Lib., Univ. of London, Chalmers papers, MS 30, ff 11–12).

[59] Sacheverell, *Account of the Isle of Man*, p. 124.

[60] George Hill, *An historical account of the MacDonnells of Antrim* (Belfast, 1873), pp 388–9; Agnew, *Merchant families*, pp 3–5.

raw materials, principally live animals. By the late seventeenth century, after the passage at Westminster of the Cattle Acts in the 1660s, which prohibited the import of live cattle into England from Ireland, the commodities exported by Irish merchants were predominantly processed goods such as butter and barrelled beef.[61] Belfast merchants were never as involved in the export of live cattle as some of the merchants operating at the other Ulster ports and therefore were not affected as much by the change.[62] Donaghadee, Carrickfergus and Coleraine, all of which exported live animals, never fully recovered.[63] Donaghadee, however, remained an important port for the export of horses to Scotland.[64]

The trade of Newry and Derry both suffered as a result of events during the Williamite War. Newry recovered well and benefited from the opening of the Newry Canal in 1741. In 1744 Harris described it as 'the largest and most trading town' in County Down.[65] Derry experienced a trade recession prior to the Williamite War and in 1687 John Davis, the Irish Society's agent, wrote to the Society about the poverty of the city.[66] Derry took longer than Newry to recover after the war, but was to become an important player in the Atlantic trade in the later eighteenth century.[67] Belfast too experienced economic problems in the early eighteenth century. Trade with Europe was affected by persistent warfare and in the domestic market it was often difficult to sell luxury goods because of general economic instability.[68] In March 1705 Isaac Macartney wrote to Henry Caldwell of Ballyshannon, 'Wee have no trade here [Belfast] all things [being] dead (God send better times).'[69] In early 1705 Macartney received a consignment of currants and raisins from Sir Edmund Harrison of London, but although all were sold they did not fetch their full value because of the 'deplorable' condition of Ireland, 'many good families' being unable to 'get as mutch as will buy them necessary bread and cloathes'.[70] Several parcels of raisins that came to Belfast from Cadiz, via Scotland, had to be sent to Dublin in 1705 because they could not be sold at Belfast, and there are other examples around the same time of luxury foodstuffs being sent to Dublin for the

---

61 Raymond Gillespie, *The transformation of the Irish economy* (Dundalk, 1991), pp 38, 42–5. There was a temporary lapse in the prohibition on Irish livestock at the start of our period, 1679–81, but even then Belfast and the northern ports of Ulster were far less active in the trade than their southern counterparts: Donald Woodward, 'The Anglo-Irish livestock trade of the seventeenth century', *Irish Historical Studies*, xviii (1973), pp 499–521.

62 Agnew, *Merchant families*, pp 117–18.

63 Ibid., pp 3–4, 118.

64 Young, *Historical notices of old Belfast*, p. 141; [Smith & Harris], *Antient & present state of Down*, p. 65.

65 Gillespie, *Early Belfast*, pp 159–60; [Smith & Harris], *Antient & present state of Down*, p. 94.

66 T. H. Mullin, *Ulster's historic city Derry, Londonderry* (Coleraine, 1986), p. 42.

67 Gillespie, *Early Belfast*, pp 159–60; Robert Gavin, William Kelly and Dolores O'Reilly (eds), *Atlantic gateway: the port and city of Londonderry since 1700* (Dublin, 2009).

68 John McBride to Robert Wyllie, 7 July 1704 (NLS, Wod. Fol., xxvi, f. 339); Gillespie, *Early Belfast*, pp 128–9, 156; idem, 'The early modern economy, 1600–1700' in Liam Kennedy and Philip Ollerenshaw (eds), *Ulster since 1600: politics, economy and society* (Oxford, 2013), pp 23–4; Agnew, *Merchant families*, p. 116.

69 Isaac Macartney to Henry Caldwell, 26 Mar. 1705 (PRONI, D501/1, p. 76).

70 Isaac Macartney to Sir Edmund Harrison, 14 Apr. 1705 (ibid., pp 85–6).

same reason.[71] In May 1706 Macartney informed Nicholas Lincoln of Dublin that wine, brandy, vinegar, prunes and almonds were all plentiful and cheap at Belfast because there was 'little consumption and no money stirring' and wrote to George Lamie of Dungannon to see if he could sell any there.[72]

It was important for merchants to try and import only what would sell, and sell quickly. They needed, therefore, to know and appreciate the particular needs and tastes of the local market. The home market for luxury goods was always small and commonly swamped by an over-supply of similar commodities arriving at the same time. While this may have to some extent been due to bad luck, with two ships loaded with the same commodity arriving at the one time, it was nevertheless often hard to avoid because of the seasonal nature of trade which meant that specific goods, such as tobacco and wine, could only be imported at certain times of the year.[73] Although profits from trade could be substantial for a successful merchant, there were also considerable risks. At all times there was the danger of shipwreck because of storms and uncharted seas, as well as ships being blown off course, or lost, and delays caused by adverse weather. Providential escapes from shipwreck had an impact on some Presbyterian merchants. Hugh Rainey, a merchant of Magherafelt, endowed a school there in fulfilment of a pledge he had made when he survived a shipwreck and John Black of Bordeaux, who was born in Belfast in 1682, spent each anniversary of a similar event in grateful prayer.[74]

Risks and difficulties increased in times of war. England was at war with France between 1689 and 1697 (the War of the League of Augsburg) and again between 1702 and 1713 (the War of the Spanish Succession). The progress of the war effort and its impact on trade were mentioned by merchants in their correspondence.[75] Isaac Macartney wrote to William Sloane in London on 27 November 1704 that the state of trade was bad owing to the war.[76] Some markets were closed but the Belfast merchants managed to overcome this by having two sets of papers on board their ships or by registering the ships in the names of residents from neutral or, even, enemy countries.[77] During wartime there was also the risk of impressments of the crew on board ships and privateers posed another danger. The war with France brought French privateers into the Irish Sea and even into Belfast Lough.[78] In May 1706 a ship belonging to James Lenox of Derry and a Scottish bark were taken by

[71] Ibid.; Isaac Macartney to James Livingston, 14 Apr. 1705 (ibid., p. 85); same to René St Fleurant, 16 & 21 July, 13 Aug. 1705 (ibid., pp 144, 147, 167–8).

[72] Isaac Macartney to Nicholas Lincoln, 18 May 1706 (ibid., p. 313); same to George Lamie, 6 May 1706 (ibid., p. 310).

[73] Agnew, *Merchant families*, p. 112.

[74] Notes on the Rainey family (LHL, Joy MS, 10); will of Hugh Rainey, 1707 (NAI, Prerogative will book, 1706–8, MFGS 41/2, ff 212–14); annotated pencil drawings relating to a shipwreck witnessed by John Black, c.1725 (PRONI, Black papers, D4457/362); Agnew, *Merchant families*, p. 134.

[75] Isaac Macartney to William Sloane, 27 Nov. 1704 (PRONI, D501/1, pp 20–1); same to Robert Stewart, 24 June 1706 (ibid., pp 328–9); same to Daniel Hays, 13 July 1706 (ibid., p. 331).

[76] Isaac Macartney to William Sloane, 27 Nov. 1704 (PRONI, D501/1, pp 20–1).

[77] Agnew, *Merchant families*, pp 116–17.

[78] Isaac Macartney to William Galbraith, 21 May 1705 (PRONI, D501/1, p. 112); Agnew, *Merchant families*, p. 134.

two privateers at the mouth of Belfast Lough.[79] Pirates presented a further risk. Joseph Bigger, a merchant of Belfast, was a passenger on the *Friendship* of Belfast when it was taken by pirates off Virginia.[80]

Merchants entered into partnerships in both cargoes and ships in order to reduce the risks of overseas trading. Trading partnerships usually only lasted until the return of the ship, and normally the cargo on board ships was shared between two and eight partners.[81] The leading merchants often had shares in a number of different trading ventures at the one time, and it was less risky to have a small stake in a number of simultaneous ventures than to invest all of their capital in a single trading venture. Once a cargo had been gathered the merchant then needed to arrange shipping. This could involve chartering a vessel, but many of the leading merchants located in Ulster port towns were also shipowners. Even Robert Murdoch of Newry had a ship, *The Robert*, and a half-share in 'the Mary and Ann sloop', both of which he bequeathed to his son Ephraim.[82] Most ships were owned by syndicates, though the ship-owning partnerships tended to be more long-term than the trading partnerships.[83] A list of Belfast-owned ships survives from c.1659–63. Leaving aside the 11 gabbarts, that is, lighters, of between 6 and 18 tons, which were used to load and unload cargoes, the average tonnage of the other 18 ships was 55 tons. Only three of the ships were over 100 tons: the *Adventure* (120 tons), *Insiquin* (150 tons), and *Antelope* (200 tons), while the other 15 were all less than 60 tons. The *Antelope* was owned by eight merchants, of whom at least six were Presbyterian and one an Anglican. Very few of the ships had a single owner and those that did were under 30 tons.[84] Another list dated 1682–6 gives 67 Belfast-owned ships, but despite the increase, only nine were of 100 tons or more.[85] The 1659–63 list gives the location of where the ships were built. All 11 of the gabbarts and five of the ships were built at Belfast and three of the ships at Coleraine. The remaining ships were built at a variety of other locations, not only in Britain and Europe, but also in America.[86] Belfast and Coleraine, as well as Derry, had a shipbuilding industry in the seventeenth century. The ships built at Coleraine tended to be larger than those at Belfast, probably because the Coleraine shipbuilders had access to the larger oaks in the north west of the province. The *Adventure*, for instance, which had a capacity of 120 tons, was built at Coleraine, while the largest ship built at Belfast, and used by the Belfast merchants in 1663, was 50 tons. Masts and other materials for rigging

[79] Isaac Macartney to James Lenox, 27 May 1706 (PRONI, D501/1, p. 316); same to William Cairnes, 27 May 1706 (ibid.).

[80] Agnew, *Merchant families*, p. 211.

[81] Charter party, 11 Mar. [1725] (PRONI, Mussenden papers, D354/388); Agnew, *Merchant families*, p. 127.

[82] Will of Robert Murdoch, 1727 (NAI, Prerogative will book, 1726–8, MFGS 41/2, f. 332).

[83] Receipt for £150 borrowed by James Mitchell to buy John O'Neill and Hugh McCollum's proportions of the ship *Rose of Belfast*, 17 Sept. 1698 (PRONI, Antrim papers, D2977/5/1/3/16); sale of one-twentieth share in the *Donegall* of Belfast, 7 Dec. 1711 (PRONI, D271/4); Agnew, *Merchant families*, pp 127–31.

[84] Benn, *Belfast*, p. 310.

[85] 'List of the vessels, which belonged to the port of Belfast, in the years 1682, 1683, 1684, 1685, and 1686', *Belfast News-Letter*, 24–8 May 1793.

[86] Benn, *Belfast*, p. 310.

ships were imported into Belfast in the late seventeenth and early eighteenth centuries.[87] By the opening years of the eighteenth century the shipbuilders at Belfast must have been capable of building larger ships, with the *Loyal Charles* (250 tons), which was built there, launched in 1700.[88]

Even when ships arrived safely there could be problems as the provisions exported from Ulster were often perishable and sometimes arrived in an unsaleable condition.[89] The common cause was the use of unseasoned wood when packing, which gave the contents an unpleasant taste. In 1686 the Belfast corporation, in which many of the leading Belfast Presbyterian merchants were burgesses, passed a by-law that beef barrels were to be made only of seasoned wood because 'the reputacion of the trade in this towne abroad is much impaired by the insufficiency of beefe barrells'.[90] Despite the by-law, and the merchants often tasting samples of butter before they were exported, the problem of goods being in a poor condition on arrival persisted.

Merchants relied on ships' masters, supercargoes or correspondents to dispose of the goods on arrival and to reload the ships with goods for the return voyage. Belfast Presbyterian merchants often used the same correspondents, many of whom by the early eighteenth century were from either Ulster or Scotland.[91] David Butle and Isaac Macartney both used Alexander and Henry Cairnes as their correspondents at London, William Cromie at Dublin, Alexander Carstaires at Rotterdam, and the Moore brothers at Barbados.[92] As well as selling and making purchases of goods for the Ulster merchants, correspondents assisted in remittance of money and provided commercial and political intelligence. Such information on the price of different commodities and what would sell well was useful to Ulster merchants. Merchants were often the first to receive news: for instance, Isaac Macartney and Robert Lenox were apparently the first in Belfast to obtain and spread the news of Queen Anne's death in 1714.[93] Merchants also had to make assessments of the creditworthiness of their clients and sometimes on behalf of their correspondents.[94] Credit and reputation were important to the merchants.[95] Sometimes, though, dependants and correspondents could be unreliable. 'Black' George Macartney wrote to Robert Contales, his correspondent at Ostend in 1679, 'I am so ashamed that such miscarriages should fall out upon me, and others that send little boys abroad

[87] A short account of Coleraine port (PRONI, Maxwell Given papers, D2096/1/72); Benn, *Belfast*, p. 310; Agnew, *Merchant families*, p. 132; Gillespie, *Early Belfast*, p. 113.

[88] '2d. part of the annals of Belfast' (LHL, Joy MS 12, p. 5).

[89] 'Black' George Macartney to Dehulter and Vanhomrigh, 15 Oct. 1679 (PRONI, MIC19/2, pp 121–2); same to Daniel Arthur, 27 Dec. 1679 (ibid., pp 159–60); Isaac Macartney to John Innis, 15 Jan. 1704/5 (ibid., D501/1, pp 39–40); James Crawford to Alexander Stewart & Co., 14 Oct. 1726 (ibid., D654/B/2/101).

[90] Young, *Belfast town book*, p. 155.

[91] Agnew, *Merchant families*, pp 139–42, 179–92.

[92] Butle letter book (PRONI, D1449/13/1); Isaac Macartney letter book (ibid., D501/1).

[93] J. W. Kernohan, *Rosemary Street Presbyterian Church Belfast: a record of the past 200 years* (Belfast, 1923), pp 10–11.

[94] Isaac Macartney to Messrs Burton & Harrison, 11 June 1705, 19 Jan. 1705/6 (PRONI, D501/1, pp 125, 255).

[95] Agnew, *Merchant families*, pp 143–50.

have their concerns all secure, and that you living in the place should meet with such misfortune it troubles me.'[96] Macartney's son, Isaac, in 1705 wrote to William Smith, his agent at Jamaica, to complain about his sending poor but expensive sugar, making claims for extravagant living and selling Macartney's beef, herrings and butter at poor prices.[97]

Insurance on both ships and cargoes was available, but was not universally used by the merchants. Isaac Macartney, for instance, did not insure his £150 concern on the Star and the vessel was taken going from Barbados to Virginia in 1704.[98] Insurance could not be arranged in Ulster and was usually obtained through correspondents at London, principally the Cairnes brothers, or correspondents in Antwerp or Rotterdam. It provided only a means of 'mitigating rather than covering risks'. This was because underwriters seldom paid more than four-fifths of the sum insured and, as a result, merchants, if they took out any insurance, usually only insured two-thirds or less of their total stake in a venture. Making an insurance claim was also a lengthy process. Insurance on cargoes was initially more common than insurance of ships, but from the 1690s insurance of ships increased because of the heightened risk posed by privateers and thereafter was common during times of war.[99]

In the early eighteenth century William Tisdall, vicar of Belfast, and other Church of Ireland authors attacked Presbyterian merchants and accused them of confining their trade to themselves and refusing to take apprentices from Church of Ireland families.[100] Rev. James Kirkpatrick of Belfast, in replying to these charges, stated that although the Presbyterian merchants preferred their apprentices to accompany them to the meetinghouse, so that they could ensure they did not get up to any mischief when left unsupervised, they did not refuse to take apprentices from any Church of Ireland family that could afford to pay the premium. Kirkpatrick added that he was not aware of any indentures made by the leading Presbyterian merchants of Belfast or Derry that contained articles obliging their apprentices to attend the Presbyterian church.[101] In the Belfast freemen's roll there are examples of masters taking apprentices across the denominational divide and it would appear that the day-to-day business relations between the Presbyterian and Church of

---

96 'Black' George Macartney to Robert Contales, 19 Apr. 1679 (PRONI, D501/1, p. 53).
97 Isaac Macartney to William Smith, 9 June 1705 (ibid., pp 121–3).
98 Isaac Macartney to Messrs Cromie & Stevenson, 21 Oct. 1704 (ibid., p. 2).
99 Isaac Macartney to Alexander & Henry Cairnes, 8 Jan. & 17 Feb. 1704/5, 26 Mar., 7 July & 22 Sept. 1705 (ibid., pp 34, 51, 76–7, 137, 190–1); same to John Cunningham, 8 Nov. 1704 (ibid., pp 6–7); same to Andrew Clark, 8 Nov. 1704 (ibid., pp 7–8); David Butle to Alexander Cairnes, 12 Feb. 1697/8, 9 Nov. 1698 (ibid., D1449/13/1, pp 53, 58–9); James Crawford to Alexander Stewart & Co., 14 Oct. 1726 (ibid., Londonderry papers, D654/B/2/101); Francis Trimble to Alexander Stewart & Co., 7 Jan. 1727 (ibid., D654/B/2/104); Agnew, Merchant families, p. 135.
100 Bp King to Sir Robert Southwell, 28 Mar. 1702 (TCD, King papers, MS 750/2/3, f. 137); King to Abp Marsh, 14 Nov. 1699 (TCD, King papers, MS 1489/1/85–6); King to Abp Wake, 24 Mar. 1715[/16] (TCD, King papers, MS 2533/160–171); Journals of the House of Lords [of Ireland] (8 vols, London, 1779–1800), ii, 410–11; The present state of religion in Ireland (London, [1712]), p. 2; [William Tisdall], The conduct of the Dissenters of Ireland, with respect both to church and state (Dublin, 1712), pp 23–5.
101 [Kirkpatrick], Presby. loyalty, pp 433–9. See also, The present state of religion in Ireland, p. 23.

Ireland merchants in Belfast were largely cordial. In instructions given to the synod's commissioner, Rev. Francis Iredell, to counter the accusations of the Irish Convocation and House of Lords in 1711, there were four examples specified of Presbyterians who had taken Anglican apprentices, and it was mentioned that the reason why Robert Lenox of Belfast had refused to take a member of the Church of Ireland as an apprentice was 'for want of apprentice fee, not for being a conformist'. Presbyterian merchants entered into trading and shipowning partnerships with members of the Church of Ireland and included members of the Church of Ireland among their customers.[102] In 1713, 79 of the principal Church of Ireland traders of Belfast signed a declaration that their Presbyterian neighbours were not guilty of any unfair dealing.[103]

III. Income and expenditure

The wealth and income of the merchants of Ulster varied from individual to individual. In Belfast the leading Presbyterian families were the Andersons, Eccles, Chalmers, Macartneys and Smiths, while the income of the Biggers and Clugstons was more modest.[104] In the late seventeenth century the most successful of the Coleraine Presbyterian merchants were the Galts, Thompsons and Twaddells. Merchants obtained their business income through profits made in trade, premiums from apprentices, and commission paid on goods that they loaded and sold for merchants from other ports.[105] Wills can provide some indication of merchant wealth, but must be treated with caution as merchants generally counted debts, even bad debts, as assets and some of the older children may have been provided with their portion before the testator's death.[106] In 1680 Hugh Eccles of Belfast valued his substance at £4,500. He also left a house in Lisburn to his wife, Grizzell.[107] James Chalmers, in 1681, estimated his wealth to be about £3,000, after the payment of his debts and funeral expenses, and in 1684 William Smith left £3,800.[108] In 1693 James Stewart left cash bequests totalling almost £3,000 and James Anderson of Belfast left cash bequests of almost £950 in 1706.[109] Hugh Rainey of Magherafelt, a brother of William Rainey the younger of Belfast, left property worth £4,650 in 1708 and in 1719 Thomas Lyle, a merchant of Belfast, valued his worldly substance at just over £1,280.[110]

---

102 Witherow, *Hist. & lit. memls*, i, 151–2; Bp Ashe to Bp King, 12 Dec. 1699 (TCD, King papers, MSS 1995–2008/650); Agnew, *Merchant families*, pp 33, 60.

103 [Kirkpatrick], *Presby. loyalty*, pp 434–5.

104 Agnew, *Merchant families*, pp xviii, 38–9.

105 Ibid., pp 41, 150; Gillespie & Royle, *Belfast: part I*, p. 2.

106 Agnew, *Merchant families*, pp 36–7.

107 Will of Hugh Eccles, 1680 (PRONI, Clarke papers, MIC92/1).

108 Agnew, *Merchant families*, pp 36, 216, 245.

109 Abstract will of James Stewart, 1693 (PRONI, Stewart papers, D1759/3/B/1, p.7); will of James Anderson, 1706 (NAI, Prerogative will book, 1704–8, MFGS 41/2, ff 24–5).

110 Will of Hugh Rainey, 1707 (NAI, Prerogative will book, 1706–8, MFGS 41/2, ff 212–14); Thomas Ash, *The Ash Mss.*, *written in the year 1735*, ed. E. T. Martin (Belfast, 1890), p. 16; Thomas Witherow (ed.), *Two diaries of Derry in 1689* (Derry, 1888), pp xv–xvi; abstract will of Thomas Lyll (Lyle), 1719 (PRONI, Mussenden papers, D354/27).

As well as their business interests some merchants obtained income from landholdings. George Martin of Belfast, whose will was dated 1678, had property in Belfast and Lisburn, as well as at Whitehouse, Listilliard and Clough Castle, County Antrim.[111] James Anderson of Belfast purchased 732 acres in County Antrim, 558 acres in County Down, 257 acres in County Kildare, and 36 acres in County Kilkenny from the forfeiture commissioners in 1703.[112] William Haltridge, a wealthy merchant based at Dromore, had lands not only in County Down and County Armagh, but also in Scotland.[113] Many of the merchants continued to live in urban areas and continued to engage in trade after they purchased land. William Crawford purchased the manor of Florida at Kilmood, County Down, in 1692, while John Young, another Belfast merchant, bought property in County Down from the trustees of the estates of Sir Hans Hamilton in 1706–9. Both Crawford and Young continued to reside in Belfast.[114] Land, therefore, was an investment for many of the merchants, and an asset which they could sell if necessary. Landownership was also attractive as it conferred status, elevating some of the merchant families into the ranks of the gentry. John Cowan of Derry, Edward Brice, William Crawford and Isaac Macartney of Belfast were included in two lists of the gentry of Ulster compiled around 1725 and 1732. The annual income of Brice and Crawford was estimated by the compilers as £200–£300, while Isaac Macartney's annual income was estimated at £600–£700.[115] Cowan of Derry was a 'wealthy man' but in consequence of commercial losses he had to part with part of his estates, so that his remaining property, which was inherited in 1733 by his daughter, Mary, amounted only to £600 a year.[116] Isaac Macartney was the leading merchant in Belfast in the early eighteenth century, but was mired in financial difficulties in the 1730s by 'inattention to business' and involvement in the debts of his brother-in-law John Haltridge of Dromore.[117] As a result of the interconnectedness and interdependency of the merchants the fall of one merchant could lead to the failure of others. James Arbuckle of Belfast, though he had stock valued at £1,800 and shares in ships worth £800, went bankrupt because he was owed £7,000 by others.[118]

There were no banks in Ulster in the late seventeenth and early eighteenth centuries, and merchants lent money and exchanged bills of exchange. Although Isaac Macartney did not call himself a banker, the title was later claimed for him by his son. Macartney never issued banknotes but was active in the supply, exchange and presentment of bills, on behalf of a number of Dublin merchants and bankers, and Agnew has suggested that his activities as an agent of the Cairnes

[111] Agnew, *Merchant families*, p. 238.

[112] Ibid., p. 209.

[113] Ibid., p. 255.

[114] Ibid., pp 46, 219, 252.

[115] List of the gentlemen of Co. Down and Co. Antrim (Royal Irish Academy, Dublin, Upton papers, MS 24.K.19, no. 1); list of the nobility and gentry of Ulster (Lambeth Palace Lib., Gibson papers, MS 1742, ff 49–56).

[116] [Witherow], 'Londonderry family', p. 29.

[117] Chancery brief and other documents relating to the case of William Macartney, son of Isaac Macartney (PRONI, Ellison-Macartney papers, D3649/5/1B); Agnew, *Merchant families*, pp 154, 236; *HIP*, iv, 322.

[118] Barnard, *New anatomy*, pp 258–9.

brothers, who were bankers in London and Dublin, mean that it is possible to consider Macartney as another 'branch' of the Cairnes' banking business.[119] Some merchants also collected rents for the gentry. Hugh McCollum was agent or receiver for the third earl of Antrim. McCollum built Limnalary House, near Carnlough, County Antrim, about 1680. There were extensive cellars under the house and nearby a small pier where vessels could discharge cargo. McCollum was engaged in trade as well as his agency business, and he appears in the 1659–63 list of Belfast shipowners, with a share in *Helena*, a ship of 40 tons, which was built at Glenarm.[120]

Before the rise of the professional undertaker, merchants occasionally undertook the organisation of funerals, by arranging and supplying the necessary paraphernalia. In July 1705 Isaac Macartney sent Henry Maxwell of Finnebrogue a bill for £18 1s 6d, for gloves and hats supplied by Samuel Smith, as well as for wine and brandy and the hire of a velvet pall for the funeral of Maxwell's grandfather. The pall was probably obtained from the Presbyterian congregation of Belfast, of which Isaac Macartney was an elder.[121] Thomas Lyle of Belfast in 1721 sent a similar bill, amounting to the lesser total of £3 6s 7d, to Edward Pierce, a currier, for several items which had been supplied for the funeral of Pierce's wife.[122]

More than any other social group within the Presbyterian community the merchants had liquid assets, which they sometimes invested in industries or in town improvements. The trade of the Belfast merchants was highly seasonal and it was advantageous for merchants to be able to draw income from other economic ventures.[123] William Smith was a partner with the Church of Ireland merchant George Macartney of Auchinleck in an ironworks at Belfast in the 1660s, and also in the first Belfast sugar refinery.[124] Smith's sons, David and Patrick, along with their brother-in-law, Thomas Crawford, and Henry Chads the younger, set up a pottery in Belfast in 1698.[125] In 1710 Isaac Macartney leased from Lord Donegall marshy ground between the church and the River Lagan. After a scheme of improvement Macartney laid out a new residential development, Brunswick Square. He did this by granting a rent-free period to sub-tenants who in return were required to build houses of stone or brick with slate roofs. In addition, Macartney built two quays in the area, which he named Hanover Quay and George Quay. By the 1720s he was

---

[119] Agnew, *Merchant families*, pp 156–8, 168–9, 173–8.

[120] H. C. Lawlor, 'Old Glenarm', *Weekly Telegraph*, 11 Mar. 1911; Benn, *Belfast*, p. 310.

[121] Isaac Macartney to [Henry Maxwell], 2 July 1705 (PRONI, D501/1, p. 135); Agnew, *Belfast funeral register*, pp 1, 4. For William Cairnes's 'disbursements for mourning for the late Earl of Donegalls death', amounting to almost £242, see Donegall rents and payments, 1706–15 (PRONI, Maguire papers, D4512/4/4).

[122] Promissory note from Edward Pierce to pay Thomas Lyll (Lyle), 3 Nov. 1721 (PRONI, Mussenden papers, D354/406); Agnew, *Belfast funeral register*, p. 24.

[123] Gillespie, *Early Belfast*, pp 112–13.

[124] Agnew, *Merchant families*, pp 43, 233, 245.

[125] Sacheverell, *Account of the Isle of Man*, p. 125; Isaac Macartney to Andrew Skeen, 15 June 1706 (PRONI, D501/1, pp 321–2); Young, *Historical notices of old Belfast*, p. 156; Gillespie, *Early Belfast*, pp 138–40; Ruari Ó Baoill, *Hidden history below our feet: the archaeological story of Belfast* (Dundonald, 2011), pp 112, 132–5.

receiving £400 a year from his Belfast property, including the new development.[126] A number of streets and bridges in Belfast bore the name of significant merchants located in the town, such as Biggar's Lane, Clugston's Lane, Pottinger's Lane, Eccles's Bridge and Chad's Bridge. Gillespie has suggested that this may have been because they had been involved in the development or financial outlay for these improvements to the infrastructure of Belfast.[127]

It is possible to obtain a glimpse into the lifestyle of some of the merchants from items that they bequeathed in their wills or, occasionally, from references in their correspondence. The Belfast merchant Hugh Eccles left his watch to his nephew, William Rainey.[128] John Macartney, another Belfast merchant, the son of 'Brown' George Macartney, left 'his cane, ring, and watch', which were formerly his father's, to his brother George, a merchant in Dublin.[129] Robert Murdoch of Newry left his eldest son, Andrew, all 'his bodily wearing cloathes' along with his 'watch and silver headed kain and mourning sword'. He bequeathed all his silver plate to his son Ephraim, and to each of his three daughters a bed and the sheets and clothes in a trunk. The family 'christening blanket' was left to his daughter Elizabeth and all his rings were to be divided between his three daughters and his son Ephraim.[130] James Stewart of Belfast left his 'large silver tankard' to his son Theophilus, a 'smaller silver tankard' to his daughter Sarah, 'a silver tumbler, spoons and the whole of his furnishings' to his daughter Rose, and his bay gelding to Henry Chads, a merchant in Belfast.[131] John Galt of Coleraine, in his will of 1715, left his son John his 'two boole cups and ... looking glass the table and stands'.[132]

Merchants also made purchases and bequests of expensive clothes. David Butle in 1698 ordered some of the best quality 'heir plush' for breeches from Holland, and in 1677 Jane Pottinger of Belfast asked her husband, Edward, to buy her an ermine scarf and some scarlet satin ribbons to trim gloves.[133] John Moore of Belfast, who made his will in 1694, possessed an extensive wardrobe. He left his 'black suit of cloaths', along with his sword, a horse, saddle and furniture to Archibald Whitehead, half-brother of his wife, 'two suits of ratten cloaths (saving the plate buttons)' and all his shoes and stockings to his uncle William Moore, a 'suit of mourning' to Hugh Moor of Bangor, and a suit of his 'best cloaths', his 'coloured cloaths' and a 'westcoat with silver butons' to Hugh Rae.[134] Samuel Davey, a Derry merchant, in 1727 left all his 'wearing cloaths' to his brother, Walter, and his wife's 'wearing cloathes and apparell' to Mary Cowan, daughter of the Derry merchant,

---

[126] Benn, *Belfast*, pp 479, 529; T. G. Paterson, 'Belfast in 1738', *UJA*, 3rd ser., ii (1939), p. 112; Gillespie, *Early Belfast*, pp 148–51.

[127] Gillespie, *Early Belfast*, pp 103, 147.

[128] Abstract will of Hugh Eccles, 1680 (PRONI, Society of Genealogists documents, T581/1, p. 24).

[129] Benn, *Belfast*, p. 583.

[130] Will of Robert Murdoch, 1727 (NAI, Prerogative will book, 1726–8, MFGS 41/2, ff 331–3).

[131] Abstract will of James Stewart, 1693 (PRONI, Stewart papers, D1759/3/B/1, p. 71).

[132] Will of John Galt, 1715 (PRONI, D2096/1/15D).

[133] David Butle to Alexander Adare, 31 Jan. 1697/8 (PRONI, D1449/13/1, p. 53); Agnew, *Merchant families*, p. 39.

[134] Abstract will of John Moore, 1694 (PRONI, Stewart papers, D1759/3/B/1, p. 85).

John Cowan.[135] In 1705 Isaac Macartney ordered a wig and stockings from Dublin and James Anderson of Belfast, who died in 1706, left his 'new wigg', linen and books to his cousin Dr George Martin of Dublin.[136]

Merchants sometimes appeared as subscribers to books. Among the subscribers to John Watson's *Tables of exchange*, which was published at Dublin in 1727, were the Presbyterian merchants John Lenox, John Macartney, Thomas McMun, Isaac Macartney, Daniel Mussenden, John Smith, Charles Young and Hugh Young.[137] Daniel Mussenden, the leading merchant in Belfast from around 1720 to 1750, also owned a copy of Willem Sewel's English and Dutch dictionary, which was published at Amsterdam in 1708.[138] In addition to books which may have been useful to their trading activities, subscriptions to other types of books showed wider interests. James Lecky was a subscriber to John Gay's *Poems on several occasions*, which was published at Dublin in 1729, and John Lyle and John McMun, of Belfast, appear among the subscribers to Richardson Pack's *Miscellaneous works in verse and prose*, which was published in Dublin in 1726.[139]

Presbyterian merchants were accused of under-living, and thus being able to 'under-sell', their Church of Ireland counterparts.[140] While there were Presbyterian merchants, such as James Anderson of Belfast, noted for their meanness, others, such as Isaac Macartney, who was described as being 'opulent', were more extravagant.[141] In 1717 John Galt of Coleraine changed his will because of the 'disobedience' and 'extravagance' of his eldest son, John.[142] It would seem that most of the Presbyterian merchants lived reasonably comfortable lives and it was important, if they were to inspire confidence in those who entrusted them with money, that they maintained suitable outward appearances. Rev. James Kirkpatrick in 1712 wrote, 'Dissenters live suitable to their stations and circumstances, and some of 'em … are both capable and willing to give gentlemen of all persuasions (clergy and laity) as generous and liberal entertainments in their houses, as their neighbours.'[143]

IV. Religious life

The surviving correspondence of the merchants is largely concerned with their business activities and tends not to give any insight into the place of religion in

---

[135] Will of Samuel Davey, 1727 (NAI, Prerogative will book, 1726–8, MFGS 41/2, f. 339).

[136] Isaac Macartney to Messrs Cromie and Stevenson, 24 Mar. 1704/5 (PRONI, D501/1, p. 74); will of James Anderson, 1706 (NAI, Prerogative will book, 1706–8, MFGS 41/2, f. 24).

[137] John Watson, *Tables of exchange. In 2 Parts. Part Ist: English money exchanged into Irish; part 2nd Irish money exchanged into English* (Dublin, 1727).

[138] Antrim Pby Lib., B. 3. 2. 9.

[139] John Gay, *Poems on several occasions* (Dublin, 1729); Richardson Pack, *Miscellaneous works in verse and prose* (Dublin, 1726).

[140] [Tisdall], *Conduct of the Dissenters*, p. 24.

[141] Agrew, Merchant families, pp 39–40; Chancery brief and other documents relating to the case of William Macartney, son of Isaac Macartney (PRONI, Ellison-Macartney papers, D3649/5/1B).

[142] Codicil to will of John Galt, 1717 (PRONI, Maxwell Given papers, D2096/1/15D).

[143] [Kirkpatrick], *Presby. loyalty*, p. 436.

their lives.[144] Merchants could express their religious beliefs through attendance at church services and participation in the sacraments and ordinances of the church. Isaac Macartney, in a letter to Edward Brice, at Dublin, in February 1705, mentioned that he had seen Brice's wife and daughter at church in Belfast.[145] Daniel Mussenden kept a book of notes of sermons he had heard and recorded the topics of sermons given during communion celebrations.[146] Pews in churches were let to individuals and families in return for a fixed sum payable at certain times during the year, with the money contributing to the minister's stipend, and a number of merchants have recorded their payments in personal documents. William Rainey, the younger, of Belfast, for instance, noted in his diary in 1703 his purchase of half a pew in the meetinghouse, as well as the renewal of his covenant of faith before taking communion.[147] In 1698 John Black, senior, of Belfast, offered advice to his son, John, and encouraged him to:

> Shune all ocations of evill, hate lyinge swearing and Sabath breakinge; begin the day with puting up petitions to God for his blesinge on your lawfull endeavours; and end it with acknowledging such, begging mercy and thankfulnes for all his goodness. Observe your masters lawfull commands, from which withdraw not without leave. Your Christian and duetyfull cariage towards all will add much to oure comfort, whoe soe much wisheth you happines.

The young John Black had a copy of the *Confession of Faith, Directory, Larger and Shorter Catechism* with him in Dublin, 'with other good books' to help him in 'each duety', and should he have any spare time to read non-religious works, his father recommended reading certain historical books.[148] In 1698 David Butle ordered a bible covered with russet leather from Holland, and the Belfast merchant John McMun was among the subscribers to Wetenhall Wilkes's *Essay on the existence of a God*, published at Belfast in 1730 by the Presbyterian printer Robert Gardner.[149] The setting up of a printing press in Belfast had occurred in 1694 when the Presbyterian merchant, William Crawford, sovereign (mayor) of Belfast from 1693–4, invited Patrick Neill, a printer from Glasgow, to come over to the town. Crawford entered into partnership with Neill, and Neill was joined by his brother-in-law, James Blow, who acted as his assistant. The press appears to have been largely used for the publication of Presbyterian literature.[150]

---

144 An exception is the letters written by John Black of Belfast to his son, John Black, jr, which are full of religious advice: for instance, PRONI, Black papers, D4457/11 and /14.

145 Isaac Macartney to Edward Brice, 21 Feb. 1704/5 (PRONI, D501/1, pp 54–5).

146 Notebook of Daniel M[ussenden] containing sermons of Rev. John McBride and others, 1704, and details on Belfast communions, 1717–21 (PHS).

147 Extracts from William Rainey's diary, 12 & 21 Feb. 1702/3, 22 Aug. 1704 (LHL, Joy MS, 10).

148 John Black, sr, to John Black, jr, 8 Sept. 1698 (PRONI, Black papers, D4457/11).

149 David Butle to Alexander Adare, 31 Jan. 1697/8 (PRONI, D1449/13/1, p. 53); Wetenhall Wilkes, *An essay on the existence of a God* (Belfast, 1730).

150 Wesley McCann, 'Patrick Neill and the origins of Belfast printing' in Peter Isaac (ed.), *Six centuries of the provincial book trade in Britain* (Winchester, 1990), pp 125–38; J. R. H. Greeves, 'Two Irish printing families', *Proceedings of the Belfast Natural History and Philosophical Society*, 2nd ser., iv (1950–55), pp 38–44; A. S. Drennan, 'On the identification of the first Belfast printed book', *The Library*, 7th ser., i (2000), pp 193–6.

Leadership in the Presbyterian urban churches of Ulster was provided by mercantile families, with many of the leading merchants serving either as elders in the kirk session or attending the higher courts as commissioners on behalf of their congregation. Ruling elders in the Belfast Presbyterian congregations included the merchants James Arbuckle,[151] Edward Brice,[152] Henry Chads the elder,[153] John Eccles,[154] Isaac Macartney,[155] John McMun,[156] William Rainey the elder[157] and Robert Lenox.[158] Lenox's brother James Lenox was an elder at Derry,[159] as were Edward Brookes,[160] Hugh Davy,[161] Robert Harvey,[162] Horace Kennedy,[163] Henry Long[164] and Alexander Lecky.[165] In Coleraine, too, the merchants were active as members of the session and as commissioners, with the Austin,[166] Averell,[167] Bankhead,[168] Galt,[169] Leslie,[170] Thompson,[171] Todd[172] and Wylie[173] families all being represented. Although the majority of those chosen by the General Synod in 1706 to solicit subscriptions in the various presbyteries for a new missionary fund were largely drawn from gentry families, some merchants were also included, such as Henry Chads for Belfast Presbytery, John Thompson for Coleraine Presbytery and James Lenox for Londonderry Presbytery: RGSU, i, 115.

Some of the merchants remitted payments of *regium donum* to the Presbyterian ministers.[174] Thomas Crawford, a merchant and shipowner of Belfast, and an elder in the Belfast Presbyterian church, was treasurer of the *regium donum* from at least 1697 until his death in 1708, and in 1707 was appointed treasurer of the newly established General Fund, for the missionary activity of the Presbyterian

---

[151] *RGSU*, i, 289, 384, 483; ii, 3.
[152] Ibid., ii, 23, 73, 75, 80, 81.
[153] Antrim 'Meeting' mins (UTC, p. 244); *RGSU*, i, 7, 27, 75.
[154] *RGSU*, i, 515.
[155] Ibid., i, 167, 384; ii, 3.
[156] Reid, *Hist. of PCI*, iii, 213.
[157] *RGSU*, i, 16, 218.
[158] Reid, *Hist. of PCI*, iii, 213.
[159] Laggan Pby mins, 1690–1700 (PHS, pp 21, 68, 141); Sub-synod of Derry mins (PHS, pp 81, 175).
[160] Laggan Pby mins, 1690–1700 (PHS, p. 15a).
[161] Ibid., p. 18.
[162] Ibid., pp 11, 36, 121.
[163] Ibid., pp 9, 79, 175; Sub-synod of Derry mins (PHS, p. 109); *RGSU*, i, 195.
[164] Laggan Pby mins, 1690–1700 (PHS, p. 73).
[165] Ibid., p. 133.
[166] Route Pby mins (PHS, pp 244, 264, 272); *RGSU*, i, 117, 132.
[167] Antrim Pby mins, 1697–1713 (PHS, p. 226); Route Pby mins (PHS, p. 264).
[168] *RGSU*, i, 3, 27, 117–18; Route Pby mins (PHS, pp 64, 221, 240).
[169] *RGSU*, i, 3, 69, 174, 246; ii, 113; Route Pby mins (PHS, pp 30, 54, 64, 205, 240, 244, 264, 272); Antrim Pby mins, 1697–1713 (PHS, p. 220); Sub-synod of Derry mins (PHS, p. 150).
[170] *RGSU*, i, 7.
[171] Antrim Pby mins, 1697–1713 (PHS, p. 220); Route Pby mins (PHS, pp 153, 195, 214, 240, 272); *RGSU*, i, 414.
[172] Mullin, *Coleraine in Georgian times*, p. 144.
[173] Route Pby mins (PHS, pp 72, 81).
[174] Isaac Macartney to James Lenox, 11 June 1705 (PRONI, D501/1, pp 124–5); Samuel Harper to Robert Hutcheson, 21 Feb. 1722/3 (PRONI, Mussenden papers, D354/407).

church.[175] Thomas Crawford was also Belfast town clerk from 1690 to 1699, and was the brother of Rev. Andrew Crawford, minister of Carnmoney congregation, who from 1703 to 1721 was clerk of the General Synod of Ulster. Thomas and Andrew Crawford were the sons of Rev. Thomas Crawford, minister of Donegore, who died in 1670.[176] Following Thomas Crawford's death in 1708, he was succeeded as treasurer of the *regium donum*, and as treasurer for the General Fund, by another Belfast merchant and church elder, Brice Blair, a descendant of Rev. Edward Brice, the first Presbyterian minister to settle in Ireland.[177]

Other merchants had family connexions with Presbyterian ministers. Rev. John Haltridge of Islandmagee (1672–97) and Rev. Matthew Haltridge of Ahoghill (1676–1705) were brothers of the merchants William Haltridge of Dromore and Alexander Haltridge of Newry.[178] William Rainey the elder of Belfast had two sons who entered the ministry: Robert Rainey was the Presbyterian minister at Newry (1706–36), while another son, Daniel Rainey, was minister of the English Church at Amsterdam.[179] The closeness between the Presbyterian merchants and their ministers is further indicated by the bequests of money and mourning rings that many of the merchants left in their wills. William Haltridge of Dromore left £3 to his minister Rev. William Leggatt and Daniel Todd of Coleraine left £5 to Rev. Charles Lynd of New Row Presbyterian Church.[180]

Charity and poor relief were regarded as an important social and religious duty. The merchants showed support for the Presbyterian church with gifts and bequests. Edward Brice gave a set of six silver communion cups, with a Dublin hallmark of 1680, to the congregation of Ballycarry, where his grandfather had been the first minister, and David Smith of Belfast donated an expensively bound psalm book to the Presbyterian congregation of Belfast in 1705.[181] James Anderson of Belfast, in his will of 1706, bequeathed £20 towards the building of a new meetinghouse in Belfast 'for the poorer sort' and in a codicil to his will in December 1721 John Galt of Coleraine left £20 towards the ceiling and finishing of the meetinghouse at Coleraine.[182] New Row Presbyterian Church at Coleraine was built on land which belonged to the Twaddell family.[183] Though many of the merchants left money to

---

175 *RGSU*, i, 26, 124, 137, 155.

176 Young, *Belfast town book*, pp 168, 170–1, 188, 191; *RGSU*, i, 87, 89.

177 *RGSU*, i, 91, 141, 156–7, 167, 178, 181–2, 208, 346, 355; ii, 11; 'The Rev. Edward Brice of Broadisland and his descendants' in *McComb's Almanack* (1859), p. 68.

178 Agnew, *Merchant families*, pp 255–6.

179 McConnell, *Fasti*, p. 120; notes on the Rainey family (LHL, Joy MS, 10); grant and conveyance of land in the Lordship of Newry from Robert Nedham, jr, to Rev. Daniel Rainey, 12 Dec. 1732 (Newry & Mourne Museum, Reside collection, NMM:2003.7.A.13.006–007); Agnew, *Merchant families*, p. 243.

180 Abstract will of William Haltridge, 1691 (PRONI, Stewart papers, D1759/3/B/1, p. 34); abstract will of Daniel Todd, 1737 (ibid., Groves papers, T808/14132).

181 *HIP*, iii, 263; [Alexander Gordon], *Historic memorials of the First Presbyterian Church of Belfast prepared in connection with the centennial of its present meeting-house* (Belfast, 1887), p. 14. The psalm book was bound in tortoise-shell and silver.

182 Will of James Anderson, 1706 (NAI, Prerogative will book, 1704–8, MFGS 41/2, ff 24–5); codicil to will of John Galt, 1721 (PRONI, D2096/1/15D).

183 Mullin, *Coleraine in Georgian times*, p. 127.

the poor in their wills, the amounts were often small. Most bequeathed £5 or less, though Hugh Eccles left £40 to the poor of the parish of Belfast in 1680 and Hugh Rainey, a merchant of Magherafelt and an elder in the congregation of Dawson's Bridge, left detailed instructions for the endowment of a school for poor children at Magherafelt.[184] The merchants also collected money for seamen and passengers who had been captured at sea, such as for John Whitehead of Belfast who was captured by the Turks. The money collected for Whitehead in the Route Presbytery was lodged for a time in the hands of the Coleraine merchant John Galt and when collections were made for the relief of the 'Algerine slaves', that is, seamen captured by north African privateers, George Macartney's letters suggest he co-ordinated the Belfast collections in the early 1680s.[185]

The Ulster and Scottish business connexions of the Belfast Presbyterian merchant Samuel Smith were instrumental in the erection of the Third Presbyterian congregation of Belfast. Smith, a member and elder in the First congregation, had scruples about the installation of the non-subscribing minister, Samuel Haliday, and in 1722 and 1723 made two trips to Scotland to collect money for the establishment of a subscribing congregation in Belfast. Among those in Scotland who gave support to Smith's efforts were the synods of Ayr and Glasgow, the provost of Edinburgh, the countess of Stair, the earl of Atholl and the earl of Buchan. Within Ulster Smith received support from the Crommelin family of Lisburn and their Huguenot pastor, Monsieur Le Vallade, and from Aldermen Brookes and Mackey, Joseph Morrison, Robert Harvey and Captain Cunningham of Derry. Almost £1,300 was collected and in recognition of the support from Scotland three of the pews in the new church were reserved free of rent 'for ever' for Scottish sailors, merchants and shipmasters 'in regard that the good people in that country did contribute largely to the building of the meeting house'.[186]

In 1714 Smith's son, Samuel Smith, junior, and Joseph Kyle, both of Belfast, were prosecuted for being married according to the Presbyterian form. The General Synod urged them not to submit to remarriage according to the form of the established church, and pledged to cover their legal expenses. Notably the General Synod was forced to renege on this pledge to pay Smith and Kyle's legal expenses when ordinary Presbyterians in some congregations objected to money being given to such wealthy individuals.[187] The outcome of the case is unknown, though the position of Presbyterians in Ireland changed as a result of the death

---

[184] Agnew, *Merchant families*, pp 67–8, 209, 216, 238, 255; will of Hugh Eccles, 1680 (PRONI, Clarke papers, MIC92/1); Dawson's Bridge (Castledawson) sess. mins, 26 Nov., 31 Dec. 1703, 14 & 26 Jan., 25 Feb., 13 Mar. 1703/4 (PRONI, MIC1P/450C/1, pp 1–3, 5–7); will of Hugh Rainey, 1707 (NAI, Prerogative will book, 1706–8, MFGS 41/2, ff 212–14); private act of parliament settling Hugh Rainey's estate (PRONI, T67/1); *An account of charity-schools in Great Britain and Ireland, with the benefactions thereto* (London, 1711), p. 47; Witherow, *Two diaries of Derry in 1689*, pp xv–xvi.

[185] *RGSU*, i, 68, 109; [J. W.] K[ernohan], 'Presbyterian Historical Society: the Synod of Ulster and Turkey', *Irish Presbyterian*, new ser., xix, no. 1 (Jan. 1913), p. 25; Agnew, *Merchant families*, p. 68.

[186] Third Belfast Presbyterian Church building book (PRONI, MIC1P/7/8, pp 10–13); Third Belfast (Rosemary Street) Presbyterian Church treasurer's book and pew register, 1726 (ibid., T654/6, pp 107–8); Kernohan, *Rosemary Street Presbyterian Church*, pp 12–21.

[187] *RGSU*, i, 336, 404, 436–7.

of Queen Anne on 1 August 1714 when Tory ministers were replaced by Whigs. The fact that Presbyterian marriage was not recognised by the ecclesiastical courts that controlled probate may have been a factor in causing some wealthy Presbyterian families to conform to the Church of Ireland. This has already been discussed in the previous chapter in relation to the gentry, but members of some mercantile families also conformed. Although 'Black' George Macartney changed from the Church of Ireland to the Presbyterian church,[188] most of those who switched denominational allegiance moved in the other direction. Dr James Macartney, a son of the Belfast Presbyterian merchant, 'Brown' George Macartney, was a conformist and John Averell, the son of the Coleraine Presbyterian merchant Nicholas Averell, was educated at Trinity College and became bishop of Limerick.[189] Sir John Eccles, the son of a Presbyterian merchant of Belfast, was a conformist, but his second wife was a Presbyterian.[190] As with the gentry, conformity did not necessarily lead immediately to a total break with Presbyterianism.

* * * * * * *

Presbyterians were strongly represented in the mercantile elites of most Ulster towns, particularly Derry and Newry, and in the case of Belfast were in the majority by the late seventeenth century. Most of the Presbyterian merchants who operated in Ulster were of Scottish origin and had settled in Ulster during the course of the seventeenth century. Some maintained a connexion with Scotland through business activities and family relations. Connexions were important to merchants and by the early eighteenth century many of the correspondents of the Belfast merchants were from either Ulster or Scotland. The merchants of Ulster were engaged in the export of agricultural surpluses, though the economic fortunes of the merchants varied from individual to individual and from port to port. Trade was seasonal in nature and merchants had to cope with difficulties arising from persistent warfare, embargoes, privateers and shipwreck. Some merchants were engaged in other economic ventures or town improvements and many of the leading merchants were landowners, some moving easily within the ranks of the Presbyterian gentry. Like some of the younger generation of the gentry families, the descendants of certain Presbyterian merchant aldermen and burgesses of Belfast, Coleraine and Derry conformed in the long-term and relocated themselves within the establishment. The scale, however, was not as large as for the Presbyterian gentry, and like the gentry conformity was in most cases not immediate upon the enforcement of the test. Merchants provided social leadership in their locality, serving not only as burgesses but also as elders and commissioners for the congregations they attended.

---

188 [Kirkpatrick], *Presby. loyalty*, p. 436.
189 Agnew, *Merchant families*, pp 257–8; Mullin, *Coleraine in Georgian times*, p. 189.
190 Agnew, *Merchant families*, p. 224.

4

The Professions

This chapter will consider Presbyterian involvement in the professions of law and medicine. There is now an extensive literature on the professions in early modern England,[1] and historians such as Toby Barnard and Patrick Fagan have explored aspects, respectively, of Protestant and Catholic involvement in the professions in Ireland.[2] Traditionally studies of the Irish legal profession have focused on the senior law officers and judges, but in 2000 Hazel Maynard completed an informative thesis which has widened our knowledge by exploring the backgrounds and careers of the Irish members who attended the English Inns of Court during the 40 years after the Restoration.[3] I hope to build on, and extend, Maynard's work by looking at the involvement of Presbyterians in the legal profession not only in the late seventeenth century but also after 1700, particularly considering the impact of the sacramental test enacted in 1704. Irish medical historiography has tended to focus on the lives of a few notable or exceptional practitioners or on the history of particular hospitals or institutions, such as the Irish Royal College of Physicians.[4] Much of what has been written has focused on Dublin and, with the exception of

---

1   Geoffrey Holmes, *Augustan England: professions, state and society, 1680–1730* (London, 1982); Wilfrid Prest (ed.), *The professions in early modern England* (London, 1987); P. J. Corfield, *Power and the professions in Britain 1700–1850* (London, 1995); Rosemary O'Day, *The professions in early modern England, 1450–1800: servants of the commonweal* (Harlow, 2000); Robert Robson, *The attorney in eighteenth-century England* (Cambridge, 1959); Wilfrid Prest (ed.), *Lawyers in early modern Europe and America* (London, [1981]); David Lemmings, *Gentlemen and barristers: the Inns of Court and the English bar 1680–1730* (Oxford, 1990); idem, *Professors of the law: barristers and English legal culture in the eighteenth century* (Oxford, 2000); Bernice Hamilton, 'The medical professions in the eighteenth century', *Economic History Review*, new ser., iv (1951), pp 141–69; R. S. Roberts, 'The personnel and practice of medicine in Tudor and Stuart England', *Medical History*, vi (1962), pp 363–82; viii (1964), pp 217–34.
2   Barnard, *New anatomy*, pp 115–42; Patrick Fagan, *Catholics in a Protestant country: trades and professions in eighteenth-century Dublin* (Dublin, 1998), pp 77–125.
3   F. E. Ball, *The judges in Ireland, 1221–1921* (London, 1926); A. R. Hart, *A history of the king's serjeants at law in Ireland: honour rather than advantage?* (Dublin, 2000); Hazel Maynard, 'Irish membership of the English Inns of Court, 1660–1699: lawyers, litigation and the legal profession' (Ph.D. thesis, University College, Dublin, 2000).
4   T. W. Belcher, *Memoir of Sir Patrick Dun* (2nd ed., Dublin, 1866); E. St John Brooks, *Sir Hans Sloane: the great collector and his circle* (London, 1954); J. D. H. Widdess, *The Charitable Infirmary, Jervis Street, 1718–1968* (Dublin, [1968]); Eoin O'Brien (ed.), *The Charitable Infirmary, Jervis Street, 1718–1987* (Dublin, 1987); J. B. Lyons, *The quality of Mercer's: the story of Mercer's Hospital, 1734–1991* ([Dublin], 1991); O'D. T. D. Browne, *The Rotunda Hospital, 1745–1945* (Edinburgh, 1947); I. C. Ross (ed.), *Public virtue, public love: the early years of the Dublin Lying-In Hospital, the Rotunda* (Dublin, 1986); T. P. C. Kirkpatrick, *The history of Doctor Steevens' Hospital, Dublin, 1720–1920* (Dublin, 1924); Elizabeth Malcolm, *Swift's Hospital: a history of St Patrick's Hospital Dublin, 1746–1989* (Dublin, 1989); J. D. H. Widdess, *A history of the Royal College of Physicians of Ireland 1654–1963* (Edinburgh, 1963).

brief references to Dr Victor Ferguson of Belfast in Barnard's *New anatomy*,[5] there has been no exploration of Presbyterian involvement in medicine or even how the inhabitants of Ulster received medical treatment. The issue of Presbyterians and medicine, therefore, is one that requires attention. This chapter will deal separately with the two groups – lawyers and medical practitioners – but will look at similar themes, such as their social background, education and training, the nature of their work, their wealth and standing in the community, and the importance of their religious faith. Geoffrey Holmes has argued that the professions provided a primary, and unique, method of social mobility in early modern England,[6] and I will consider how far the legal and medical professions provided routes for social advancement among Ulster Presbyterians.

I. The Law

Members of the legal profession were divided between two branches that differed according to the nature of their training and the work that they undertook. Barristers qualified by attending one of the Inns of Court in England, and the King's Inns in Dublin, while attorneys usually trained by serving an apprenticeship to an attorney or clerk. Barristers constituted the upper echelon of the profession. They alone had the privilege of pleading cases in the courts and it was from their ranks that judges were chosen. The work of the attorneys was more mechanical and involved tasks such as drafting wills, marriage settlements, or executing deeds and tenancies. In practice the division was not always clear-cut, as barristers could, in addition to their advocacy in the courts, be engaged in the non-litigious activities that were more usually associated with the attorneys.

Ia. Social background and training

Entry to the Irish bar was controlled by King's Inns in Dublin. King's Inns was established in 1541, and membership was required in order to plead in Irish courts but no tuition was provided. Law in Ireland followed the English model, and was based on parliamentary statute and interpretation of case law. In contrast, Scotland retained its own distinctive system of law, based on Roman law, which meant that those wishing to practise at the Irish bar could not be trained in Scotland.[7] As a result of the Statute of Jeofailles (1542) anyone wishing to be called to the Irish bar had first to spend at least five years at an English inn.[8] The admission records of King's Inns are incomplete, with admissions from the late seventeenth century among those

---

5   Barnard, *New anatomy*, pp 129, 135–6.
6   Geoffrey Holmes, 'The professions and social change in England, 1680–1730', *Proceedings of the British Academy*, lxv (1979), pp 313–54.
7   T. C. Barnard, 'Lawyers and the law in later seventeenth-century Ireland', *Irish Historical Studies*, xxviii (1993), p. 259.
8   33 Henry VIII, c. 3 (*The statutes at large, passed in the parliaments held in Ireland* (20 vols,

which are now lost,[9] so they cannot be used to provide a reliable indication of the numbers admitted to the Irish bar. By using the admission records of the English Inns[10] along with the defective records of King's Inns we can obtain some idea of the numbers entering the upper branch of the Irish legal profession during the period. Maynard's research identified approximately 700 Irishmen entering the English Inns between 1660 and 1699.[11] Middle Temple was the most popular among the Irish students, attracting 42%, while 27% were admitted to Inner Temple, 20% to Gray's Inn and 11% to Lincoln's Inn.[12]

Students from Ulster Presbyterian families formed a very small proportion of the Irish students entering the English Inns. Only 20 entrants between 1660 and 1699 can be identified as coming from Ulster Presbyterian families.[13] In this period, therefore, Presbyterians from Ulster formed between 2% and 3% of the total Irish membership at the English Inns, and about a fifth of the entrants from Ulster.[14] No Ulster Presbyterian attended Gray's Inn and only one was admitted to Lincoln's Inn. Most (13) attended the Inner Temple, and a further six the Middle Temple. Sending sons to one of the English Inns was expensive and could cost, it has been estimated, between £1,000 and £1,500.[15] Sir Richard Cox, the elder, reckoned the Inner Temple the cheapest option out of the four Inns,[16] and that may have been why it was favoured by the Ulster Presbyterians. As we saw in chapter 2, the Presbyterian gentry in Ulster were limited in number and, by the late seventeenth century, few of the landed families of Ulster were Presbyterian. Most of the students entering the English Inns were drawn from the upper levels of society,[17] and the fact that this socio-economic group was restricted in number among the Ulster Presbyterians helps explain why they formed such a small proportion of the students being admitted to the English Inns.

1786–1804), i, 209–11); Black Book of King's Inns, Dublin, 12 Jan. 1683 (King's Inns, Dublin: microfilm, NLI, P.4909, f. 267); Barnard, 'Lawyers & the law', p. 259.

9 Edward Keane, et al. (eds), *King's Inns admission papers 1607–1867* (Dublin, 1982); Colum Kenny, 'The records of King's Inns, Dublin' in Dáire Hogan and W. N. Osborough (eds), *Brehons, serjeants and attorneys* (Dublin, 1990), pp 233–5, 242–4.

10 *Lincoln's Inn admission register, 1420–1799* (London, 1896); H. A. C. Sturgess (comp.), *Register of admissions to The Honorable Society of the Middle Temple* (3 vols, London, 1949); *The register of admissions to Gray's Inn, 1521–1889* (London, 1889). The record of admissions to Inner Temple can be searched online at: http://www.innertemplearchives.org.uk/index.asp. A list of all the Irish members at the English Inns of Court during the period 1660–99 is given in Maynard, 'Irish membership of the English Inns', pp 384–404.

11 Maynard, 'Irish membership of the English Inns', p. 2.

12 Ibid., p. 380; see also Barnard, 'Lawyers & the law', p. 121.

13 Based on an analysis of the admission records of the English Inns. I have not included John Ross from Co. Down, who entered Inner Temple in 1677, as there were a number of different Ross families in Co. Down, some of which were Presbyterian, while others were members of the established church.

14 Based on calculations against Maynard's statistics for Ulster and Irish members at the English Inns: Maynard, 'Irish membership of the English Inns', p. 2.

15 Barnard, *New anatomy*, p. 118; Peter Earle, *The making of the English middle class: business, society and family life in London, 1660–1730* (London, 1989), p. 61.

16 Barnard, *New anatomy*, p. 121.

17 Lemmings, *Gentlemen & barristers*, pp 11–14; O'Day, *The professions*, pp 136, 142, 149.

All Ulster Presbyterian students attending the English Inns came from gentry or armigerous backgrounds. The majority (14) came from County Antrim. Sir Hercules Langford (1626–83) of Belfast and Kilmackevett, County Antrim, and also of Summerhill, County Meath, sent three sons to the English Inns. His eldest son and heir, Arthur Langford (c.1652–1716), was admitted to Lincoln's Inn in 1671, after having previously studied at Trinity College in Dublin. His second son, Henry (c.1656–1725), entered the Middle Temple in 1677. The third, Theophilus, was accompanied by his cousin, Clotworthy Upton (1655–1725), to the Middle Temple, where they were both admitted in 1685.[18] Clotworthy was the fourth, but eldest surviving, son of the M.P. Arthur Upton (1623–1706) of Castle Upton, Templepatrick. His younger brother, Thomas (1677–1733), followed him to the Middle Temple, in 1700.[19] The Langfords and Uptons were both of English origin and another Presbyterian family of English origin which sent more than one member to the English Inns of Court was the Dalway family of Bellahill, Carrickfergus. Robert Dalway of Norsellstone, Carrickfergus, was admitted to Inner Temple, along with his nephew John Dalway of Bellahill, in 1677. Following John's death, without issue, in 1687, Robert succeeded to the estate at Bellahill. Two of Robert's sons followed him to the Inner Temple; the eldest, Alexander, in 1693 and the second, Henry, in 1697.[20] Both had previously studied at Trinity.[21]

The other Presbyterian students who came from County Antrim were of Scottish origin and all attended the Inner Temple. They included James Donaldson of Glenarm, who entered in 1671, John Butle of Glenarm (1673), James Donaldson of Bay, near Glenarm (1675) and Robert Adair of Ballymena (1678).[22] Archibald Adair, who entered the Inner Temple in 1695, was the third son of Rev. Patrick Adair (1624–94), the Presbyterian minister of Belfast. He too could be classed as coming from a gentry background as Rev. Patrick Adair was a relative of the

18 *Lincoln's Inn admission register*, p. 311; G. D. Burtchaell and T. U. Sadleir (eds), *Alumni Dublinenses* (new ed., Dublin, 1935), p. 481; *Middle Temple adm. reg.*, i, 196, 214; *HIP*, v, 56–7; G. E. C[okayne], *Complete baronetage* (5 vols, Exeter, 1900–4), iv, 205; Maynard, 'Irish membership of the English Inns', p. 214; *DIB* (Langford, Sir Arthur). Theophilus Langford predeceased his two older brothers, his will being proved in 1713: will of Theophilus Langford, 18 Sept. 1712 (National Archives, Kew, Prerogative Court of Canterbury wills, PROB 11/535).

19 W. H. Upton, *Upton family records: being genealogical collections for an Upton family history* (London, 1893), pp 110–11; *HIP*, vi, 454–6; *Middle Temple adm. reg.*, i, 246; Maynard, 'Irish membership of the English Inns', p. 214; *ODNB* (Upton, Arthur); *DIB* (Upton, Arthur (1623–1706)). The Langfords, however, were moderates in their Presbyterianism: see above, p. 64, n. 41.

20 Sir Bernard Burke, *A genealogical and heraldic dictionary of the landed gentry of Great Britain and Ireland* (4th ed., London, 1863), p. 333; Samuel McSkimin, *The history and antiquities of the county of the town of Carrickfergus*, ed. E. J. McCrum (new ed., Belfast, 1909), p. 474–7; Maynard, 'Irish membership of the English Inns', pp 212–13, 399, 403–4. Maynard mistakenly describes Robert and John Dalway as brothers.

21 Burtchaell & Sadleir, *Alumni Dublinenses*, p. 207.

22 Maynard, 'Irish Membership of the English Inns', pp 214–15, 399; 'The Inner Temple admissions database' (http://www.innertemplearchives.org.uk/index.asp) (28 June 2013); Agnew, *Merchant families*, pp 12, 215. For the history of the Donaldson family in Co. Antrim see: George Hill, *An historical account of the MacDonnells of Antrim* (Belfast, 1873), p. 362, n. 18 and H. C. Lawlor, 'Historical sketch of old Glenarm', *Weekly Telegraph*, 25 Mar., 1 Apr. 1911.

Adairs of Ballymena.[23] The three Presbyterian students supplied by County Down all attended Inner Temple. They were William Fairlie of Killyleagh (in 1676), Hans Trail of Drumnaconnor, near Killyleagh (1677) and John Shaw of Ballyganaway, Donaghadee (1695).[24] The two students of Presbyterian background from County Fermanagh were father and son Daniel and Gilbert Eccles, who were admitted to Inner Temple in 1670 and 1693 respectively, and who were connected to the Belfast merchant family of the same name.[25] The remaining Presbyterian student attending the English Inns during the period 1660–1700 was David Cairnes, second surviving son of David Cairnes, of Knockmany, County Tyrone, who was admitted to Middle Temple in 1668.[26] Between 1700 and 1704 only one Presbyterian student entered the English Inns, Archibald Edmonstone of Redhall, Ballycarry, later M.P. for Carrickfergus, who was admitted to Middle Temple in December 1700.[27]

In the later seventeenth century the English Inns provided only a very basic, and somewhat haphazard, formal training to those who wished to become barristers.[28] In the early part of the century training had centred around public lectures (called readings) and moots.[29] The readings were given by the benchers to the student members of the Inns and the moots involved 'mock trials' or discussion of a hypothetical case by the law students so that they could develop skills that would be useful to them in their future careers. Public lectures were not given after 1684 and in fact many of the practising barristers no longer continued to reside or eat at the Inns.[30] There was still some opportunity for students to engage in oral exercises, even into the early eighteenth century, though these had become mere formalities and were not taken seriously by the students. Some of the certificates in the Black Books of King's Inns, belonging to students seeking admittance to King's Inns

---

[23] Maynard, 'Irish members at the English Inns', pp 217, 403; 'The Inner Temple admissions database'; ODNB (Adair, Patrick); McConnell, Fasti, p. 4; Classon Porter, 'Congregational memoirs: no. IV – Cairncastle', Christian Unitarian, iv (1866), p. 190.

[24] Maynard, 'Irish membership at the English Inns', pp 222, 399, 403; 'The Inner Temple admissions database'; David Stewart, The story of Kilmore Presbyterian Church (Belfast, 1932), p. 19; 'Shaw' in 'Notes on families and places mostly in the eastern part of Co. Down', comp. Rev. David Stewart, 1938 (PRONI, Stewart papers, D1759/3/A/1, p. 17).

[25] Maynard, 'Irish membership of the English Inns', pp 231, 398, 403; 'The Inner Temple admissions database'; H. B. Swanzy, 'The Eccles family', UJA, ix (1903), p. 144; extract from Sir Robert Douglas's 'History of the Eccles family' (PRONI, D2081/2/1). By the eighteenth century some branches of the Eccles family had conformed to the Church of Ireland: Agnew, Merchant families, pp 223–5.

[26] Maynard, 'Irish membership of the English Inns', pp 226–7, 385; Middle Temple adm. reg., i, 20; HIP, iii, 358; H. C. Lawlor, A history of the family of Cairnes or Cairns and its connections (London, 1906), pp 109, 144; ODNB (Cairnes, David). In the Middle Temple admission register David Cairnes is stated to be the son of John Cairnes of Parsonstown. This, however, must be incorrect as according to the family history by H. C. Lawlor David's father was David Cairnes of Knockmany. John Cairnes was the father of David Cairnes, jr's, cousins William, Sir Alexander and Sir Henry Cairnes.

[27] HIP, iv, 107; Middle Temple adm. reg., i, 249.

[28] Barnard, 'Lawyers & the law', p. 260; O'Day, The professions, p. 149; Paul Lucas, 'A collective biography of students and barristers of Lincoln's Inn, 1680–1804: a study in the "aristocratic resurgence" of the eighteenth century', Journal of Modern History, xlvi, no. 2 (1974), pp 227–8.

[29] Lemmings, Gentlemen & barristers, p. 75.

[30] Ibid., pp 25, 40.

in 1674–9 and 1704–5, refer to exercises performed by the students while at the English Inns.[31] In the main, however, students were left to their own devices and taught themselves through reading legal textbooks, law digests and the statutes.[32] Irish students had the additional burden of having to familiarise themselves with the statutes of the Irish parliament, which did not apply in England.[33] By the time Robert Dalway wrote his will in 1699 he had acquired a number of law books, which he bequeathed to his son Alexander who had also been at the Inner Temple.[34] The library of the Presbytery of Antrim has a volume of Irish statutes which had belonged to Thomas Upton. Though these may have been intended by Upton to help him in his legal practice, they may equally have been acquired because of his activity as a member of the Irish parliament.[35] While at the Inns students were encouraged to attend the courts at Westminster to observe procedure, and opportunities were available for conscientious students, who wished to avail of it, to discuss what they observed in the courts or read in their private studies. This was a useful means of correcting errors or inaccuracies in their knowledge and helped develop fluency of speech and skill in public speaking.[36] After five years spent in this way an Irish student was able to apply to be admitted as a member of King's Inns in Dublin, and thus enter the Irish bar. Some students, however, remained a further two years at the English Inns in order to be called to the English bar.[37]

The students who entered the Inns were not all intent on pursuing a legal career. Instead some attended to receive a 'gentlemanly' and social education that would prepare them, it was thought, for a future role as a justice of the peace or Member of Parliament.[38] It is necessary, therefore, to make a distinction between non-professional students and those who were serious about making the law their career. This distinction can by made by looking at the records of the Inns to see whether a student was called to the bar and also by looking at the records of the Irish chancery court, the only Irish court for which records survive, to see which of them practised in Ireland. This double check is necessary because not all those called to the bar went on to practise.[39] Of the 21 Ulster Presbyterian students between 1660 and 1704 only six went on to pursue a legal career: David Cairnes (called 1673),[40] Hans

---

[31] Ibid., p. 25; Black Book of King's Inns, Dublin (King's Inns, Dublin: microfilm, NLI, P.4909, ff 48–52, 321–3); Kenny, *King's Inns*, p. 160.

[32] Lemmings, *Gentlemen & barristers*, p. 98.

[33] Barnard, 'Lawyers & the law', p. 260.

[34] Will of Robert Dalway, 1699 (PRONI, Castle Stewart papers, D1618/8/5).

[35] Antrim Pby Lib., B. 2. 7. 16; *HIP*, vi, 456–7; idem, *Professors of the law*, pp 131, 141.

[36] Lemmings, *Gentleman & barristers*, p. 107; idem, *Professors of the law*, pp 131, 141.

[37] Generally students had to spend seven years at an English inn to be eligible for a call to the English bar, but from 1682 to 1688 Middle Temple reduced this to six years: Lemmings, *Gentlemen & barristers*, pp 63, 262.

[38] Lemmings, *Gentlemen & barristers*, p. 8; Maynard, 'Irish membership at the English Inns', p. 3; E. M. Johnston-Liik, *MPs in Dublin: companion to the history of parliament 1692–1800* (Belfast, 2006), p. 27.

[39] Corfield, *Power & the professions*, pp 88, 90.

[40] Black Book of King's Inns, Dublin (King's Inns, Dublin: microfilm, NLI, P.4909, f. 167); Keane, et al., *King's Inns admission papers*, p. 71.

Trail,[41] Henry Langford (called 1682),[42] Robert Dalway (called 1684),[43] Theophilus Langford (called 1694)[44] and Thomas Upton (called 1704).[45]

In the spring of 1704 the Irish parliament passed an act 'to prevent the further growth of popery', which included a clause imposing a sacramental test on all those holding any public office under the crown.[46] The test subsequently became a measure of fitness to practise at the Irish bar. In May 1704 an entry recorded in the Black Book of King's Inns declared that:

> It is this day ordered that noe person be admitted to the barr and practice as barrister untill he shall produce an authentique certificate of his receiveing the sacrament according to the useage of the Church of Ireland as by law established before his said admittance pursuant to the late act.[47]

This new regulation meant that in future any Presbyterians who wished to enter the upper branch of the legal profession, and be called to the bar, had either to conform to the established church or at least receive the sacrament of communion once a year in the Church of Ireland.

Only five of the members admitted to the English Inns of Court between 1704 and 1730 had Presbyterian fathers from Ulster.[48] All attended the Middle Temple. They were Randolph (Randal) Brice of Lisburn, son of the late M.P. of Lisburn of the same name, who entered in 1710; Alexander Henderson, fourth son of John Henderson, of Donoughmore, County Donegal, who entered in 1714; James Blackwood, second son of John Blackwood, of Ballyleidy, County Down, who entered in 1715; James Stevenson, son and heir of Hans Stevenson, of Killyleagh, County Down, who entered in 1721; and Alexander McAulay (or Macaulay), son and heir of Alexander McAulay, of Drumnegessen, near Coleraine, County Antrim, who entered in 1722.[49] Only two out of the four – James Blackwood and Alexander McAulay – were called to the Irish bar, in 1721 and 1729 respectively,

---

[41] The exact date Trail was called to the bar is unknown, but he first appeared in the Irish court of chancery in 1683: chancery bill books, viii, 1677–1682 (NAI, MFGS 57/002, f. 142).

[42] T. C. Martin (ed.), *Minutes of parliament of the Middle Temple*, iii: *1650–1703* (London, 1905), p. 1346.

[43] Massereene to Secretary Jenkins, 23 Feb. & 20 June 1683 (*CSPD, 1683*, pp 74, 332); Jenkins to Massereene, 5 May 1683 (ibid., p. 234); *A calendar of the Inner Temple records*, ed. F. A. Inderwick, iii: *12 Charles II. (1660)–12 Anne (1714)* (London, 1901), pp 205, 209.

[44] *Minutes of parliament of the Middle Temple*, iii, 1423.

[45] Keane, *King's Inns admission papers*, p. 488; 'An alphabetical list of members of King's Inns' (NAI, MFS/42/10). One of the James Donaldsons educated at Inner Temple may also have become a barrister as a James Donaldson appeared in the Irish court of chancery in Trinity term 1682 and Michaelmas term 1684: chancery bill books, ix, 1682–7 (NAI, MFGS 57/002, ff 18, 143).

[46] J. G. Simms, 'The making of a penal law (2 Anne, c. 6), 1703–4', *Irish Historical Studies*, xii (1960), pp 105–18.

[47] Black Book of King's Inns, Dublin (King's Inns, Dublin: microfilm, NLI, P.4909, f. 322); B. T. Duhigg, *History of the King's Inns; or, an account of the legal body in Ireland, from its connexion with England* (Dublin, 1806), p. 258; Kenny, *King's Inns*, pp 163–4.

[48] This does not include Daniel Eccles of Fintona, Co. Tyrone, who entered Middle Temple in June 1717: *Middle Temple adm. reg.*, i, 279. The Eccles, originally Presbyterian, later conformed.

[49] *Middle Temple adm. reg.*, i, 266, 274–5, 289, 291. Though Hans Stevenson (d. 1713) was a Presbyterian, his son James was a conformist.

and these two were therefore obliged to conform, either fully or occasionally, to the Church of Ireland.[50] Alexander McAulay is known to have been a full conformist, as in surviving lists of the gentry in Ulster in the mid-1720s and early 1730s it is stated that the eldest son of Alexander McAulay, senior, was, unlike his father, a Churchman.[51] The younger Alexander actually became a leading ecclesiastical lawyer. He was vicar-general of Ossory, a judge of the consistorial court of Dublin from 1746 until his death in 1766, and from 1751 was governor of Erasmus Smith's schools and other charities. He owed the offices he held to the established church and endeavoured to support the established clergy over the unpopular issue of tithes. In 1763 he published a pamphlet in support of the clergy's claims to tithes, under the title *A treatise on tillage and property inviolable*.[52]

Ib. Legal practice and income

Any study of legal practice in Ireland is hampered by the destruction of many of the relevant court records during a fire at the Irish Public Record Office in 1922, with the records of the courts of king's bench, common pleas and exchequer all being destroyed. The only court for which original records survive, in any extent, is the court of chancery, for which bill books are available in the National Archives of Ireland.[53] The six Ulster Presbyterian barristers were all, except Theophilus Langford, active in the court of chancery. It is possible that Theophilus was active in one of the other courts for which records do not survive, and as barristers did not usually specialise in advocacy in a particular court,[54] the other five barristers may have also been active in one or more of the other courts as well.

David Cairnes was the first of the six Presbyterian lawyers to qualify, and was active in the Irish court of chancery from the late 1670s. He was joined there by Hans Trail in 1683, Robert Dalway and Henry Langford in 1687, and Thomas Upton in 1705.[55] Most of the clients the Presbyterian barristers represented in the court of chancery came from Ulster, and it would appear that in the setting up of a legal practice, family relations and neighbours were often an important source of business. Henry Langford, for instance, represented his brother Arthur Langford in 1687–8 in cases against Sir Neale O'Neale, Anne Burley and John, Viscount Massereene.[56] The disputes between the Hamiltons over the Clanbrassil inheritance

---

[50] Keane, *King's Inns admission papers*, pp 38, 300; Arthur Dobbs to Alexander McAulay, 22 June 1732 (PRONI, D162/26).

[51] List of the gentlemen of Co. Down and Co. Antrim (Royal Irish Academy, Dublin, Upton papers, MS 24.K.19, no. 1); list of the nobility and gentry of Ulster (Lambeth Palace Lib., Gibson papers, MS 1742, f. 50).

[52] George Hill, 'Gleanings in family history from the Antrim coast', *UJA*, viii (1860), p. 201; *HIP*, v, 162.

[53] Chancery bill books, viii–xviii, 1677–1722 (NAI, MFGS 57/002–6).

[54] Barnard, 'Lawyers & the law', p. 263.

[55] Chancery bill books, ix, 1682–7 (NAI, MFGS 57/002, ff 83 (Trail), 138 (Dalway)); ibid., x, 1687–92 (ibid., MFGS 57/003, f. 7 (Langford)); ibid., xiii, 1701–05 (ibid., MFGS 57/004, f. 422 (Upton)); Maynard, 'Irish membership at the English Inns', p. 226.

[56] Chancery bill books, x, 1687–92 (NAI, MFGS 57/003, ff 7, 28, 31, 44, 77).

in County Down provided ample case work for a number of barristers in the court of chancery, including the Presbyterian barristers Robert Dalway, Henry Langford and Hans Trail.[57] Trail was connected to the Hamiltons through his mother, Mary, who was the daughter of John Hamilton of Hamilton's Bawn, County Armagh.[58]

David Cairnes, born in 1645, was one of the sons of David Cairnes of Knockmany, County Tyrone. By 1680 he had set up legal practice in Derry, splitting his time between Derry, Knockmany and Dublin, where he was engaged in advocacy in the courts and present as a member of the Irish parliament, representing Derry between 1692 and 1699.[59] Cairnes was elected a burgess of Derry in 1680 and played a key role during the siege of the city.[60] He was agent for the Irish Society in Derry and in 1690–1 made several journeys to London in relation to Derry city and its recovery after the siege. While in London he had his portrait painted, reputedly by Kneller, which says something of his wealth and success or, at least, of his view of himself.[61] In the Irish chancery court Cairnes represented the London Society on a number of occasions, including legal disputes with William King, bishop of Derry, over lands and fishery rights.[62] Henry Langford, interestingly, acted as counsel to King in the dispute with the Irish Society and was legal adviser to King on the Act of Resumption in 1700. The Langfords, however, had always been more moderate in their Presbyterianism.[63]

In addition to work provided at the central law courts in Dublin, there were also opportunities nearer home, provided by assizes and quarter sessions, as well as manor courts and borough courts. Recorderships in corporation boroughs were often a useful supplement to incomes. David Cairnes was appointed recorder of Derry in 1691,[64] and Thomas Upton held the same position from 1707 until his death in 1733.[65] In the early 1700s the Presbyterian barrister Henry Langford was

[57] Ibid., ix, 1682–7 (ibid., MFGS 57/002, f. 83 (Trail)); ibid., x, 1687–92 (ibid., MFGS 57/003, f. 57 (Trail)); ibid., xi, 1692–6 (ibid., MFGS 57/003, f. 284 (Dalway)); Hans Stevenson to Lieutenant Hans Stevenson, 1 Feb. 1695/6 (NLI, Stevenson correspondence, MS 1702, p. 54); Maynard, 'Irish membership at the English Inns', p. 299.

[58] A short account of the Trail family of Blebe, Scotland, and their descendants (PRONI, T273/1); pedigree and genealogical notes relating to the Hamilton family, 1603–1827 (NLI, MS 8792 (1)).

[59] Lawlor, History of the Cairnes, p. 144; HIP, iii, 358.

[60] Derry corp. mins (PRONI, LA/79/2/AA/1, p. 66); Lawlor, History of the Cairnes, pp 144, 156–63.

[61] Derry corp. mins (PRONI, LA/79/2/AA/2, pp 54–5, 110); Coleraine corp. mins (PRONI, LA/25/2/AA/1A, pp 273, 309); A concise view of the origin, constitution and proceedings of The Honorable Society of the Governor and Assistants of London, of the New Plantation in Ulster, within the realm of Ireland, commonly called The Irish Society (London, 1842), p. 77; Lawlor, History of the Cairnes, p. 164.

[62] Chancery bill books, xi, 1692–6 (NAI, MFGS 57/003, ff 127, 161–2); ibid., xii (MFGS 57/004, ff 110–11, 113); Lawlor, History of the Cairnes, p. 165; Maynard, 'Irish membership at the English Inns', p. 299.

[63] DIB (Langford, Sir Arthur); Raymond Gillespie, 'Dissenters and Nonconformists, 1661–1700' in Kevin Herlihy (ed.), The Irish Dissenting tradition 1650–1750 (Blackrock, Co. Dublin, 1995), p. 19.

[64] HIP, iii, 358.

[65] Ibid., vi, 456; J. L. J. Hughes (ed.), Patentee officers in Ireland 1173–1826: including high sheriffs, 1661–1684 and 1761–1816 (Dublin, 1960), p. 132.

Figure 9   Portrait of David Cairnes (1645–1722) of Knockmany and Derry
(From portrait reputedly painted by Sir Godfrey Kneller.)

the recorder of Coleraine, though the government did not initially sanction his
appointment. He was succeeded by his cousin, Thomas Upton, in March 1711.[66] A
dispute occurred in 1710 between two rival factions for control of the Coleraine
borough and as a result Upton was removed from the recordership in May 1711.[67]
Presbyterian barristers were active in a number of other public roles in which their

[66]   Coleraine corp. mins (PRONI, LA/25/2/AA/1A, pp 177, 179, 186, 212, 215, 220, 306–7); *HIP*,
vi, 456.
[67]   T. H. Mullin, *Coleraine in by-gone centuries* (Belfast, 1976), p. 169.

legal training and experience probably proved an asset. David Cairnes, Robert Dalway, Henry Langford and Thomas Upton all served as members of the Irish parliament.[68] Langford was sheriff of County Meath in 1690, was sworn as a burgess of Trim in 1698, and in 1699 was appointed by the English Parliament as one of the seven commissioners chosen to examine the handling of the Irish forfeitures.[69]

When the test clause was introduced in 1704 two of the Presbyterian barristers had already died: Hans Trail in 1692 and Robert Dalway in 1699.[70] The last appearance of Henry Langford in the court of chancery was in Michaelmas term 1706.[71] David Cairnes, who died in 1726, was present once in Trinity term 1705, once in Michaelmas term 1710 and once in Michaelmas term 1711.[72] Though barristers qualified before 1704 were not subject to the sacramental test contained in the Black Book of King's Inns, it would appear that the Presbyterian barristers qualified before the test kept a lower profile in the courts after 1704. Henry Langford moved to England, where he purchased an estate at King's Kerswell, Devon, in 1710. He succeeded to the baronetcy following the death of his brother, Sir Arthur Langford in 1716, and in 1716–17 was sheriff of Devon.[73] It would appear that Thomas Upton (1677–1733), though qualified before 1704, conformed to the Church of Ireland. He was awarded an LL.D. (*speciali gratia*) by Trinity College, Dublin, in 1718 and held a number of other public appointments after 1704 which would have been impossible had he remained a Presbyterian. These included the post of king's counsel from 1715, commissioner of the revenue appeals (1717–33), counsel to the barrack board (by 1721–33), and governor of the Dublin workhouse (1732–33). He also acted as justice of assize for the Connaught circuit in Lent 1730.[74]

No fee books are known to survive for any of the Ulster Presbyterian lawyers and this makes it difficult to be precise about the income they earned. What is clear is that they did not usually rely solely on fees drawn from legal practice. It has already been mentioned that David Cairnes served as agent for the Irish Society, and while the annual retainer he received is unknown, his successor was paid £200 *per annum*.[75] Thomas Upton's wealth was estimated at £200 in 1713. Upton's salary as recorder of Derry was £40 *per annum* and his position as counsel to the barrack board gave him £100 *per annum*.[76] He was also bequeathed £1,000 by his cousin Sir Arthur

[68] HIP, iii, 358; iv, 5; v, 56–7; vi, 456–7.

[69] Ibid., v, 57; J. G. Simms, The Williamite confiscation in Ireland 1690–1703 (London, [1956]), p. 98; Eileen Black (comp. & ed.), Kings in conflict: Ireland in the 1690s (Belfast, 1990), pp 289–90.

[70] A short account of the Trail family of Blebe, Scotland, and their descendants (PRONI, T273/1); Stewart, Story of Kilmore Presbyterian Church, p. 19; HIP, iv, 5.

[71] Chancery bill books, xiv, 1706–10 (NAI, MFGS 57/004, f. 69).

[72] Ibid., xiii, 1701–5 (MFGS 57/004, f. 388); ibid., xv, 1710–12 (MFGS 57/005, ff 37, 68, 82, 249).

[73] Will of Henry Langford, 1725 (N.A., Prerogative Court of Canterbury wills, PROB 11/601/331); G.E.C., Complete baronetage, iv, 204; HIP, v, 56–7. Sir Henry Langford's portrait, painted by William Gandy c.1710, is held at the Royal Albert Memorial Museum, Exeter.

[74] Burtchaell & Sadleir, Alumni Dublinenses, p. 831; Hughes, Patentee officers, p. 132; HIP, vi, 456; the lords justices to Dorset, 1 Aug. 1732 (PRONI, Wilmot papers, T3019/101).

[75] T. H. Mullin, Coleraine in Georgian times (Belfast, 1977), pp 30–1.

[76] A list of the peers and members of the House of Commons of Ireland, [late 1713] (PRONI,

Langford.[77] The Presbyterian barristers drew income from the estates they owned. Robert Dalway inherited the family estate at Bellahill in 1687 after the death of his nephew, John, without issue.[78] David Cairnes inherited lands at Knockmany, County Tyrone, from his father, as well as the 'Sixtown estate' of Raveagh, County Londonderry.[79] He added to this by a fortuitous marriage with Margaret Edwards, by which he obtained 'considerable property' in Derry and its suburbs.[80] Hans Trail of Drumnaconnor, County Down, was the second son of Lieutenant-Colonel James Trail of Tollychin, near Killyleagh, County Down. When Lieutenant-Colonel Trail died in 1663, he was succeeded at Tollychin by his eldest son, John, while Hans was left lands at Drumnaconnor and Raleagh, along with a corn mill and tuck mill which were situated at the latter location. When Hans died in 1692 he left Drumnaconnor to his eldest son, James, along with £70 to each of his daughters, Elizabeth, Mary and Matilda, and £90 to his younger son, Robert.[81]

Although attorneys were more numerous than barristers less information can be found about them in the surviving sources. Alexander Harper, a Presbyterian from County Down, worked as 'a little attorney in the manor court' and leased property of £6 *per annum*.[82] Matthew Gledstanes, a Presbyterian attorney, is known about only through the inscription of his name on an early eighteenth-century headstone.[83] The Gledstanes owned property at Fardross, County Tyrone.[84] Matthew was the son of James Gledstanes, a captain during the Siege of Derry, and his mother was Ann Galbraith, but apart from Matthew's death, at the age of 30, on 19 October 1708, nothing is known about him or his legal practice.[85] Other known Presbyterian attorneys include Hugh Hamill, later M.P. for Lifford (1692–3, 1703–9), and George Butle Conyngham, who inherited the Springhill estate in 1721.[86] William Roulston's study of Strabane during the late seventeenth century did not uncover any attorneys located there, and he suggests that this was perhaps because Strabane was not an assize town.[87] Dublin, along with the assize towns, probably provided the best place for attorneys to reside, in regard to potential earnings, and a little is known about two further attorneys, with Ulster Presbyterian connections, who lived and worked in Dublin.

Blenheim papers, T4311); Derry corp. mins (PRONI, LA/79/2/AA/3A, pp 117, 133, 153, 187, 247, 259, 275); *HIP*, vi, 456.

77 Will of Arthur Langford, 1715 (PRONI, T168/1, p. 8).

78 Burke, *Genealogical & heraldic dictionary of the landed gentry* (1863), p. 333.

79 Lawlor, *History of the Cairnes*, p. 144.

80 Ibid., p. 151, n. 1; *HIP*, iii, 358.

81 Abstract will of James Trail, 1662 (PRONI, Stewart papers, D1759/3/B/1, pp 118–19); abstract will of Hans Trail, 1691 (ibid., p. 120); Stewart, *Story of Kilmore Presbyterian Church*, p. 19.

82 Notes on the Co. Down militia, c.1719 (PRONI, Ward papers, D2092/1/3, f. 30); Barnard, *New anatomy*, p. 125.

83 David Stewart, 'Notes on Presbytery of Antrim mins' (PRONI, Stewart papers, D1759/1/A/3, p. 518).

84 Young, *Fighters of Derry*, pp 151–2.

85 Stewart, 'Notes on Presbytery of Antrim' (PRONI, D1759/1/A/3, p. 518).

86 *HIP*, iv, 323; Agnew, *Merchant families*, p. 215.

87 W. J. Roulston, *Restoration Strabane, 1660–1714: economy and society in provincial Ireland* (Dublin, 2007), p. 46.

James Alexander acted as an attorney in Dublin for some of the leading Presbyterian families of County Down, including the Kennedys of Cultra. In David Kennedy's will a bond is mentioned as having been made by James Alexander.[88] Attorneys in the seventeenth and eighteenth centuries, as well as being employed to draw up the documents connected with property transactions, often arranged mortgages for their clients. Attorneys drew fees for preparing the bonds and often made loans from money that was in their hands, on which they could earn interest.[89] James Alexander died in 1701 and when drawing up his will the only debt he remembered was David Kennedy's bond of £180. He wrote in his will, 'I hope Mr. Kenedy will be reasonable in his demands, in regard he had lodging and dyett [diet] at my house severall times that he was in Dublin.'[90]

Samuel Martin, an attorney in the court of common pleas, was a son of the Belfast Presbyterian merchant George Martin. Samuel moved to Dublin, where he was made a freeman in 1679, and after spending a short time as a merchant, set up in Dublin as an attorney. His legal career was aided by the support of Sir Audley Mervyn, serjeant-at-law and speaker of the Irish Commons, who was a relation of Samuel's wife, Elizabeth. Martin, like other Belfast Presbyterians who settled in Dublin, lived in Capel Street, where he attended the Presbyterian church and built up a thriving legal practice. In 1687 the Antrim 'Meeting' contemplated asking him to present to the Irish government a representation of their grievances. He acted for the Belfast corporation in the same year and for the Presbyterian General Synod in 1705, as well as handling the business of a number of Ulster Presbyterian gentry and mercantile families.[91]

Ic. Religious life

The religious life of the Presbyterians engaged in the legal profession is obscure and only a limited number of references have been found. The only Presbyterian barrister mentioned in the *Records of the General Synod of Ulster* is Robert Dalway, who was appointed in 1699 as a member of a committee to investigate a scandal relating to Rev. Stafford Pettigrew, minister of Ballyeaston.[92] The wills of three of the Presbyterian barristers give brief glimpses into their religious life and illustrate the obligatory absence from home that barristers suffered in order to pursue a legal career. Hans Trail of Drumnaconnor, County Down, stipulated that he wished to

[88] 'Presbyterian Historical Society', *Irish Presbyterian*, xviii, no. 4 (Apr. 1912), p. 61.

[89] Holmes, *Augustan England*, pp 157–8; Michael Birks, *Gentlemen of the law* (London, 1960), pp 182, 185, 187; Corfield, *Power & the professions*, p. 73.

[90] 'Presbyterian Historical Society', *Irish Presbyterian*, xviii, no. 4 (Apr. 1912), p. 61. James Alexander's son, John, was Presbyterian minister of Plunket Street Presbyterian Church, Dublin, 1730–1743, and was moderator of the General Synod in 1734: Bailie, *Hist. of congns*, p. 440.

[91] Agnew, *Merchant families*, pp 34, 55, 57, 184, 239; *RGSU*, i, 3, 101; Antrim 'Meeting' mins (UTC, pp 240–1); Young, *Belfast town book*, p. 158; Samuel Martin to Robert Stewart, 1 Nov. 1681, 2 Dec. 1682 (PRONI, Castle Stewart papers, D1618/15/2/41, /43); [Alan Brodrick] to Thomas Brodrick, 24 June 1714 (Surrey History Centre, Midleton papers, 1248/3/187–8); W. D. Killen, *History of congregations of the Presbyterian Church in Ireland …* (Belfast, 1886), p. 128.

[92] *RGSU*, i, 40; see also Antrim Pby mins, 1697–1713 (PHS, p. 118).

be buried at the church in Killyleagh 'if he die near that place', but he died in 1692 in Dublin, and was buried at St. Michael's there. He left 50s to be distributed to the poor of Killyleagh.[93] David Cairnes left 30s and a gold mourning ring worth 14s, which was to have his initials, 'DC', engraved on it, along with the date of his death, to each of the Presbyterian ministers that he was accustomed to hearing. The ministers concerned were, his 'most esteemed friend', Rev. Joseph Boyse, minister of Wood Street Presbyterian Church in Dublin, Rev. Samuel Ross, minister of Derry, and Rev. Nehemiah Donaldson, at Castlederg.[94] Cairnes's daughter, Mary, married Rev. Richard Choppin of Dublin and two of Cairnes's nieces also married Presbyterian ministers.[95]

Robert Dalway in his will of 1699 distributed the contents of his two houses, at Bellahill, County Antrim, and Dublin. Among bequests to his son, Alexander, he left his 'great English Bible with Clerks annotations now in Dublin' and to his other son, Henry, he left his 'large other English Bible now at Bellahill'.[96] Dalway also bequeathed £16 to be split into four equal portions and distributed amongst the poor of St. Michan's, Dublin, and three County Antrim parishes. He left a further £20 to Rev. Elias Travers, a Presbyterian minister in Dublin, 'to be disposed of as he thinks fit', and requested that Travers and Dr Duncan Cumyng, whom he described as his 'good friends', would, as opportunity offered, be 'aiding to his executors by their good and Christian advice'. Dalway ended his will with a long section which shows his concern for the religious well-being of his children and highlights the commonly held belief that the father was expected to offer religious instruction to the household:

By virtue of the authority God has given to me as a Christian husband and father I injoyne and require my wife children and grandchildren that they be diligent and constant in the great work of Christianity, repentance, faith, love, admiring the perfections of God and those that wonderfully appear in Christ in redeeming sinners; that they attend all his ordinances, serve and call on God dayly in their families and closets, be helps and encouragements to a gospell ministry and charitable to the poore, and this I leave on their consciences as the last and earnest request and command of a Christian dying husband and father, wishing the blessing of the almighty and leaveing my blessing with them.[97]

* * * * * * *

Presbyterian involvement in the legal profession, at least in its upper branch, was modest. Only six Presbyterian barristers from Ulster have been identified as active during the period 1660 to 1704. The barristers received much of their work from Ulster clients, who they are known to have represented in the Irish

---

93 Abstract will of Hans Trail, 1691 (PRONI, Stewart papers, D1759/3/B/1, p. 120).

94 Lawlor, History of the Cairnes, pp 168–71.

95 Ibid., pp 168–9; McConnell, Fasti, pp 122, 124.

96 Will of Robert Dalway, 1699 (PRONI, Castle Stewart papers, D1618/8/5); Barnard, 'Libraries & collectors', p. 120. The Bible with annotations was probably Samuel Clarke, The Old and New Testament, with annotations and parallel Scriptures (London, 1690).

97 Will of Robert Dalway, 1699 (PRONI, Castle Stewart papers, D1618/8/5).

court of chancery. After 1704, as a result of the test, Presbyterians entering the legal profession were obliged to conform, though without other evidence, it is not possible to assess the sincerity of those who did conform. The Presbyterians who entered the legal profession before 1704 came from gentry families and many owned or inherited lands. In addition to their legal practice they often engaged in other public activities, serving as recorders for Ulster corporations or, in the case of four of the barristers, as members of the Irish parliament. Presbyterian barristers were often absent from their homes in Ulster because of the necessity of being present at the law courts in Dublin, and even for the attorneys the most lucrative opportunities were often located in the Irish capital. As a result of their absence from Ulster, and because of their low number, Presbyterian barristers did not have a significant role in the administration of the Presbyterian church in Ulster, though they could indicate and express their religious beliefs and piety through attendance at churches in both Ulster and Dublin, and through charitable bequests made in their wills.

II. Medicine

In the early modern period patients had a variety of options available to them when requiring medical advice or treatment. There was a tripartite division in the practice of 'official' medicine, which included physicians, surgeons and apothecaries. Physicians usually held a university degree and were theoretically concerned with diagnosis and prescription. The surgeons were trained by apprenticeship or through service in the armed forces and performed operations and manual work, such as the removal of tumours, amputation of limbs or bloodletting. Apothecaries prepared and sold the medicines that were prescribed by the physicians. In practice the demarcations between the three groups were not always clear, especially in rural areas, where if there was only one medical practitioner available, he may have undertaken all of the roles. In addition, apothecaries increasingly not only supplied drugs but also offered medical advice and prescribed medicines without the aid of a physician.[98]

All three branches of orthodox medical practice were open to Presbyterians as, in contrast to the upper branch of the legal profession, no sacramental test applied.[99] Since a law of Henry VIII's reign, ecclesiastical authorities had the power to issue licences for the practice of medicine and surgery. This, however, does not appear to have been an obstacle as in the late seventeenth and early eighteenth century most practitioners were not licensed by the diocesan authorities.[100] During the reign of Queen Anne, for instance, the bishop of Limerick issued only six medical licences.[101] Many of the medical practitioners have left little trace of their

---

98 Holmes, *Augustan England*, pp 166–8; Hamilton, 'Medical professions in the eighteenth century', pp 159–60; journal of the RCPI, i (RCPI Lib., p. 216).
99 Barnard, *New anatomy*, p. 128.
100 3 Hen. VIII, c. 11 [1511] (*The statutes at large of England and of Great-Britain* (10 vols, London, 1851), ii, 7); Ian Mortimer, 'Diocesan licensing and medical practitioners in south-west England, 1660–1780', *Medical History*, xlviii (2004), p. 49.
101 Barnard, *New anatomy*, p. 131.

existence. No directories cover Ulster during the period between 1680 and 1730, and the first Belfast directory was not published until 1807.[102] The Belfast freemen's roll, which might have given some idea of the numbers involved in the medical profession, unfortunately has a gap from February 1682 to November 1723.[103] One source which offers some insight into the number of medical practitioners located in Belfast is the funeral register kept by the Belfast Presbyterian congregation during the period 1712 to 1736. The doctors mentioned in the funeral register are Dr [John] Alexander, Dr John Anderson, Dr [James] Correy, Dr [George] Cromie, Dr Delap, Dr Henry Duncan, Dr [Victor] Ferguson, Dr [James] Macartney, Dr Archibald McNeall, Dr [John] Peacock, Dr [Andrew] Smith and 'the doctor of the armey', who all lived in Belfast,[104] and 'Docter Weare, in Antriam'.[105] In addition, three apothecaries are mentioned: John Ferguson and James Reed, both of Belfast, and John Steel from Donagheady.[106]

It cannot, however, be assumed that all of the medical practitioners in the funeral register were Presbyterians, as the mort cloths of the Presbyterian congregation were lent to members of the Church of Ireland. Certainly, Dr James Macartney must have been a conformist. Although Dr Macartney's father, 'Brown' George Macartney, was a Presbyterian merchant who lived in Belfast, Dr Macartney must have conformed to the Church of Ireland as he became a burgess of Belfast in 1715 and died in 1726 while serving as sovereign (mayor) of the town – an office he could not have held, because of the test clause, unless he had been at least an occasional conformist.[107] The funeral register also illustrates the imprecise separation between the three branches of medicine, with Dr Henry Duncan described in one entry as 'Mr Henery Duncan, doct' and in another as 'Doctr Doncan, potegar' (that is, apothecary).[108] Belfast was, therefore, reasonably well supplied with medical practitioners in the early eighteenth century, but we will also need to consider medical provision elsewhere in Ulster.

IIa. Education and training

There were no facilities in the British Isles for the education of physicians until 1726, when a medical faculty was established at Edinburgh University. Most students studied in Europe, principally in the universities of the United Provinces or France. France was popular particularly with Catholics from southern Ireland, and

---

[102] *Merchants in plenty: Joseph Smyth's Belfast directories for 1807 and 1808*, introd. J. R. R. Adams (Belfast, 1991).

[103] Young, *Belfast town book*, pp 246–94.

[104] Agnew, *Belfast funeral register*, pp 13–17, 20, 22–8, 31, 35–6, 39–40. The 'doctor of the armey' was probably John Campbell, an Ulsterman, who was physician-general to the army in Ireland from 1714–17: E. A. Underwood, *Boerhaave's men: at Leyden and after* (Edinburgh, 1977), p. 146.

[105] Agnew, *Belfast funeral register*, p. 22.

[106] Ibid., pp 12, 15, 28–9, 32, 34.

[107] Agnew, *Merchant families*, pp 257–8; RGSU, i, 159.

[108] Agnew, *Belfast funeral register*, pp 17, 24.

the Dutch universities attracted Protestants throughout the kingdom.[109] Although the British universities had, from their foundation, the right to confer degrees in medicine, medical teaching had not received much attention from the university authorities and many of the professorships were titular. In the rare cases when teaching was given it was often theoretical and tuition had to be obtained from private anatomical teachers or local practising surgeons.[110] Leiden University was the premier medical institution in Europe at this time, particularly under its celebrated professor, Herman Boerhaave, who was appointed *lector* (reader) in 1701, and became professor of botany and medicine in 1709. In 1714 he was appointed professor of practical medicine, and in 1718 was also appointed to the chair of chemistry, thus holding three medical chairs simultaneously.[111] The chair of anatomy at Leiden was held from 1719 to 1770 by Bernard Siegfried Albinus, who was regarded as 'the greatest anatomist of his day'.[112] In addition to the reputation of its professors, Leiden was attractive to medical students for a number of other reasons. The facilities were impressive. The university boasted not only an anatomical theatre and clinical training, but also a renowned botanical garden and a well-stocked library, while the city was noted for printing and bookselling.[113]

The presence of Scottish merchants settled at Leiden and its neighbouring Dutch cities facilitated the students by providing places for them to lodge and enabled them to receive money and post from home.[114] George Cromie, who studied medicine at Leiden in the early eighteenth century, was a nephew of the Belfast merchant, Isaac Macartney, who supplied money to Cromie through Alexander Carstaires, Macartney's correspondent at Rotterdam.[115] Students were able to attend the English (Scottish) church at Leiden, whose minister from 1716 to 1758 was Rev. Thomas Gowan, the son of an Ulster Presbyterian minister, and himself minister of Drumbo before settling at Leiden in 1716.[116] One of the Scottish

---

[109] R. W. Innes-Smith, 'English-speaking students of medicine at continental universities', intro. H. T. Swan, (http://www.rcpe.ac.uk/library/read/people/english-students) (12 Jan. 2013).

[110] O'Day, *The professions*, p. 191; Underwood, *Boerhaave's men*, pp 76–8, 83–5, 102, 106, 108, 124–5; J. D. Mackie, *The University of Glasgow 1451–1951: a short history* (Glasgow, 1954), p. 169; W. S. Craig, *History of the Royal College of Physicians of Edinburgh* (Oxford, 1976), pp 25–6; G. A. Lindeboom, *Herman Boerhaave: the man and his work* (London, 1968), pp 368–9; John Kerr, *Scottish education, school and university, from early times to 1908* (Cambridge, 1910), pp 263–4.

[111] F. R. Jevons, 'Boerhaave's biochemistry', *Medical History*, vi (1962), p. 343; Underwood, *Boerhaave's men*, pp 6–8.

[112] Underwood, *Boerhaave's men*, p. 10; Holmes, *Augustan England*, p. 176; Kees van Strien and Witte de Withlaan, 'A medical student at Leiden and Paris: William Sinclair 1736–38', *Proceedings of the Royal College of Physicians of Edinburgh*, xxv (1995), p. 295; Esther Mijers, 'Scotland and the United Provinces, c.1680–1730: a study in intellectual and educational relations' (Ph.D. thesis, St. Andrews Univ., 2002), p. 284.

[113] Mijers, 'Scotland & the United Provinces', pp 36, 62, 70; G. A. Lindeboom, *Boerhaave and Great Britain* (Leiden, 1974), p. 17; R. W. Innes Smith, *English-speaking students of medicine at the University of Leyden* (Edinburgh, 1932), p. xix.

[114] Mijers, 'Scotland & the United Provinces', pp 51–2.

[115] Isaac Macartney to Alexander Carstaires, [c. Jan/Feb. 1705], 9 July 1705 (PRONI, D501/1, pp 44–5, 141–2); same to George Cromie, 14 Aug. 1706 (ibid., p. 344); same to Robert Milling, 19 Aug. 1706 (ibid., p. 344).

[116] *RGSU*, i, 109, 394–5, 420.

students who studied at Leiden described Gowan as 'a man of very good sense' who was 'very well beloved by the students'. Gowan visited the students at their lodgings and also acted as an informer to the English government of the presence of undesirable students, such as those involved in Jacobite activities.[117] The students at Leiden came from throughout the British Isles, as well as from across Europe and the American colonies.[118] Innes Smith identified about 2,000 English-speaking medical students at Leiden between 1575 and 1875.[119] Nationality was not a barrier to receiving an education there, as lectures were given in Latin, a language known and used by the educated classes of all nationalities.

Students usually completed their medical studies at Leiden in two years or less, and this must have been another important factor attracting British students to study medicine there or at one of the other continental universities.[120] In contrast, at Oxford it took at least 12 years before a student could graduate as a doctor of medicine, because of the requirement to complete a four-year arts course, followed by study for a bachelor of medicine, before one could begin to study for a doctorate. Even then much of his practical training had to be obtained outside the university.[121]

The matriculation albums of Leiden University often give the nationality of the students, with 'Scoto-Hibernus' being used to describe Ulster-Scots.[122] It is impossible, however, without other evidence, to definitively state that all those described as 'Scoto-Hibernus' were Presbyterian. In addition, some of the students from Ulster were sometimes described as 'Hibernus' (Irish) or 'Scotus' (Scottish); for example, John Williamson, a Presbyterian doctor who practised at Antrim, was described as 'Hibernus' when matriculating at Leiden in 1723, and Gabriel King, a Presbyterian doctor based at Armagh, was described as 'Scotus' when entering the university in 1719.[123] Of those known from other evidence to have been Presbyterian (or the offspring of Presbyterian parents), most graduated elsewhere even though they had studied medicine for a period at Leiden: at Rheims in France, or to a lesser extent, Utrecht or Harderwijk in the United Provinces. Dr Gabriel King and Dr John Williamson both graduated at Rheims after studying at Leiden,[124] for the simple reason that it was cheaper to graduate there. Adam Murray, a Scottish medical student who studied at Leiden in the mid-1720s estimated that an M.D. from Rheims cost 'at least £8 or £9 sterling', while an M.D. at Leiden cost approximately £17 to £18. In addition it was customary for students at Leiden to pay for a meal for their professors and friends after graduation and this may have more

---

117 Van Strien & De Withlaan, 'A medical student at Leiden & Paris', p. 300; "Le Connû" (a government spy in Holland) to [George Tildon or Anthony Corbiere?], 11 May 1723 (HMC, *Townshend MSS*, p. 193).
118 Lindeboom, *Boerhaave & Great Britain*, p. 16.
119 Innes Smith, *English-speaking students.*
120 Underwood, *Boerhaave's men*, p. 57; Lindeboom, *Herman Boerhaave*, p. 37.
121 Holmes, *Augustan England*, pp 176–7; Underwood, *Boerhaave's men*, p. 2.
122 *Album studiosorum Academiae Lugduno Batavae MDLXXV–MDCCCLXXV* (The Hague, 1875).
123 Innes Smith, *English-speaking students*, pp 133, 250; 'King, Gabriel' (RCPI, Kirkpatrick archives); *RGSU*, i, 489; ii, 152; Innes-Smith, 'English-speaking students of medicine at continental universities'.
124 Innes Smith, *English-speaking students*, pp 133, 250.

than doubled the cost of graduation.[125] It was for this reason, therefore, that many students, not just Presbyterians from Ulster, travelled to Rheims where, because they did not know the professors and students, they did not feel obliged to provide a feast. Rheims offered three types of degrees: one for those who wanted to practise in Rheims itself, another for French citizens who wanted to practise in their native town or county, and a third for non-French students intending to practise in their home countries. The latter involved a short oral examination and the examination and graduation could be completed in a single day.[126]

Other Presbyterian medical students graduating from Rheims after study at Leiden were Upton Peacock, Andrew Smith and Samuel Moore. Peacock was the eldest son of Dr John Peacock of Belfast and Mary Upton, daughter of Arthur Upton of Castle Upton, Templepatrick. He entered Glasgow University in 1713, where he was described as 'Scoto-Hibernus'; at the age of 22 was admitted to the medical faculty at Leiden, described as 'Hibernus'; and graduated M.D. at Rheims in 1718.[127] Andrew Smith (1697–1753) came from a mercantile background. His father, also Andrew, was a merchant of Belfast and later Dublin, and his grandfather was the wealthy Belfast merchant Samuel Smith. Andrew entered Glasgow University in 1715 and matriculated at Leiden in 1720. He graduated M.D. at Rheims in 1722.[128] Samuel Moore was the son of James Mure of Roddans, who had settled in Ireland from Scotland, where the Mure family had been heavily involved in supporting the Covenanters, with the result that their properties at Rowallan, Caldwell and Glanderston had been confiscated. Although James Mure later returned to Scotland his son, Samuel, remained in Ulster where he practised as a physician in Counties Donegal and Londonderry. Samuel studied first at Glasgow University, where his brother-in-law, Alexander Dunlop, was one of the professors. He changed his surname from the Scottish 'Mure' to the Irish 'Moore', and when graduating as M.A. from Glasgow in 1724 used the spelling 'Moore'. He then travelled to Leiden University, which he entered in 1729, at the age of 24. Two years later he graduated from Rheims with his doctorate.[129]

An Ulster Presbyterian student who also graduated from Rheims, but for whom there is no evidence of study at Leiden, was Dr Samuel Cornwall. Described as 'Hibernus', he graduated with his medical doctorate from Rheims in 1699.

---

[125] Van Strien & De Withlaan, 'A medical student', pp 644–5; Lindeboom, *Herman Boerhaave*, p. 39.

[126] Laurence Brockliss, 'Medicine, religion and social mobility in eighteenth- and early nineteenth-century Ireland' in James Kelly and Fiona Clark (eds), *Ireland and medicine in the seventeenth and eighteenth centuries* (Farnham, 2010); Van Strien & De Withlaan, 'A medical student', pp 644–5.

[127] Benn, *Belfast*, p. 576; Agnew, *Belfast funeral register*, p. 43; Innes Smith, *English-speaking students*, p. 179; *Munimenta alme Universitatis Glasguensis*, iii, 201; Underwood, *Boerhaave's men*, p. 51; Esther Mijers, 'Irish students in the Netherlands, 1650–1750', *Archivium Hibernicum*, lix (2005), p. 71.

[128] Philip Crossle, 'Smith' in 'Families and local history: a scrapbook' (PHS); Agnew, *Belfast funeral register*, p. 53; Innes Smith, *English-speaking students*, p. 215.

[129] Genealogy of the Mure/Moore family (PRONI, Moore papers, D1999/1, pp 5, 8); R. K. Moore, *The Moores of Derry and Oakover* (Perth, Australia, 2003), pp 19–22; Innes Smith, *English-speaking students*, p. 163; *Munimenta alme Universitatis Glasguensis*, iii, 56, 163; Mijers, 'Irish students in the Netherlands', p. 73.

Cornwall was the son of Rev. Gabriel Cornwall, Presbyterian minister of Ballywillan (1655–90), who lived at Maddybenny, County Londonderry. He was described as 'of Curreen in Co. Tyrone' and probably practised in County Londonderry and County Tyrone.[130] Another Presbyterian doctor who practised in County Tyrone was Dr Thomas Cairnes, the son of William of Killyfaddy, County Tyrone. He entered Leiden in 1704, at the age of 29, and then travelled to Utrecht where he graduated in 1705. Several copies of Cairnes's thesis for his doctorate survive. It is entitled 'De pleuritide et peripneumonia' (on pleurisy and inflammation of the lungs). Thomas dedicated the thesis to his uncle, the barrister David Cairnes, and to his father's cousins, the Ulster Presbyterian bankers and gentlemen, William, Alexander and Henry Cairnes.[131]

Intending physicians sometimes undertook private practical training either before or after completing their university education. Dr William Stephens, who practised in Dublin, must have received training from the Presbyterian physician Dr Duncan Cumyng, for among those to whom he dedicated his Leiden thesis in 1716 were 'Duncan Cuming, M.D., of Dublin, his teacher'.[132] Stephens, who later became a chemistry lecturer at Trinity College, Dublin, was the son of an Anglican parson, and this, therefore, is an example of co-operation between Churchmen and Presbyterians. Many medical students rounded off their studies with practical training in one of the large Paris hospitals[133] and both Victor Ferguson of Belfast and Duncan Cumyng spent some time training in France. Ferguson, writing in 1721, described how in his earlier years he had the 'opportunity of seeing some of the foreign churches, particularly the Church of France', and he may have studied under the French chemist Nicolas Lemery, a Calvinist who in 1686 converted to Catholicism.[134] James Macartney, son of the Belfast Presbyterian merchant 'Brown' George Macartney, spent some time in London 'for his improvement in the studie of medicine'. So too did George Cromie, son of the Belfast and Dublin merchant Francis Cromie, who attended Trinity in 1701, and after spending some time in Holland went to London 'for his further and better improvement', before returning to the continent to study medicine at Leiden and graduate as a doctor of medicine from the University of Harderwijk in 1708.[135]

---

130 J. E. Mullin, The kirk of Ballywillan since the Scottish settlement (Belfast, 1961), pp 28, 30; Innes-Smith, 'English-speaking students of medicine at continental universities'.
131 Lawlor, History of the Cairnes, pp 107, 110–11; Innes Smith, English-speaking students, p. 39; Mijers, 'Irish students in the Netherlands', p. 70; Thomas Cairnes, Disputatio medica inauguralis de pleuritide et peripneumonia (Utrecht, 1705).
132 Innes Smith, English-speaking students, p. 223.
133 Van Strien & De Withlaan, 'A medical student', pp 294, 639.
134 Joseph Boyse, The works of the reverend and learned Mr. Joseph Boyse, of Dublin (2 vols, London, 1728), i, 316; [James Kirkpatrick], A vindication of the Presbyterian ministers in the north of Ireland; Subscribers and Non-Subscribers: from many gross and groundless aspersions cast upon them, in a late scandalous libel, entituled, an account of the mind of the synod at Belfast. 1721 (Belfast, 1721), p. 3; Victor Ferguson to [Hans Sloane], 14 May 1698 (BL, Sloane MS 4037, f. 73).
135 John McBride to Sloane, 16 Jan. 1702, 15 Jan. 1703 (BL, Sloane MS 4038, ff 288–9; Sloane MS 4039, ff 229–30); Agnew, Merchant families, pp 257–8; Innes-Smith, 'English-speaking students of medicine at continental universities'.

A Fraternity of Physicians was established in Ireland in 1654. It was granted a royal charter by Charles II in 1667, becoming the College of Physicians in Dublin, and in 1692, after a new charter was granted by William and Mary, was renamed the King and Queen's College of Physicians in Ireland. Under the terms of the 1692 charter no one was to practise physic in Dublin, or within seven miles of the city, unless either a fellow or licentiate of the college. In the rest of Ireland only those who had graduated from the universities of Dublin, Oxford or Cambridge could practise without licence. Anyone else had to obtain a licence from the College, which was only granted after the undertaking of an examination and the payment of a fee. The college's control outside Dublin was limited, however, because it lacked the necessary administrative apparatus, and most physicians outside Dublin practised without the licence.[136] Nevertheless, there was some Presbyterian engagement with the college. Duncan Cumyng was a fellow of the college before the 1692 charter, perhaps from as early as 1685, and Victor Ferguson was also a fellow of the college. Cumyng was particularly active[137] and served as president from October 1699 to October 1700.[138] Ferguson, though a fellow from 1698 until his death in 1723, does not appear to have taken any role in the college and is not listed as attending any of its meetings.[139] Fellows of the college were elected from the order of candidates. One with Presbyterian connections was Upton Peacock. After graduating from Rheims in 1718, Peacock submitted himself to the Irish College of Physicians for examination. They found him 'sufficiently qualify'd to practice physick' and after paying a fee of £7 10s and a further 5s 5d for the college's servant, he was admitted as a candidate of the College in 1721. From 1725 until his death in 1744 Peacock was physician general to the army in Ireland, but was never elected a fellow of the college.[140] Another Ulsterman, Dr John Campbell, was physician general to the army in Ireland from 1714 to 1717. Campbell was admitted as a candidate of the Royal College of Physicians in 1712, but his denominational affiliation or background is unknown.[141]

Surgeons and apothecaries usually trained by apprenticeship with an existing practitioner, though some surgeons trained through service in the armed forces. Both options provided a less expensive way of entering the medical profession compared to the costs involved in training to become a physician. Most of the surgeons and apothecaries who trained by apprenticeship probably received all of their training in Ulster, but there were some who undertook or completed their training in Britain. George McGhee, a surgeon based at Strabane, for instance, had an apprentice named William Benson in 1716,

---

[136] J. F. Fleetwood, *The history of medicine in Ireland* (Dublin, 1983), pp 33–4; Widdess, *History of the Royal College of Physicians of Ireland*, pp 1, 33–5.

[137] Journal of the RCPI, i, 1692–1717; ii, 1717–23 (RCPI Lib.); 'Cumings, Duncan' (RCPI, Kirkpatrick archives).

[138] Journal of the RCPI, i (RCPI Lib., pp 90–102).

[139] Ibid., i, 76; ii, 41.

[140] Ibid., ii, 23; Innes Smith, *English-speaking students*, p. 179; Underwood, *Boerhaave's men*, pp 51, 146–7.

[141] Journal of the RCPI, i (RCPI Lib., p. 156); Innes Smith, *English-speaking students*, p. 40; Underwood, *Boerhaave's men*, pp 146–7.

and in 1730 William Clugston was an apprentice with the Belfast apothecary Henry Duncan.[142] John Love, a Presbyterian merchant at Strabane, travelled to Glasgow with his brother-in-law, Alexander Herkes, in 1693 in order to arrange an apprenticeship with a surgeon there for his nephew, Thomas.[143] A number of letters survive from Dr Victor Ferguson and the Presbyterian ministers Rev. John McBride of Belfast and Rev. James Bruce of Killyleagh, written to Sir Hans Sloane in London.[144] Sloane was born at Killyleagh, County Down, in 1660 and it is possible that McBride and Ferguson had known him before he moved to London. The letters to Sloane were written on behalf of a number of individuals who, usually after completing some preliminary training in Ulster, hoped to spend some time improving their skills under a London master or by gaining some employment there. The letters from McBride and Bruce usually refer to the young men's moral character, while the letters of introduction from Ferguson refer to their competency and medical skill. There was a tradition in some families of the sons of doctors following their fathers into the medical profession, and examples also exist where members from the one family were engaged in different branches of the medical profession. In such cases this would have enabled training for the younger generation. James Anderson, son of 'Doctor' John Anderson, a Belfast apothecary, also trained as an apothecary and Victor Ferguson's son, John, and nephew, William, were both apothecaries.[145] In 1715 Victor Ferguson wrote to Sloane, 'Having one only son I'm anxious to improve him to my power' and he asked Sloane for advice on where to obtain the 'best glasses now made for the discovery of insects in water'.[146]

---

[142] Roulston, *Restoration Strabane*, p. 45; Young, *Belfast town book*, p. 292. For an example of an apprenticeship agreement see PRONI, D238/58, which apprenticed John Campbell of Dromore to the Armagh apothecary Joseph Boyd in 1738. Boyd was a member of the Presbyterian church at Armagh: T. G. F. Paterson, 'Presbyterianism in Armagh', *Seanchas Ardmhacha: Journal of the Armagh Diocesan Historical Society*, xix (2003), p. 148. For the medical activities of McGhee, see: Diary of Rev. William Homes [Holmes], 1688–1746 (New England Historic Genealogical Society, Mss A 1996, pp 14–17).

[143] Roulston, *Restoration Strabane*, p. 45.

[144] Victor Ferguson to Sloane, 10 May 1700 (BL, Sloane MS 4038, f. 14), introduces a Mr Taylor, a surgeon; Ferguson to Sloane, 30 Dec. 1700 (ibid., f. 117), introduces James Boyd of Glastry, Co. Down, who was 'bred ane apothecrarie' at Belfast; John McBride to Sloane, 16 July 1701 (ibid., f. 189), introduces John Stevens, an apothecary, who was the son of a Monaghan merchant; James Bruce to Sloane, 15 Dec. 1704 (ibid., MS 4039, f. 405), introduces Alexander Wylie; Ferguson to Sloane, 27 Mar. 1705 (ibid., MS 4040, f. 16), introduces his brother George's son; McBride to Sloane, 28 Jan. 1706 (ibid., f. 122), introduces William Rodgers, an apothecary; McBride to Sloane, 3 Nov. 1712 (ibid., MS 4043, f. 202), introduces the bearer of the letter whose name is not specified; Ferguson to Sloane, 29 Oct. 1713 (ibid., f. 200), introduces James Anderson who sought to be appointed a journeyman in an apothecary's shop; Bruce to Sloane, 28 Aug. 1725 (ibid., MS 4048, f. 51), introduces Thomas Orr, the son of the Rev. Thomas Orr, Presbyterian minister of Comber, Co. Down, who had been educated 'att Belfast ane apothecarey and surgeon'.

[145] Victor Ferguson to Sloane, 29 Oct. 1713 (BL, Sloane MS 4043, f. 200); Agnew, *Belfast funeral register*, p. 13; Victor Ferguson to Sloane, 27 Mar. 1705 (BL, Sloane MS 4040, f. 16); The MacCarthy Mor, 'The Fergusons of Belfast: a short account of the ancestry of H.R.H. the duchess of York', *Familia*, ii, no. 2 (1986), pp 20–1.

[146] Victor Ferguson to Sloane, 10 Aug. 1715 (BL, Sloane MS 4044, f. 84).

Although licences from diocesan authorities were rarely granted in the early eighteenth century, the licence of one Presbyterian does survive. In 1718 John Thomson, who was born at Shilvodan, near Connor, County Antrim, was issued with a licence by William Walkingham, chancellor of Connor, and Edward Smyth, bishop of Down and Connor, 'to exercise the art or mystery of chyurgery in any place or upon any person within the diocess of Connor'. An important qualification for the diocesan licences seems to have been the character of the candidate, with Thomson's licence referring not only to his 'knowledge cunning and experience in the art and science of chyurgery' but also his 'honest life and good conversation'. After practising for a while as a surgeon Thomson, in 1730, became the Presbyterian minister at Carnmoney.[147]

IIb. Medical practice, income and status

There was no such thing in the early modern period as belonging to a single medical practice. Individuals used a number of different medical practitioners, depending on their personal wealth, the nature of the illness and the specialty of the practitioner. This is well illustrated in the diary of Rev. John Kennedy, Presbyterian minister of Benburb. In May 1724 Kennedy obtained Dr Smith from Minterburn, Country Tyrone.[148] In June 1726 his son, James Kennedy, was bled by Joseph Lawson.[149] When Mrs. Kennedy was ill in April 1729 her breast was lanced by William Woods.[150] At the same time as his wife's illness Kennedy's six eldest children and the family servant, Peg Olipher, all had measles. Kennedy went to Armagh on 7 April 1729 to obtain medicine from a Dr McLasly. He spent the night at McLasly's and returned home the following day when he administered the medicine to the children and servant himself. A couple of days later a local nurse was brought in to the Kennedy home to care for the sick members of the family, and on 15 April Kennedy returned to Armagh to obtain more medicine, which he again administered himself. On 6 June 1729 Kennedy returned to Armagh, this time to pay the doctor for the drugs.[151] Patients made use of self-medication and families accumulated accredited cures over generations, which were often recorded in handwritten recipe books. Rev. Archibald Maclaine of Banbridge recorded a number of medical treatments in his commonplace book, and in the final pages of the diary of Rev. Robert Landess, the Presbyterian minister of Ballymoney (1672–86), there are recorded 'singular remedies' and 'physical receipts'.[152] Among the receipts in Landess's diary were a

---

[147] Licence to practice surgery granted to John Thomson, 10 Mar. 1718 (PHS, Rev. John Thomson papers); R. H. Bonar, *Nigh on three and a half centuries: a history of Carnmoney Presbyterian Church* (Newtownabbey, 2004), p. 29.
[148] Diary of Rev. John Kennedy (PHS, p. 18).
[149] Ibid., pp 91–2.
[150] Ibid. (p. 179).
[151] Diary of Rev. John Kennedy (PHS, pp 18, 91–2, 179–80, 184).
[152] Archibald Maclaine memorandum book, 1728–40 (Southern Historical Collection, Manuscripts Department, Wilson Library, University of North Carolina at Chapel Hill, Collection No. 2313); Robert Lamond, 'Seventeenth century receipts', *Scottish Historical Review*, xiii (1916), pp 219–28.

remedy for gout, another to ease any pain in the head, one for pains in the ear, three for toothache, three for 'guttish payne', two to stay vomiting, three for coughs and one for colic.[153]

Medical knowledge was primitive by modern standards. It was largely based on the theories of Hippocrates and Galen. The human body was conceived of as being filled with four basic substances, called humours, which were in balance when a person was healthy. The four humours were identified as blood, black bile, yellow bile and phlegm. Ill-health resulted from an imbalance in one or more of the four humours and the person would remain ill, it was believed, until the balance was restored. Methods of treatment like bloodletting, emetics and purges, which were commonly used in the late seventeenth and early eighteenth centuries, were aimed at removing a harmful excess of a particular humour. Bloodletting was a common treatment which was employed to treat a large number of ailments. William Rainey, a Presbyterian merchant in Belfast, for instance, was bled in the foot in 1703 because he was suffering from 'sore eyes'.[154] Bloodletting, though ordered by physicians, was carried out by surgeons or barbers. Rev. Michael Bruce, minister of the Presbyterian congregation at Holywood, County Down, suffered from asthma and gout. In 1735 he was troubled with swollen legs and thighs. Along with his wife, Bruce went to Belfast and spent ten days there so that he could be near the doctor. The doctor ordered issues to be put in his legs.[155] This involved an incision and the creation of an artificial ulcer, with the purpose of causing a discharge.

Another common treatment was hydrotherapy.[156] This involved the drinking or use of water to soothe pains or treat various other ailments. In August 1721 Mrs Anne Hamilton of Tollymore was suffering from heart palpitations. Dr Cumyng of Dublin advised her to take 'stell [steel] and spaw waters', but after taking them for two months she found no benefit but rather an increase in her disorder. She wrote to Sloane in London to obtain his advice, and a number of her other letters to Sloane contain further references to the use of hydrotherapy by both Mrs Hamilton and her children.[157] Epistolary consultation was an option for the literate and wealthy and was common in Europe and America in the early modern period.[158] Patients and their families wrote to Sir Hans Sloane in London for advice or to report on a

---

153 Lamond, 'Seventeenth century receipts', pp 225–8.

154 Extracts from William Rainey's diary, 1703 (LHL, Joy MS, 10).

155 Samuel Haliday, A sermon occasioned by the death of the Reverend Mr. Michael Bruce (Belfast, 1735), pp 30–1; Michael Bruce to James Trail, [c.1731/2], 26 Jan. 1731/2 (PRONI, Bruce papers, T3041/1/A/7–8); W. B. Armstrong, The Bruces of Airth and their cadets, appendix, p. cxxxix.

156 Alexander Dalway to Richard Dobbs, 19 May 1694 (PRONI, Dobbs papers, D162/10); '2d. part of annals of Belfast', p. 4 (LHL, Joy MS, 12); Hill, Historical account of the MacDonnells, pp 383–4; W. J. Cordner, 'Some old wells in Antrim and Down', UJA, 3rd ser., iii (1940), pp 157–60.

157 Anne Hamilton to Sloane, 4 Sep. 1710, 15 & 23 Mar. 1714, 10 Aug. 1721 (BL, Sloane MS 4042, f. 174; MS 4043, ff 238, 242; MS 4046, ff 112–13).

158 See, for instance, Laurence Brockliss, 'Consultation by letter in early eighteenth-century Paris: the medical practice of Étienne-François Geoffroy' in A. L. Berge and Mordechai Feingold (eds), French medical culture in the nineteenth century (Amsterdam, 1994), pp 79–117; L. W. Smith, 'Reassessing the role of the family: women's medical care in eighteenth-century England', Social History of Medicine, xvi (2003), pp 327, 331–2.

Figure 10   Portrait of Rev. Dr James Kirkpatrick
In later life, Rev. Dr James Kirkpatrick, minister of Templepatrick
(1699–1706) and Belfast (1706–43), combined his ministerial duties with work
as a physician.

course of treatment that they were undergoing, while medical practitioners wrote to him to obtain a second opinion.

Rev. James Kirkpatrick, minister of Templepatrick Presbyterian Church (1699–1706) and Belfast (1706–43), received the degrees of M.D. and D.D. from Glasgow University in 1732.[159] Kirkpatrick's M.D. was not honorary but was awarded only

---

[159] W. I. Addison (comp.), *A roll of the graduates of the University of Glasgow from 31st December, 1727 to 31st December, 1897* (Glasgow, 1898), p. 314.

after an oral examination.[160] In later life he combined the work of a physician with ministerial duties.[161] In 1739 he published a medical treatise, dedicated to the Royal College of Physicians, Dublin, which gave an account of the alleged success of Mrs Stephens's medicine for the dissolution of gallstones.[162] Another Presbyterian minister who had a medical degree was Rev. Alexander Colvill, jr, of Dromore, Co. Down, who was awarded his M.D. by Glasgow University in 1728.[163]

Through a series of letters written to Sir Hans Sloane we can obtain some insight into the medical practice of the Belfast physician Victor Ferguson. Ferguson did not confine himself to the town but developed a large country practice. As a result, he spent much time on horseback travelling round the surrounding rural area and told Sloane that he spent 'much time in conference abstract from our trade when in houses of note'.[164] In 1698 he wrote to Sloane about the illness of the son of James Hamilton of Bangor, who subsequently died.[165] The Hamiltons of Bangor were members of the Church of Ireland. Although the majority of the patients treated by the Presbyterian doctors were probably Presbyterian, patients did not restrict themselves to using only doctors of their own religious persuasion. The Belfast curate Mr Fairfoul, for instance, was attended by Ferguson, and Duncan Cumyng of Dublin attended the dying William Conolly.[166]

Another of Ferguson's patients was Mr William Nevin of Millisle, near Donaghadee, in County Down. Nevin suffered from headaches after a fall from his horse and had almost lost his sight as a result of two cataracts. Ferguson wrote to Sloane to obtain the name of the best oculist in either London or France, as he hoped that Nevin would regain his sight by couching of his eyes. Ferguson also mentioned that he had been called on to treat a species of epilepsy which he had never read of.[167]

Physicians sought to increase their knowledge through reading. Rev. Joseph Boyse stated that the Dublin doctor Duncan Cumyng attained much skill through 'the fruit of his great reading, penetrating judgment, and accurate observations'.[168] In his letters to Sloane, Ferguson often asked Sloane to send him the latest medical publications that were available in London.[169] He informed Sloane that he had the

---

[160] Glasgow University Meeting (Senate) mins, 1730–49 (GUA 26631, pp 16–21). For the context of the conferring of the two degrees on Rev. Kirkpatrick, a Non-Subscriber, see Anne Skoczylas, *Mr Simson's knotty case: divinity, politics, and due process in early eighteenth-century Scotland* (London, 2001), pp 334–5.

[161] [Alexander Gordon], 'Belfast: list of ministers: First Presbyterian Church', *Disciple*, iii (1883), p. 83; *ODNB* (Kirkpatrick, James (c.1676–1743)).

[162] James Kirkpatrick, *An account of the success of Mrs. Stephens's medicines for the stone, in the case of James Kirkpatrick, Doctor of Divinity, M.A.* (Belfast, 1739), pp iv–vi.

[163] Glasgow Univ. Faculty Meeting mins, 1727–30 (GUA 26631, pp 35–6).

[164] Victor Ferguson to Sloane, 14 May 1698 (BL, Sloane MS 4037, f. 73).

[165] Brooks, *Sir Hans Sloane*, p. 141.

[166] [Kirkpatrick], *Presby. loyalty*, p. 442; Barnard, *New anatomy*, p. 129.

[167] Victor Ferguson to Sloane, 23 July 1700 (BL, Sloane MS 4038, f. 38).

[168] Boyse, *Works*, i, 315.

[169] Victor Ferguson to Sloane, 14 July 1691, 4 Feb. 1697, 14 May & 18 Sept. 1698, 13 Nov. 1699, 23 July 1700 (BL, Sloane MS 4036, f. 106; MS 4037, ff 35, 73, 119; MS 4075, f. 124; MS 4038, f. 39).

'marrow of all ancient and modern authors till about 1688' and wanted 'nothing but what is new and of value tending to physick directly or indirectly'. He also desired Sloane to send the best microscope for herbs, as he went on forays into the Ulster countryside with William Sherard (1659–1728), a botanist who was staying with Sir Arthur Rawdon at Moira in County Down.[170] Plants were an important component in early modern medicines, hence the need for medical practitioners to have some familiarity with herbs and plants. In a letter of 1697 Ferguson asked when Sloane intended to publish his natural history of Jamaica, and inquired if Sir Robert Sibbald's natural history of Scotland was to be improved and republished and whether anyone was planning to refine Willem Piso's natural history of Brazil.[171]

Physicians and surgeons made their living by charging fees for their work. Apothecaries, theoretically, did not charge for diagnosis or advice but rather for the drugs that they sold. Fee or case books do not survive for any of the Presbyterians engaged in the medical profession in the late seventeenth and early eighteenth centuries. We are, however, able to gain some idea of their wealth from surviving wills and from occasional references to unpaid medical bills mentioned in executors' accounts and other similar sources. Drugs which were supplied by the Belfast apothecary, John Ferguson, for the wife of Edward Pierce, for instance, cost 3s 6d in 1721.[172] The account of charges owing after the death of Mary Pottinger included £1 16s 8d for Dr Ferguson's attendance and 1s 3d for a visit by Dr Cromie and a schedule of debts discharged by James Montgomery, esq., included 6s to Hugh Montgomery, an apothecary at Donaghadee, and £2 6s to Dr Ferguson.[173] Skilled and well-connected physicians could enjoy substantial wealth. It was not uncommon for well-established physicians to be landowners, and some were involved in giving loans, and therefore we cannot assume they lived only on the proceeds of their medical practice. Dr Hugh Kennedy was probably the leading medical practitioner in Belfast in the late seventeenth century. Among his patients were the Donegall family. Dr Kennedy, a Presbyterian, was present at the earl of Donegall's funeral in 1675 and Donegall left Kennedy a legacy of £200. The Kennedy family purchased an estate at Cultra from the earl of Clanbrassil in 1671 and Dr Kennedy married Mary Upton, a daughter of Arthur Upton, a leading figure among the Presbyterian gentry.[174] In 1705 the Kennedy lands were let to tenants upon leases of three lives and 31 years,

---

170 Ferguson had a copy of John Ray's *Synopsis methodica stirium Britannicarum*, which was published in 1690, and had read Richard Morton's *Phthisiologia*, on tuberculosis, which was published in 1689, though he did not own a copy of the work himself. He borrowed Clopton Havers's *Osteologia nova, or, some new observations of the bones*, and asked Sloane to send him a copy of Robert Boyle's *Medicina hydrostatica* and Thomas Tryon's *New art of brewing beer, ale, and other liquor so as to render them more healthful*: Victor Ferguson to Sloane, 14 July 1691 (BL, Sloane MS 4036, f. 106); ODNB (Sherard, William).

171 Victor Ferguson to Sloane, 4 Feb. 1697 (BL, Sloane MS 4037, f. 25).

172 Promissory note from Edward Pierce to pay Thomas Lyll (Lyle), 3 Nov. 1721 (PRONI, Mussenden papers, D354/406).

173 Hamilton Maxwell to Agmondisham Vesey, 3 Feb. 1721/2 (PRONI, Kirk papers, T2524/13); a schedule of debts discharged by James Montgomery (ibid., Montgomery papers, T1030/9/A).

174 Benn, *Belfast*, pp 720–1; Con Auld, *Holywood Co. Down: then and now* (Holywood, 2002), pp 32–3.

for the sum of £297 16s 5d.[175] After Dr Kennedy's death his widow subsequently married Dr John Peacock of Belfast. The Peacocks' daughter, Anne, married George Butle Conyngham, who inherited the Conyngham estate at Springhill, County Londonderry, in 1721. On his deathbed in 1712 Dr John Peacock estimated his wealth to be £500, which he directed to be divided between his three children.[176]

Dr Victor Ferguson, in his will dated 25 October 1723, bequeathed six of the best chairs in his parlour, along with his large silver salver, six silver spoons, six silver forks and six silver-handled knives, to his daughter, Mary, and her husband, Captain James McCullogh. Ferguson had a house in Broad (now Waring) Street in Belfast and in the early eighteenth century the street boasted substantial houses, each with a garden. Ferguson's will also mentioned £500 which he had loaned to the earl of Donegall and £150 loaned to Patrick Shaw, a County Antrim attorney.[177]

Apothecaries and surgeons usually earned less and commanded smaller fees than physicians. Nevertheless, some were men of means and status. The dean of Kilmore wrote that in 1712 there were only two Presbyterian inhabitants in Belturbet of note, one of whom was 'Hansard the apothecary'.[178] James Boyd of Glastry, County Down, who trained in London as an apothecary in the early years of the eighteenth century, was left £100 in his father's will of 1719.[179] Neil McNeill, an apothecary in Belfast, was described variously as 'apothecary', 'doctor' and 'gentleman'. He was of sufficient standing in his local community to be elected a burgess of Belfast in 1702, but was among the ten Presbyterian burgesses of Belfast disqualified by the test and removed from office in 1707.[180] James Morrison, a Presbyterian apothecary, resided in Gracious Street in Derry and was appointed one of the sheriffs of the city in 1678, and his relative William Morrison, also an apothecary, was chosen as a burgess of the same corporation in 1689.[181] Thomas Adams, an apothecary at Coleraine, had lands which extended to over 57 acres. Adams, however, got into financial difficulty because of debts that he was unable to pay. He appealed to Route Presbytery in February 1702 for assistance to support him 'in his distress'd condition and want'. The presbytery, aware of the lands and houses that Adams possessed, advised him to first sell his effects and pay off his debts. Only then, if he did not have sufficient means to make a living, did the presbytery promise to contribute to his assistance, though in recognition of the 'poor condition' of Adams's wife and children they also agreed to refer the case to the sub-synod.[182]

---

[175] Stevenson, *Two centuries of life in Down*, pp 232–3.

[176] Benn, *Belfast*, p. 576; Agnew, *Belfast funeral register*, p. 43; Mina Lenox-Conyngham, *An old Ulster house: Springhill and the people who lived in it* (Belfast, 2005), pp 21–2, 24–5.

[177] Will of Victor Ferguson, 1723 (NAI, Prerogative will book, 1728–9, MFGS 41/4, ff 260–2).

[178] Dr Marsh to Matthew Handcock, 17 Dec. 1712 (PRONI, Crossle papers, T780/1, p. 1).

[179] Victor Ferguson to Sloane, 30 Dec. 1700 (BL, Sloane MS 4038, f. 117); abstract will of Thomas Boyd, 1719 (PRONI, Stewart papers, D1759/3/B/1, p. 5).

[180] Agnew, *Belfast funeral register*, p. 55; Young, *Belfast town book*, pp 193, 232, 235.

[181] Belfast Public Art Gallery and Museum, *Catalogue of Irish tokens: 17th, 18th and 19th centuries* (Belfast, 1913), p. 25; Derry corp. mins (PRONI, LA/79/2/AA/1, p. 45; LA/97/2/AA/2, p. 7).

[182] Route Pby mins (PHS, pp 25, 36); T. H. Mullin, *Coleraine in by-gone centuries*, pp 151–2.

IIc. Religious life

Some doctors were very prominent in the affairs of the Presbyterian church, and their religious beliefs could impact on their medical practice. Dr Cumyng used not only drugs and other medical treatments, but also prayed for the recovery of his patients. When such means failed Cumyng ascribed it to the 'rebukes of providence to himself', and when his prescriptions were effective he always remembered to thank God through prayer. In cases he judged to be terminal, Cumyng warned patients of their approaching death and helped them to make preparation for it.[183] As a fellow of the Royal College of Physicians in Dublin, Cumyng took his turn with the other fellows to attend the sick boys of the Bluecoat Hospital in Dublin, which was done free of charge.[184] Cumyng had a stated hour when the poor could come to him for free consultation, and devoted all the fees he received on Sundays to religious and charitable causes.[185] Ferguson's faith also affected his practice as a physician. According to Rev. Samuel Haliday, Ferguson was 'the blessing of many who were ready to perish, whom he fed, clothed and lodged … without prospect of a reward in this world', curing their diseases and endeavouring also to 'impress their minds' with a 'serious sense of true religion'.[186]

Ferguson was an elder in Second Belfast. He represented the congregation as ruling elder at the General Synod in 1710, 1717 and 1718, and appeared at the General Synod as a commissioner for Ballinderry congregation, County Antrim, in 1712 and for Dromara congregation, County Down, in 1714.[187] John Peacock was an elder of Lisburn and, later, First Belfast and represented the latter at the General Synod in 1710.[188] John Williamson was one of the commissioners who appeared at the General Synod from Antrim congregation in 1719 and in 1730 Gabriel King attended the General Synod as a commissioner seeking supplies for Armagh Presbyterian Church.[189] Other doctors mentioned in the synod minutes were George Martin and a Dr Somerville.[190]

Duncan Cumyng was a prominent member of Wood Street Presbyterian Church in Dublin. He had studied theology for a short time before deciding to train to become a physician and he retained a keen interest in divinity throughout his life.[191] We can obtain further insight into his religious life from the sermon preached at his funeral by Joseph Boyse, minister of Wood Street, who at the time of Cumyng's death had known the doctor for 40 years. Cumyng had settled in Dublin in 1684

---

[183] Boyse, *Works*, i, 316.

[184] Journal of the RCPI, i (RCPI Lib., p. 135).

[185] Boyse, *Works*, i, 316.

[186] Samuel Haliday, *A letter to the Reverend Mr. Gilbert Kennedy; occasion'd by some personal reflections, contain'd in his answer to Mr. Haliday's reasons against the imposition of subscription to the Westminster-Confession, or any such human tests of orthodoxy* (Belfast, 1725), p. 12.

[187] *RGSU*, i, 190, 274, 328, 413, 449.

[188] Lisburn sess. mins, 29 Jan., 23 Mar. 1698/9, 1 June 1699 (PRONI, MIC1P/159/6); *RGSU*, i, 190. He also appeared as a commissioner: *RGSU*, i, 144, 148, 159, 178–9.

[189] *RGSU*, i, 489; ii, 152.

[190] Ibid., i, 55; ii, 152.

[191] Thomas Emlyn, *The works of the Rev. Thomas Emlyn* (3 vols, London, 1746), i, 17; Boyse, *Works*, i, 315.

and according to Boyse was a regular attender at services. Cumyng kept a monthly record of his own carriage towards God and God's instances of providence towards him. He made diligent enquiry into matters of doctrine and was reputedly able to defend the faith as well as many ministers.[192] In 1702 Cumyng was the first to notice the heretical views of Rev. Thomas Emlyn, who was prosecuted for Unitarianism.[193] Each day Cumyng spent time reading the Bible, which he studied with the aid of the 'best' commentaries, and he often discussed what he had read, and his thoughts on it, with his friends. Cumyng was diligent in private prayer. He kept a note of his prayer requests and 'strictly observ'd what returns were made to 'em'. At the start of each new year Cumyng renewed his covenant with God, and in later years, after he married and had children, included his family in his covenants. He took his religious duties as head of the household very seriously. Each Sunday evening he spent an hour examining his children and servants and instructed them in the principles and duties of the Christian religion. When his children were older he reminded them of their baptismal bonds and persuaded them to make 'a solemn and deliberate renewal of their covenant with God at his holy table'. Cumyng also encouraged young candidates for the Presbyterian ministry whom he thought were of sufficient religious character and ability. He supported the work of the Societies for the Reformation of Manners and was active in obtaining contributions to support the work of the societies established in Great Britain for the propagation of Christian knowledge. Cumyng supported the establishment of the Presbyterian General Fund and was among those who gave a substantial financial contribution to get it established. He was also involved in the erection of a charity school at Wood Street.[194]

The importance of religion in the lives of some of the doctors is indicated by their charitable giving and bequests, as well as their reading activities. Cumyng was greatly affected by the suffering of fellow Protestants, which he had observed while receiving his training on the continent, and when he settled in Dublin he gave support to the Huguenots who settled there after the revocation of the edict of Nantes.[195] When Cumyng died in 1724 he left money to the school of his native parish of Edinkillie, in Moray, Scotland.[196] Victor Ferguson left £5 to the poor of Belfast, to be distributed among them at the discretion of Rev. James Kirkpatrick and Colonel Edward Brice, an elder of First Belfast.[197] In 1722 Cumyng and Dr Upton Peacock both subscribed for a Dublin edition of the French theologian Lewis Ellies du Pin's *New history of ecclesiastical writers*.[198] Peacock was also one of the subscribers to Antonio Gavin's *Master-key to popery*, an anti-Catholic tirade attacking Romish doctrine and practices, which was published at Dublin in 1724.[199]

---

[192] Boyse, *Works*, i, 315.

[193] Emlyn, *Works*, i, 17.

[194] Boyse, *Works*, i, 315–17; C. H. Irwin, *A history of Presbyterianism in Dublin and the south and west of Ireland* (London, 1890), pp 33–5.

[195] Boyse, *Works*, i, 315–16.

[196] 'Cuming, Duncan' (RCPI, Kirkpatrick archives).

[197] Will of Victor Ferguson, 1723 (NAI, Prerogative will book, 1728–9, MFGS 41/4, f. 261).

[198] Lewis Ellies du Pin, *A new history of ecclesiastical writers* (Dublin, 1722), vol. i.

[199] Antonio Gavin, *A master-key to popery* (Dublin, 1724).

Ferguson had a copy of *The sanctuarie of a troubled soule*, a devotional title by Sir John Hayward.[200] Both Cumyng and Ferguson gave their support to the publication of works written by Presbyterian ministers. Joseph Boyse's sermon on the death of Queen Anne in 1714 was subsequently published at the instigation of Dr Cumyng.[201] Ferguson was very much involved with the Belfast Society, acting as its lay secretary. In 1721 Ferguson's minister, Rev. James Kirkpatrick, wrote *A vindication of the Presbyterian ministers in the north of Ireland*. The work is often referred to as *Ferguson's Vindication* because it was Ferguson who caused it to be published.[202] In the preface to the pamphlet Ferguson stated that he had carefully perused the records of the Presbyterian church from its first foundation, which indicates an interest in the history of the Presbyterian church as it had developed in Ireland.[203]

Not all Presbyterian doctors were necessarily as religious or pious as Cumyng or Ferguson. Dr Thomas Cairnes of Dunmore, County Tyrone, has been described by H. C. Lawlor, the historian of the Cairnes family, as a 'disreputable person'. His uncle, the lawyer David Cairnes, referred in his will to the 'unjust doings and carriage' of Thomas Cairnes towards his wife. These 'doings' are not specified but it is known that Thomas Cairnes had an illegitimate child and it is possible that the comment in the will may have, at least in part, referred to that.[204]

* * * * * *

Presbyterians were involved at all levels of the medical profession and although it is impossible to give exact numbers it is nevertheless possible to state that there were more Presbyterian physicians than barristers. Belfast was particularly well supplied by medical practitioners, but there were also Presbyterian physicians active in Counties Antrim, Armagh, Down, Donegal, Londonderry and Tyrone, and though often located in towns, they commonly had a large remit that included the surrounding rural areas. Physicians usually held a university degree and although many of the Ulster Presbyterian physicians had been educated at Leiden they usually chose to graduate from Rheims where the cost of graduation was less. Surgeons and apothecaries trained through apprenticeship to an existing practitioner or through service in the armed forces, and although many served their apprenticeship in Ulster there are examples of young men from Ulster being apprenticed to masters in Scotland or London. Though most of the physicians in Ulster were not licensed by the Irish Royal College of Physicians, in Dublin, there was some involvement by Presbyterians in the affairs of the college, with the Presbyterian physicians Duncan Cumyng and Victor Ferguson both being elected

---

[200] Antrim Pby Lib., B. 13. 9. 19.
[201] Boyse, *Works*, i, 317.
[202] [Kirkpatrick], *A vindication of the Presbyterian ministers*, p. 3; Witherow, *Hist. & lit. memls*, i, 160.
[203] [Kirkpatrick], *A vindication of the Presbyterian ministers*, p. 4. The Adair MS, on the history of Presbyterianism in Ireland until 1670, appears to have been in the hands of Dr Victor Ferguson as his initials appear on marginal notes of the manuscript and also refers to manuscripts relating to early Presbyterianism in Ulster which were in his possession: Adair manuscript (PHS, pp 92, 146, 152, 154, 157, 159–62, 173, 179, 181, 184, 239, 272).
[204] Lawlor, *A history of the Cairnes*, pp 111, 169–70.

fellows of the college, and the former also serving as its president. The leading physicians enjoyed a high social status, married well, and were reasonably wealthy. Even some of the apothecaries were of sufficient status to be chosen as burgesses or sheriffs. The existence of alternative medicine did not negate the existence of a recognised profession of medicine and most of the Presbyterian physicians took their medical practice seriously. They sought to extend their medical knowledge through reading, experiment, observation, and correspondence with leading London doctors such as Sir Hans Sloane, who was a president of the Royal Society. Some of the Presbyterian doctors of Scottish origin maintained their affinity with their homeland. Cumyng, for instance, left money to the school of his native Scottish parish and also contemplated being buried there. Others such as Samuel Moore, however, who changed his name from the Scottish 'Mure' to the Irish 'Moore', exhibit less of a concern for their Scottish heritage. Many physicians were active in the life of their congregation and their religious beliefs impacted not only on their personal but also their professional lives.

* * * * * * *

Presbyterian professionals were important because, alongside the leading merchants, they added to the number and character of the prominent in Ulster Presbyterian society. After the passage of the test clause the higher branches of the legal profession were closed to Presbyterian recruits unwilling to conform, at least occasionally, but all levels of medical practice remained open to Presbyterians despite the technical requirement that medical practitioners be licensed by bishops. The professions were never an exclusive or distinctly discrete group and shared certain similarities with the Presbyterian gentry. Most physicians, and practically all barristers, came from gentry backgrounds and, though they were urban-based, professionals were similar to landed gentry in lifestyle and social activities. There were also similarities between the secular professions and the Presbyterian ministry, who both underwent a similar educational process which involved study outside the province. They shared the common experience of education at grammar school and university or inn, and even some of those in the lower branches of the legal and medical professions underwent lengthy and demanding training that could involve time spent outside Ulster. The cost of entering the leading branches of the law and medicine was substantial, which helped to restrict recruitment to the gentry or other wealthy families. Those aspiring to enter the secular learned professions did not have the same opportunities that were provided by the presbyteries for poorer students studying divinity, and it may be, therefore, that the leading professionals were of higher social origins than the ministers. At the lower levels of the secular professions there were opportunities for those of more humble origins who had the talent but lacked the necessary status or capital. Social advancement, however, took time and often was not confined to a single generation. As a result of the close links between the gentry and those at the top of the professions, when gentry families conformed to the established church, they were not giving way to a distinctly new, emerging, middle class, but groups with which they were already connected and with whom they already shared certain characteristics.

5

The Lower Orders

The Presbyterian elite, in terms of the ministers, gentry, merchants and professionals has already been considered. This chapter is concerned with those at the lower levels of the social and occupational structure. Material for reconstructing the lives of these non-elite groups is not abundant and when they do appear in the surviving sources it is usually as observed rather than observers. Nevertheless, because they formed the largest group in Presbyterian society they cannot be ignored. Contemporaries and modern historians have both recognised the importance of the middling and lower orders to Irish Presbyterianism. Bishop William King of Derry recognised that the bulk of the common people in Ireland were either Dissenters or 'Papists', and Toby Barnard has stated that Presbyterian congregations derived their strength from the middle and lower orders.[1] Within the last five decades, social historians have shown an increasing interest in the historically less-articulate members of early modern English society but only more recently has an interest for the topic developed among historians of Ireland. Barnard considers the lower orders in his *New anatomy* and servants of the gentry in The King's and Queen's Counties (modern-day Laois and Offaly) are given attention in a doctoral thesis by Daniel Beaumont.[2] The poor, and poor relief, have been the subject of articles by David Dickson, Rowena Dudley and Rosalind Mitchison, and have been the focus of an excellent, though rarely cited, thesis by Patrick Fitzgerald.[3] Though these works are useful for comparison and contain material of general application, the following is the first time that there has been focused attention on late seventeenth- and early eighteenth-century Presbyterian traders, craftsmen, farmers, servants and poor relief.

---

[1]   Abp King to Bp John Stearne, 25 Sept. 1714 (TCD, King papers, MS 2536/75); Barnard, *New anatomy*, p. 17.
[2]   Barnard, *New anatomy*, pp 279–327; D. M. Beaumont, 'The gentry of The King's and Queen's Counties: Protestant landed society, 1690–1760' (2 vols, Ph.D. thesis, TCD, 1999), pp 169–81.
[3]   David Dickson, 'In search of the old Irish poor law' in Rosalind Mitchison and Peter Roebuck (eds), *Economy and society in Scotland and Ireland, 1500–1939* (Edinburgh, 1988), pp 149–59; Rowena Dudley, 'The Dublin parishes and the poor: 1660–1740', *Archivium Hibernicum*, liii (1999), pp 80–94; Rosalind Mitchison, 'Permissive poor laws: the Irish and Scottish systems considered together' in S. J. Connolly, *et al.* (eds), *Conflict, identity and economic development: Ireland and Scotland, 1600–1939* (Preston, 1995), pp 161–71; P. D. Fitzgerald, 'Poverty and vagrancy in early modern Ireland 1540–1770' (Ph.D. thesis, QUB, 1994). See also R. L. Greaves, *God's other children: Protestant Nonconformists and the emergence of denominational churches in Ireland, 1660–1700* (Stanford, Calif., 1997), pp 241–46.

I. Traders and craftsmen

A few tradesmen and craftsmen were present in many of the rural villages of Ulster, but the majority lived and worked in the larger urban areas and county towns. The Belfast freeman's roll, which extends from 1635 to 1682 and 1723 to 1796, shows the diversity of trades practised in the town. There were large numbers of butchers, chandlers, coopers, cordwainers (shoemakers) and tanners, as well as carpenters, tailors, masons and alesellers, who were admitted as freemen of the corporation. By the 1680s there were also goldsmiths, watch- and clockmakers, two gunsmiths, a sugar baker, bookbinder and stationer.[4] Similarly, the corporation minute books of Derry exhibit the same variety in the trades practised by the inhabitants of the city. On 15 January 1691 a retailer, tobacco-spinner, two tailors and a baker were admitted as freemen; in May 1692 there were two cordwainers, two glovers and a chapman; in April 1694 a butcher and a currier; in January 1700 a tailor and seven weavers; and on 2 July 1706 two wigmakers.[5] It is impossible, however, in the absence of other evidence to determine the denominational affiliation of those admitted as freemen in either Belfast or Derry. The Adair family of Ballymena, whose head until at least 1704 was a member of the Presbyterian church, sought to develop Ballymena by attracting a wide range of tradesmen to settle in the town. Among those obtaining leases from the Adairs during the last two decades of the seventeenth century were carpenters, glovers, shoemakers, smiths, turners, and innkeepers, as well as a butcher, currier, cutler, mason, tailor and weaver.[6] However, as with the freedom, although the Adairs were themselves Presbyterian, we are unable to state definitively that the lessees were of the same religious denomination as their landlord.

The First and Second Presbyterian congregations of Belfast shared as their joint property a selection of mort cloths (or palls) and mourning cloaks which they loaned to members of their own congregations, as well as to people living in other places as far away as Counties Armagh, Londonderry and Tyrone. Though the majority of those who hired the funeral gear were probably members of the Presbyterian church, there were also some Anglicans. The funeral register, which survives for the period from 1712 to 1736, contains details of around 2,000 deaths, and in many cases provides the occupation and place of residence of those recorded.[7] Benn analysed the register and found that along with the death of 72 Belfast merchants, there were also those of 36 mariners, 23 carpenters or ship-carpenters, 18 coopers, 17 tailors, 16 carmen, 12 shoemakers, 12 butchers, 10 glovers and a variety of other trades and crafts.[8]

Occasionally Presbyterian baptismal registers include references to the occupations of some of the fathers who had their children baptised. In Antrim congregation John Mills, a pewterer, had his son baptised in November 1678, and other trades

4   Young, *Belfast town book*, pp 246–93.
5   Derry corp. mins (PRONI, LA/79/2/AA/2, pp 64, 71, 109, 178; LA/79/2/AA/3A, p. 53).
6   Adair leases, 1680–99 (PRONI, Adair papers, D929/HA12/F2/1/6, /12–13, /24, /27, /29, /35, /46, /61, /64, /79, /105–6; D929/HA12/F2/2/12, /24–25, /27, /44, /48).
7   Agnew, *Belfast funeral register*.
8   Benn, *Belfast*, p. 585.

mentioned include a baker, chandler, glover, loader, nailer, maltster, tanner and weaver.[9] In the baptism records of Larne and Kilwaughter it is recorded that the son of a shoemaker was baptised in June 1721 and in February 1726 the son of Robert Workman, a miller.[10] Records which allow us to glimpse the occupational structure of a particular congregation survive for only one Presbyterian church – Third Belfast. A third Presbyterian congregation was formed in Belfast in 1723 and the pew register of the church contains not only the names of the householders who formed the original members but also the price of the seats and in most cases the occupation of their holders. Recorded in the pew register were: farmers (12), most of whom lived on the edge of the town; shoemakers (11); weavers (8); maltsters (7); alesellers, coopers, mariners and tobacconists (6 each); bricklayers, tailors and hucksters (5 each); bakers and carpenters (4 each); schoolteachers, chandlers, blacksmiths and carmen (3 each); butchers, glovers, millers and ship-carpenters (2 each); and one each of the following: an apothecary, barber, bookseller, button maker, clockmaker, distiller, glazier, hatter, labourer, linen-draper, mason, mealman, potter, printer, saddler, sword cutler, tanner and waterman.[11]

These records make clear just how many objects were produced locally for a local market. Urban craftsmen supplied clothing, footwear, domestic and household essentials, as well as the tools and implements necessary for outdoor and agricultural activities. Dr Thomas Molyneux visited Belfast in 1708 and described it as a 'thriving, well-peopled town' with 'a great many new houses and good shops in't. The folks seemed all very busy and employed in trade, the inhabitants being for the most part merchants, or employ'd under 'em, in this sea port.'[12] The pew register of Third Belfast, though it recorded 22 merchants, only named one shopkeeper.[13] As mentioned in chapter 3, 'merchant' was a term which had a wide application and could include both retailers and those engaged in wholesale or foreign trade. The international trade of the merchants in port towns such as Belfast, Coleraine, Derry and elsewhere gave rise to a number of ancillary occupations which were important to the provisions trade in which the Ulster Presbyterian, and Anglican, merchants were primarily engaged. A large number of mariners or sailors were often located in port towns and Belfast was no exception as is apparent from their significant presence in its funeral and pew registers. Coopers made the coops or casks in which

---

9 W. S. Smith, 'Early register of the old presbyterian congregation of Antrim', *UJA*, v (1899), p. 181.

10 Larne & Kilwaughter sess. mins (PRONI, MIC1B/6A/1B, pp 104, 112).

11 Third Belfast (Rosemary Street) Presbyterian Church treasurer's book and pew register, 1726 (PRONI, T654/6, pp 60–119). Occupations are also contained in the Third Belfast Presbyterian Church building book (PRONI, MIC1P/7/8, pp 5–8). According to a hostile source the Presbyterian congregation at Drogheda, in 1712, included Widow Ballantine (innkeeper), Robert Adair ('a tobacco pipe maker from the North, a man of no substance'), Archibald Campbell ('a journyman taylor, no housekeeper, and of no substance'), Jonathan Lunn ('of no substance'), Thomas Marsden (cooper), John French (cobbler), Arthur Caesar ('a poor man, no housekeeper'), an unnamed journeyman shoemaker from Derry and an unnamed servant to an alderman: petition to the Lords Justices of Ireland from Narcissus, Abp of Armagh (PRONI, Crossle papers, T780/1, p. 47).

12 Young, *Historical notices of old Belfast*, p. 155.

13 Third Belfast treasurer's book & pew register, 1726 (PRONI, T654/6, pp 60–119).

the butter and beef to be exported were stored after being salted, while the main function of carmen (or carriers) in places like Belfast was to draw loads of goods to and from the quay to the marketplace. James Warke, a member of Third Belfast, was a beef salter and John Magown, another member of the same congregation, a butter buyer.[14] Curriers purchased and prepared animal hides for the tanners who then turned the hides into leather. Much of the leather was made to order by cordwainers who cut and sewed the leather into shoes and boots for the home market, but tanned leather was also significant among the products exported from Belfast, as was tallow which the chandlers of the town would have been involved in preparing.[15] Molyneux's statement concerning Belfast alludes to the construction of new houses in the town and five of the pewholders in Third Belfast were bricklayers, while one was a mason.[16] In the seventeenth century most homes (and church buildings) were thatched, but from the early eighteenth century slates began to replace thatch on the homes of those who could afford it. In some areas the change was slow. In Glenarm all the houses, with three exceptions, were thatched rather than slated in 1683, while in Belfast only ten were slated in 1700 and two decades later the houses in Bridge Street, Belfast, were still all thatched. Nevertheless, two slaters were resident in Belfast during the years when the funeral register was compiled.[17]

Belfast had ship-carpenters and ropemakers[18] but the principal manufactures related to textiles and brewing activities. Rev. John Abernethy in 1733 wrote, 'All who know the present state of Ireland will acknowledge, that it is supported chiefly by the linen manufacture, and it is certain that that manufacture is principally carried on by the Dissenters in the north.'[19] Though Quakers such as Louis Crommelin played a key role in the development of the linen industry, many contemporaries, including Anglicans such as Rev. William Tisdall, pointed out the dominant position of Presbyterians among the weavers of Ulster.[20] Although the weaving of fine linen cloth required the skill of expert craftsmen, low grade or coarser cuts were produced by women in the countryside who supplemented family incomes by spinning and weaving cloth which they were then able to sell. Almost all the inhabitants of Islandmagee in the late seventeenth century were Presbyterian and when writing about the area in 1683 Richard Dobbs stated that the women located there spent their time 'in spinning and making linen cloth, and some ordinary woollen for their family's use'.[21] Though restrictive legislation, enacted in 1699, placed heavy duties on the export of manufactured wool, the

---

14 Ibid., pp 73, 106.

15 Benn, *Belfast*, pp 317–18.

16 Third Belfast treasurer's book & pew register, 1726 (PRONI, T654/6, pp 86, 95–6, 118).

17 George Hill, *An historical account of the MacDonnells of Antrim* (Belfast, 1873), p. 382; Young, *Belfast town book*, pp xi–xii; Agnew, *Belfast funeral register*, pp 18, 33.

18 Agnew, *Belfast funeral register*, pp 12, 16, 18, 22, 25–6, 30–1, 37–8; Third Belfast treasurer's book & pew register, 1726 (PRONI, T654/6, pp 70, 77).

19 John Abernethy, *Scarce and valuable tracts and sermons, occasionally published, by the late reverend and learned John Abernethy, M.A.* (London, 1751), p. 66.

20 [William Tisdall], *The conduct of the Dissenters of Ireland, with respect both to church and state* (Dublin, 1712), pp 17–18.

21 Hill, *Historical account of MacDonnells*, p. 380.

home market was not affected.[22] After the founding of the first newspaper in the north of Ireland, the *Belfast Newsletter*, in 1737, tradesmen and shopkeepers were able to advertise their products through the press. In 1739 Adam Dickson of Newry advertised his handiwork as follows: 'Adam Dickson, hosier, just from Newry, grand-son of the late Rev. Archebald Dickson, [Presbyterian minister] of Saintfield, deceas'd, makes and sells all sorts of best loom stockings, at reasonable rates. He is to be found at the house of Mr. James Micklerath, shopkeeper, near the market-house in Belfast.'[23]

Brewing and distilling were generally undertaken on a small scale, and were often connected with inns and even private houses.[24] Taverns and inns had an important social and economic function, providing both accommodation for travellers and entertainment for locals. They served as places for county business in county towns such as Carrickfergus where, in 1683 Dobbs noted, 'the greatest trade now is in taverns and ale-houses'.[25] A smaller number of traders and craftsmen were involved in the production and retail of luxury items which appealed to, and could be afforded by, the wealthy of society. In addition to printers,[26] bookbinders[27] and stationers,[28] Belfast by the early 1730s also had a coffeehouse and playhouse.[29] Large quantities of tobacco were imported from North America into Ulster by the Belfast merchants. This supplied employment for tobacco spinners who increasingly appeared among the freemen of the town from 1675 onwards.[30] The Malcolm family who attended Third Congregation were prominent tobacconists in Belfast, as was William Stevenson, and the death of John Cairns, 'a snuf man', is recorded in the Belfast funeral register in 1732.[31]

Although there were tailors' and cordwainers' shops in villages and towns, journeymen also travelled from house to house carrying their tools and making clothes and shoes from material provided by the householders. Rev. John Kennedy, the Presbyterian minister of Benburb, for instance, had shoemakers in residence at his home for three days who were employed in making shoes for members of his family in 1726.[32] There were also travelling merchants and chapmen who roamed the countryside with their selection of goods, and occasionally they are mentioned

---

[22] *HIP*, i, 301.

[23] *Belfast Newsletter*, 22 May 1739.

[24] List of licences for 'ale, wine and strong waters', Belfast walk, 1683–4 (PRONI, Groves papers, T808/14891); T. H. Mullin, *Ulster's historic city Derry, Londonderry* (Coleraine, 1986), p. 83.

[25] Hill, *Historical account of MacDonnells*, p. 388.

[26] Third Belfast treasurer's book & pew register, 1726 (PRONI, T654/6, p. 67); Agnew, *Belfast funeral register*, pp 21, 25; Raymond Gillespie, *Early Belfast: the origins and growth of an Ulster town to 1750* (Belfast, 2007), pp 141–3.

[27] Young, *Belfast town book*, p. 285; Agnew, *Belfast funeral register*, pp 20, 39–41.

[28] Young, *Belfast town book*, pp 259, 285; Agnew, *Belfast funeral register*, p. 32.

[29] Agnew, *Belfast funeral register*, pp 35–6.

[30] Young, *Belfast town book*, pp 278, 284–6; Gillespie, *Early Belfast*, p. 116.

[31] Third Belfast treasurer's book & pew register, 1726 (PRONI, T654/6, pp 68, 77, 81); J. W. Kernohan, *Rosemary Street Presbyterian Church Belfast: a record of the past 200 years* (Belfast, 1923), p. 20; Agnew, *Belfast funeral register*, pp 15, 19, 23, 38.

[32] Diary of Rev. John Kennedy (PHS, p. 100). See also Rev. Kennedy's accounts, 1729–31 in 'Miscellanea by J[ohn] K[ennedy], 1699–1725' (PHS); James Trail's accounts, 30 August 1732 (PRONI, D1460/1).

in discipline cases recorded in session minute books. Mary Brown of Ballymena confessed adultery with 'John Kelly a traveling merchant' in 1710, while Anne McLeslie of Ballycarry congregation confessed fornication with a man who 'wrought days in the neighbourhood and particularly at the couper trade'. In February 1731 Isobel McCluny appeared before Ballycarry kirk session for 'uncleanness' with Robert McCalah, a 'wool comber and a stroler through the countrey', 'but whither it be adultery or fornication we can[no]t tell'.[33]

Entry into most crafts and trades was through service as an apprentice. The adolescent apprentice was bound by a legal contract, or indenture, to serve a master or mistress for a period of usually seven years' duration. Apprenticeship indentures took a standardised form, whether it was for a smith or a clockmaker, and set out the duties expected of the two parties, the apprentice and his master. Masters agreed not only to teach and instruct the apprentice in their craft but also to provide him with lodging, food and clothes. Apprentices lived in the home of their master and masters were responsible for their apprentices' welfare, conduct and religious life. In the indentures the apprentice promised to serve his full term and not to waste or lend, without his master's knowledge, any of the master's goods or tools. The apprentice also promised to remain celibate during his time of servitude, not to contract marriage, not to engage in cards or dice, and not to 'haunt or use' taverns or alehouses 'unless it be about his master's business'. The parents or guardians of the apprentice paid a fee, or premium, to the master for the training of the apprentice and since apprentices did not usually receive any wages the free labour of the apprentice could be an asset to the master's income, if not in the early years, certainly by the third or fourth year.[34] The success of the training varied, probably depending on the aptitude of the apprentice and the dedication and character of the master. In corporation towns the municipalities offered some degree of regulation,[35] but this was not the case where apprentices served masters located in villages and non-corporate towns. Corporation guilds, where they existed, may also have had a supervisory role. A guild of tailors and glovers was established in Carrickfergus in 1670 and a 'fraternity of trade', consisting of 36 tradesmen, in Derry in 1735.[36]

---

[33] Antrim Pby mins, 1697–1713 (PHS, p. 474); Ballycarry sess. mins, 20 Sept. 1719, 21 Feb. 1730/31 (PRONI, CR3/21/1). For similar references in Burt sess. mins, see K. M. Middleton, 'Religious revolution and social crisis in southwest Scotland and Ulster, 1687–1714' (Ph.D. thesis, TCD, 2010), pp 225, 256.

[34] Matthew Dutton, The law of masters and servants in Ireland (Dublin, 1723), pp 73, 232, 243–4; Belturbet corp. mins, 1657–c.1730 (Cavan County Archives, BC/1, pp 92, 103); Samuel McSkimin, The history and antiquities of the county of the town of Carrickfergus: from the earliest records till 1839, ed. E. J. McCrum (new ed., Belfast, 1909), pp 408–9; Barnard, New anatomy, pp 306–9; Rosemary O'Day, The professions in early modern England, 1450–1800: servants of the commonweal (Harlow, 2000), pp 24–5.

[35] For instance, Derry corp. mins (PRONI, LA/79/2/AA/1), p. 38.

[36] W. H. Crawford, 'The creation and evolution of small towns in Ulster in the seventeenth and eighteenth centuries' in Peter Borsay and L. J. Proudfoot (eds), Provincial towns in early modern England and Ireland: change, convergence and divergence (Oxford, 2002), p. 104; Mullin, Ulster's historic city Derry, p. 73. See also: 'The declaration of the members of the Committee of Freemen who are Handicraft Tradesmen of the Society in Londonderry' to Thomas Upton and George Tomkins, 17 July 1727 (PRONI, Lenox-Conyngham papers, D1449/12/47).

A casual entry in the Belfast funeral register on 30 May 1722 which mentions 'the capt[ain] of the tealoars' (tailors), 'capt[ain] of the beackears' (bakers) and the 'capt[ain] of the show-mackers' (shoemakers), and a reference in the building book of Third Belfast to the 'wardens of the corporation of taylors', suggests a degree of organisation among the artisans of Belfast.[37] Apprenticeship was one of the commonest methods of acquiring freedom in a corporation, which brought with it the right to trade within the bounds of the municipality. Edward Carloe, for instance, was admitted a freeman of Derry in May 1692 after a seven-year apprenticeship to a glover and Richard Crookshanks was admitted to the freedom the following week after he had served seven years as an apprentice to his brother, a mariner.[38] Once apprenticeship was finished the young man was then able to become a journeyman (that is a hired worker paid by the day) to either his master or another of the same trade. After gaining skill and experience a journeyman could set up as a master on his own, though not all journeymen were able to save sufficient capital. In the various trades the masters were counted among the 'quality', as Barnard terms it,[39] but, in contrast to the principal merchants, it was rare for craftsmen to become rich enough to be able to buy estates or grant loans to members of the local gentry.

II. Farming and rural Ulster

Agriculture and farming were central to the economy and daily life in Ireland. Most people in Ulster lived in rural areas and engaged in farming activities on farms of varying sizes and quality. Even in the towns there was a close connexion with the countryside and many town residents grew vegetables on garden plots for their own domestic use. Whilst farming was undeniably important to seventeenth- and early eighteenth-century Presbyterianism, farmers are nevertheless the social grouping that is hardest to trace in the extant primary sources. Even when it is possible to uncover tenant farmers in contemporary rentals and other estate records, it is unfortunately often extremely difficult to ascertain their precise religious affiliation.

Late Stuart and early Hanoverian Ulster was an important period of transition in Irish agriculture.[40] The influx, particularly of Scottish Presbyterians, in the 1690s, and the resultant increase in population, encouraged a more intensive use of land. In the early seventeenth century Ulster had been the most backward of the Irish provinces, but this input of capital – both human and financial – led to investment in activities to further clear woods, drain bogs, and improve the fertility of the ground by use of lime and other fertilisers.[41] Ulster, however, was not equally prosperous and parts of Fermanagh and the west of Donegal remained undeveloped

---

[37] Agnew, *Belfast funeral register*, p. 77; Kernohan, *Rosemary Street Presbyterian Church*, p. 19.
[38] Derry corp. mins (PRONI, LA/79/2/AA/2, pp 71, 73).
[39] Barnard, *New anatomy*, p. 280.
[40] Raymond Gillespie, *The transformation of the Irish economy 1550–1700* ([Dublin], 1991); idem (ed.), *Settlement and survival on an Ulster estate: the Brownlow leasebook 1667–1711* (Belfast, 1988), pp xxv–xxxiii.
[41] W. H. Crawford, 'Economy and society in eighteenth century Ulster' (Ph.D. thesis, QUB, 1982), pp 51–4.

and the majority of their inhabitants poorer than their north-eastern counterparts. In general, though, the more backward parts of Ulster did not have as high a proportion of Presbyterians and the Presbyterians' independent means often meant they were able to obtain better lands.[42]

The townland was the usual tenurial unit and landlords preferred to rent these blocks of land, of approximately 200–400 acres, to a single head tenant, who then sublet this, in whole or part, to smaller tenants. Alternatively, a group of smaller tenants sometimes clubbed together and took the holding in partnership. In Ireland at this time there was a noted dearth of strong farmers able to rent and stock a substantial holding equivalent to the yeomen of England, and in their absence the 'head' tenants assumed greater importance. Though modern historians have tended to be more indulgent of them, there was some criticism levelled at these middlemen in the early eighteenth century, for instance, from the Belfast-born Presbyterian James Arbuckle, who denounced this 'sort of idle half gentry, half commonalty', as the 'very pest and bane' of Ireland. Below those renting from a head tenant were the peasant cottiers who rented a few acres in exchange for cash or labour, which allowed them to grow some crops to feed their families, and at the very bottom were the labourers who invested their earnings in a small patch of ground which they rented only for a season.[43]

A detailed leasebook for the manor of Castledillon in Armagh, from around the end of the seventeenth century, gives us a glimpse of the system in operation.[44] Unusually it also includes the religion of the tenants. Among the Presbyterian head tenants were William Murra leasing 298 (English) acres, William Dicky leasing 139 acres and James Clarke leasing 55 acres. Following Murra's death his wife sold her 'interest' to James Marshall, a pack merchant of Armagh, and she re-married James McComb, another Presbyterian. The Dickys too fell on hard times following the death of William Dicky, during the Williamite War. His widow 'was poor' and a third of their lands on Grange townland was granted to a relative, John Dicky, who was a Presbyterian elder, while the remaining part was held by William's son, also called John. The son, John, was described as 'a very laborious sober good tenant' and his holding of 92½ acres as 'pretty inclosed'. It produced good corn though the pasture was 'course and shrubby', and he had 'a good house and outhouses' and 'good convenience of turf from an adjacent bogg'. The Dickys farmed their entire holdings themselves and did not have sub-tenants. James Clarke's land was in Mullanasilla townland. It too was well enclosed with 'ash and sally trees' and had access to turf. He was described as 'an honest man' who paid his 'rent well' and his 'mud and watled wall' house was well situated, with outbuildings and garden, the 'mault kilne very convenient except [for] water'. The land yielded chiefly oats. Clarke's under-tenants were Murtagh McCloskey, an Anglican, and 'Widdow Donnelly Papist', with two 'small sod wall-houses' near the road.

---

42 L. M. Cullen, *The emergence of modern Ireland 1600–1900* (London, 1981), pp 55–6.

43 S. J. Connolly, *Divided kingdom: Ireland 1630–1800* (Oxford, 2008), pp 358–9; Ian McBride, *Eighteenth-century Ireland: the isle of slaves* (Dublin, 2009), pp 123–4; [James Arbuckle], *The Tribune* (Dublin, 1729), pp 126–8.

44 Leasebook of the manor of Castledillon, Co. Armagh, with observations by William Molyneux, c.1700 (PRONI, MIC80/3).

Among the Presbyterian under-tenants on the Castledillon estate there was great variety. At the top of the pile was the Presbyterian minister of Armagh, Rev. John Hutcheson, who had a holding of just over 100 acres. On this he had a 'good strong house of stone and lime with a good cow house and stable and barne but all ruinous by reason the present tenant has not incouragment being only tenant at will'. He also had a 'pretty garden and orchard'. George Johnson, who was described as 'an industrious man', leased 63 acres for £13 *per annum*, and on this he had 'a good house of stone and lime, barn, cowhouse and malt house'. He was also building a stable, contemplating enlarging his cowhouse, and had undertaken a number of other improvements. Others held their holdings (varying from 48 to 80 acres) in joint-partnership, often with another Presbyterian, though in one case with a member of the Church of Ireland. For some of the Presbyterian under-tenants, many of whom held 'at will', farming was not their sole occupation. Robert McFirland, a mason, held 32 acres, with an 'old stone and clay house', orchard and garden, with 'a little plantation of sallyes'; Andrew Kerr, a weaver, held 9 acres; and John Kennedy, a butcher, just over 7 acres. At the very bottom were those who held only a house and garden, such as James Job, a weaver, who, for 10s had a 'small mud wall cabin' and garden in the town of Castledillon. If they were lucky, like John Rantin, they also, in addition to their house and garden, had 'grazing of a cow and firing'.

As the eighteenth century progressed the standard tenurial arrangement was to hold land by lease for three lives. Many of the poor, however, were simply holding 'at will' from year to year. Though tenants were careful not to antagonise landlords by claiming tenant right in this period, there was an underlying 'understanding' that a sitting tenant would be given the first opportunity to renew his lease and complaints did appear before the kirk session when an individual tried to obtain land over the head of the occupying tenant.[45] As the Presbyterian agent of a County Antrim estate complained in 1722: 'if they doe not cume to a new agreemt you need not feor tenants, but [deal with] none untill they have left the land for our foolish peple in this cuntorey thincks it a great sin to tacke land while the other tenant is in poustione.'[46]

Across Ulster a mixed agrarian economy prevailed. Cattle farming was the chief commercial enterprise on pastoral farms, though sheep and horses were also kept. Commercial dairying was located particularly in the hinterlands of the port towns, with women being engaged in butter production in order to sell to supplement family incomes. In Lisburn, for instance, many of the original members of the Presbyterian congregation that was set up in the late 1680s were under-tenants engaged in the manufacture and sale of butter to Belfast merchants.[47] Grazing was

---

[45] Letterbook of Isaac Macartney, 1705 (PRONI, Lenox-Conyngham papers, D501/1, pp 220–1); Memorandum of Thomas Addi of Donaghadee, c.1730 (ibid., Murray of Broughton papers, D2860/25/3/35); Aghadowey sess. mins (PHS, p. 44); W. H. Crawford, 'Landlord-tenant relations in Ulster, 1609–1820', *Irish Economic and Social History*, ii (1975), p. 11; Middleton, 'Religious revolution', pp 254–5.

[46] Hamilton Maxwell to Agmondisham Vesey, 15 Aug. 1722 (PRONI, Kirk-Vesey papers, T2524/17).

[47] Crawford, 'Economy & society', p. 65; David Dickson, *New foundations: Ireland 1660–1800* (2nd ed., Dublin, 2000), p. 125; George Chambers, 'Milk processing in Co. Fermanagh from the

most predominant in hillier and mountainous areas such as the Down uplands and the Antrim Hills. The major products of farming in the latter region were horses and sheep. Most of the woollens produced in Ulster were, and had always been, for domestic use and with the population increase and the increased demand for clothing some new tuck mills were built, for example, at Ballymena in 1709, though most were small enterprises.[48] The main crops were oats, barley and, in poorer ground, potatoes. In Ulster, the area under tillage was expanding and by the 1720s and 1730s the southern Ulster counties of Monaghan and Cavan had undergone a transition from pastoral to a greater proportion of arable farming. In 1738 it was observed of Monaghan, 'The grain that this county produces is wheat, bear [bere, i.e. winter barley], barly, rey [rye] and oats, [and] there is also plenty of potatoes, not only sufficient to support the inhabitants, but likewise to supply some of the neighbouring counties, with bear, barly and oatmeal.'[49] Oats formed the predominant part of what was largely a grain-based diet, though there were local and seasonal variations, such as fish in coastal areas. Oats were eaten in the form of bread and as porridge. Potatoes were important (though not yet dominant), particularly with the poorer elements of society because of the large yields that could be achieved from small plots of ground, though they tended only to be eaten in winter and early spring. Barley was used in brewing and for making whiskey.[50] In 1739 Dean William Henry singled out the Scotch planters for their improvement of their lands in the Inishowen area of County Donegal. He wrote:

> I can't pass by ... without observing to the honour of the Scotch planters who settled in this county, the indefatigable pains they have been at in tilling and manuring the ground. Tho' there is scarce any county in the kingdom whose soil is naturally more discouraging to the husbandman; they have, by continual labour, by liming, shelling, and dunging, as it were forced nature and made it fruitful to maintain a great number of people, and to afford some barley also for exportation.[51]

Farms tended to be smaller in Ulster than elsewhere in Ireland, and even in the richer lowland areas acreages of ten to twelve acres were common. This partly was due to pressure for land, but more particularly to the existence of farmer-weavers. As our 1739 observer records: 'the farmer contents himself with no more land than necessary to feed his family and depends on the industry of his

seventeenth century until the present day' in E. M. Murphy and W. J. Roulston (eds), *Fermanagh: history and society* (Dublin, 2004), pp 525–7; Sir George Rawdon to Lord [Conway], 2 Mar. 1681 (*CSPD, 1680–1681*, p. 193).

48 Crawford, 'Economy & society', pp 66, 79; H. D. Gribbon, *The history of water power in Ulster* (Newton Abbot, 1969), pp 55–8.

49 Dickson, *New foundations*, p. 125; Crawford, 'Economy & society', p. 69; Archdeacon Cranston and Mr Lucas, 'Co. Monaghan', 1738/9, in 'Topographical and statistical returns from various respondents sent to Walter Harris and the Physico-Historical Society of Ireland' (Armagh Public Library, P001498343).

50 Richard Dobbs's observations about Carrickfergus, 1683 (PRONI, D162/6); L. M. Cullen, *An economic history of Ireland since 1660* (London, 1981), p. 70.

51 Dean William Henry's topographical descriptions of several counties, 1739 (PRONI, MIC198/1, pp 68–9).

wife and daughters to pay by their spinning, the rent, and lay up riches.'[52] Rents were commonly due in May and November. The November rent, in normal conditions, was usually easier met as it followed the harvest, but traditionally for those living a marginal existence, the May rent could only be paid by selling their cattle while lean. As a result of the development of the linen manufacture, however, linen could be spun over the winter months and woven into cloth and then sold to pay the rent. Without having to sell their cattle before being fattened, a higher price could be achieved for them at market later in the year.[53] The core of the linen industry was in the 'linen triangle' in south-east Ulster, though it gradually spread into Tyrone, Monaghan and Cavan. Spinning of linen yarn, which was less economically remunerative than weaving, was also a feature of County Londonderry, from which yarn was exported to Manchester and Lancashire.[54]

A farming life could, however, be a precarious one. Harvest failure was not uncommon, and there were also cattle murrains and the impact of changes in the demands of export markets to contend with. When such occurrences allied with a downturn in the linen industry there was widespread suffering and this was one of the stimulants for emigration in the late 1710s and late 1720s.[55]

III. Servants

Domestic and agricultural servants formed a large proportion of those in employment in the eighteenth century and domestic service, in particular, offered one of the chief openings for young women seeking employment.[56] Servants, however, were not a homogeneous group. They could be permanent or temporary. Some were hired by the year or part of the year and seasonal labourers were important in farm work.[57] The surviving evidence, though limited, suggests that servant-keeping was widespread in the late seventeenth and early eighteenth centuries, with many households above the labouring poor employing one or more.[58] Not only members

---

[52] Ibid., p. 69; L. M. Cullen, *Anglo-Irish trade, 1660–1800* (Manchester, 1968), p. 9; Gillespie, *Early Belfast*, pp 128–9; Liam Kennedy and Philip Ollerenshaw (eds), *Ulster since 1600: politics, economy and society* (Oxford, 2013), p. 162.

[53] John Cary, *Some considerations relating to the carrying on of the linen manufacture in the kingdom of Ireland* (London, 1704), p. 12.

[54] Arthur Dobbs, *An essay on the trade and improvement of Ireland* (Dublin, 1729), i, 32–3; ii, 13, 75; Dean William Henry's topographical descriptions (PRONI, MIC198/1, p. 98); Connolly, *Divided kingdom*, pp 354–5.

[55] McSkimin, *History & antiquities of Carrickfergus*, p. 77; Gillespie, 'Settlement & survival', pp xxxii–xxxiii; F. G. James, 'Derry in the time of George I: selections from Bishop Nicolson's letters, 1718–1722', *UJA*, 3rd ser., xvii (1954), pp 181–2.

[56] Beaumont, 'Gentry of The King's & Queen's Counties', i, 169; *HIP*, i, 255.

[57] Dutton, *Law of masters & servants*, p. v.

[58] Religious census of Sir John Rawdon's estates, Moira, Co. Down, 1716 (Huntington Library, Hastings papers, HAM Box 75, folder 32); Beaumont, 'Gentry of The King's & Queen's Counties', i, 173; Mary O'Dowd, 'Women and paid work in rural Ireland, c.1500–1800' in Bernadette Whelan (ed.), *Women and paid work in Ireland, 1500–1930* (Dublin, 2000), p. 19.

of the Presbyterian gentry,[59] but also ministers,[60] merchants,[61] professionals[62] and those further down the social scale kept servants.[63] The gentry, however, usually employed the greatest number of servants for both indoor and outdoor tasks. Indoor servants may have included a housekeeper, butler, groom, footmen or waiting maids and outdoor servants included gardeners, huntsmen and park keepers. Where more than one servant was employed, the servants formed into a hierarchy, depending on the importance of their role or length of service. In small establishments where the number of servants was less there was less specialisation of duties and the one or two servants employed had to undertake a multiplicity of tasks. The type of servants employed by a household changed and developed with the particular needs of the employing family. Nurses and tutors were important in gentry households when there were young children. When the children had grown up nurses could be retained as maids, though tutors tended to move to another family.[64]

Most permanent servants, like apprentices, lived in the home of their master. Employers provided their servants not only with lodging and wages, but also food and clothing.[65] Often there were additional benefits, such as gratuities from parting guests. Many employers paid for medicines or medical assistance for their servants during times of sickness, as servants were often regarded as part of the family.[66] One of the richest sources for the lives and conditions of servants, both male and female, employed by a Presbyterian in this period is the brief series of accounts kept by Rev. John Kennedy, minister of Benburb, between 1728 and 1733. Kennedy's accounts give the names of the servants, as well as short-term tradesmen, employed, dates of commencement and wages and other expenses incurred. The accounts show Kennedy to have been a conscientious and caring employer. The expenses listed include various garments such as stockings, shoes and overcoats which he supplied

---

[59] See above, p. 75.

[60] Templepatrick sess. mins (PRONI, CR4/12/B/1, p. 211); Monaghan Pby mins (PHS, pp 297, 342); James Reid, *Formal Christians and secession from them consider'd; being a sermon preach'd on 2 Tim. 3. 5. at the opening of a synod at Belfast, January 6. 1718–19* (Belfast, 1729), p. 23; Philip Crossle, 'Gordons in County Down: Rev. Alexander Gordon of Rathfriland', *Banbridge Chronicle*, 19 Mar. 1913.

[61] Extracts from William Rainey's diary, 11 Dec. 1688 (LHL, Joy MS, 10); abstract will of James Stewart, 1693 (PRONI, Stewart papers, D1759/3/B/1, p. 71); will of John Galt, 1715 (ibid., Maxwell Given papers, D2096/1/15D); Young, *Belfast town book*, p. 292.

[62] Will of Robert Dalway, 1699 (PRONI, Castle Stewart papers, D1618/8/5); will of Theophilus Langford, 1713 (N.A., Prerogative Court of Canterbury wills, PROB 11/535).

[63] Templepatrick sess. mins (PRONI, CR4/12/B/1, pp 190, 225); Carnmoney sess. mins, 18 Feb. 1704/5 (ibid., MIC1P/37/4); Antrim Pby mins, 1697–1713 (PHS, pp 327, 341, 357); Ballycarry sess. mins, 15 Apr. 1707, 11 June 1707 (PRONI, CR3/31/1); Larne & Kilwaughter sess. mins (ibid., MIC1B/6A/1B, p. 137); Connor sess. mins, 17 Mar. 1724 (PHS); religious census of Sir John Rawdon's estates, Moira, Co. Down, 1716 (Huntington Library, Hastings papers, HAM Box 75, folder 32); Peter Carr, '*The most unpretending of places': a history of Dundonald, County Down* (Dundonald, 1987), p. 80.

[64] Beaumont, 'Gentry of The King's & Queen's Counties', i, 171.

[65] Blackwood cash book, 1720–39 (PRONI, Dufferin and Ava papers, D1071/A/B/2/1).

[66] Beaumont, 'Gentry of The King's & Queen's Counties', i, 176, 178–9; HIP, i, 255, 257; Peter Earle, *The Making of the English middle class: business, society and family life in London, 1660–1730* (London, 1989), p. 219; J. A. Sharpe, *Early modern England: a social history 1550–1760* (2nd ed., London, 1997), p. 60; Dutton, *Law of masters & servants*, p. 80; O'Dowd, 'Women & paid work', p. 17.

to his servants, as well as books and bibles.[67] As with masters and apprentices, those with servants in their household were expected to take care of their religious, as well as physical, well-being. Catherine, countess of Granard, took a keen interest in all 'her domestic affairs' and according to her minister, Rev. Robert Craghead, her house, 'tho' it was sometimes very numerous, no confusion was to be seen, no licentiousness or irregularities among servants were conniv'd at'.[68] Servants were expected to participate in family worship and in cases where they were of the same religious denomination as their employer would have accompanied them to the Presbyterian meetinghouse.[69] The pew register of Third Belfast includes four examples of employers who purchased seats for their servants separate from the family pew, but in most cases servants sat in the same pew as the family they served.[70]

Employers could become attached to their servants. In January 1720 a serving maid of James Trail of Killyleagh sought leave to visit her sister who was unwell. Trail not only granted the request but ordered a horse for her and sent a servant boy to accompany her there and back again. On their return the maid was drowned when attempting to cross a river. In his autobiography, Trail wrote her death 'was very afflicting ... but I have good hopes concerning her [salvation]. I have not had many servants if any, that I had a better opinion of. I bless God for the preservation of the other servant'.[71] Faithful and long-standing servants were commonly remembered in the wills of their masters and mistresses.[72] This often involved monetary legacies to make provision for the loyal servant in old age. Robert Dalway of Bellahill, Carrickfergus, in his will of 1699 wrote, 'I count my selfe under some obligations to leave some little thing to my late servant Mary Eglesome' and bequeathed her £6.[73] The amounts granted usually varied with the rank of the servant and the wealth and generosity of the employer. David Kennedy of Cultra in 1697 left an annuity of only £1 to his housekeeper, Agnes Creighton, a widow, and Robert Given, a merchant of Killowen, County Londonderry, left £3 to his servant, Mary Beggs. Sir Arthur Langford, an unmarried squire, was significantly more generous. Langford bequeathed to his servants Thomas Granger £200, John Fagan £100 and George Boasman £100.[74] The testator sometimes had an ulterior motive. James Stewart, a Presbyterian 'merchant' in Belfast, who composed his will in 1693, left £20 to

---

[67] These accounts are recorded in 'Miscellanea by J[ohn] K[ennedy], 1699–1725' (PHS). Another good example is the Blackwood cash book, 1720–39 (PRONI, Dufferin and Ava papers, D1071/A/B/2/1), which records purchases of shoes, boots, clothing and occasionally reading material for their servants.

[68] Robert Craghead, *A funeral sermon on the occasion of the death of the right honourable Catherine, countess dowager of Granard* (Dublin, 1714), p. 23.

[69] Antrim Pby mins, 1697–1713 (PHS, p. 336); autobiography of James Trail (PRONI, D1460/1, openings 14–15); Beaumont, 'Gentry of The King's & Queen's Counties', i, 175.

[70] Third Belfast treasurer's book & pew register, 1726 (PRONI, T654/6, pp 64, 98, 110).

[71] Autobiography of James Trail (PRONI, D1460/1, opening 28).

[72] Beaumont, 'Gentry of The King's & Queen's Counties', i, 176; *HIP*, i, 256–7; will of James Anderson, 1706 (NLI, Prerogative will book, 1706–8, MFGS 41/2, f. 25).

[73] Will of Robert Dalway, 1699 (PRONI, Castle Stewart papers, D1618/8/5).

[74] Abstract will of David Kennedy, 1697 (PRONI, Stewart papers, D1759/3/A/1, p. 7); abstract will of Robert Given, 1757 (ibid., D1759/3/B/1, p. 107); will of Arthur Langford, 1715 (ibid., T168/1, pp 8–9).

his servant William Anderson 'if he remains so long as to look after my children's business'.[75] Gifts to faithful servants could include bequests of clothes or a reduction of rent if the servant held property owned by their employer. Henry Dalway of County Antrim left a grey coat trimmed with gold to his 'old servant James Brae' and James Stewart ordered in his will that John Morrow, 'an honest servant', was to have the house he lived in rent free for two years.[76]

Periods of service in any one household, however, were often brief and some servants, unlike apprentices whose servitude lasted seven years, did not stay long in the one place.[77] By a statute of 1715, an employer who discharged a servant was obliged to supply the servant with a certificate stating that the person therein named was his or her servant, and if desired the master or mistress could also include a comment about the character and behaviour of the servant.[78] Among the testimonials received by Ballynahinch congregation, County Down, between 1715 and 1734 were five which had been granted by masters, one of whom lived in Belfast.[79] The reasons why servants left a particular household varied: some left to get married or were sick or pregnant. Others moved in order to obtain better wages or conditions elsewhere, or because they simply sought a change or wanted another type of job.[80] In some cases, however, servants were forced to leave as a result of misconduct and occasionally cases appeared before the Presbyterian kirk session in which employers were concerned about, or dissatisfied with, the actions of their servants. In February 1705 George Carr reported his maid, Sarah Gordon, to Carnmoney session 'for absenting from his family at unseasonable hours'. Gordon was rebuked and exhorted to carry more suitably which she promised to do.[81] Other examples of servant misconduct included gossiping about the household, bringing people into the house without permission or stealing from their employer. In May 1704 Templepatrick kirk session rebuked Letitia Montgomery, maid to their minister, Rev. James Kirkpatrick, for giving away goods belonging to her master, including wheat and beef, a crime aggravated by the fact it had been committed on a Sunday.[82] Two years later James Hamilton and his wife appeared before Templepatrick kirk session and stated that when they returned from worship they noticed that some items in their house had gone missing. Their maid, Helen Lowrimur, accused Elizabeth Thompson of coming into the Hamilton home and taking away beef and some lint. Jean Grahame then appeared before the session and stated that when she came to the Hamilton's

75 Abstract will of James Stewart, 1693 (PRONI, Stewart papers, D1759/3/B/1, p. 71).

76 Will of Henry Dalway, 1720 (PRONI, Castle Stewart papers, D1618/8/14); abstract will of James Stewart, 1693 (ibid., Stewart papers, D1759/3/B/1, p. 71).

77 Barnard, New anatomy, pp 302, 306–7; O'Dowd, 'Women & paid work', pp 18–19; HIP, i, 256; Earle, Making of the English middle class, p. 221; Rosemary O'Day, The family and family relationships, 1500–1900: England, France and the United States of America (Basingstoke, 1994), p. 186.

78 2 George I, c. 17 (The statutes at large, passed in the parliaments held in Ireland (20 vols, 1786–1804), iv, 403); Dutton, Law of masters & servants, p. 25.

79 Ballynahinch testimonials, 8 Nov. 1715, 7 Mar., 25 Aug. 1716, 4 Nov. 1718, 27 Feb. 1719.

80 Connor sess. mins, 17 Mar. 1724 (PHS); Earle, Making of the English middle class, pp 225, 228; Sharpe, Early modern England, p. 60.

81 Carnmoney sess. mins, 18 Feb., 21 Mar. 1704/5 (PRONI, MIC1P/37/4).

82 Templepatrick sess. mins (ibid., CR4/12/B/1, p. 211).

home Lowrimur had offered her salt which she refused. The session judged the evidence of 'the little girle' Lowrimur insufficient and Elizabeth Thompson's reputation was vindicated.[83]

The intimacy between servants and employers, usually all living under one roof, could lead to incidents where masters abused the power vested in them.[84] Cases where masters seduced or raped servant girls came before the kirk session and higher courts of the church. In February 1705 James McBride was rebuked by the Presbytery of Antrim for committing adultery with his servant, Jean Henry, and two years later the same presbytery rebuked James Neil of Templepatrick for adultery committed with his maid, 'Marrion Lemin'.[85] Rev. Thomas Futt, minister of Ballyclare, sought the advice of the presbytery in a case where an unmarried housekeeper was strongly suspected of fornication with a servant girl but no sufficient proof could be found. The presbytery determined that the master and servant both be rebuked for 'unseemly carriage' and be ordered not to live 'any longer together'.[86] In 1707 Rev. Stafford Pettigrew of Ballyeaston proposed the case of William Jackson who had attempted to rape his servant maid, Martha Hill. On this occasion the presbytery voted that Jackson be required to confess his fault publicly during Sunday worship.[87]

Whether or not Presbyterians employed, or were employed by, members of other religious denominations is an important question, bearing as it does on everyday inter-relations between Anglicans and Presbyterians. James Kirkpatrick, minister of Belfast, when countering the accusations of William Tisdall, in 1713, asserted that Presbyterians did not 'persecute any man for his conformity' and that Presbyterian householders 'entertain servants that are conformists in their families, without any such certificates, and employ conformist labourers and tradesmen'.[88] Barnard has suggested that only in north-east Ulster and the grandest houses elsewhere was it possible for servants to be exclusively Protestant.[89] Documents in the Hastings papers, relating to the estates of Sir John Rawdon, suggest that while most households were made up of the same confessional group, there were households that employed servants of a different religious persuasion. In Brookhill William Brown, Thomas Betty and Daniel Diall, all three Presbyterian, each employed one Catholic servant, and John Montgomery and John McCullogh, other Presbyterian householders, employed one or more Anglican servants. Five Church of Ireland householders in Brookhill employed at least one Presbyterian servant. Nine out of the eleven Quaker families residing there employed non-Quakers, including Presbyterians. This was probably a result of the smallness

[83] Ibid., p. 225.
[84] S. D. Amussen, *An ordered society: gender and class in early modern England* (New York, 1988), p. 159.
[85] Antrim Pby mins, 1697–1713 (PHS, pp 276, 357).
[86] Ibid., p. 327.
[87] Ibid., p. 341. For further material relating to cases that appear before the kirk session concerning employers and servants, see: R. M. Browne, 'Kirk and community: Ulster Presbyterian society, 1640–1740' (M.Phil. thesis, QUB, 1999), pp 147–50.
[88] [Kirkpatrick], *Presby. loyalty*, pp 557–8.
[89] Barnard, *New anatomy*, p. 294.

of the Quaker community in the area compared to the other denominations. In the townland of Clare (parish of Moira, County Down) Widow Dixon, a Presbyterian, employed a Catholic boy, while George Hill, another Presbyterian, employed two female Catholic servants, and Thomas Sankey and Fergus Fowler, both Presbyterian, employed members of the Church of Ireland. These references suggest that households were not always denominationally exclusive, and even in parishes where Presbyterians formed the largest proportion, such as Clare where there were 373 Presbyterian inhabitants, 323 Catholics and 289 members of the Church of Ireland, Presbyterians both employed, and were employed by, members of other religious persuasions.[90]

IV. The poor and poor relief activities

The poor were a diverse group. Included could be the elderly, the ill, widows, orphans, the unemployed and vagrants. For some, poverty was only temporary and dependence often marked a particular stage in life, with the young and elderly prevalent on many poor lists. Ireland lacked the legislation which in England made the poor the responsibility of the parish in which they resided. However, the appointment of cess for poor relief was undertaken on a voluntary basis in many Irish parishes and there were other official mechanisms for relieving the plight of the worthy poor and prosecuting non-resident beggars. Surviving grand jury records suggest that jurors were primarily concerned with policing and prosecuting the idle poor rather than distributing charity to those who had legitimate reasons for poverty.[91] In 1707 the County Antrim jury laid down steps to be taken to deal with the problem of beggars. Parishes were required to register beggars permitted to beg within their bounds and to give them a badge or ticket bearing the name of the parish. Those found begging without the badge, or outside their authorised parish, were to be either 'stripd nak'd from the middle upward and to be openly whipt till their bodies shall be bloody. Or be putt into the stocks two daies and two nights and there to have only bread and water'.[92] Many towns had stocks or a pillory, though the municipal records suggest these were used infrequently, with whipping being more common. 'Whip' or 'bang beggars', or beadles and constables, were employed to regulate beggars and vagrants and to whip unlicensed, non-resident, beggars from the district. The death of the Belfast bang beggar, for instance, is recorded in the Belfast funeral register in June 1733.[93]

---

[90] Religious census of Sir John Rawdon's estates, Moira, Co. Down, 1716 (Huntington Library, Hastings papers, HAM Box 75, folder 32).

[91] Co. Antrim grand jury presentment books, 1711–21, 1727–61 (PRONI, ANT/4/1/1, ANT/4/1/3); Fitzgerald, 'Poverty & vagrancy', p. 315.

[92] Derriaghy vestry mins (PRONI, MIC1/32/1).

[93] Fitzgerald, 'Poverty & vagrancy', pp 355, 363–4, 367; Toby Barnard, 'The eighteenth-century parish' in Elizabeth FitzPatrick and Raymond Gillespie (eds), *The parish in medieval and early modern Ireland: community, territory and building* (Dublin, 2006), p. 315; Agnew, *Belfast funeral register*, p. 38.

An act of 1707 permitted the state to carry out enforced transportation of the vagrant poor to the colonies, but the numbers involved were small.[94] Some towns, such as Armagh, Derry and Downpatrick, had bridewells or houses of correction for the incarceration of beggars.[95] Measures laid down by County Monaghan grand jury to regulate the poor of the county in 1700 included a recommendation that any found guilty of leaving a parish with illegitimate children be committed to jail or to the house of correction.[96] Corporations took action against the non-resident poor, while making provision to help their own.[97] In 1700 vagrants in Coleraine were warned by the corporation that those who 'had notis to leve the town' but who had not done so were to have 'their cabbings' 'puld down within tenn dayes after notis given them'.[98] At Lifford, County Donegal, in 1722 it was decided that 'no vagabonds, vagrants, or day labourers should from hence-forth be entertaind in this corporation as residenters by any person whatsoever until that said person or persons so coming into town do first apply to the magistrate for present, and produce a certificate of his good behaviour in such places as he formerly came'.[99] Derry corporation maintained a list of pensioners, amounting to £20 per year, whose names were drawn up annually, usually in February or March, and approved by the council. In addition, Derry corporation gave out money in one-off payments to those requiring temporary relief.[100] One of those who received relief from Derry corporation in 1707 was Robert Shennan, a Presbyterian apothecary, who had resigned as an alderman of the corporation on account of the test in 1704.[101] Manors also concerned themselves with overseeing the poor. Among the rules governing the manor court of Florida, County Down, was one that the inhabitants should present 'all vagabonds and idlers that will not work and have not of their own to maintain them'.[102] In rural areas which lacked the regulation and oversight that the corporation provided to urban centres, the Church of Ireland vestry often provided an alternative mechanism to regulate the poor within the parish.[103] Parish vestries were asked to administer bequests, and some of these, according to the specifications

[94] 6 Anne, c. 11 (*The statutes at large, passed in the parliaments held in Ireland* (20 vols, 1786–1804), iv, 144–6); Fitzgerald, 'Poverty & vagrancy', pp 246–7.
[95] Fitzgerald, 'Poverty & vagrancy', pp 386–7; Avril Thomas, *Derry–Londonderry: Irish historic towns atlas* (Dublin, 2005), p. 21; R. H. Buchanan and Anthony Wilson, *Downpatrick: Irish historic towns atlas* (Dublin, 1997), p. 10.
[96] Clones Parish Church vestry mins (PRONI, MIC1/147A/1, pp 198–201).
[97] Fitzgerald, 'Poverty & vagrancy', pp 329, 333–4; Belturbet corp. mins, 1657–c.1730 (Cavan County Archives, BC/1, pp 127, 143, 254–6).
[98] Coleraine corp. mins (PRONI, LA/25/2/AA/1A, pp 187–8).
[99] Lifford court and borough book (PRONI, Erne papers, D1939/18/9, p. 46).
[100] Derry corp. mins (PRONI, LA/79/2/AA/1, pp 27, 37, 64, 87–8, 90, 101–3; LA/79/2/AA/3A, pp 11, 18, 27, 35–6, 38, 40, 45–6, 56, 65, 74, 82, 106–7, 109–10, 135, 140, 155, 159, 171, 189, 224–5, 248, 261, 277, 291–2, 306–7, 319–20).
[101] Derry corp. mins (PRONI, LA/79/2/AA/3A, p. 82); Young, *Fighters of Derry*, p. 166.
[102] Articles for the grand jury in the manor of Florida, [c.1690] (PRONI, Gordon papers, D4204/F/2/1).
[103] J. J. Marshall (ed.), *Vestry records of the Church of St. John, Parish of Aghalow Caledon, Co. Tyrone 1691–1807* (Dungannon, 1935), pp 17–20; Fitzgerald, 'Poverty & vagrancy', pp 271–80; T. G. F. Paterson, 'A County Armagh mendicant badge inscribed "Shankill Poor 1699"', *UJA*, x (1947), pp 110–14; Gerard MacAtasney, 'Provision for the poor in the pre-famine era' in A. J.

of the testator, were granted to the inhabitants of the parish irrespective of their religious denomination.[104]

The Presbyterian church also administered charity, with each congregation assuming responsibility for the poor among its own members. Money for relief was derived from various sources. The principal means was through voluntary church collections. These were taken up at Sunday services, and in some cases at the mid-week lecture day. The method of collection varied; in some cases at the church door, in others at the churchyard gate, during the service, or by door-to-door visitation. Only heads of households were expected to give,[105] and according to their means, usually under the watchful eye of the elders. A few congregations were rebuked during presbyterial visitations for not showing enough liberality to the poor.[106]

At Dundonald in County Down the weekly collections in 1679 averaged 1s 8d, but it some weeks did not rise to 1s.[107] Larger amounts were collected at communion services, and special collections were occasionally organised when a particular need arose which could not be met from regular income. One of the problems with church, or service, collections was that there was a tendency for greatest need to coincide with least supply, and during the famine of 1729 Larne session found that they had 'nothing at all in the [poor] box' for the 'necessity of the poor in such a hard time'.[108] Some congregations tried to overcome this difficulty by investing the money they had available, and distributing the interest. This was particularly common with larger bequests which kirk sessions were often asked to administer by wealthy testators. In 1715 John Shaw, esq., of Ballyganaway, Donaghadee, County Down, bequeathed £100 to the minister of Carnmoney for the poor of the parish. The money was lent to Clotworthy Upton, a ruling elder in the neighbouring congregation of Templepatrick, bearing interest at 6% *per annum*, which was paid half-yearly. On 14 January 1719 among those who received money from the Shaw bequest were 'a family in great distress', 'a family shipwreckt' and 'a hopeful scholar'.[109]

It was common practice for those of means to leave money to the poor of the parish in which they lived or congregation where they worshipped.[110] Some also

Hughes and William Nolan (eds), *Armagh: history and society* (Dublin, 2001), pp 779–82; Barnard, 'The eighteenth-century parish', p. 312.

[104] Derriaghy vestry mins (PRONI, MIC1/32/1, pp 13, 17, 20); Fitzgerald, 'Poverty & vagrancy', p. 295; Barnard, 'The eighteenth-century parish', p. 312.

[105] Barkley, 'History of the eldership', i, pp iii–iv; Lisburn sess. mins, 13 Dec. 1688, 17 & 31 Jan., 14 & 28 Feb. 1688[/9], 8, 24 & 31 Oct., 21 Nov., 12 & 26 Dec. 1689, 9 & 30 Jan. 1689[/90], 29 May, 12 & 25 June, 16 July 1690 (PRONI, MIC1P/159/6); Carr, 'The most unpretending of places', p. 79.

[106] Antrim Pby mins, 1697–1713 (PHS, pp 59, 77).

[107] Carr, 'The most unpretending of places', p. 79.

[108] Larne & Kilwaughter sess. mins (PRONI, MIC1B/6A/1B, p. 30).

[109] Carnmoney sess. mins, 27 Apr. 1716 (PRONI, MIC1P/37/6); R. H. Bonar, *Nigh on three and a half centuries: a history of Carnmoney Presbyterian Church* (Newtownabbey, 2004), pp 302–3.

[110] For instance, abstract will of Thomas Lyll (Lyle), 1719 (PRONI, Mussenden papers, MIC510/1); will of Arthur Graham, 1732 (ibid., Bryson collection, D4006/3); will of Ann Conyngham, 1744 (ibid., Lenox-Conyngham papers, D1449/1/59A); will of Daniel Mussenden, 1756 (ibid., Mussenden papers, MIC510/1).

made bequests of a different nature which benefited the poor. Hugh Rainey, a wealthy merchant at Magherafelt and an elder in Castledawson congregation, as a result of a vow made to God for protection and favour, by will in 1707, devoted half of his estate to fund a charity for 24 boys, sons of parents who 'were of good repute and are reduced to poverty'. After three years' instruction the boys were to be given a suit of clothes and 50s for an apprentice fee.[111] In 1720 Henry Dalway of County Antrim left £5 to the Presbyterian congregations of Ballyclug, Carrickfergus and Templecorran for 'the buying of Bibles and the Westminster Confession of Faith, and catechism's for the poor'.[112]

Much more difficult to measure are gifts made directly to the poor while donors were still alive, but such philanthropy was a feature of at least some lives. The church courts also imposed fines on members for neglecting to attend or carry out appointments and the funds so derived, though small, were a supplement to the poor relief given by the church.[113] Finally, some congregations such as Ballynahinch, Belfast, Drumbo and Larne, possessed mort cloths which were used to drape over coffins on the journey from the deceased's home to the burying plot. As well as being used in the funerals of the poor, the income derived from the rental of these mort cloths was granted to the living poor. The hire of the funeral equipment which belonged to First Belfast, for instance, brought in about £50 a year, most of which was used for charitable purposes.[114]

The presbyteries and synods occasionally concerned themselves with poor relief, particularly, if not exclusively, with ministers' widows or orphans, those overseas requiring relief, those who had a petition or recommendation, and those who had suffered as a result of fire.[115] Most Presbyterian relief, however, was carried out at the session level. The elders, who knew intimately the circumstances and character of every member of their congregation, were able to grant sums according to need, either through regular payments or occasional assistance. The latter was usually for larger sums than the regular instalments and it was uncommon for regular pensioners to be granted supplementary payments as well. There were thus in effect two separate groups of recipients, which the Lisburn session minutes refer to as 'weekly and extraordinary' poor.[116] In Aghadowey congregation in January 1703 eight

---

111 Will of Hugh Rainey, 1707 (NAI, Prerogative will book, 1706–8, MFGS 41/2, ff 212–14); Thomas Witherow (ed.), *Two diaries of Derry in 1689* (Derry, 1888), pp xv–xvi. The school survives to this day as Rainey Endowed School.

112 Will of Henry Dalway, 1720 (PRONI, Castle Stewart papers, D1618/8/14).

113 Lisburn sess. mins, 30 Jan. 1700[/01] (PRONI, MIC1P/159/6), 1 Oct. 1719 (ibid., MIC1P/159/8); *RGSU*, i, 202; General Pby (Dublin Pby) mins, 1730–9, pp 15, 59, 63–4 (in private hands).

114 Ballynahinch accounts, 15 June, 3 July, 17 Oct. 1720, 14 & 21 May, 22 Oct. 1721, 5 Mar. 1727, 17 Nov. 1728, 25 May, 20 July, 17 & 31 Aug., 13 Oct., 14 & 28 Dec. 1729, 25 Jan., 1, 8 & 15 Feb., 5 Apr., 4 Oct., 21 Dec. 1730; Agnew, *Belfast funeral register*; Benn, *Belfast*, pp 574–6; Drumbo extracts, 15 Feb. 1701 (PRONI, Stewart papers, D1759/1/D/1); Larne & Kilwaughter sess. mins (ibid., MIC1B/6A/1B, pp 300–1); Ballymoney sess. mins (ibid., CR3/1/B/1, p. 8).

115 Down Pby mins (PHS, pp 215–16, 248, 300); Monaghan Pby mins (PHS, pp 17, 69); Sub-synod of Derry (PHS, pp 72, 87, 93, 107, 115, 127, 223, 247, 300); *RGSU*, i, 5, 8, 11, 13–14, 49, 87, 104, 137–8, 232, 272–3, 337, 393–4; ii, 9, 17–18.

116 Lisburn sess. mins, 24 Nov. 1698, 11 June 1702 (PRONI, MIC1P/159/6).

pensioners were granted sums of between 6d and 3s.[117] In every case the amount given, though small, was granted according to need and carefully judged. The amount of relief given also varied according to rank. During the second decade of the eighteenth century, Ballynahinch congregation was more generous to distressed gentlewomen than to the generality of its female pensioners.[118] The local poor did not always benefit in cash and sometimes other forms of assistance were offered. On occasion the session supplied food,[119] shoes or clothes,[120] and there are instances of books and bibles being bought and given to the poor.[121] Medical treatment was also provided[122] and the sessions concerned themselves with the burial of the poor by supplying, or contributing towards the cost of, coffins or winding sheets.[123]

Since kirk sessions had finite resources they had to make judgements about the worthiness of individuals and families seeking assistance, and to discriminate between deserving and undeserving cases. This led to the prioritising of certain groups. A common feature of poor lists was the preponderance of female over male recipients, though there were exceptions, for instance, at Ballynahinch and Burt, where more men were aided than women.[124] Women were especially vulnerable if widowed or unmarried because few employment opportunities existed for them.[125] The elderly were also much more likely to be relieved than those of working age. Surviving poor lists do not record the age of recipients but sometimes describe them as 'old' or 'elderly',[126] and though widows were not necessarily old, their presence in many cases could probably be taken as an indication of age. Help was also granted to poor families with young children, as well as to orphans,[127] and steps were taken

---

117 Aghadowey sess. mins (PHS, p. 3).

118 Ballynahinch accounts, 1711–17.

119 Ibid., 18 Sept. 1715.

120 Ibid., 19 Aug. 1705; Armagh sess. mins (PRONI, Stewart papers, D1759/1/B/1, pp 17, 19); J. M. Barkley, 'The evidence of old Irish session-books on the sacrament of the Lord's Supper', *Church Service Society Annual*, no. 22 (May 1952), p. 30.

121 Armagh sess. mins (PRONI, Stewart papers, D1759/1/B/1, pp 16, 19); Ballynahinch accounts, 26 Sept. 1708, 18 Mar. 1716, 23 Nov. 1718, 24 May 1732; expenditure book of Third Presbyterian Church, Belfast, 1733–9 (PRONI, MIC1P/7/4, p. 16); Barkley, 'Evidence of old Irish session-books', p. 30; 'Extracts from the Presbytery of Munster', *Christian Moderator*, no. 3 (July 1826), p. 71; Middleton, 'Religious revolution', p. 260.

122 Armagh sess. mins (PRONI, Stewart papers, D1759/1/B/1, p. 18).

123 Ibid., pp 12, 15, 18–21; Ballynahinch accounts, 24 Nov. 1706, 16 Feb. 1707, 29 Jan., 22 Oct. 1710, 25 Feb. 1711, 2 Mar. 1712, 5 Apr. 1713, 28 Feb. 1714, 9 Jan., 6 Feb. 1715, 5 May, 24 Nov. 1717, 6 July 1718, 24 Jan. 1720, 29 Jan. 1721, 24 June 1722, 31 Jan. 1725; Templepatrick sess. mins (PRONI, Stewart papers, D1759/2/B/2, p. 100); Kirkdonald sess. mins (PHS, pp 9, 35, 39, 60, 83); expenditure book of Third Presbyterian Church, Belfast, 1733–9 (ibid., MIC1P/7/4, pp 2, 6, 12, 20); Barkley, 'History of the eldership', ii, 67, 122, 144; idem, 'Evidence of old Irish session-books', pp 29–30.

124 Ballynahinch accounts, 1704–34; Greaves, *God's other children*, p. 242.

125 Fitzgerald, 'Poverty & vagrancy', pp 298–9. Widows were, for instance, the dominant group receiving poor relief in the congregation of Third Belfast in the 1730s: expenditure book of Third Presbyterian Church, Belfast (PRONI, MIC1P/7/4).

126 Ballynahinch accounts, 30 Nov. 1707, 17 Apr. 1709, 12 Nov. 1710, 9 Dec. 1711, 20 Jan., 24 Feb. 1712, 24 Oct. 1714, 12 Feb. 1716, 13 May 1717, 17 Jan. 1720, 27 Aug. 1721, 7 Oct. 1724, 7 Mar. 1725, 5 Oct. 1726, 12 Oct. 1729, 5 Apr. 1730; Kirkdonald sess. mins (PHS, pp 9, 58).

127 Ballynahinch accounts, 23 July, 8 Oct. 1710, 16 Dec. 1711, 31 Jan., 30 May, 22 Aug., 15 Nov.

to ensure that illegitimate children were maintained. Nurses were paid to rear foundlings[128] and some of the adolescents who had been maintained throughout their childhood were helped into modest apprenticeships,[129] which helped reduce the need for continued assistance. Another group frequently found among those requiring poor relief from the Presbyterian church were those who suffered from illness, injury or physical disablement. In Dundonald among those who received aid in 1684 were a 'poor cripple man carried on a barrow, named John Kennedy' and an Irish man who had part of his tongue cut out by Gaelic Irish bandits.[130] The blind[131] and mentally ill[132] were also provided with relief.

Most Presbyterian relief probably went to needy Presbyterians. Although Presbyterians were accused in the early eighteenth century of confining their charity to their own denomination,[133] session minutes and surviving poor lists do demonstrate that at least some of the payments were granted to non-Presbyterians. Armagh congregation, for example, in 1707 granted 3s 7d 'to vagrants and people of other religions'.[134] In his reply to Tisdall's accusations, the Presbyterian minister of Second Belfast, Rev. James Kirkpatrick, pointed out that while only six of the ninety-seven who received poor relief from the Presbyterian congregations in Belfast were members of the Church of Ireland, this was only because 'no more of 'em apply'd to the elders, but went to their own minister' instead.[135] Patrick Fitzgerald has suggested that, although the Presbyterian records are not as voluminous as those of the Church of Ireland, the trend suggested is that Presbyterians showed greater liberality to poor migrants.[136] A common phrase in many Presbyterian poor lists

1714, 30 Jan., 20 Feb., 8 May, 29 May, 5 June, 7 Aug., 5–6 Nov., 4 Dec. 1715, 5 Feb., 6 May, 14 May, 5 Aug., 19 Nov. 1716, 24 Feb., 29 Apr., 18 Aug. 1717, 30 Aug. 1724, 15 Nov. 1730, 22 Aug., 17 Oct. 1731; Carnmoney sess. mins, 14 July 1697, 10 Feb. 1707/8 (PRONI, MIC1P/37/4); Kirkdonald sess. mins (PHS, p. 11); Lisburn sess. mins, 16 Apr. 1691 (PRONI, MIC1P/159/6); Down Pby mins (PHS, p. 300); Barkley, 'History of the eldership', ii, 144–5.

128 Armagh sess. mins (PRONI, Stewart papers, D1759/1/B/1, p. 16); Ballynahinch accounts, 10 Dec. 1721, 8 May, 22 Dec. 1723, 11 May 1724, 20 May 1725; Templepatrick sess. mins (PRONI, Stewart papers, D1759/2/B/2, p. 34); Kirkdonald sess. mins (PHS, p. 59); Barkley, 'History of the eldership', ii, 55.

129 Lisburn sess. mins, 30 Sept. 1703 (PRONI, MIC1P/159/6).

130 Kirkdonald sess. mins (PHS, p. 24).

131 Ballynahinch accounts, 22 Dec. 1706, 17 Aug., 7 Sept., 5 Oct., 2 Nov., 21 Dec. 1707, 18 Jan., 15 Feb., 4 & 18 Apr., 9 May, 20 June, 18 July, 15 Aug., 26 Sept., 31 Oct., 5 Dec. 1708, 2 & 30 Jan., 13 Feb., 27 Mar., 17 Apr., 15 May, 19 June, 17 July, 11 Sept. 1709, 22 Jan., 10 Sept. 1710, 18 Mar., 3 June 1711, 23 Mar., 25 May 1712, 29 Apr., 8 July, 30 Sept., 30 Dec. 1716, 3 Mar., 4 Dec. 1717, 2 Feb., 30 Mar., 19 Oct., 30 Nov. 1718, 28 June 1719, 22 May, 12 June, 31 July 1720, 31 Dec. 1721, 8 Aug. 1725; Kirkdonald sess. mins (PHS, pp 3, 28, 43, 47, 82).

132 Ballynahinch accounts, 19 Aug., 21 Oct. 1705, 12 May, 11 Aug. 1706, 7 Aug., 13 Nov. 1709, 9 Sept., 2 Dec. 1716, 17 Mar., 5 May, 14 July, 4 Dec. 1717, 30 Mar., 20 July 1718, 8 Feb. 1719, 16 May 1720, 5 Feb. 1721, 3 Feb. 1723, 4 Apr. 1725, 26 Oct. 1726, 29 Dec. 1728; Kirkdonald sess. mins (PHS, p. 34); Down Pby mins (PHS, p. 248); Barkley, 'Evidence of old Irish session-books', p. 30.

133 [Tisdall], Conduct of the Dissenters, pp 24–5.

134 Armagh sess. mins (PRONI, Stewart papers, D1759/1/B/1, p. 12).

135 [Kirkpatrick], Pres. loyalty, pp 440–1.

136 Fitzgerald, 'Poverty & vagrancy', p. 296.

was grants made to a 'stranger' or 'strange object'.[137] Although there was always the problem of the professional beggar, genuine cases were protected by a certificate from the supplicant's local session. The higher courts of the church kept records of the signatures of each minister within their bounds, which could be consulted if there was any doubt about the authenticity of a testimonial.[138] Recommendations were also accepted from non-ministers. Among those receiving aid from Dundonald session were one who possessed a letter of recommendation from Lord Granard, another recommended by the mayor of Carrickfergus and a Huguenot recommended by the mayor of Derry.[139] At Armagh a Palatine minister received 6s 4d in 1712 and in 1726 seven men from Charleville, County Cork, were given 7s 'upon a briefe on account of their loss by fire'.[140] These and other examples present in poor lists demonstrate that though most Presbyterian charity benefited the local Presbyterian poor, Presbyterians did not confine their charity in this way.

* * * * * * *

Presbyterians were engaged in a wide range of trades and crafts. Entry to most of these was through service as an apprentice. Domestic service was also an important sector of employment, particularly for young Presbyterian women. As apprentices and servants usually lived in the home of their master or mistress this meant that those who lived in a particular household were not necessarily related by blood, but could be connected by a contractual relationship whereby the servant or apprentice received material benefit for the work and service that they offered to the employing family. Heads of households had an important role in Presbyterian society and were responsible not only for the physical well-being of their family and residing employees but also the religious and spiritual welfare of all those who resided under their roof. The Presbyterian system also made provision for those at the lowest and most precarious levels of Presbyterian society, through the collection and allocation of poor relief. Such relief, though primarily financial, could also involve food, clothing, subsidised or free schooling and the provision of religious reading material.

---

[137] Armagh sess. mins (PRONI, Stewart papers, D1759/1/B/1, pp 12–13, 15); Carnmoney sess. mins, 22 Aug. 1697 (PRONI, MIC1P/37/4); Kirkdonald sess. mins (PHS, p. 34); Lisburn sess. mins, 29 Nov., 13 & 27 Dec. 1688, 9 July 1691, 12 July 1693 (PRONI, MIC1P/159/6).
[138] *RGSU*, i, 49–50, 100.
[139] Kirkdonald sess. mins (PHS, pp 25, 27–8).
[140] Armagh sess. mins, 5 Mar. 1712, 27 Mar. 1726 (PRONI, Stewart papers, D1759/1/B/1, pp 17, 22).

6

Organisation and Religious Practice

This chapter is concerned with how the different social groups within Presbyterianism organised and worshipped together as a distinctive ecclesiastical community within Ulster society. It will also consider where power lay in Presbyterian society.

I. Power and authority

The Presbyterian church was governed through a system of representative committees known as 'courts'. At the local level was the kirk session, which consisted of the minister and a number of elders. There was no fixed number of elders and it was usually dependent on the size of the congregation. The elders were termed 'ruling elders' and were unpaid, while the minister, termed a 'teaching elder', was paid a stipend. Kirk sessions met regularly and supervised not only the moral and spiritual life of the congregation but also poor relief, congregational education and maintenance of church property. In Ballycarry and Templepatrick deacons were appointed as well as elders, though they were chiefly concerned with the temporal affairs of the congregation rather than its spiritual welfare.[1] In addition to ordinary business meetings, some sessions held special meetings for prayer and theological discussion. The elders were assigned a particular district, or 'quarter', over which they had supervision, and at Larne and Lisburn the elders of each district met together in prayer fellowships.[2] At Larne and Kilwaughter, as a result of a resolution agreed on 30 November 1733, the session held meetings in the form of 'conference which might tend to their knowledge and edification'. On 13 December 1733 they discoursed 'of privat judgment, of a haritek [heretic]; and the trinity' and on 28 December 1733 discoursed 'of the covenant of grace, of the imputation of Christs righteousnes, and whither a person was oblidged to belive any thing as an article of the Christian faith, which he could not understand, and lastly of the imputation of Adams first sin to all his posterity'. However, such meetings at Larne came to an abrupt end after 4 April 1734 as a result of differences among the members.[3]

The kirk session was the lowest judicatory. Its discipline extended to all members of the congregation, except the minister. Above the kirk session was the presbytery,

---

[1] Ballycarry sess. mins, 12 May 1704 (PRONI, CR3/31/1); Templepatrick sess. mins (ibid., CR4/12/B/1, pp 179, 195, 250); W. T. Latimer, 'The old session-book of Templepatrick Presbyterian Church', *Journal of the Royal Society of Antiquaries of Ireland*, xxv (1895), p. 131.
[2] Barkley, 'History of the eldership', ii, 115; Lisburn sess. mins, 10 & 14 May, 22 & 29 Oct. 1696, 14 Mar. 1696/7, 16 May 1697, 19 May 1698, 5 June 1699, 16 May, 31 Oct. 1700, 29 Jan. 1701[/02] (PRONI, MIC1P/159/6).
[3] Larne & Kilwaughter sess. mins (PRONI, MIC1B/6A/1B, pp 160–1).

which was composed of the ministers and one elder from each congregation. Originally congregations were assigned to a presbytery because of geographical propinquity but by the third decade of the eighteenth century agreement in opinion and theological outlook were more often considered. Presbyteries examined, licensed and ordained candidates for the ministry, provided services for vacant congregations, heard appeals against kirk session decisions, and supervised the work of ministers within their boundaries. The next higher court, above the presbytery, was the sub-synod. Three sub-synods were created in 1702: Belfast, Laggan and Monaghan.[4] Sub-synods met for consultation, advice and the hearing of appeals. The General Synod of Ulster, which met, usually annually, from 1690 onwards, was the highest judicatory and the court of final appeal against any of the decisions taken by the lower courts. The General Synod also appointed a number of committees, including a fixed, or standing, committee which met when required during the year to deal with any emergencies that occurred between the yearly meetings of the synod.

Presbyterians depended on ministers for the conduct of worship services, for preaching, marriage and the administration of the sacraments of baptism and communion. Unlike the representative elder who was elected by the kirk session to attend the higher courts, the minister was permanently a member of such higher courts by virtue of his office and training. As a result of his education and ordained status a minister could be viewed as a man apart from his congregation but in many ways was connected to his congregation, living and farming among them, and in many cases drawn from the same socio-economic background. Though not the only members of the Presbyterian community to receive a higher education, the ministers occasionally, because of their knowledge, were called upon to provide services, such as will-making or offering medical advice or assistance, to their congregation.[5] In some instances the progressive farming practices of certain ministers helped to introduce 'improvement' in their locality.[6] Ministers could also provide social leadership in their communities, and this was enhanced after the defection of Presbyterian gentry families. Tisdall blamed Presbyterian ministers for encouraging Presbyterians to disrupt Anglican burial services and though Kirkpatrick stated that this was 'the practice but of a few' he did not deny that it had taken place in certain instances.[7] At Rathfriland in County Down, in 1716, a meeting organised by Quakers was disturbed by a 'mob of [Presbyterian] boys, partly instigated by the Presbyterian priest, one Robert Gordon, and his elder, Robert Little, who went about to hinder their party coming to the meeting'. The Quakers preached in the streets instead but were stoned by the young Presbyterian men.[8]

Unlike the Church of Ireland and the Catholic Church, Presbyterian congregations in Ulster permitted the active participation of the laity at all levels of

4 *RGSU*, i, 58.
5 See above, p. 52.
6 *HIP*, i, 267.
7 [William Tisdall], *The conduct of the Dissenters of Ireland, with respect both to church and state* (Dublin, 1712), pp 65–6; [Kirkpatrick], *Presby. loyalty*, p. 525.
8 Thomas Story, *A journal of the life of Thomas Story* (Newcastle-upon-Tyne, 1747), pp 540–1.

church government, not only at the local level in the kirk session where the laity dominated, but also in the higher courts, where laymen were eligible to attend in equal numbers to the ministers. The meetings of each court were chaired by a chairman known as the 'moderator', and it was always a minister who held this position. No individual minister, however, was superior to, or exercised authority over, a colleague, and the moderators were always elected for a short period, usually a year, their authority consisting solely of maintaining the forms of debate during the meeting of the court and handling correspondence between meetings. The importance of the ministers at the higher courts was further underscored by their meeting as a block, separate from the elders, in what was termed an 'interloquitur'.[9] Additionally, the kirk session could not meet without a minister.[10] The attendance of lay elders was only compulsory at the kirk session, while the presence of ministers was obligatory at all levels unless there was a valid excuse for their absence. While ministers and elders were almost always present at meetings of the Laggan Presbytery, elders were not present at the Presbytery of Antrim until after James II's declaration of indulgence in 1687.[11] Although every congregation was entitled to be represented at the higher courts by an elder in addition to the minister, in practice the surviving records show that the courts above the kirk session were clerically dominated, as the attendance record of the lay elders was poor. Between 1672 and 1679, Raymond Gillespie has calculated, the average lay attendance at the Laggan Presbytery was 5.6 while the clergy averaged ten. There were occasions when no elders were present and on only five occasions were there ten or more elders.[12] In December 1687 the Presbytery of Antrim instructed ministers supplying vacant congregations to select an elder to attend the meetings of the presbytery, but in 1695 the Presbytery of Laggan ordered that elders from 'desolat', that is vacant, congregations were to be excluded from meetings of presbytery.[13] In terms of the elders who did attend, there was a considerable turnover in personnel, while the ministerial group remained substantially the same.[14] Some congregations had a rotation system whereby elders attended in alphabetical order or in terms of seniority,[15] and though the synod recommended that elders go in their turns to three successive presbyteries, or six months together, this was not popular with, and consequently not followed by, many sessions because 'some is not in a

---

9 See, for example, *RGSU*, i, 25, 44, 61, 336, 442; R. L. Greaves, *God's other children: Protestant Nonconformists and the emergence of denominational churches in Ireland, 1660–1700* (Stanford, Calif., 1997), pp 175–6.

10 Ballycarry sess. mins, 18 July 1705, 3 Feb. 1731/32; Barkley, 'History of the eldership', i, 45–6; ii, 125, 140.

11 Antrim 'Meeting' mins, 1671–91 (PRONI, Stewart papers, D1759/1/A/2); Laggan Pby mins, 1672–95 (ibid., D1759/1/E/2); Greaves, *God's other children*, pp 163–4.

12 Raymond Gillespie, 'The Presbyterian revolution in Ulster, 1660–1690' in W. J. Shiels and Diana Wood (eds), *The churches, Ireland and the Irish ...* (Oxford, 1989), p. 165. See also Greaves, *God's other children*, pp 419–20.

13 Antrim 'Meeting' mins (UTC, p. 247); Laggan Pby mins, 1690–1700 (PHS, p. 74).

14 Gillespie, 'Presbyterian revolution', p. 165.

15 Carnmoney sess. mins, 2 Feb. 1697/8 (PRONI, MIC1P/37/4); Connor sess. mins, 5 Dec. 1708 (PHS).

capacity to attend presbyteries so long together'.[16] No distinction, however, was drawn between ministers and lay elders, who could vote and speak on the same basis in all judicatories. On certain occasions the votes of the elders made a significant difference; for instance, during the Subscription Controversy.[17] It was the lay elders who forced through the motion for voluntary subscription in 1721 and at a meeting of the General Synod at Dungannon in 1723 Clotworthy Upton, a ruling elder from Templepatrick, brought the accusation that the Non-Subscribers 'maintain principles which open a door to lett in all errors and heresys into this church'.[18] Dr Henry Winder, an Englishman who was present at the synod,[19] wrote that the Subscribers 'had all along a vast majority, for the elders were a dead weight' upon the Non-Subscribers, and similar sentiments were expressed by the Dublin minister Joseph Boyse who hoped the moderate subscribers might succeed in preventing a rift, provided they were not outnumbered by the 'dead weight of the ruling elders'.[20] Elders tended to be more conservative than ministers and in June 1726 the exclusion overture, which separated the nonsubscribing Presbytery of Antrim from the General Synod, was passed by a majority in which, significantly, the votes of the elders rather than the ministers determined the outcome.[21]

The kirk session had an important role in the appointment of a minister. The session nominated the candidate and, if he was approved by the congregation on hearing him preach on a certain number of occasions, the session supplicated the presbytery to obtain his ordination or installation. If more than one candidate was considered the session decided which should be nominated by holding a congregational poll, presided over by a minister of the presbytery.[22] In April 1733 the session at Connor met after sermon and agreed 'to sett up Mr — Willson in the Presbytery of Letterkeney and Mr —Inch in the Presbytery of Straban that the congregation may com to apole [that is, a poll] and to stand to the one of those who the majoritey shall fall upon'.[23] In 1733 a rule was approved by the General Synod which meant that from then on any candidate needed not only the support of two-thirds of the congregation but the voters' subscriptions should amount to two-thirds of the stipend proposed for the maintenance of the minister.[24] Rev. William Campbell suggested that this regard to 'the rank and wealth of voters' was 'founded on the presumption of better education, and therefore better judgement' but it may also

---

[16] *RGSU*, i, 22; Barkley, 'History of the eldership', ii, 124.

[17] Joseph Boyse to Thomas Steward, n.d. (Magee College, Derry, Steward papers, MSS 46, no. 17).

[18] *A narrative of the proceedings of seven General Synods of the northern Presbyterians in Ireland, with relation to their differences in judgment and practice, from the year 1720 to the year 1726* (Belfast, 1727), pp 45–6; *RGSU*, ii, 50–65.

[19] *RGSU*, ii, 57.

[20] Winder quoted in Robert Allen, 'The principle of nonsubscription to creeds and confessions of faith as exemplified in Irish Presbyterian history' (2 vols, Ph.D. thesis, QUB, 1944), i, 228; Joseph Boyse to Thomas Steward, [c.1725] (Magee College, Derry, Steward papers, MSS 46, no. 18).

[21] *RGSU*, ii, 104–5, 108–9; *A narrative of the proceedings of seven General Synods*, pp 291–2.

[22] Barkley, 'History of the eldership', i, 47–8.

[23] Connor sess. mins, 1 Apr. 1733 (PHS).

[24] *RGSU*, ii, 187.

have been to prevent the election of a minister who was opposed by a minority large or wealthy enough to set up a separate congregation.[25]

Rev. Kirkpatrick wrote that the elders were 'all chosen by the people', but in reality elders were nominated by the session and then approved by the congregation.[26] This could be done either by announcing from the pulpit on three successive Sundays the names of those whom the session sought to make elders and thus allow time for any objections to be made,[27] or by dispatching existing elders through the congregation to see if any would object to a certain individual entering the session.[28] In some cases potential elders were also approved by the presbytery, which was made a rule by the General Synod in 1707.[29] Those elected and approved were appointed by the minister by prayer or simply invited to take their place in the session.[30] At Lisburn new elders had to serve a probationary period before becoming full elders.[31] Congregations did, however, take seriously their role in approving elders and in 1706 Golan (Fintona) congregation complained to Monaghan Presbytery that their minister 'had thrust in some elders upon them which they are not satisfy'd with', while at Larne and Kilwaughter in the early 1720s James Hadden was forced to demit his eldership, because 'his quarter was not satisfied with him'.[32]

Elders were not necessarily senior, that is elderly, members of the congregation, as the election of a student by Carnmoney in 1711 demonstrates.[33] The occupation of all elders serving in this period is unknown, but what is clear is that ordinary Presbyterians rather than the gentry predominated. Women were not appointed as ministers or lay elders, but could appeal the decisions of a court on the same basis

---

[25] William Campbell, MS 'Sketches of the history of Presbyterians in Ireland' (1803), p. 159 (PHS); McCracken, 'Ecclesiastical structure', p. 100.

[26] [Kirkpatrick], *Presby. loyalty*, p. 501; Carnmoney sess. mins, 12 & 21 Apr., 12 May 1686, 7 Sept. 1706, 12 Nov., 1 Dec. 1710 (PRONI, MIC1P/37/4); Connor sess. mins, 23 Dec. 1710 (PHS); Lisburn sess. mins, 26 Feb. 1701[/2] (PRONI, MIC1P/159/6); Templepatrick sess. mins (ibid., CR4/12/B/1, p. 195); Barkley, 'History of the eldership', i, pp ii, 36; ii, 115.

[27] Aghadowey sess. mins (PHS, pp 5–6); Larne & Kilwaughter sess. mins (PRONI, MIC1B/6A/1B, pp 136, 140); Lisburn sess. mins, 1 June 1699, 18 Feb. 1703/4 (ibid., MIC1P/159/6); autobiography of James Trail (ibid., D1460/1, opening 25).

[28] Carnmoney sess. mins, 14 Apr. 1697, 15 Apr. 1702, 15 Dec. 1706, 11 Jan. 1706/7, 6 & 18 Mar. 1710/11 (PRONI, MIC1P/37/4); Lisburn sess. mins, 14 Mar. 1696/7, 25 Apr., 16 May 1697, 29 Jan., 23 Mar. 1698/9 (ibid., MIC1P/159/6); Templepatrick sess. mins (ibid., CR4/12/B/1, p. 195).

[29] Laggan Pby mins, 1690–1700 (PHS, pp 46, 49); Carnmoney sess. mins, 9 Nov., 15 Dec. 1706, 25 Jan., 20 Feb. 1710/11 (PRONI, MIC1P/37/4); Monaghan Pby mins (PHS, p. 230); Killyleagh Pby mins (PRONI, Stewart papers, D1759/1/D/10, pp 32a, 51); Gillespie, 'Presbyterian revolution', p. 168; *RGSU*, i, 135.

[30] Lisburn sess. mins, 23 Dec. 1694, 18 Feb. 1703/4 (PRONI, MIC1P/159/6); Carnmoney sess. mins, 15 Feb. 1706/7 (PRONI, MIC1P/37/4); Templepatrick sess. mins (PRONI, CR4/12/B/1, p. 250); Barkley, 'History of the eldership', i, 39–40; J. W. Lockington, 'An analysis of the practice and procedure of Irish Presbyterianism' (Ph.D. thesis, QUB, 1980), p. 91.

[31] Lisburn sess. mins, 10 & 31 Jan. 1688[/9], 19 Feb. 1690[/1], 19 Feb., 2 Mar. 1692/3, 17 May 1694, 24 May 1702 (PRONI, MIC1P/159/6).

[32] Monaghan Pby mins (PHS, p. 123); Larne & Kilwaughter sess. mins (PRONI, MIC1B/6A/1B, p. 137).

[33] Carnmoney sess. mins, 6 Mar. 1710/11 (PRONI, MIC1P/37/4).

as men.[34] Heads of households had an important role, as they were responsible for disciplining all those in their charge, overseeing the religious, spiritual and moral development of their family, servants and apprentices, and during presbyterial visitations they were questioned about the conduct of the minister and elders.[35]

An area where power and authority was particularly important was church discipline. While most of the discipline cases brought before the session and other courts concerned 'fornication' or adultery, there were also a variety of other offences such as Sabbath-breaking,[36] marital difficulties,[37] over-consumption of alcohol,[38] disputes between neighbours,[39] theft,[40] dishonesty in business dealings,[41] and seeking to outbid a fellow Presbyterian for land on which he was regarded as having first claim.[42] Before a guilty person was absolved he or she had to acknowledge the fault before the session, and in more serious offences, such as fornication and adultery, also acknowledge it publicly before the congregation on three successive Sundays. Presbyteries were consulted in difficult cases. There could be local variations on the number of appearances considered necessary to be made before the congregation and sometimes the sentence was dependent on the notoriety of the case; for example, if an offence occurred a long time ago the session could be more lenient.[43] A person was able to clear him- or herself by an oath of purgation, administered with much seriousness, and great care was taken that there should be no perjury so that where there was any doubt the accused would not be permitted to take the oath.[44]

There is some debate about the degree to which offenders submitted to church discipline. Latimer noticed a growth of non-submission in Templepatrick congregation in the late seventeenth century, but this may have been a result of disruption to normal church discipline during the period of the Williamite War and its immediate aftermath, and he concludes that the majority nevertheless did submit.[45]

---

[34] A. R. Holmes, *The shaping of Ulster Presbyterian belief and practice 1770–1840* (Oxford, 2006), p. 224.

[35] Antrim Pby mins, 1697–1713 (PHS, p. 338).

[36] Lisburn sess. mins, 26 Dec. 1697 (PRONI, MIC1P/159/6); Carnmoney sess. mins, 15 Feb., 24 Mar. 1701/2 (ibid., MIC1P/37/4); Templepatrick sess. mins (ibid., CR4/12/B/1, pp 194, 231); Monaghan Pby mins (PHS, p. 102).

[37] Carnmoney sess. mins, 14 July 1697 (PRONI, MIC1P/37/4).

[38] Lisburn sess. mins, 29 Dec. 1698 (PRONI, MIC1P/159/6); Templepatrick sess. mins (ibid., CR4/12/B/1, pp 189–90); Aghadowey sess. mins (PHS, p. 126).

[39] R. H. Bonar, *Nigh on three and a half centuries: a history of Carnmoney Presbyterian Church* (Newtownabbey, 2004), p. 293.

[40] Lisburn sess. mins, 15 Jan. 1688/9, 24 Feb. 1708/9 (PRONI, MIC1P/159/6); Barkley, 'History of the eldership', ii, 138.

[41] Connor sess. mins, 14 Oct. 1716 (PHS).

[42] Aghadowey sess. mins (PHS, pp 44–5); R. M. Browne, 'Kirk and community: Ulster Presbyterian society, 1640–1740' (M.Phil. thesis, QUB, 1999), p. 178; Hamilton Maxwell to Agmondisham Vesey, 15 Aug. 1722 (PRONI, Kirk papers, T2524/17).

[43] Greaves, *God's other children*, p. 236.

[44] Carnmoney sess. mins, 4 Sept. 1698 (PRONI, MIC1P/37/4); Templepatrick sess. mins (ibid., Stewart papers, D1759/2/B/2, p. 82); Templepatrick sess. mins (PRONI, CR4/12/B/1, pp 182, 184); Connor sess. mins, 15 Jan. 1719 (PHS).

[45] Latimer, 'The old session-book of Templepatrick', p. 134; [Alexander Gordon], 'Congregational memoirs: Templepatrick', *Disciple*, ii (1882), pp 111–12, 136–8, 173.

Citing a few examples, Patrick Griffin has asserted that the early eighteenth century witnessed a crisis of discipline and the breakdown of the cohesiveness of the Presbyterian system,[46] but most historians, basing their conclusions on a larger volume of evidence, have concluded that the discipline of the church was generally accepted.[47] Most session records have not survived, but of those that are extant the number continually refusing to submit to discipline was small. There are various reasons why discipline was generally accepted. First, it was an established tradition and reflected the attitudes and views of the majority of Presbyterians. Second, some forms of behaviour that left members open to discipline had consequences for the whole community, such as pre- or extra-marital sex which could lead to illegitimate children whose upkeep could become a burden on congregational funds, and a common phrase in many discipline cases, recorded especially in the session books of Carnmoney and Lisburn, was that it was an offence not only 'against God' but also to 'his people'.[48] Some offences came before the session because the minister or elder noticed or had been informed about it or because a member of the congregation laid a charge against another member, but as well as this some members came forward of their own accord.[49]

Corporal punishment lay at the heart of eighteenth-century criminal justice and petty thieves were often whipped.[50] The law of the church, in contrast, was more humane.[51] Church discipline consisted of persuasion, or admonition and rebuke. The final sanction that the church possessed was excommunication, which deprived the offender of the sacraments of the church as well as all social dealings with his or her neighbours, as Presbyterians would not trade or commune with one under this penalty.[52] In areas where Presbyterians dominated the population such a sanction could be harmful to an individual's livelihood and subsistence. The session was responsible for granting testimonials. Such certificates testified to the holder's character and whether they were free from censure. In the absence of a satisfactory certificate it was difficult to obtain work and impossible to be admitted into full communion in another Presbyterian congregation.[53] Excommunicants could be

---

[46] Patrick Griffin, 'Defining the limits of Britishness: the "new" British history and the meaning of the Revolution Settlement in Ireland for Ulster's Presbyterians', *Journal of British Studies*, xxxix (2000), pp 278–80; idem, *The people with no name: Ireland's Ulster Scots, America's Scots Irish, and the creation of a British Atlantic world, 1689–1764* (Princeton, 2001), pp 37–47.

[47] J. M. Barkley, 'The Presbyterian minister in eighteenth century Ireland' in J. L. M. Haire, *et al.*, *Challenge and conflict: essays in Irish Presbyterian history and doctrine* (Antrim, 1981), p. 53; J. C. Beckett, *Protestant Dissent in Ireland 1687–1780* (London, 1948), p. 142; Browne, 'Kirk & community'.

[48] Carnmoney sess. mins, 12 May 1686 (PRONI, MIC1P/37/4); Lisburn sess. mins, 10 Jan. 1688[/9], 26 Mar. 1693, 17 May 1696, 31 Oct. 1700 (ibid., MIC1P/159/6).

[49] Barkley, 'History of the eldership', i, pp vi, 80–1.

[50] Belturbet corp. mins, 13 Jan. 1709 (Cavan County Archives, BC/1, p. 195); J. A. Sharpe, 'Crime and punishment' in H. T. Dickinson, (ed.), *A companion to eighteenth-century Britain* (Oxford, 2002), pp 361–2.

[51] Barkley, 'History of the eldership', i, p. v.

[52] [Kirkpatrick], *Presby. loyalty*, p. 556; Barkley, 'History of the eldership', i, 253–6.

[53] Templepatrick sess. mins (PRONI, CR4/12/B/1, p. 181); [Kirkpatrick], *Presby. loyalty*, pp 555–6; Peter Carr, *'The most unpretending of places': a history of Dundonald, County Down* (Dundonald, 1987), p. 79.

isolated in the wider community because their names were announced from the pulpits of the district and there are examples of sessions seeking information and the instigation of searches for offenders in other counties.[54] Excommunication, however, was always a last resort and every effort was made by the session to try and bring the offender to admit their sin. The prime aim of church discipline was always redemptive rather than punitive.[55] Another sanction which the church possessed was the withholding of baptism from a newborn child until its parent or parents submitted. Many Presbyterians believed that infants would not thrive if they were not baptised and baptism exercised a powerful grip over popular imagination.[56] Many cases appeared before the session simply because the offender wanted to have an illegitimate child baptised. The consciences of the guilty could also prick them into coming forward. In 1703 Michel Paul of Templepatrick congregation appeared before the session charged with committing adultery but 'obstinately denied' it until 1712 when he voluntarily appeared before the session because of 'the conviction and terror of his conscience, from the remarkable judgments of God upon his family, viz: extreme poverty, and that one of his hopefull children was suddenly struck blind, and the other turn'd an idiot'.[57] Church discipline was given added credence because ministers and elders had also to submit to discipline. Private censures of ministers and elders were carried out at church courts and during presbyterial visitations the congregation was able to comment on the conduct of both their minister and elders.[58]

There was some negotiation between heads of families, elders and ministers, but ultimately power was in the congregation. Although the General Synod of Ulster had agreed to pay the legal expenses of two wealthy Presbyterian merchants from Belfast who were prosecuted for being married according to the Presbyterian form, the synod was forced to renege on this offer when objections were raised against financial assistance being given to such wealthy individuals.[59] The Subscription Controversy also displayed the power of the laity. Seventeen memorials were presented to the General Synod when it met in 1721 which asked that all members of the synod, and of the inferior courts, should be obliged to subscribe to the *Westminster Confession*.[60] Pressure from congregations led several ministers of a

---

[54] Carnmoney sess. mins, 14 July 1697 (PRONI, MIC1P/37/4); Connor sess. mins, 8 May 1701, 26 Feb. 1711/12 (PHS); Gillespie, 'Presbyterian revolution', p. 162.

[55] Templepatrick sess. mins (PRONI, Stewart papers, D1759/2/B/2, pp 64–7, 75); Barkley, 'History of the eldership', i, p. v; Bonar, *Nigh on three & a half centuries*, pp 296–8.

[56] L. M. Ballard, *Forgetting frolic: marriage traditions in Ireland* (Belfast, 1998), p. 135; Leah Leneman and Rosalind Mitchison, *Sin in the city: sexuality and social control in urban Scotland 1660–1780* (Edinburgh, 1998), p. 31; K. M. Middleton, 'Religious revolution and social crisis in southwest Scotland and Ulster, 1687–1714' (Ph.D. thesis, TCD, 2010), p. 259.

[57] Templepatrick sess. mins (PRONI, CR4/12/B/1, p. 254).

[58] Lisburn sess. mins, 13 Mar. 1690/[1], 8 June 1693 (PRONI, MIC1P/159/6); Laggan Pby mins, 1672–95 (UTC, pp 14, 57, 195–7); Route Pby mins (PHS, p. 60); Antrim Pby mins, 1697–1713 (ibid., pp 300, 338); Down Pby mins (ibid., pp 24–5, 122, 364); Strabane Pby mins (UTC, pp 6, 9, 15–16, 20); Killyleagh Pby mins (PRONI, Stewart papers, D1759/1/D/10, pp 19, 31, 70, 81, 106); *RGSU*, i, 56, 67, 274–6, 383; Barkley, 'History of the eldership', i, p. v.

[59] *RGSU*, i, 336, 339, 404, 436–7.

[60] Ibid., ii, 7–8.

moderate disposition to make a voluntary subscription rather than lose members of their congregations. After the synod of 1721 Irish correspondents such as Rev. Alexander McCracken of Lisburn, an extreme Subscriber, informed the Scottish historian Robert Wodrow that 'severall of the Belfast Society are broke off from their non-subscribing, and by the weight of their people have, since the synod, signed the Confession of faith' because 'their congregations told them plainly if they did not subscribe, they could not in conscience adher to them as their pastors'.[61] Rev. John Abernethy noted that the laity were 'reproaching or deserting ministers, meerly on the score of subscribing or nonsubscribing'.[62]

The majority of the Presbyterian laity favoured subscription, though a minority, particularly from the wealthier and more educated sectors of society, gave support to, and had sympathies with, New Light ideas and nonsubscription.[63] Rev. George Lang of Loughbrickland informed Wodrow in May 1721 that 'the major part of the wealth[y]' in First Belfast were on the side of Rev. Samuel Haliday, a Non-Subscriber. Wodrow noted that Haliday and Kirkpatrick, 'being in a toun, and in a collegiat life' had 'the best congregations of any' of the Non-Subscribers and that the 'gentry and rich people' were favourable to the Non-Subscribers' sentiments and provided them with financial contributions. Charles Mastertown, the subscribing minister of Third Belfast, confessed in 1724 that the Non-Subscribers had the 'chief men in town'.[64] Most lay people, however, supported the Old Light cause. Kirkpatrick noted, 'nothing is more common amongst poor country-people, and amongst all who are ignorant of the state of the controversy, than to vent their jealousies against the Non-Subscribers, and to say plainly, that there must be something at the bottom of their Non-Subscribing.'[65] Ordinary and poorer Presbyterians were less likely to read the pamphlets connected with the Subscription Controversy and, therefore, relied on received tradition as had been taught to them through catechising based on the Westminster formularies.

Members of the laity who were dissatisfied with nonsubscribing ministers petitioned the superior courts of the church and managed to secure, if numbers were sufficient, separate congregations. Third Belfast was created for the subscribers of Belfast and in 1726 its list of catechisable persons amounted to 1,420 of whom 609 were communicants.[66] In 1724 the people of Connor opposed the participation of a nonsubscribing minister in the ordination of their new minister, and when a

---

61 Wodrow, *Analecta*, ii, 351; Alexander McCracken to [Robert Wodrow], 12 Oct. 1721 (NLS, Wod. Lett. Qu., xx, f. 251); George Lang to Robert Wodrow, 4 Nov. 1721 (ibid., f. 254).
62 [John Abernethy], *Seasonable advice to the Protestant Dissenters in the north of Ireland* (Dublin, 1722), p. 35.
63 I. R. McBride, *Scripture politics: Ulster Presbyterians and Irish radicalism in the late eighteenth century* (Oxford, 1998), pp 8, 47–8; Griffin, *The people with no name*, pp 56–8; Finlay Holmes, *The Presbyterian Church in Ireland: a popular history* (Blackrock, co. Dublin, 2000) p. 59.
64 George Lang to Robert Wodrow, 23 May 1721 (NLS, Wod. Lett. Qu. xx, f. 245); Wodrow, *Analecta*, iii, 468; McBride, *Scripture politics*, p. 48.
65 [James Kirkpatrick], *A vindication of the Presbyterian ministers in the north of Ireland; Subscribers and Non-Subscribers* (Belfast, 1721), p. 17.
66 Third Belfast (Rosemary Street) Presbyterian Church list of catechisable persons, 1725–42 (PRONI, T654/7); J. W. Nelson, 'The Belfast Presbyterians 1670–1830: an analysis of their political and social interests' (Ph.D. thesis, QUB, 1985), pp 118, 121.

nonsubscribing minister was sent by the presbytery he was barred from entry to the church.[67] Nonsubscribing ministers whose congregations lost members because of their views included Rev. Thomas Nevin of Downpatrick who lost 80 families in 1726, Rev. John Abernethy of Antrim who lost around 90 families in the same year, Rev. Thomas Shaw of Ahoghill who lost around 100 families residing in east Portglenone, and Rev. John Mears of Newtownards. By 1727 Rev. Michael Bruce was left with only 10 or 12 families at Holywood.[68] Even some of the moderate subscribers were affected. Rev. John Elder, though he professed willingness to subscribe the confession again, claimed that the Non-Subscribers were guilty of neither heresy nor impiety in practice and lost members of his congregation in consequence. At Coleraine Rev. Robert Higginbotham, another moderate, lost 90 families who in 1727 formed themselves into a new congregation, and at Comber in County Down the majority (100 out of 120 families) detached themselves from their minister, Rev. John Orr. When the Presbytery of Down refused to sanction this action, and after Orr joined the Presbytery of Antrim, those against Orr, who formed the bulk of the congregation, took possession of the meetinghouse and prevented Orr from officiating.[69] The Presbyterian laity's demand for doctrinal orthodoxy may help explain the rapid expansion of the Seceding Presbyterian church in the century after 1740.[70]

II. Belief and practice

Worship at church services brought together under a single roof Presbyterians from all social groups. As Raymond Gillespie has written, Presbyterian worship was 'a meeting of the community as well as a meeting for worship'.[71] Seating in churches reflected the social hierarchy. Dawson's Bridge, County Londonderry, for example, stated in 1701 that 'each man in his own proportion should have the choice of his seate according to his payment'.[72] Well-to-do people tended to sit towards the front and in Third Belfast the elders and chief members of the congregation were seated

---

[67] Reid, *Hist. of PCI*, iii, 214; Witherow, *Hist. & lit. memls*, ii, 8–10.

[68] Wodrow, *Analecta*, iii, 468; iv, 56; Robert McBride to Robert Wodrow, 9 Sept. 1726 (NLS, Wod. Lett. Qu., xxii, f. 118); Joseph Boyse to Thomas Steward, 1 Nov. 1726 (Magee College, Derry, Steward papers, MSS 46, no. 21); M. A. Stewart, 'John Abernethy (1680–1740): a reappraisal', *Bull. PHSI*, xxxii (2008), pp 16–17; Reid, *Hist. of PCI*, iii, 251; Charles Mastertown to Robert Wodrow, 9 Sept. 1726 (NLS, Wod. Lett. Qu., xxii, f. 120); Trevor McCavery, *Newtown: a history of Newtownards* (Belfast, 1994), p. 81; McBride, *Scripture politics*, pp 47–8.

[69] John Elder, *Reasons for moderation in the present debates amongst Presbyterians in the north of Ireland* (Belfast, 1725); Aghadowey sess. mins (PHS, pp 135–6); Witherow, *Hist. & lit. memls*, i, 300–1; Griffin, *The people with no name*, p. 53; Mr M[astertown] to William McKnight, 28 July 1726 (NLS, Wod. Lett. Qu., xxii, f. 113); Robert McBride to Robert Wodrow (ibid., f. 118); Joseph Boyse to Thomas Steward, 1 Nov. 1726 (Magee College, Derry, Steward papers, MSS 46, no. 21); 'Notes by Rev. David Stewart' in unfoliated appendix to Killyleagh Pby mins, 1725–32 (PRONI, Stewart papers, D1759/1/D/10); Reid, *Hist. of PCI*, iii, 225.

[70] David Hempton and Myrtle Hill, *Evangelical Protestantism in Ulster society, 1740–1890* (London, 1992), p. 70.

[71] Gillespie, 'The Presbyterian revolution', p. 163.

[72] Route Pby mins (PHS, p. 14).

nearest to the pulpit.[73] As a result of the symbolic importance of placement in the church, conflicts sometimes occurred over seating.[74]

There were normally two services on Sunday. Examples survive of those who were negligent in their attendance and were called before the session as a result of profaning the Sabbath. At Templepatrick elders were appointed to go through the congregation during Sunday worship and report any who stayed away unnecessarily.[75] In March 1708 some of the members of the congregation, including 'many young ones', confessed 'guilt in the profanation of the Lord's day', and the Connor session book recorded in 1717 that, 'a very uncomely and sinfull custom has crept into this congregation (viz) that many in the time of sermon frequent the houses of the towns not regarding the Lords day'.[76] By and large, however, the laity did attend Sunday services. By modern standards, Sunday services and sermons were long.[77] Surviving sermons, either in print or manuscript, suggest a strongly biblical emphasis and a systematic and logical arrangement, with points and sub-points.[78] Psalms were sung unaccompanied and 'lined' by a precentor. Rev. Joseph Boyse of Dublin disliked the practice but regarded it as a necessary evil because some of the people had no psalm books, and some were unable to read and had not committed the psalms to memory.[79] Many churches also had a mid-week lecture, but this was generally not as well attended as the Sunday services, particularly in rural congregations where it was difficult to take people away from agricultural work.[80] In 1706 Antrim session complained to the presbytery during a visitation that 'as to lecture days the country part of the parish doth not keep them well'.[81] Before the Williamite War many congregations had societies for prayer, but in the aftermath of the war, though some survived or were revived, in many cases the numbers involved had declined and did not return to pre-1688 levels.[82]

Sabbath observance entailed not only presence at worship services but also setting aside the whole day for religious devotions. Heads of households were responsible for ensuring that family worship was maintained on the Sabbath and

---

[73] Third Belfast (Rosemary Street) Presbyterian Church treasurer's book and pew register, 1726 (PRONI, T654/6, pp 60–119); J. W. Kernohan, *Rosemary Street Presbyterian Church Belfast: a record of the past 200 years* (Belfast, 1923), pp 17–21.

[74] Strabane Pby mins (UTC, pp 3, 137, 192); Griffin, *The people with no name*, pp 33–4.

[75] Templepatrick sess. mins (PRONI, CR4/12/B/1, pp 193, 231, 250); Latimer, 'The old session-book of Templepatrick', pp 131–2.

[76] Templepatrick sess. mins (PRONI, CR4/12/B/1, p. 231); Connor sess. mins, 15 May 1717 (PHS).

[77] R. S. Tosh, 'Presbyterian worship through the ages', *Bull. PHSI*, xxviii (2001–3), p. 2; T. H. Mullin, 'Old customs and practices in the Irish Presbyterian Church', *Bull. PHSI*, xxix (2004–5), p. 23.

[78] Sermons by Rev. John Mackenzie, 1689 (PHS); sermon book of Rev. Seth Drummond, 1705–7 (ibid.); ministerial notebook of Rev. John Kennedy, 1710–60 (ibid.).

[79] Joseph Boyse, *Remarks on a late discourse of William Lord Bishop of Derry; concerning the inventions of men in the worship of God* (Dublin, 1694), p. 28; Raymond Gillespie, '"A good and godly exercise": singing the Word in Irish dissent, 1660–1701' in Kevin Herlihy (ed.), *Propagating the word of Irish Dissent 1650–1800* (Dublin, 1998), pp 25–6, 28.

[80] Antrim Pby mins, 1697–1713 (PHS, pp 33, 43–4, 55, 59, 166).

[81] Ibid., p. 318.

[82] Ibid., pp 44, 55, 59, 166; [Gordon], 'Templepatrick', *Disciple*, ii (1882), p. 207.

during the week. Ministers and elders visited every home to see that household worship was practised.[83] Around the turn of the eighteenth century the people of Ballyclare and Cairncastle were regarded as generally observing family worship, but their neighbours at Ahoghill, Duneane and Glenarm were rebuked for not giving it sufficient attention.[84] In 1699 Antrim session desired the presbytery to admonish its congregation in relation to family worship, 'there being some that are carless as to that, either neglecting it altogether or going about it but seldom'.[85]

Examples do survive, though, of parents, even from lower social levels, who gave attention to the education of their children, not only in the rudiments of reading and writing but also in religious instruction. Thomas Gent, a printer, born in Ireland in 1693, to parents whom he described later in life as 'rich in grace, tho' not in shining ore', was given a Presbyterian baptism, and his parents saw to it that he 'learnt reading, writing, arithmetic, and Latin, and that he read his Bible and was God-fearing'.[86] James Hamilton, a murderer, born in the parish of Kilmore, County Down, described, in his speech from the gallows, how his parents took 'an early care' of his education and taught him 'to read the scriptures and to write'.[87] James Dunbar, who was executed for high treason in 1725, displayed a similar religious upbringing and like Hamilton his speech before execution was filled with scriptural allusions and quotations. Dunbar described how his father, a farmer, 'liv'd in the fear of God', 'attended the meetings constantly with his family', and did his best to bring 'up all under his care in the fear and service of God'. It was his father who taught Dunbar the *Catechism* and the psalm book and brought him up to the age of 16. Dunbar's speech also contained advice for his own children. He advised his son to keep away from '[lewd] women strong drink, and Sabbath breaking' and recommended that his children 'neglect not to pray in secret every morning, and at night'.[88]

Care was taken to instruct young people in the faith through a process of catechising before they were admitted for the first time to the Lord's Supper.[89] Bishop King alleged that of some 800 Presbyterians that he encountered only four had any knowledge of their *Catechism* and many could not say the Creed, nor the Lord's Prayer or the Ten Commandments.[90] Presbyterian ministers, such as Joseph Boyse of Dublin and Robert Craghead of Derry, were not prepared to accept these allegations, however, and pointed out that the members of the established church were equally ignorant. Boyse wrote that the Presbyterian ministers 'of the north of Ireland, and those in Scotland, do (speaking generally) outstrip all those we know of in the Christian world as to their unwearied catechising those under their charge',

---

[83] Carnmoney sess. mins, 2 Feb. 1697/8 (PRONI, MIC1P/37/4).

[84] Antrim Pby mins, 1697–1713 (PHS, pp 44, 55, 59, 166, 304).

[85] Ibid., p. 77.

[86] *ODNB* (Gent, Thomas (1693–1778)).

[87] James Hamilton, *The last speech and dying words of James Hamilton. In the parish of Kilmore in the County of Down; who was executed at Downpatrick for the bloody and heinous murder of William Lammon* (Glasgow, 1714), pp 2–3.

[88] James Kelly, *Gallows speeches from eighteenth-century Ireland* (Dublin, 2001), pp 176, 178–82.

[89] Connor sess. mins, 2 Nov. 1716 (PHS).

[90] William King, An *admonition to the dissenting inhabitants of the diocese of Derry* (Dublin, 1694), pp 5–6.

and in 1726 Rev. Samuel Hemphill wrote that 'the ministers in the north take some pains to explain the principles of religion', whereby 'many private Christians, can give a rational account of that abridgement of the Christian faith'.[91] Craghead claimed that the poor would rather 'pinch themselves' than do without a bible, and that those who could not read were assisted by their neighbours.[92] For the illiterate biblical knowledge was also available through attendance at church services where there were not only Bible readings, but prayers filled with biblical quotations and allusions, and where the sole praise was from the psalms.[93]

Presbyterian literacy was probably higher than for the other denominations in Ulster. When a call was drawn up by Coleraine congregation in 1673, out of a total of 33 signatories only three were marksmen.[94] In 1718 when Rev. William Boyd of Macosquin was sent to America with a commission to find what encouragement would be given to prospective emigrants planning to settle in New England, the memorial he carried had 319 signatories, nine of whom were Presbyterian ministers and a further three who were educated at Scottish universities. Only 13 signed the commission with their marks – a literacy rate (in this respect) of 95%. Given that the majority of the signatories were small farmers and labourers this would indicate a reasonable standard of popular education.[95] There was though probably a higher literacy rate among men than women and among urban dwellers than those based in rural areas. On the Adair estate, around Ballymena, in the late seventeenth century, though 31 out of 33 tradesmen were able to sign their leases, only a third of the farmers and yeomen were able to do the same.[96]

Presbyterian congregations usually had one or more schools attached to them, which were run and overseen by the session, which not only appointed the teachers but ensured the orthodoxy of the religious instruction provided.[97] The education

[91] Boyse, *Remarks on a late discourse*, p. 85; Samuel Hemphil[l], *A letter to the Rev'd. Mr. Samuel Haliday: wherein his scheme of minnisterial [sic] communion, in the seventh page of his introduction, to his Reasons against subscription to the Westminster Confession of Faith is examin'd, and compar'd* (Dublin, 1726), p. 22.

[92] Robert Craghead, *An answer to a late book, intituled, a discourse concerning the inventions of men in the worship of God. By William Lord Bishop of Derry* (Edinburgh, 1694), p. 86.

[93] Raymond Gillespie, *Devoted people: belief and religion in early modern Ireland* (Manchester, 1997), p. 75.

[94] 'An account of Presbyterianism in Coleraine, Co. Londonderry, from the seventeenth century' (PRONI, Maxwell Given papers, D2096/1/79, p. 15).

[95] E. L. Parker, *The history of Londonderry, comprising the towns of Derry and Londonderry, N. H.* (Boston, 1851), pp 35, 317–21; Graeme Kirkham, 'Literacy in north-west Ulster, 1680–1860' in Mary Daly and David Dickson (eds), *The origins of popular literacy in Ireland: language change and educational development 1700–1920* (Dublin, 1990), p. 74; J. A. McIvor, *Popular education in the Irish Presbyterian Church* (Dublin, 1969), p. 32.

[96] Toby Barnard, 'Learning, the learned and literacy in Ireland, c.1660–1760' in idem *et al.* (eds), *A miracle of learning: studies in manuscripts and Irish learning: essays in honour of William O'Sullivan* (Aldershot, 1998), p. 221; Raymond Gillespie, *Reading Ireland: print, reading and social change in early modern Ireland* (Manchester, 2005), p. 41; Kirkham, 'Literacy in north-west Ulster', pp 74–7.

[97] Down Pby mins (PHS, p. 72); Bp King to Abp Boyle, 30 Aug. 1700 (PRONI, DIO/4/29/2/1/2); J. C. Beckett, 'William King's administration of the Diocese of Derry, 1691–1703', *Irish Historical Studies*, iv (1944). p. 178; Barkley, 'History of the eldership', i, p. iv; ii, 116–17, 120–2; Aghadowey sess. mins (PHS, pp 49–50).

of poor children was paid or subsidised by the session, or higher courts,[98] which occasionally provided bibles and other books to poor congregants.[99] As with attendance at the weekday lecture, it was sometimes harder to ensure the attendance of rural-based children. At Antrim the 'land-ward part of the congregation' was admonished in 1699 for not encouraging the schools of the congregation through failure to send their children.[100] There was, however, the potential for a poor man's son who had the necessary talent to receive a university education, financed by the church.[101] Presbyterian congregational schools identified boys with the potential for university study and even in these congregational schools, primarily concerned with the rudiments of reading and writing, Latin instruction was sometimes given or actively sought by the congregation. When it was suggested at Larne, in 1701, that Patrick Plunkett set up a school to teach English some objected that they already had English instruction and that 'there is more need to have a master that can teach Latin'.[102]

Those able to read could acquire reading material in various ways. A printing press was established at Belfast in 1694,[103] but both before and after that books were regularly imported into Ulster, particularly from Scotland to Belfast and Derry.[104] The *Catechism* was available at markets and chapmen carried reading material among their wares. Tisdall stated in 1712 that for 20 years he had observed 'the Scotch strolers and pedlars, who go from house to house, all over the country selling small ware' and 'have generally a Scotch Directory and Solemn League and Covenant along with them, which they still expose to sale among their other toys', and in the same year Convocation made a similar complaint that seditious books

[98] Armagh sess. mins (PRONI, Stewart papers, D1759/1/B/1, pp 12, 15, 21–2); Ballynahinch accounts, 6 Jan. 1723, 18 Oct. 1724, 2 Nov. 1730; Lisburn sess. mins, 30 Jan. 1700[/1], 6 May, 10 June 1703 (PRONI, MIC1P/159/6); Templepatrick sess. mins (ibid., CR4/12/B/1, p. 187); Kirkdonald sess. mins (PHS, pp 29, 31, 36, 43, 80, 86); Laggan Pby mins, 1690–1700 (ibid., pp 18, 118, 130); Monaghan Pby mins (ibid., p. 147); Sub-synod of Derry mins (ibid., p. 238).

[99] Armagh sess. mins (PRONI, Stewart papers, D1759/1/B/1, pp 16, 19); Ballynahinch accounts, 26 Sept. 1708, 18 Mar. 1716, 23 Nov. 1718, 24 May 1732; J. M. Barkley, 'The evidence of old Irish session-books on the sacrament of the Lord's Supper', *Church Service Society Annual*, no. 22 (May 1952), p. 30.

[100] Antrim Pby mins, 1697–1713 (PHS, p. 77).

[101] Monaghan Pby mins (PHS, p. 147).

[102] Barkley, 'History of the eldership', ii, 120.

[103] J. R. R. Greeves, 'Two Irish printing families', *Proceedings and Reports of the Belfast Natural History and Philosophical Society*, 2nd ser., iv (1950–55), pp 38–44; Wesley McCann, 'Patrick Neill and the origins of Belfast printing' in Peter Isaac (ed.), *Six centuries of the provincial book trade in Britain* (Winchester, 1990), pp 125–38; Gillespie, *Reading Ireland*, pp 78–9; A. S. Drennan, 'On the identification of the first Belfast printed book', *The Library*, 7th ser., i (2000), pp 193–6; Raymond Gillespie, *Early Belfast: the origins and growth of an Ulster town to 1750* (Belfast, 2007), p. 141.

[104] Port Glasgow customs book, 16 & 26 Mar., 22 June, 6 & 22 July 1681 (NAS, E/72/19/2, pp 7–8, 13–14); Port Glasgow customs book, 1 & 22 Dec. 1681, 1 Feb. 1682 (ibid., E/72/19/6); Port Glasgow customs book, 3 & 27 Oct. 1685 (ibid., E72/19/11); Port Glasgow customs book, 1 Apr. & 11 June 1686 (ibid., E72/19/13); Port Glasgow customs book, 22 Apr., 19 June & 12 Sept. 1690 (ibid., E72/19/19); Portpatrick customs book, 21 Feb., 9 & 19 May, 10 June, 5 & 9 Aug., & 20 Oct. 1682 (ibid., E72/10/7); Gillespie, *Reading Ireland*, p. 87; idem, *Early Belfast*, p. 141.

were 'handed thro the kingdom' 'by pedlars and vagabonds'.[105] At Templepatrick sermon books, which had been given by the local squire, were distributed free of charge by the session to the poor.[106] In Larne in January 1729 the session agreed that nothing that had been lost, except books, was to be announced in the meetinghouse,[107] and there are occasionally fleeting references in session minutes to those below the gentry and merchant elite being involved in reading, usually of religious material.[108] It was not only religious reading material, though, that circulated. It was brought to the attention of the General Synod in 1718 that 'several obscene ballads printed in Belfast' were 'dispers'd through the countrey' and the synod appointed Rev. James Kirkpatrick to 'represent to the printers that the ministers and several other godly persons take just offense at these ballads, and therefore advise them not to print such papers for the future'.[109]

The Presbyterian church recognised two sacraments – baptism and communion – which were deemed to have biblical sanction. Marriage, though not a sacrament, was to be conducted by a minister of the word, as couples were to 'marry only in the Lord'.[110] During this period the validity of marriages conducted by Presbyterian ministers was called into question and some of the Presbyterian ministers were prosecuted by the ecclesiastical courts for performing illegal ceremonies.[111] A valid marriage was particularly important for the upper classes as it affected the legitimacy of children and inheritance.[112] Rev. John McBride of Belfast, in October 1713, wrote that while the poorer groups among the Presbyterians were willing to be married by Presbyterian ministers, some of the wealthier members married in the Church of Ireland to avoid questions about the

[105] [Tisdall], *Conduct of the Dissenters*, p. 67; *The present state of religion in Ireland* (London, [1712]), p. 10; Samuel McSkimin, *The history and antiquities of the county of the town of Carrickfergus*, ed. E. J. McCrum (new ed., Belfast, 1909), p. 76; Bp King to Abp Wake, 2 June 1719 (TCD, King papers, 750/5/171–72); King to Wake, 1 Aug. 1719 (BL, Add MS 6117, no. 46); Raymond Gillespie, 'The world of Andrew Rowan: economy and society in Restoration Antrim' in Brenda Collins, *et al.* (eds), *Industry, trade and people in Ireland, 1650–1950* (Belfast, 2005), p. 18; idem, *Reading Ireland*, pp 88–90.
[106] Templepatrick sess. mins (PRONI, CR4/12/B/1, p. 223).
[107] Larne & Kilwaughter sess. mins (PRONI, MIC1B/6A/1B, p. 140).
[108] Templepatrick sess. mins (PRONI, CR4/12/B/1, p. 223); Middleton, 'Religious revolution', p. 268.
[109] *RGSU*, i, 478–9.
[110] *Westminster Confession of Faith* (1646), ch. 24, and *The directory for the publick worship of God* (published with the *Confession*), pp 387–8.
[111] Laggan Pby mins (UTC, p. 36); *RGSU*, i, 313, 412; Bp King to Bp Edward Smith, 3 Dec. 1700 (TCD, King papers, MS 750/2/2/27); King to Mr [Thomas] Lawson, 11 Feb. 1700[/1] (ibid., MS 750/2/2/66); John McMun to [Robert Wodrow], 8 Apr. & 9 June 1702 (N.L.S., Wod. Lett. Qu., ii, ff 26, 52); Antrim Pby mins, 1697–1713 (PHS, p. 172); Alexander McCracken to [Robert Wodrow], 21 July & 13 Oct. 1704 (N.L.S., Wod. Lett. Qu., ii, ff 109–10); William Hair to [Robert Wodrow], 4 Dec. 1712 (ibid., Wod. Lett. Qu., xx, f. 183); Gilbert Kennedy to Robert Wodrow, 5 Oct. 1716 (ibid. f. 217); George Lang to Robert Wodrow, 13 Oct. 1716 (ibid., f. 221); Bp Nicolson to Abp Wake, 17 Jan. 1719/20 (Christ Church, Oxford, Wake papers, xiii: microfilm, Institute of Historical Research Library, London, XR.129/18); Sub-synod of Derry mins (PHS, pp 211–12); Witherow, *Hist. & lit. memls*, i, 71; Beckett, *Protestant dissent*, pp 117–21.
[112] Petition from the B[ishop] of D[own] to the Lords Justices in Ireland, Sept. 1698 (PRONI, T525/12).

validity of their marriage.[113] Clotworthy Upton, for instance, obtained a licence from the faculty office of the archbishop of Canterbury for his marriage in 1692 to his first wife Lady Mary Boyle, daughter of the second earl of Orrery.[114] With regard to marriages conducted within the Presbyterian church, banns announcing any intended marriage were publicly proclaimed three times, usually on successive Sundays after sermon, though an overture of the General Synod in 1712 allowed one of the proclamations to be given on a lecture day. Banns were proclaimed in the couple's respective congregations and the procedure was important in preventing bigamy and allowed time for objections to be made or impediments to be investigated. If one of the parties belonged to another congregation a testimonial was required from the minister of the other church testifying that the bearer was eligible for marriage.[115] Cases of breach of promise to marry also came before the session.[116] For a valid marriage consent of parents was necessary. The 1712 overture stated that any minister who married persons without the publication of banns or without the consent of parents or guardians was to be suspended from office for six months. Parents, however, were not permitted to be unreasonable.[117]

Evidence suggests that marriages did not necessarily take place in the church itself and many couples were married in the parental home or the home of the minister. Marriages were celebrated at all hours and at least three of the couples married in Antrim between 1711 and 1716 were 'maryed at night'.[118] Marriages could be regarded as irregular for various reasons, including not only lack of parental approval and the failure to publish banns, but also if the couple eloped, were married in the Church of Ireland or Catholic Church, or if they were married by a defrocked minister.[119] Mary Armstrong, for instance, who was married by 'Priest

---

[113] William Hair to Robert Wodrow, 4 Dec. 1712 (Wodrow, *Corresp.*, i, 484, n. 1).

[114] G. E. Cokayne and E. A. Fry (eds), *Calendar of marriage licences issued by the Faculty Office. 1632–1714* (London, 1905), p. 120. The marriage licence itself would have been given to the couple, and is now lost, but Lambeth Palace Lib. holds associated documents, namely marriage allegations. The allegation was a sworn statement to the effect that both parties were free and available to marry. The allegation for the Upton and Boyle marriage appears in the Chester and Armytage calendar, and is available to view at Lambeth. Another Ulster Presbyterian gentleman who obtained a marriage licence from the faculty office of the archbishop of Canterbury was Alexander Cairnes, for his marriage to Elizabeth Gould in 1698: Cokayne & Fry, *Calendar of marriage licences*, p. 155.

[115] *RGSU*, i, 276; Barkley, 'History of the eldership', i, pp iii, 61–2; ii, 58, 61, 68, 126.

[116] Templepatrick sess. mins (PRONI, CR4/12/B/1, p. 174); Aghadowey sess. mins (PHS, pp 69–70, 88); Carnmoney sess. mins, 27 Nov. 1713 (PRONI, MIC1P/37/5); Connor sess. mins, 12 Oct. 1714 (PHS).

[117] Aghadowey sess. mins (PHS, pp 88, 122); Connor sess. mins, 12 Oct. 1704, 6 Sept. 1719 (PHS); Templepatrick sess. mins (PRONI, CR4/12/B/1, p. 259); Sub-synod of Derry mins (PHS, p. 99); *RGSU*, i, 276; Barkley, 'Marriage and the Presbyterian tradition', *Ulster Folklife*, xxxix (1993), p. 36; idem, 'The Presbyterian minister', p. 52.

[118] Diary of Rev. William Homes, 1688–1746 (New England Historic Genealogical Society, Mss A 1996, p. 11); W. S. Smith, 'Early register of the old Presbyterian congregation of Antrim', *UJA*, v (1899), p. 187; Rosemary ffolliott, 'Irish social customs of genealogical importance', *Irish Ancestor*, x, no. 1 (1978), p. 19; Mullin, 'Old customs', p. 25.

[119] Barkley, 'Marriage & the Presbyterian tradition', p. 35.

O Hammil', was rebuked at Templepatrick for 'symbolizing with idolators' and in the same congregation James Kennedy was rebuked in 1721 for 'his sin and folly in his unorderly marriage in goeing to a buckle beggar'.[120] The validity of marriage in the Church of Ireland or Catholic Church, however, was not questioned and the offender was readmitted to the privileges of church membership after expressing sufficient sorrow and repentance. Kirk sessions also dealt with marital unfaithfulness and marriage breakdown.[121] The Westminster standards made provision for divorce, but only on the grounds of adultery and desertion.[122] Only one example survives during the period where the session recommended divorce. In 1698 Carnmoney session advised Alexander Collbeart 'to seek counsel whether he may not be divorced seeing she [his wife] wil not cohabit with him'.[123]

Large families were common, but infant mortality was high. Despite acts against private baptism made by the session of Aghadowey in 1711 and the Presbytery of Strabane in 1718, private baptism continued to occur, with parents not wanting to expose a young child to the cold.[124] The diary of Rev. Robert Gordon, minister of Rathfriland, who had 26 children, would suggest that baptism was carried out at an early age, with most of his children baptised within three days of birth.[125] Presbyterian baptism was administered by an ordained minister to the children of believing parents and, much more rarely, to adults. At least one of the parents had to be a believer in order for the child to be baptised and though it was usually the father who presented the child for baptism, in cases where he was not a member of the church or was under censure the child could be presented by a sponsor, who was often a relative.[126] One of the rare cases of adult believers' baptism was in 1678 when the Laggan Presbytery instructed Rev. Robert Campbell to confer with a young Letterkenny man who had not been baptised, and ordered him to baptise the young man if satisfied with the candidate's profession of faith.[127]

In most congregations, except during the disruptions of the 1680s,[128] communion was celebrated once or twice a year, in sacramental occasions of three or four days' duration. The session determined when communion should be celebrated, and it would be intimated to the congregation at least three Sundays before the actual event. Communion involved more than just the Sunday service when

---

[120] Templepatrick sess. mins (PRONI, CR4/12/B/1, pp 222, 294).

[121] Antrim Pby mins, 1697–1713 (PHS, p. 314).

[122] Barkley, 'Marriage & the Presbyterian tradition', pp 37–8; *The Westminster Confession of Faith* (1646), ch. 24:6.

[123] Carnmoney sess. mins, 3 & 25 Aug., 19 Oct. & 7 Dec. 1698 (PRONI, MIC1P/37/4); Barkley, 'Marriage & the Presbyterian tradition', pp 37–8.

[124] Aghadowey sess. mins (PHS, p. 91); Strabane Pby mins (UTC, p. 25); ffolliott, 'Irish social customs', p. 18.

[125] Diary of Rev. Robert Gordon, 1707–44 (PHS); Diary of Rev. William Homes (New England Historic Genealogical Society, Mss A 1996, pp 11–13, 20).

[126] Typescript copy of First Armagh baptisms, 1 Apr. 1708, 7 Nov. 1710, 7 Jan. 1710/11, 13 June & 21 [Aug.] 1711, 1 & 29 May 1712 (NLI, MS 1395, pp 4, 15–16, 19–20, 23–4); Barkley, 'History of the eldership', i, p. iii.

[127] Laggan Pby mins, 1672–95 (UTC, p. 156). Another example of adult baptism can be found in Lisburn Presbyterian Church's register of baptisms (PRONI, MIC1P/159/7, p. 41).

[128] Antrim 'Meeting' mins (UTC, p. 193).

the sacrament was itself administered. It began with a fast day which was usually held mid-week. Some congregations, in addition, kept the Saturday before the communion as a day of preparation and the Monday afterwards was always kept as a day of thanksgiving.[129] This undoubtedly led to a heightened sense of occasion, though people did not necessarily attend the sermons given on each of these days. Though a collection was taken each day, the amount collected usually peaked on the communion Sabbath itself.[130]

It was customary for communicants to travel to other congregations when communion was being celebrated, and this swelled the numbers participating. Those attending from neighbouring congregations had to have proof that they were members of good standing in their own congregations, through possession of a testimonial or the approval of their own minister who may have accompanied them in order to assist at the administration of the sacrament in his colleague's church.[131] In many cases church buildings were unable to accommodate the numbers and a relay system was used to administer the sacrament, and platforms, often referred to as 'tents', were erected outside the meetinghouse from which neighbouring ministers addressed those who had just received, or were waiting their turn to receive, the elements.[132] The numbers attending the Sunday communion could be high. Some Church of Ireland sources suggest numbers as high as 5,000,[133] while Presbyterian estimates, because they issued tokens to their own members, were probably more accurate. About 600 communicants from Carnmoney attended the service at their own church in 1697 and at Burt in County Donegal 984 communicants were recorded at one service in the 1690s.[134] Such large numbers gave rise to opportunities for non-religious sociability and some came to meet friends. Rev. Gordon Scott, an Anglican rector, suggested that the Presbyterians came to communion

[129] Boyse, *Remarks on a late discourse*, p. 136; Seth Drummond's sermon notebook, 4 Aug. 1706 (PHS, pp 1–2 (first pagination)); Daniel M[ussenden]'s book of sermons, 1717–18 (PHS); Aghadowey sess. mins (ibid., p. 32); Carnmoney sess. mins, 22 Aug. 1697 (PRONI, MIC1P/37/4); Connor sess. mins, 14 Oct. 1707 (PHS); Lisburn sess. mins, 11 June 1691, 2 June 1692, 1 June 1693, 12 June 1694 (PRONI, MIC1P/159/6); diary of Rev. John Kennedy, 1714–37 (PHS, p. 1).

[130] Armagh sess. mins (PRONI, Stewart papers, D1759/1/B/1, p. 14); Boyse, *Remarks on a late discourse*, p. 136; Gillespie, *Devoted people*, p. 101; Tosh, 'Presbyterian worship through the ages', p. 4.

[131] Boyse, *Remarks on a late discourse*, pp 136–7; Lisburn sess. mins, 9 June 1692 (PRONI, MIC1P/159/6); Rev. Gordon Scott to Bp King, 11 June 1694 (TCD, Lyons (King) papers, MSS 1995–2008/359); Bp Synge to Abp Wake, 4 Mar. 1715[/16] (Christ Church, Oxford, Wake papers, xii: microfilm, Institute of Historical Research Library, London, XR.129/17); autobiography of James Trail (PRONI, D1460/1, openings 22, 25–6); commonplace book belonging to Samuel Hyndman and others (PHS). From the 1690s, however, Presbyterian church leaders attempted to reduce large assemblies at communion by trying to limit the number of ministers participating to three or four. It was not, however, until the mid-eighteenth century that communions became generally based on a single congregation: *RGSU*, i, 22; S. J. Connolly, *Divided kingdom: Ireland 1630–1800* (Oxford, 2008), p. 280.

[132] Raymond Gillespie, 'Dissenters and Nonconformists, 1661–1700' in Kevin Herlihy (ed.), *The Irish Dissenting tradition 1650–1750* (Blackrock, Co. Dublin, 1995), pp 24–5.

[133] Bp King to Abp Boyle, 30 Aug. 1700 (PRONI, DIO/4/29/2/1/12); Bp Synge to Abp Wake, 4 Mar. 1715/16 (BL, Add. MS 6117, no. 18).

[134] Carnmoney sess. mins, 22 Aug. 1697 (PRONI, MIC1P/37/4); Gillespie, 'Dissenters & Nonconformists', p. 24.

'like crowds to a fair' and the rebuke of two men by Templepatrick session 'for their unseasonable drinking on the communion Moonday night' is further evidence of the associated opportunities for socialising.[135] Occasionally a complaint was made at presbyterial visitations that at communions people stood 'off that minister and session would allow', but whether this was because they devalued the sacrament or felt unworthy to receive it is unclear.[136]

Fast days were not only associated with communion preparation, but were also appointed, along with days of thanksgiving, by sessions,[137] presbyteries[138] and synods.[139] In some cases they were also appointed by the government, which declared fasts on a national basis, especially in times of crisis such as war or famine. During the 1690s eight such fasts were proclaimed by the state.[140] Days of fasting and humiliation for the success of the military campaign during the War of the Spanish Succession were appointed in the opening years of the eighteenth century, along with days of thanksgiving, and notes survive from sermons preached on these occasions by the Presbyterian minister of Ramelton, Rev. Seth Drummond.[141] Ramelton also observed the day of public thanksgiving, on 1 May 1707, appointed by the government for the Anglo-Scottish union.[142] Presbyterians, in common with other Protestants, believed that crises such as famine were the result of God's intervention in the world and expressed divine displeasure at sin. It seemed natural, therefore, as a community to pray to God for forgiveness and relief.[143] Fast days were marked by worship (both public and private), abstinence from food and cessation of work.[144]

The fasts appointed by the Presbyterian church were for both general and specific reasons. Reasons included the ordination of a minister[145] or elders,[146] bad weather,[147]

---

[135] Rev. Gordon Scott to Bp King, 11 June 1694 (TCD, Lyons (King) papers, MSS 1995–2008/359); Templepatrick sess. mins (PRONI, CR4/12/B/1, p. 208); Gillespie, 'Dissenters & Nonconformists', p. 25.

[136] Antrim Pby mins, 1697–1713 (PHS, pp 33, 44, 55, 77, 318).

[137] Lisburn sess. mins, 9 Jan. 1689[/90], 29 Jan. 1690[/1] (PRONI, MIC1P/159/6); Ballycarry sess. mins, 11 Apr. 1711 (ibid., CR3/31/1); Connor sess. mins, 13 May 1713 (PHS).

[138] Laggan Pby mins, 1672–95 (UTC, pp 5, 9, 28–9, 68, 74, 121, 163–4, 183–4, 201–2); Laggan Pby mins, 1690–1700 (PHS, p. 214); Antrim Pby mins, 1697–1713 (PHS, p. 534); Down Pby mins (PHS, p. 137).

[139] Sub-synod of Derry mins (PHS, pp 177, 184); RGSU, i, 26, 31, 53, 61–2, 72, 87–8, 154, 277–8, 338, 366; ii, 88, 99–101, 109, 146.

[140] Gillespie, Devoted people, pp 48–50.

[141] Seth Drummond's sermon notebook (PHS, pp 12–15, 31–4, 77–9, 95–6, 105–6 (all second pagination)).

[142] Ibid., pp 107–9 (second pagination).

[143] Gillespie, Devoted people, pp 49–50; C. G. Brown, The social history of religion in Scotland since 1730 (London, 1987), p. 107.

[144] Rev. Andrew Rowan account book, 1672–80 (PRONI, Rowan papers, D1614/3, p. 20); Gillespie, Devoted people, pp 49–50; A. W. G. Brown, 'Irish Presbyterian theology in the early eighteenth century' (Ph.D. thesis, QUB, 1977), pp 531–2; Greaves, God's other children, p. 232.

[145] RGSU, i, 57, 67; Down Pby mins (PHS, p. 17).

[146] Templepatrick sess. mins (PRONI, CR4/12/B/1, p. 179); Lisburn sess. mins, 18 Feb. 1703/4 (ibid., MIC1P/159/6).

[147] RGSU, i, 31; ii, 100; Killyleagh Pby mins (PRONI, Stewart papers, D1759/1/D/10, p. 2); autobiography of James Trail (PRONI, D1460/1, opening 30).

food shortages,[148] the state of the poor,[149] the decay of religion,[150] the persecution of Christians abroad[151] and the conversion of the Irish.[152] Kirk sessions were able to appoint fasts for specific local reasons. Connor appointed a day of humiliation on 9 May 1713 'upon the consideration of a great mortality and sickness in the congregation' and two years earlier Ballycarry had appointed a day for prayer and humiliation 'upon account of the bad season for saving of the food and also upon account of the witchcraft and other sins that abound in this part of the country'.[153] The latter referred to the trial and conviction of alleged witches at Carrickfergus that year, one of whose principal victims was the widow of the Presbyterian minister of Islandmagee.[154]

Alongside what would now be regarded as orthodox beliefs, Presbyterians in the early modern period gave credence to superstitious or alternative beliefs which could be held alongside the official teachings of the church. Such alternative beliefs were used to help explain or deal with the uncertainties of life. Witchcraft and other accusations, such as charming, came before the Presbyterian sessions, as well as the higher courts.[155] The Presbytery of Antrim in 1684 considered how to deal with the seventh son's curing of the evil, while in November 1699 Rev. John McGachin, minister of Enniskillen and Magherabuoy, sought the advice of Laggan Presbytery on how to proceed with those who 'use charmers and charms in caring of their sick'.[156] Objects, as well as people or places, were resorted to in order to achieve healing, prognostication or harm.[157]

* * * * * * *

Though power ultimately lay with the congregation, the Presbyterian church in the early eighteenth century was not as democratic as it would later become. Elders,

[148] Down Pby mins (PHS, p. 137); Charles Mastertown to Robert Wodrow, 4 Feb. 1729 (NLS, Wod. Lett. Qu., xxii, f. 161).

[149] Down Pby mins (PHS, p. 137); RGSU, ii, 146.

[150] RGSU, ii, 99–101, 109; 'Extracts from the minutes of a MSS dated 1700–01 containing early minutes of Larne and Kilwaughter session', in unfoliated section at the end of Larne & Kilwaughter sess. mins, 1720–69 (PRONI, MIC1B/6A/1B, 19 May 1700).

[151] RGSU, i, 31; 'Extracts from the minutes of a MSS dated 1700–01 containing early minutes of Larne and Kilwaughter session' (PRONI, MIC1B/6A/1B, 19 May 1700).

[152] RGSU, i, 440.

[153] Connor sess. mins, 13 May 1713 (PHS); Ballycarry sess. mins, 19 Apr. 1711 (PRONI, CR3/31/1).

[154] [William Tisdall], The Islandmagee witches … [ed. Samuel McSkimin] ([Belfast, 1822]); Young, Historical notices of old Belfast, pp 161–4; McSkimin, History & antiquities of Carrickfergus (1909), pp 73–4.

[155] Connor sess. mins, 5 May 1701 (PHS); Carnmoney sess. mins, 27 June, 8 July & 4 Oct. 1702 (PRONI, MIC1P/37/4); Aghadowey sess. mins (PHS, p. 8); Antrim Pby mins, 1697–1713 (PHS, pp 444–5).

[156] Antrim 'Meeting' mins (UTC, pp 180, 193); Laggan Pby mins, 1690–1700 (PHS, p. 188).

[157] Carnmoney sess. mins, 1 Aug. 1703 (PRONI, MIC1P/37/4); Templepatrick sess. mins (ibid., CR4/12/B/1, pp 260–1, 263); George Hill, An historical account of the MacDonnells of Antrim (Belfast, 1873), p. 383; Browne, 'Kirk & community', pp 179–181; Gillespie, Devoted people, pp 64, 74, 118.

for instance, were selected by the session and the congregation simply asked if they acquiesced, and from 1733 a social distinction was created when in the election of a minister a two-thirds majority of both men and money was required. Nevertheless, the Presbyterian church, in what was a hierarchical and deferential period, was more democratic than its largest rivals, the Church of Ireland and the Catholic Church, and in contrast to these two denominations the Presbyterian laity could participate at all levels of church government. Sunday services at the meetinghouse were generally well attended and most Presbyterians submitted to the authority of their church and its discipline process. Aspects of their worship, particularly their celebration of the communion sacrament, helped to forge and maintain a corporate religious identity among the Presbyterians and marked them out as a distinctive religious community within late Stuart and early Hanoverian Ulster.

Conclusion

Ulster Presbyterians were drawn from all social groups below the aristocracy. The majority lived at the middling and lower levels, and this present study has for the first time brought into focus, in detail, who these non-clerical, lesser Presbyterians actually were and how they contributed to the Presbyterian denomination and society more widely. During the period the social profile of Presbyterianism was undergoing transformation. The linen industry was slowly beginning to change the economic context, and would lead to social mobility, though developments did not come to full fruition until the decades after 1730. Instead the most important social change in this period was the decline of the Presbyterian gentry. The number of Presbyterian gentry families in Ulster was never huge, but in the generation after the enactment of the sacramental test clause, in 1704, the number declined sharply. Conforming was not confined to the landed elite and extended, to a lesser degree, to the leading mercantile families and professionals. The impact, however, was more noticeable among the Presbyterian gentry.

Afterwards the gap left in the social leadership by the defection of the gentry was filled by the ministers and merchants. Though not the only Presbyterians to receive a higher education, ministers had always been the dominant group among the Presbyterians' intellectual elite. The Presbyterian church, however, was never run by an oligarchy and the structure of church government allowed for the participation of the laity at all levels and in the kirk session they formed the majority. Some of the gentry were elders, though their more usual role had been as commissioners to the higher courts when issues of finance or vacancy relating to their local congregation were under discussion. The majority of the lay elders, therefore, were drawn from the middling and lower orders, though in the urban congregations the merchants had an important role to play. The transition in the Presbyterian social elite was gradual and as the landed gentry conformed they did not give way to a distinctly new, emerging middle class. There were, and always had been, close links between the gentry and those at the top levels of trade and the professions. The professions were never an exclusive or distinctly discrete group and, like the leading merchants, shared characteristics with the gentry. Many of the physicians, and practically all the barristers, came from gentry backgrounds, and, though urban-based, the professionals resembled the gentry in lifestyle and social activities.

The Ulster Presbyterians were a distinctive and significant community within Ireland. They were largely Scottish in origin and in addition to being distinguished by ethnicity, their difference from their Anglican and Catholic neighbours was also displayed in their own religious views, and audible in some of their vocabulary and dialect. In some respects, the Presbyterian church in Ulster, by its unique system of church government, may be said to have formed an alternative establishment. Their ecclesiastical structure provided a framework to administer social discipline, as well as educate their children, and provide for their poor. This does not mean that there were no similarities between Presbyterians, Anglicans and even Catholics, and, as has been shown in the preceding chapters, Presbyterians, at least in the upper levels of society, were as concerned with material culture as Barnard has shown their Anglican counterparts to be. They engaged in the same recreational activities, bought the latest books and fashions, not only from Britain and Ireland, but also Europe and, therefore, were part of the 'consumer revolution' gripping Europe and North America.

This book has also exhibited the complexities in the connexion of Ulster Presbyterianism with Scotland. The institutions of the Ulster Presbyterian church, though modelled on the Presbyterian church in Scotland, were distinct, and the flowering of Presbyterian historiography in Ulster in this period under the Belfast minister Rev. Patrick Adair suggests a self-confidence and an interest in the history of Scottish Presbyterianism, particularly in the way in which it had developed in Ireland. The experience of Presbyterians in Ulster differed from their co-religionists in Scotland because while, after 1690, the Presbyterians in Scotland formed the established church, in Ireland they did not. As far as can be demonstrated with the ministers, gentry and merchants who formed the upper social strata of Presbyterian society, the greatest connexions were with south-west Scotland rather than Scotland as a whole, as most individuals in these social groups were descended from immigrants who had arrived in Ulster from Ayrshire and the Galloway region. Scottish immigration declined after this period and was never again to be as large as it was in the late 1690s. Though Scottish universities remained important until the nineteenth century with respect to ministerial education, within the Synod of Ulster, Scotland became less important as a pool for ministerial recruitment as the number of Ulster-born Presbyterian ministers grew.

In addition, Ulster Presbyterians had contacts with Presbyterians in the south of Ireland, in England, and with the world outside the British Isles. Aspiring barristers were obliged to spend at least five years at one of the four English Inns of Court and the apprenticeship of some surgeons and apothecaries was served under masters in London. Many of the Ulster Presbyterian physicians were educated at Leiden, a select number of wealthier Presbyterians undertook a grand tour of Europe, and the merchants had correspondents based at European ports. Increasingly, too, as a result of emigration, the Ulster Presbyterians were forging links across the Atlantic with British North America. Scottish culture was thus becoming one rather than necessarily the only culture with which Ulster Presbyterianism engaged.

The connexion with Scotland, however, was not totally extinguished, as demonstrated in the later eighteenth century when Edinburgh supplanted Europe as the leading place for the education of Ulster Presbyterian medical students, and by the importation of other branches of Presbyterianism originating in Scotland into Ulster, such as the Seceders from the 1740s onwards. The history of the Seceders in Ireland is an area which requires re-investigation by historians but an important factor in its success may be that as the Scottish link was becoming less significant for the Synod of Ulster there were some traditional and conservative Presbyterians in Ulster to whom the secession church appealed because of its potential to reinforce the traditional link with Scotland.

This study has been concerned with the re-creation of the social structure and experiences of a single denomination, in a particular locality, and within a specific period. There are areas that I have not had the space to explore in detail, such as the relationship between Presbyterians and the other denominations in Ulster. The official relationship between the Presbyterian church in Ulster and these denominations, including the less numerically significant Dissenting groups, such as the Quakers, who kept good records, have yet to be explored. Preliminary findings suggest that while in the abstract and on the wider scale Presbyterians could harbour apprehensions about Catholics or Anglicans, they were nevertheless able to engage, and even have harmonious relations, with non-Presbyterians who were directly known to them. Presbyterians employed and housed Anglicans and Catholics as servants, leased property to and from Anglicans, bought goods from, and provided professional services to, them. These points of contact and co-operation and not only the flashpoints and conflicts have yet to be investigated and analysed by historians of early eighteenth-century Ireland. The Catholics in Ulster during this period have also yet to be dissected in the style undertaken here for the Presbyterians and pioneered by Barnard in his studies of the Protestant Ascendancy. Useful insights could then be achieved by undertaking comparative studies between the religious groups in Ulster and elsewhere, and I hope that my findings will allow the circumstances and experiences of Presbyterians in Ulster to be compared with those in Dublin, elsewhere in Ireland, Britain, Europe and North America. With regard to Ulster Presbyterianism itself, a gap still remains in the historiography between the end of the period covered here and the excellent studies of Presbyterianism in the late eighteenth and early nineteenth centuries undertaken by Ian McBride and Andrew Holmes. Nevertheless, it is hoped that the present study will give a clearer understanding of a distinctive group normally overlooked in the historiography, and taken along with Barnard's work on Anglican Protestants, will give a more accurate picture of Irish Protestantism in this period.

Bibliography

Primary sources

Manuscript material

Northern Ireland

Armagh Public Library

P001498149, Dopping papers
P001498343, Topographical and statistical papers of the Physico-Historical Society
of Ireland, c.1738–45

Belfast Central Library

Bigger collection

Linen Hall Library, Belfast

Joy MSS

Magee College Library, University of Ulster, Derry

MSS 46, Steward correspondence, 1699–1749

Newry and Mourne Museum

Reside collection

Presbyterian Historical Society, Belfast

Adair manuscript
Aghadowey session minutes, 1702–61
Antrim 'Meeting' minutes, 1654–8
Antrim Presbytery minutes, 1697–1713
Commonplace book belonging to Samuel Hyndman and others, c.1688–1710
Connor session minutes, 1693–1735

Copy of diary of Rev. Robert Gordon, 1707–44
Copy will of Rev. Thomas Fultowne (Fulton), 1688
Diary of Rev. John Cook, 1698–1733
Diary of Rev. John Kennedy, 1714–37
Down Presbytery minutes, 1707–15
Dundonald (Kirkdonald) session book, 1678–1713
Genealogies, 3 (Genealogical notes on various Ulster families)
Irish letters, 1701–25 (transcripts from Stirling and Wodrow papers)
Laggan Presbytery minutes, 1690–1700
Letters of William Stewart and Rev. John Richardson, 1701, 1705
Licence to practise surgery issued by the chancellor of Connor and the bp of Down
    and Connor, 1718
Ministerial card index
Ministerial notebook of Rev. John Kennedy, 1710–60
'Miscellanea' – notebooks of Rev. John Kennedy, 1699–1725
Monaghan Presbytery minutes, 1702–12
Notebook of Daniel M[ussenden] containing sermons of Rev. John McBride and
    others, 1704, and details on Belfast communions, 1717–21
Rev. Seth Drummond sermon notebook, 1705–7
Route Presbytery minutes, 1701–06
Scrapbook on 'Families and local history'
'Sketches of the history of Presbyterians in Ireland' by William Campbell (1803)
Sub-synod of Derry minutes, 1706–36

Private Collection

The Dublin Presbytery minute book, 1730–9

Public Record Office of Northern Ireland, Belfast

ANT/4/1/1, 3, Co. Antrim grand jury presentment books, 1711–21, 1727–67
CR3/15/D/1, Testimonials received in Carnmoney Presbyterian Church,
    1708–25
CR3/31/1, Ballycarry session minutes, 1704–80
CR4/12/B/1, Templepatrick session book 1646–88, 1697–1743
CR4/12/C/1, Lease of Templepatrick meetinghouse, 1693
D1, Map and survey of lands in the Cookstown area belonging to the primate of
    Armagh and held by William Stewart of Killymoon, 1726
D2–3, Maps of estate of William Stewart of Killymoon, 1731 and 1736
D162 [Viewed as MIC533], Dobbs papers
D238/58, Agreement for apprenticeship to an apothecary, 1738
D271/2–4, Leases and correspondence relating to Belfast, 1685–1892
D302/1, List of high sheriffs of the counties of Ireland (Londonderry excepted),
    1302–1891
D354 [Viewed as MIC510], Mussenden papers
D501/1, Isaac Macartney's out-letter book, 1704–7
D654, Londonderry papers

D929, Adair papers

D1071, Dufferin and Ava papers

D1449, Lenox-Conyngham papers

D1460/1, Autobiography of James Trail, c.1690–1742, including farming accounts, notes on books of the Bible, and a list of books belonging to Trail

D1618, Castle Stewart papers

D1759 [Viewed as MIC637], Rev. David Stewart papers

D1769/60/2/3, Copy will of Arthur Maxwell, 1720

D1939, Earl of Erne papers

D1999, Moore papers

D2092, Ward papers

D2096, Maxwell Given papers

D2624/2, Rent roll of estate of Sir Arthur Langford, 1700

D2860, Murray of Broughton papers

D2977, Antrim papers

D3000/72/1, Typescript notes on the Smith, Perry and Robinson families

D3045, Young papers

D3649, Ellison-Macartney papers

D4006/3, Will of Arthur Graham, 1732

D4108, Salters' Company Irish estate records

D4204, Gordon papers

D4457, Black papers

D4512, Maguire papers

DIO/1/22/1, Account and memorandum book of Bp Hutchinson, 1721–30

DIO/4, Armagh diocesan records

HAR/1/G/1/13/1, Belfast customs register, 1682–7

LA/25/2/AA/1A–C, Coleraine corporation minute books, 1672–1710

LA/79/2/AA/1–4, Derry corporation minute books, 1673–1736

LPC/944, Copy will of Henry Stewart of Killymoon, 1717

LPC/1034, Copy will of Patrick Agnew, 1724

LPC/1302, Copy will of Hugh Henry, 1743

MIC1/32/1, Derriaghy vestry minutes, 1696–1758

MIC1/147A/1, Clones Parish Church vestry minutes, 1688–1823, with baptismal and marriage records

MIC1B/6A/1B, Larne and Kilwaughter session book, 1700–1 and 1720–1769

MIC1P/7, Rosemary Street Presbyterian Church, Belfast records

MIC1P/37/4–6, Carnmoney session minutes, 1686–1748, with baptisms (1726–60), marriages (1727–58), testimonials granted and received (1708–26), and poor relief lists (1716–84)

MIC1P/53/1, Killyleagh Presbyterian Church baptisms and marriages, 1692–1757

MIC1P/159/6–8, Lisburn session minutes, 1688–1709, 1711–63, with registers of baptisms, 1692–1732, and marriages, 1688–96, 1711–19

MIC1P/450C/1, Dawson's Bridge (Castledawson) session minutes, 1703–29

MIC19/2, George Macartney out-letter book, 1679–81

MIC80/3/4, Leasebook of the manor of Castledillon, Co. Armagh, with observations by William Molyneux

MIC92/1, Clarke papers

MIC139/1, Petty cash book of Samuel Boyce, Ballyrashane, Co. Londonderry, 1731–60

MIC147/8, Letters to James Hamilton of Tollymore, Co. Down, 1679, 1683–96.

MIC223/146–66, State papers of Ireland, 1679–1733

MIC720/1, Thomson narrative

T67/1, Will and private act of parliament settling Hugh Rainey's estate, 1707

T168/1, Copy will of Sir Arthur Langford, 1715

T273/1, A short account of the family of Trail of Blebe and their descendants, 1647–1868

T448/1, Transcripts of State Papers relating to Ireland, 1715–16

T525, Wodrow transcripts

T581/1, Society of Genealogists documents

T654/6–7, Third Belfast (Rosemary Street) Presbyterian Church pew register (1726–67) and list of catechisable persons (1725–42)

T659/1, Transcripts of State Papers relating to Ireland, 1727–9

T780/1, Crossle papers

T808, Groves papers

T828, Nicholson papers

T1030, Montgomery papers

T1053/1, Antrim (Non-Subscribing) Presbytery minutes, 1783–1834

T1073, Black papers

T1075/6, Miscellaneous matters in Armagh Registry

T1451/1, Map and survey of estate of James Ross of Portavo, Co. Down, 1731

T1809/1, Letter of James Murray of New York to Rev. Baptist Boyd of Co. Tyrone, from *The Pennsylvania Gazette*, 1737

T2521/3, Dean William Henry's topographical accounts, c.1739

T2524, Kirk papers

T2807, Somers papers

T2825, Castletown papers

T2929, Rossmore papers

T3019, Wilmot papers

T3041, Bruce papers

T3161, Lenox-Conyngham papers

T3411/1, Printed list of members of the Irish parliament, with MS annotations, late 1713

T3729/1, Rent roll of Lady Blayney, Co. Monaghan, 1790, with details of leases 1706–99

Queen's University Library, Belfast

B1–6, 8–10, B12.6–10, B13–15, Antrim Presbytery Library, MS marks of ownership

MS 23, Allen collection

Union Theological College Library, Belfast

Antrim 'Meeting' minutes, 1671–91

Chambre, Robert, 'An explanation of the Shorter Catechisme of the Reverend Assembly of Divines' (1680)

Laggan Presbytery minutes, 1672–95 (with gap 1681–90)

Lecture notes of John King, 1710–13
Strabane Presbytery minutes, 1717–40

Republic of Ireland

Cavan County Archives Service, Johnston Central Library and Farnham
Centre, Cavan

BC/1, Belturbet corporation minute book, 1657–c.1730

Cork City and County Archives

U87, Cork (Princes Street) Presbyterian minutes, 1717–57, register of baptisms,
1717–99, and other records

National Archives of Ireland, Dublin

MFGS 41/2, Prerogative will books, 1706–8, 1726–8
MFGS 41/4, Prerogative will book, 1728–9
MFGS 57/002–6, Court of chancery bill books, 1677–1722
MFS/42/10, Lodge MS

National Library of Ireland, Dublin

D. 19,724, Copy will of John Blackwood, 1698
D. 19,725, Copy will of John Blackwood, 1720
MS 1395, Typescript of First Armagh baptisms and marriages, 1707–29
MS 1702, Typescript copy of Stevenson correspondence, 1621–1715 (principally
    1694–1710)
MS 8734, Stewart papers
MS 8792, Genealogical notes on Hamilton family, 1603–1827, and correspondence
    of the Hamilton and Rowan families
MSS 20,867–70, 21,961, Bruce papers
MSS 41,575–82, Smythe of Barbavilla papers
P 3053, Microfilm copy of Dublin Society minute books, 1731–46, register and
    letter book, 1731 and 1736, and treasurer's book, 1731–39
P 4909, Microfilm copy of Black Book of King's Inns, Dublin, 1607–1730

Royal College of Physicians of Ireland, Library, Dublin

College journals, i–ii, 1692–1743
Kirkpatrick archives

BIBLIOGRAPHY

Royal Irish Academy, Dublin

MS 24.K.19, no. 1, List of gentlemen of Counties Antrim and Down [c.1725] (Upton papers)

Trinity College, Dublin

MSS 750, 1489, 2533, 2536–7, King letter-books
MSS 1995–2008, Lyons (King) papers

England

Bodleian Library, Oxford

MSS Carte, 40, 45, 146, 168, 216, 221, Carte papers

British Library, London

Add. MS 6116, Copies of letters to Bp Nicolson, 1697–1721
Add. MS 6117, Letters to Abp Wake from Abp King and Abp Synge, 1703–26
Add. MS 24120, Wotton papers
Add. MSS 61466, 61495, 61510, 61534, 61579, 61611, 61638–40, 61643, 61649–50, Blenheim papers
Sloane MSS 4036–40, 4043–4, 4046–8, 4052, 4054, 4056–7, 4060, 4062, 4075, 4078

Christ Church, Oxford

Wake papers, xii–xiv [consulted on microfilm in the Institute of Historical Research, London, XR.129/16–20]

Lambeth Palace Library

MS 1742, Gibson papers

Leicestershire, Leicester and Rutland Record Office

DG7 IRE.9, Finch MSS

BIBLIOGRAPHY

National Archives, Kew, London

PROB 11, Prerogative Court of Canterbury wills

Senate House Library, University of London

MS 30, Chalmers papers

Surrey History Centre

1248/1–7, Midleton papers

Warwickshire County Record Office, Warwick

CR 136 B/280–3, 285–6, 288–9, 291–3, 295, 298–9, Newdegate papers

Scotland

Glasgow Archives Service

GUA 26631: Glasgow University Faculty meeting minutes, 1702–20
GUA 26634: Glasgow University Faculty meeting minutes, 1720–27
GUA 26635: Glasgow University Faculty meeting minutes, 1727–30
GUA 26639: Glasgow University meeting minutes (Senate), 1730–49
GUA 30159: Glasgow University Bill of Suspension, 1717

Glasgow University Library, Special Collections

MS Gen 207, Stirling papers
MS Gen 343, 'Cases answered by the societys of the students of divinity under Mr. James Wodrow'

Mitchell Library, Glasgow

CH2/171/7–9, Glasgow Presbytery minutes, 1687–1723

National Archives of Scotland, Edinburgh

CH2/165/2, Synod of Galloway minutes, 1689–1712
CS96/1726, Letter book of Gilbert Robertson, merchant, Edinburgh, 1690–4

CS96/3074, Ledger of an anonymous Greenock merchant, 1707–12
E72/10/5–14, Glasgow customs books, 1680–91
E72/19/1–23, Port Glasgow customs books, 1680–96
E72/20/6–19, Portpatrick customs books, 1680–92
GD154, Agnew family of Lochnaw papers
GD220, Montrose muniments
GD406, Hamilton papers
RH15/19, Maxwell papers

National Library of Scotland, Edinburgh

Acc. 7043, Maxwell of Monreith papers
MS 3740, ff 176–9, Extracts from letters from the north of Ireland, 1704–5
Wodrow papers

Royal College of Physicians, Library, Edinburgh

MS list of donations to the library, 1682–1724

Netherlands

Leiden University Library, Leiden

AHM 8 (Olim Mus.7), 'Album amicorum aangelegd door Samuel Haliday', 1706–8

U.S.A.

Baker Library, Harvard Business School, Boston

MSS: 766, Macpheadris and Warner papers

Huntington Library, Manuscripts Department, San Marino, California

HAM Box 75, folders 32–3, 36; Box 79, folders 7, 9, 18, Hastings papers

New England Historic Genealogical Society, Boston

Mss A 1996, Diary of Rev. William Homes [Holmes], 1688–1746

BIBLIOGRAPHY

Wilson Library, University of North Carolina at Chapel Hill

2313, Archibald Maclaine memorandum book, c.1728–40

Printed material

Contemporary or near-contemporary publications

Abernethy, John, *Religious obedience founded on personal persuasion. A sermon preach'd at Belfast the 9th of December. 1719* (Belfast, 1720)
—, *Scarce and valuable tracts and sermons* ... (London, 1751)
Anon., *An account of charity-schools in Great Britain and Ireland, with the benefactions thereto* (London, 1711)
[Arbuckle, James], *The Tribune* (Dublin, 1729)
Binning, Hugh, *The works of the Rev. Hugh Binning* (Project Gutenberg EBook, 2008)
Boyse, Joseph, *Remarks on a late discourse of William Lord Bishop of Derry; concerning the inventions of men in the worship of God* (Dublin, 1694)
—, *A sermon preach't before the Societies for Reformation in Dublin* ... (Dublin, 1698)
—, *A sermon on the occasion of the death of the late Sir Arth. Langford, Bar. Preach'd at Woodstreet, Dublin, April the 8th, 1716* (London, 1717)
—, *The works of the reverend and learned Mr. Joseph Boyse, of Dublin* ... (2 vols, London, 1728)
Cairnes, Thomas, *Disputatio medica inauguralis de pleuritide et peripneumonia* (Utrecht, 1705)
Calamy, Edmund, *Memoirs of the life of the late Revd. Mr. John Howe* (London, 1724)
Cobham, James, *Preparation for death describ'd in a sermon occasion'd by the* ... *death of* ... *Mrs. Anna-Helena Edmonstone* ... (Belfast, 1711)
[Cornwall, Gabriel], *An essay on the character of the late Mr. William Bruce* ... (Dublin, 1755)
Craghead, Robert, *An answer to a late book, intituled, a discourse concerning the inventions of men in the worship of God* ... (Edinburgh, 1694)
—, *A funeral sermon on the* ... *death of* ... *Catherine, countess dowager of Granard* ... (Dublin, 1714)
Disposition and tailzie, by Archibald Edmonstone of Duntreath, to Archibald Edmonstone, his eldest son, and the other heirs therein mentioned ([Edinburgh, 1769])
Dobbs, Arthur, *An essay on the trade and improvement of Ireland* (Dublin, 1729)
Donaldson, Nehemiah, *A funeral sermon preach'd on the occasion of the death of Thomas Edwards esq; of Castle-Gore in the County of Tyrone* ... (Dublin, [1721])
Duchal, James, *A sermon on* ... *the* ... *death of the late Reverend Mr. John Abernethy, a Protestant-dissenting minister, first in Antrim, and next in Dublin* ... *with an appendix, containing some brief memoirs of the lives and characters of the late Revd. Messieurs Thomas Shaw, William Taylor, Michael Bruce, and Samuel Haliday* ... (Dublin, 1741)
Dutton, Matthew, *The law of masters and servants in Ireland* ... (Dublin, 1723)
Elder, John, *Reasons for moderation in the present debates amongst Presbyterians in the north of Ireland* (Belfast, 1725)

Emlyn, Thomas, *A sermon preach'd before the Societies for Reformation of Manners in Dublin* ... (Dublin, 1698)

—, *The works of Mr. Thomas Emlyn* (3 vols, London, 1746)

G[owan], T[homas], *Ars sciendi sive logica nova methodo disposita, et novis praeceptis aucta* (London, 1681)

—, *Logica elenctica, sive, summa controversiarum, quae circa materiam & praecepta logicae, agitari solent in qua etiam novae aliquot quaestiones tractantur* (Dublin, 1683)

Haliday, Samuel, *Reasons against the imposition of subscription to the Westminster-Confession; or, any such human tests of orthodoxy* ... (Belfast, 1724)

—, *A letter to the Reverend Mr. Gilbert Kennedy; occasion'd by some personal reflections, contain'd in his answer to Mr. Haliday's reasons against the imposition of subscription to the Westminster-Confession* ... (Belfast, 1725)

—, *A sermon occasioned by the death of the Reverend Mr. Michael Bruce* ... (Belfast, 1735)

Hamilton, James, *The last speech and dying words of James Hamilton. In the parish of Kilmore in the County of Down; who was executed at Downpatrick for the bloody and heinous murder of William Lammon* ... (Glasgow, 1714)

Hemphil[l], Samuel, *A letter to the Rev'd. Mr. Samuel Haliday: wherein his scheme of minnisterial [sic] communion, in the seventh page of his introduction, to his reasons against subscription to the Westminster Confession of Faith is examin'd* ... (Dublin, 1726)

An historical description of Carolina North and South being an account of its discovery, settlement, and progress; its climate, soil, situation, productions, trade, and commerce ... (Belfast, 1717)

Hutcheson, Francis, *A system of moral philosophy* ... *to which is prefixed some account of the life, writings, and character of the author, by the Reverend William Leechman* (2 vols, Glasgow, 1755)

Iredell, Francis, *A sermon preached before the Societies for the Reformation of Manners in Dublin, April 22 1701* (Dublin, 1701)

Kennedy, Gilbert, *A defence of the principles and conduct of the Reverend General Synod of Ulster. Being an answer to a pamphlet published by the Reverend Mr. Samuel Haliday: containing his reasons against the imposition unto the Westminster Confession* ... (Belfast, 1724)

King, William, *An admonition to the dissenting inhabitants of the diocess of Derry* ... (Dublin, 1694)

Kirkpatrick, James, *The saint's life and death. In a sermon preach'd on occasion of the* ... *death of* ... *Arthur Upton esq* ... (Belfast, 1706)

—, *An essay by way of elegy, on the Hond: Arthur Upton esq; of Castle-Upton* ... (Belfast, 1707)

—, *An historical essay upon the loyalty of Presbyterians in Great-Britain and Ireland from the Reformation to the present year* ... ([Belfast], 1713)

[Kirkpatrick, James], *A vindication of the Presbyterian ministers in the north of Ireland; Subscribers and Non-Subscribers: from many gross and groundless aspersions cast upon them, in a late scandalous libel, entituled, an account of the mind of the synod at Belfast* ... (Belfast, 1721)

Kirkpatrick, James, *An account of the success of Mrs. Stephens's medicines for the stone, in the case of James Kirkpatrick, Doctor of Divinity* ... (Belfast, 1739)

Livingston, William, *The blessings of a long life well spent and happily concluded: a sermon preach'd at Temple---patrick* ... *on the occasion of the* ... *death of Mrs. Dorothy Upton* ... (Belfast, 1721)

[Logan, Allan], *An enquiry into Professor Simson's sentiments on the doctrine of the Trinity, from his papers in the process against him* (Edinburgh, 1729)

Maclaine, Archibald, *A sermon occasioned by the death of the Reverend Mr. Robert Rainey* ... (Belfast, 1736)

Makemie, Francis, *An answer to George Keith's libel. Against a catechism published by Francis Makemie* ... (Boston, 1694)

McBride, John, *A sermon before the provincial synod of Antrim. Preached June 1. 1698* ([Belfast], 1698)

[McBride, John], *A vindication of marriage, as solemnized by Presbyterians, in the north of Ireland* ... ([Dublin?], 1702)

[McBride, John], *A sample of jet-black prelatick calumny. In answer to a pamphlet, called, True-bleu Presbyterian loyalty* ... (Glasgow, 1713)

A narrative of the proceedings of seven General Synods of the northern Presbyterians in Ireland, with relation to their differences in judgment and practice, from the year 1720 to the year 1726 ... (Belfast, 1727)

Petty, Sir William, *Sir William Petty's political survey of Ireland* ... (2nd ed., London, 1719)

The present state of religion in Ireland ... (London, [1712])

Reid, James, *Formal Christians and secession from them consider'd* ... (Belfast, 1729)

Richardson, John, *A short history of the attempts that have been made to convert the popish natives of Ireland, to the establish'd religion* ... (London, 1712)

Sacheverell, William, *An account of the Isle of Man, its inhabitants, language, soil, remarkable curiosities, the succession of its kings and bishops, down to the present time* (London, 1702)

Sinclare, Alexander, *A sermon preach'd before the Societies for Reformation of Manners in Dublin, April the 11th, 1699* (Dublin, 1699)

[Smith, Charles and Harris, Walter], *The antient and present state of the County of Down* (Dublin, 1744)

Story, George, *A true and impartial history of the most material occurrences in the kingdom of Ireland during the two last years. With the present state of both armies* (2nd ed., London, 1693)

Story, Thomas, *A journal of the life of Thomas Story* ... (Newcastle-upon-Tyne, 1747)

[Synge, Edward], *An account of the erection, government and number, of charity-schools in Ireland* (Dublin, 1717)

[Tisdall, William], *The conduct of the Dissenters of Ireland, with respect both to church and state* ... (Dublin, 1712)

Weld, Nathaniel, *A sermon before the Societies for the Reformation of Manners in Dublin: preached in New-Row* ... (Dublin, 1698)

Later publications, source compilations and calendars

'Abstracts of wills', *Irish Ancestor*, ii (1970), pp 117–27; iii (1971), pp 92–101

Adair, Patrick, *A true narrative of the rise and progress of the Presbyterian Church in Ireland*, ed. W. D. Killen (Belfast, 1866)

Addison, W. I. (comp.), *A roll of the graduates of the University of Glasgow from 31st December, 1727 to 31st December, 1897* ... (Glasgow, 1898)

—, *The matriculation albums of the University of Glasgow from 1728 to 1858* (Glasgow, 1913)

Agnew, Jean (ed.), *Funeral register of the First Presbyterian Church of Belfast* (Belfast, 1995)

Album studiosorum Academiae Lugduno Batavae MDLXXV–MDCCCLXXV accedunt nomina curatorum et professorum per eadem secula (The Hague, 1875)

Album studiosorum Academiae Rheno-Trajectinae MDCXXXVI–MDCCCLXXXVI (Utrecht, 1886)

Ash, Thomas, *The Ash Mss., written in the year 1735 ... and other family records*, ed. E. T. Martin (Belfast, 1890)

Austen-Leigh, R. A., *The Eton College register 1698–1752 ...* (Eton, 1927)

Berwick, Edward (ed.), *The Rawdon papers ...* (London, 1819)

Boulter, Hugh, *Letters written by his Excellency Hugh Boulter ...* (2 vols, Oxford, 1769–70)

Buckley, James, 'The free schools of Ulster in 1673', *UJA*, ix (1903), pp 54–6

Burtchaell, G. D. and Sadleir, T. U. (eds), *Alumni Dublinenses: a register of the students, graduates, professors and provosts of Trinity College in the University of Dublin (1593–1860)* (new ed., Dublin, 1935)

Calendar of State Papers, Domestic: Charles II (1660–85), *James II* (1685–89), *William III* (1689–1702), *Anne* (1702–6)

A catalogue of the graduates in the Faculties of Arts, Divinity, and Law, of the University of Edinburgh, since its foundation (Edinburgh, 1858)

Coghill, Marmaduke, *Letters of Marmaduke Coghill, 1722–1738*, ed. D. W. Hayton (Dublin, 2005)

Cokayne, G. E. and Fry, E. A. (eds), *Calendar of marriage licences issued by the Faculty Office. 1632–1714* (London, 1905)

Erskine, J. G. W. (ed.), 'The will of the Rev. Patrick Adair, Belfast', *Bull. PHSI*, xii (1993), pp 31–2

Eustace, P. B. (ed.), *Registry of Deeds Dublin: abstracts of wills, i: 1708–1745* (Dublin, 1956)

Faithful contendings displayed: being an historical relation of the state and actings of the suffering remnant in the church of Scotland ... (Glasgow, 1780)

Foster, Joseph, *The register of admissions to Gray's Inn, 1521–1889 ...* (London, 1889)

Gillespie, R. G. (ed.), *Settlement and survival on an Ulster estate: the Brownlow leasebook 1667–1711* (Belfast, 1988)

Historical Manuscripts Commission: *Buccleuch & Queensbury MSS*, ii; *Downshire MSS*, i; *Egmont MSS: diary*, i; *Finch MSS*, ii–iv; *Ormonde MSS*, n.s., v–viii; *Portland MSS*, v–x; *Townshend MSS*

'Horse-racing in Antrim in 1710', *UJA*, vii (1901), p. 158

Inderwick, F. A. (ed.), *A calendar of the Inner Temple records, iii: 12 Charles II. (1660)–12 Anne (1714)* (London, 1901)

James, F. G., 'Derry in the time of George I: selections from Bishop Bicolson's letters, 1718–1722', *UJA*, 3rd ser., xvii (1954), pp 173–86

The journals of the House of Commons, of the kingdom of Ireland ... (2nd ed., 13 vols, Dublin, 1763–82)

Journals of the House of Lords [of Ireland] (8 vols, London, 1779–1800)

Keane, Edward, Phair, P. B. and Sadleir, T. U. (eds), *King's Inns admission papers 1607–1867* (Dublin, 1982)

King, C. S. (ed.), *A great archbishop of Dublin: William King, D.D., 1650–1729* (London, 1906)

Lamond, Robert, 'Seventeenth century receipts', *Scottish Historical Review*, xiii (1916), pp 219–28

Lincoln's Inn admission register, 1420–1799 (London, 1896)

Lowry, T. K. (ed.), *The Hamilton manuscripts* ... (Belfast, [1867])

[MacLysaght, Edward], 'Doneraile papers: interim report', *Analecta Hibernica*, no. 15 (1944), pp 333–62

Marshall, J. J. (ed.), *Vestry records of the Church of St. John, Parish of Aghalow Caledon, Co. Tyrone 1691–1807* (Dungannon, 1935)

Martin, T. C. (ed.), *Minutes of parliament of the Middle Temple* ..., iii: *1650–1703* (London, 1905)

[Mitchelburne, John], *Ireland preserved; or, the Siege of Londonderry and Battle of Aughrim* ..., ed. John Graham (Dublin, 1841)

Montgomery, William, *The Montgomery manuscripts: (1603–1706)* ..., ed. George Hill (Belfast, 1869)

Munimenta alme Universitatis Glasguensis: records of the University of Glasgow from its foundation till 1727 (4 vols, Glasgow, 1854)

Pitassi, Maria-Cristina, *Inventaire critique de la correspondence de Jean-Alphonse Turrettini* (6 vols, Paris, 2009)

Precedents and abstracts from the journals of the Trustees of the Linen and Hempen Manufactures of Ireland, to the Twenty-fifth of March, M,DCC,XXXVII (Dublin, 1784)

Records of the General Synod of Ulster, from 1691 to 1820 (3 vols, Belfast, 1890–98)

The records of the Honorable society of Lincoln's Inn: the Black books, iii: *From A.D. 1660 to A.D. 1775* ([London], 1899)

The register of the Privy Council of Scotland (16 vols, Edinburgh, 1908–70)

Roberts, R. A. (ed.), *A calendar of the Inner Temple records*, iv: *I George I. (1714)–24 George II. (1750)* (London, 1933)

Schlenther, B. S. (ed.), *The life and writings of Francis Makemie, father of American Presbyterianism (c.1658–1708)* (New York, 1999)

Sterry, Sir Wasey, *The Eton College register 1441–1698* ... (Eton, 1943)

Stringer, Arthur, *The experienced huntsman* ..., ed. James Fairley (Belfast, 1714; repr. 1977)

Sturgess, H. A. C. (comp.), *Register of admissions to the Honourable Society of the Middle Temple* ... (3 vols, London, 1949)

Swift, Jonathan, *Journal to Stella*, ed. Harold Williams (2 vols, Oxford, 1948)

—, *The correspondence of Jonathan Swift, D.D.*, ed. David Woolley (4 vols, 1999–2007)

[Tisdall, William], *The Islandmagee witches* ... [ed. Samuel McSkimin] ([Belfast, 1822])

Wackernagel, H. G. (ed.), *Die matrikel der Universität Basel* (5 vols, Basel, 1951–80)

Witherow, Thomas (ed.), *Two diaries of Derry in 1689* ... (Derry, 1888)

Wodrow, Robert, *Life of James Wodrow, A.M.* ... (Edinburgh, 1828)

—, *Analecta: or materials for a history of remarkable providences, mostly relating to Scotch ministers and Christians*, ed. M[atthew] L[eishman] (4 vols, Glasgow, 1842–43)

—, *The correspondence of Rev. Robert Wodrow* ..., ed. Thomas McCrie (3 vols, Edinburgh, 1842–43)

—, *Early letters of Robert Wodrow 1698–1709* ..., ed. L. W. Sharp (Edinburgh, 1937)

Young, R. M. (ed.), *The town book of the corporation of Belfast, 1613–1816* (Belfast, 1892)

—, 'A Belfast cookery book of Queen Anne's time', *UJA*, 2nd ser., ix (1898), pp 114–21

BIBLIOGRAPHY

Electronic

Ballynahinch Presbyterian Church baptisms, 1696–1735 (http://freepages.genealogy.rootsweb.ancestry.com/~rosdavies/WORDS/BallynahinchPresbyterianBirths.htm) (12 Jan. 2013).

Ballynahinch Presbyterian Church marriages, 1696–1733 (http://freepages.genealogy.rootsweb.ancestry.com/~rosdavies/WORDS/BallynahinchPresbyterianMarriages.htm) (12 Jan. 2013).

Ballynahinch Presbyterian Church record of certificates and testimonials, 1715–34 (http://freepages.genealogy.rootsweb.ancestry.com/~rosdavies/WORDS/BallynahinchPresbTestimonials.htm) (12 Jan. 2013).

Ballynahinch Presbyterian Church account of collections and disbursements, 1704–34 (http://freepages.genealogy.rootsweb.ancestry.com/~rosdavies/WORDS/BallynahinchPresbyDisburse.htm) (12 Jan. 2013).

Secondary sources

Books

Adams, J. R. R., *The printed word and the common man: popular culture in Ulster 1700–1900* (Belfast, 1987)

Agnew, Jean, *Belfast merchant families in the seventeenth century* (Dublin, 1996)

Akenson, D. H., *God's peoples: covenant and land in South Africa, Israel, and Ulster* (Ithaca, New York, 1992)

Allen, Robert, *The Presbyterian College Belfast 1853–1953* (Belfast, 1954)

Amussen, S. D., *An ordered society: gender and class in early modern England* (New York, 1988)

Anderson, John (comp.), *Catalogue of early Belfast printed books, 1694 to 1830* ([3rd ed.], Belfast, 1890; suppt., Belfast, 1894; suppt., Belfast, 1902)

Anderson, R. D., Lynch, Michael and Phillipson, Nicholas, *The University of Edinburgh: an illustrated history* (Edinburgh, 2003)

Armstrong, W. B., *The Bruces of Airth and their cadets* (Edinburgh, 1892)

Auld, Con, *Holywood Co. Down: then and now* (Holywood, 2002)

Bahlman, D. W. R., *The moral revolution of 1688* (New Haven, 1957)

Bailie, W. D. (ed.), *A history of congregations in the Presbyterian Church in Ireland 1610–1982* (Belfast, 1982)

Ball, F. E., *The judges in Ireland, 1221–1921* (2 vols, London, 1926)

Ballard, L. M., *Forgetting frolic: marriage traditions in Ireland* (Belfast, 1998)

Bardon, Jonathan, *Belfast: an illustrated history* (Dundonald, 1982)

—, *A history of Ulster* (new ed., Belfast, 2001)

—, *The Plantation of Ulster: the British colonisation of the north of Ireland in the seventeenth century* (Dublin, 2011)

Barkley, J. M., *A short history of the Presbyterian Church in Ireland* (Belfast, [1959])

—, *The eldership in Irish Presbyterianism* ([Belfast], 1963)

Barnard, Toby, *Irish Protestant ascents and descents, 1641–1779* (Dublin, 2002)

—, *A new anatomy of Ireland: the Irish Protestants, 1649–1770* (London, 2003)

—, *The kingdom of Ireland, 1641–1760* (Basingstoke, 2004)

—, *Making the grand figure: lives and possessions in Ireland, 1641–1770* (London, 2004)

—, *Improving Ireland? Projectors, prophets and profiteers, 1641–1786* (Dublin, 2008)

Barr, W. N. C., *Derriaghy: a short history of the parish* (rev. ed., Belfast, 2006)

Barry, Jonathan and Brooks, Christopher (eds), *The middling sort of people: culture, society and politics in England, 1550–1800* (Basingstoke, 1994)

Bartlett, Thomas and Hayton, D. W. (eds), *Penal era and golden age: essays in Irish history, 1690–1800* (Belfast, 1979)

Bassett, G. H., *County Down guide and directory 1886* (Dublin, 1886)

Beckett, J. C., *Protestant Dissent in Ireland 1687–1780* (London, 1948)

Beckett, J. C. and Glasscock, R. E. (eds), *Belfast: the origin and growth of an industrial city* (London, 1967)

Beckett, J. V., *Coal and tobacco: the Lowthers and the economic development of West Cumberland, 1660–1760* (Cambridge, 1981)

Belfast Public Art Gallery and Museum, *Catalogue of Irish tokens: 17th, 18th and 19th centuries* ([Belfast], 1913)

Bell, J. B. A., *A history of Garmany's Grove Presbyterian Church* ([Newry], 1970)

Benn, George, *A history of the town of Belfast from the earliest times to the close of the eighteenth century* (London, 1877)

Birks, Michael, *Gentlemen of the law* (London, 1960)

Black, Eileen (comp. and ed.), *Kings in conflict: Ireland in the 1690s* (Belfast, 1990)

Blaney, Roger, *Presbyterians and the Irish language* (Belfast, 1997)

Bonar, R. H., *Nigh on three and a half centuries: a history of Carnmoney Presbyterian Church* (Newtownabbey, 2004)

Borsay, Peter and Proudfoot, Lindsay (eds), *Provincial towns in early modern England and Ireland: change, convergence and divergence* (Oxford, 2002)

Boyce, D. G., Eccleshall, Robert and Geoghegan, Vincent (eds), *Political discourse in seventeenth- and eighteenth-century Ireland* (Basingstoke, 2001)

Brett, C. E. B., *Buildings of County Antrim* (Belfast, 1996)

Brooke, Peter, *Ulster Presbyterianism: the historical perspective 1610–1970* (Dublin, 1987)

Brooks, E. St John, *Sir Hans Sloane: the great collector and his circle* (London, 1954)

Brown, A. L. and Moss, Michael, *The University of Glasgow: 1451–1996* (Edinburgh, 1996)

Brown, A. W. G., *The great Mr. Boyse: a study of the Reverend Joseph Boyse minister of Wood Street Church, Dublin 1683–1728* ([Belfast], 1988)

Brown, Michael, McGrath, C. I. and Power, Thomas (eds), *Converts and conversion in Ireland, 1650–1850* (Dublin, 2005)

Buchanan, R. H. and Wilson, Anthony, *Downpatrick: Irish historic towns atlas* (Dublin, 1997)

Burke, Sir Bernard, *A genealogical and heraldic dictionary of the landed gentry of Great Britain and Ireland* (London, 1863; 1912)

—, *A genealogical and heraldic dictionary of the peerage and baronetage ...*, ed. A. P. Burke (London, 1900)

Camblin, Gilbert, *The town in Ulster: an account of the origin and building of the towns of the province ...* (Belfast, 1951)

Carr, Peter, *'The most unpretending of places': a history of Dundonald, County Down* (Dundonald, 1987)

—, *Portavo: an Irish townland and its peoples: part one: earliest times to 1844* (Belfast, 2003)

Cochran, L. E., *Scottish trade with Ireland in the eighteenth century* (Edinburgh, 1985)

C[okayne], G[eorge] E[dward] (ed.), *Complete baronetage* (5 vols, Exeter, 1900–6)

Collins, Brenda, Ollerenshaw, Philip and Parkhill, Trevor (eds), *Industry, trade and people in Ireland, 1650–1950: essays in honour of W. H. Crawford* (Belfast, 2005)

A concise view of the origin, constitution and proceedings of the Honorable Society of the Governor and Assistants of London, of the New Plantation in Ulster, within the realm of Ireland, commonly called The Irish Society (London, 1842)

Connolly, S. J., *Religion, law, and power: the making of Protestant Ireland 1660–1760* (Oxford, 1995)

—, *Divided kingdom: Ireland 1630–1800* (Oxford, 2008)

Connolly, S. J., Houston, R. A. and Morris, R. J. (eds), *Conflict, identity and economic development: Ireland and Scotland, 1600–1939* (Preston, 1995)

Corfield, P. J., *Power and the professions in Britain 1700–1850* (London, 1995)

Costecalde, Claude and Gallagher, Jack (eds), *Hunting in Ireland: a noble tradition* ([Holywood, Co. Down], 2004)

Coxe, William, *Memoirs of the duke of Marlborough, with his original correspondence* … (new ed., 3 vols, London, 1847–8)

Cragg, G. R., *The church and the age of reason 1648–1789* (London, 1990)

Craig, W. S., *History of the Royal College of Physicians of Edinburgh* (Oxford, 1976)

Crawford, W. H., *The impact of the domestic linen industry in Ulster* (Belfast, 2005)

Crompton, J., *A compendious system of chronology* … (Belfast, 1823)

Cullen, K. J., *Famine in Scotland: the 'ill years' of the 1690s* (Edinburgh, 2010)

Cullen, L. M., *Anglo-Irish trade, 1660–1800* (Manchester, 1968)

—, *An economic history of Ireland since 1660* (London, 1981)

—, *The emergence of modern Ireland 1600-1900* (London, 1981)

Cullen, L. M. and Furet, François (eds), *Ireland and France 17th–20th centuries: towards a comparative study of rural history* (Paris, 1980)

Cullen, L. M. and Smout, T. C. (eds), *Comparative aspects of Scottish and Irish economic and social history 1600–1900* (Edinburgh, [1977])

Dickinson, H. T. (ed.), *A companion to eighteenth-century Britain* (Oxford, 2006)

Dickson, David, *New foundations: Ireland 1660–1800* (2nd ed., Dublin, 2000)

—, *Old world colony: Cork and South Munster 1630–1830* (Cork, 2005)

Dickson, R. J., *Ulster emigration to Colonial America, 1718–1775* (London, 1966)

Donaldson, John, *The barony of Upper Fews in the county of Armagh* (1838; repr. Crossmaglen, 1993)

Duhigg, B. T., *History of the King's Inns; or, an account of the legal body in Ireland, from its connexion with England* (Dublin, 1806)

Durand, Mortimer, *The life of Field-Marshal Sir George White* … (2 vols, Edinburgh, 1915)

Earle, Peter, *The Making of the English middle class: business, society and family life in London, 1660–1730* (London, 1989)

Edmonstone, Archibald, *Genealogical account of the family of Edmonstone of Duntreath* (Edinburgh, 1875)

Fagan, Patrick, *Catholics in a Protestant country: trades and professions in eighteenth-century Dublin* (Dublin, 1998)

Falloon, Jane, *Throttle full open: a life of Lady Bailey, Irish aviatrix* (Dublin, 1999)

Fitzgerald, Patrick and Lambkin, Brian, *Migration in Irish history, 1607–2007* (Basingstoke, 2008)

FitzPatrick, Elizabeth and Gillespie, Raymond (eds), *The parish in medieval and early modern Ireland: community, territory and building* (Dublin, 2005)

Fleetwood, J. F., *The history of medicine in Ireland* (Dublin, 1983)

Fletcher, A. J. and Gillespie, Raymond (eds), *Irish preaching 700–1700* (Dublin, 2001)

Forbes, John, *Memoirs of the earls of Granard*, ed. George Arthur Hastings[-Forbes] (London, 1868)

Ford, Alan, McGuire, James and Milne, Kenneth (eds), *As by law established: the Church of Ireland since the Reformation* (Dublin, 1995)

Gavin, Robert, Kelly, William and O'Reilly, Dolores, *Atlantic gateway: the port and city of Londonderry since 1700* (Dublin, 2009)

The Georgian Society records of eighteenth century domestic architecture and decoration in Dublin (5 vols, Dublin, 1969)

Gibson, James and Lumsden, James, *Two discourses delivered before the First Presbyterian Congregation, Strabane, on leaving their old and entering their new church, October, 1872* (Belfast, [1872])

Gill, Conrad, *The rise of the Irish linen industry* (Oxford, 1925)

Gillespie, Raymond, *Colonial Ulster: the settlement of east Ulster 1600–1641* (Cork, 1985)

—, *The transformation of the Irish economy 1550–1700* ([Dublin], 1991)

—, *Devoted people: belief and religion in early modern Ireland* (Manchester, 1997)

—, *Reading Ireland: print, reading and social change in early modern Ireland* (Manchester, 2005)

—, *Early Belfast: the origins and growth of an Ulster town to 1750* (Belfast, 2007)

Gillespie, Raymond and Foster, R. F. (eds), *Irish provincial cultures in the long eighteenth-century: making the middle sort: essays for Toby Barnard* (Dublin, 2012)

Gillespie, Raymond and O'Sullivan, Harold (eds), *The Borderlands: essays on the history of the Ulster-Leinster border* (Belfast, 1989)

Gillespie, Raymond and Royle, S. A. (eds), *Belfast: part 1, to 1840: Irish historic towns atlas* (Dublin, 2003)

[Gordon, Alexander], *Historic memorials of the First Presbyterian Church of Belfast prepared in connection with the centennial of its present meeting-house* (Belfast, 1887)

Gordon, Alexander, *Historic memorials of the Remonstrant Presbyterian Congregation of Templepatrick* (Belfast, 1899)

Greaves, R. L., *God's other children: Protestant Nonconformists and the emergence of denominational churches in Ireland, 1660–1700* (Stanford, Calif., 1997)

Green, E. R. R., *The industrial archaeology of County Down* (Belfast, 1963)

Gregory, Jeremy, *Restoration, reformation and reform, 1660–1828: archbishops of Canterbury and their diocese* (Oxford, 2000)

Gribbon, H. D., *The history of water power in Ulster* (Newton Abbot, 1969)

Griffin, Patrick, *The people with no name: Ireland's Ulster Scots, America's Scots Irish, and the creation of a British Atlantic world, 1689–1764* (Princeton, 2001)

Haakonssen, Knud (ed.), *Enlightenment and religion: rational dissent in eighteenth-century Britain* (Cambridge, 1996)

Haire, J. L. M., *et al.*, *Challenge and conflict: essays in Irish Presbyterian history and doctrine* (Antrim, 1981)

Hamilton, George, *A history of the house of Hamilton* (Edinburgh, 1933)

Hamilton, Walter, *Dated book-plates (ex libris) with a treatise on their origin and development* (London, 1895)

Hardy, W. J., *Book-plates* (2nd ed., London, 1897)

Harvey, K. J., *The Bellews of Mount Bellew: a Catholic gentry family in eighteenth-century Ireland* (Dublin, 1998)

Hayton, D. W., Cruickshanks, Eveline and Handley, Stuart, *The history of parliament: the House of Commons 1690–1715* (5 vols, Cambridge, 2002)

Heal, Felicity and Holmes, Clive, *The gentry in England and Wales, 1500–1700* (Basingstoke, 1994)

Hempton, David, *The church in the long eighteenth century* (London, 2011)

Hempton, David and Hill, Myrtle, *Evangelical Protestantism in Ulster society, 1740–1890* (London, 1992)

Herlihy, Kevin (ed.), *The Irish Dissenting tradition 1650–1750* (Blackrock, Co. Dublin, 1995)

—, *The religion of Irish Dissent 1650–1800* (Blackrock, Co. Dublin, 1996)

—, *The politics of Irish Dissent 1650–1800* (Dublin, 1997)

—, *Propagating the Word of Irish Dissent 1650–1800* (Dublin, 1998)

Hill, George, *An historical account of the MacDonnells of Antrim* (Belfast, 1873)

Hogan, Dáire and Osborough, W. N. (eds), *Brehons, serjeants and attorneys: studies in the history of the Irish legal profession* (Dublin, 1990)

Holmes, A. R., *The shaping of Ulster Presbyterian belief and practice 1770–1840* (Oxford, 2006)

Holmes, Finlay, *The Presbyterian Church in Ireland: a popular history* (Blackrock, Co. Dublin, 2000)

Holmes, Geoffrey, *Augustan England: professions, state and society, 1680–1730* (London, 1982)

Holmes, R. F. G., *Our Irish Presbyterian heritage* ([Belfast], 1985)

Horn, D. B., *A short history of the University of Edinburgh: 1556–1889* (Edinburgh, 1967)

Houston, R. A. and Whyte, I. D. (eds), *Scottish society 1500–1800* (Cambridge, 1989)

Hughes, A. J. and Nolan, William (eds), *Armagh: history and society* (Dublin, 2001)

Hughes, J. L. J. (ed.), *Patentee officers in Ireland 1173–1826: including high sheriffs, 1661–1684 and 1761–1816* (Dublin, 1960)

Hunt, M. R., *The middling sort: commerce, gender, and the family in England, 1680–1780* (London, 1996)

Innes Smith, R. W., *English-speaking students of medicine at the University of Leyden* (Edinburgh, 1932)

Irwin, C. H., *A history of Presbyterianism in Dublin and the south and west of Ireland* (London, 1890)

Jenkins, Philip, *The making of a ruling class: the Glamorgan gentry 1640–1790* (Cambridge, 1983)

Jocelyn, Robert, earl of Roden, *Tollymore: the story of an Irish demesne* (Belfast, 2005)

Johnston-Liik, E. M., *History of the Irish parliament 1692–1800* (6 vols, Belfast, 2002)

—, *MPs in Dublin: companion to the history of parliament 1692–1800* (Belfast, 2006)

Kelly, James, *'That damn'd thing called honour': duelling in Ireland 1570–1860* (Cork, 1995)

—, *Gallows speeches from eighteenth-century Ireland* (Dublin, 2001)

Kelly, James and Clark, Fiona (eds), *Ireland and medicine in the seventeenth and eighteenth centuries* (Farnham, 2010)

Kennedy, Liam and Ollerenshaw, Philip (eds), *Ulster since 1600: politics, economy and society* (Oxford, 2013)

Kenny, Colum, *King's Inns and the kingdom of Ireland: the Irish 'inn of court' 1541–1800* (Blackrock, Co. Dublin, 1992)

Kernohan, J. W., *Rosemary Street Presbyterian Church Belfast: a record of the past 200 years* (Belfast, 1923)

Kerr, John, *Scottish education school and university from early times to 1908* (Cambridge, 1910)

Killen, W. D., *The ecclesiastical history of Ireland: from the earliest period to the present times* (2 vols, London, 1875)

—, *History of congregations of the Presbyterian Church in Ireland* ... (Belfast, 1886)

Kilroy, Phil, *Protestant Dissent and controversy in Ireland 1660–1714* (Cork, 1994)

[Kimber, Edward], *The new peerage* ... (3rd ed., 3 vols, London, 1784)

Lawlor, H. C., *A history of the family of Cairnes or Cairns and its connections* (London, 1906)

Lemmings, David, *Gentlemen and barristers: the Inns of Court and the English bar 1680–1730* (Oxford, 1990)

—, *Professors of the law: barristers and English legal culture in the eighteenth century* (Oxford, 2000)

Leneman, Leah and Mitchison, Rosalind, *Sin in the city: sexuality and social control in urban Scotland 1660–1780* (Edinburgh, 1998)

Lenox-Conyngham, Mina, *An old Ulster house: Springhill and the people who lived in it* (Belfast, 2005)

Lindeboom, G. A., *Herman Boerhaave: the man and his work* (London, 1968)

Lockhart, Audrey, *Some aspects of emigration from Ireland to the North American colonies between 1660 and 1775* (New York, 1976)

Loughrey, Patrick (ed.), *The people of Ireland* (Dublin, 1988)

Loughridge, Adam, *The Covenanters in Ireland: a history of the Reformed Presbyterian Church in Ireland* (Belfast, 1984)

Mackie, J. D., *The University of Glasgow 1451–1951: a short history* (Glasgow, 1954)

Maguire, W. A. (ed.), *Kings in conflict: the revolutionary war in Ireland and its aftermath, 1689–1750* (Belfast, 1990)

Malcomson, A. P. W., *The pursuit of the heiress: aristocratic marriage in Ireland 1740–1840* (Belfast, 2006)

Maxwell, Constantia, *Country and town in Ireland under the Georges* (Dundalk, 1949)

McBride, Ian, *Eighteenth-century Ireland: the isle of slaves* (Dublin, 2009)

McBride, I. R., *Scripture politics: Ulster Presbyterians and Irish radicalism in the late eighteenth century* (Oxford, 1998)

McCall, Hugh, *Ireland and her staple manufactures: being sketches of the history and progress of the linen and cotton trades as well as other details connected with the northern province* (2rd ed., Belfast, 1865)

McCavery, Trevor, *Newtown: a history of Newtownards* (Belfast, 1994)

McClelland, Aiken, *A short history of First Dromara Presbyterian Church* (Belfast, 1963)

McConnell, James, *Fasti of the Irish Presbyterian church*, rev. S. G. McConnell, ed. F. J. Paul and David Stewart (Belfast, 1951)

McCreery, Alexander, *The Presbyterian ministers of Killileagh: a notice of their lives and times* (Belfast, 1875)

McCrie, Thomas (ed.), *Miscellaneous writings, chiefly historical* (Edinburgh, 1841)

McDowell, R. B. and Webb, D. A., *Trinity College Dublin 1592–1952: an academic history* (Cambridge, 1982)

McIvor, J. A., *Popular education in the Irish Presbyterian church* (Dublin, 1969)

McKee, W. J. H., *Aspects of Presbyterianism in Cookstown* (Belfast, 1995)

McMaster, R. K., *Scotch-Irish merchants in Colonial America* ([Belfast], 2009)

McSkimin, Samuel, *The history and antiquities of the county of the town of Carrickfergus* … (Belfast, 1823), ed. E. J. McCrum (new ed., Belfast, 1909)

Miller, K. A., Schrier, Arnold, Boling, B. D. and Doyle, D. N., *Irish immigrants in the land of Canaan: letters and memoirs from Colonial and Revolutionary America, 1675–1815* (Oxford, 2003)

Mingay, G. E., *The gentry: the rise and fall of a ruling class* (London, 1976)

Moody, T. W. and Vaughan, W. E. (eds), *A new history of Ireland: iv: Eighteenth-century Ireland 1691–1800* (Oxford, 1986)

Moore, R. K., *The Moores of Derry and Oakover* (Perth, Australia, 2003)

Mullin, J. E., *The kirk of Ballywillan since the Scottish settlement* (Belfast, 1961)

Mullin, T. H., *The kirk and lands of Convoy since the Scottish settlement* (Belfast, 1969)

—, *Aghadowey: a parish and its linen industry* (Belfast, 1972)

—, *Coleraine in by-gone centuries* (Belfast, 1976)

—, *Coleraine in Georgian times* (Belfast, 1977)

—, *Ulster's historic city Derry, Londonderry* (Coleraine, 1986)

Murphy, E. M. and Roulston, W. J. (eds), *Fermanagh: history and society* (Dublin, 2004)

Ó Baoill, Ruari, *Hidden history below our feet: the archaeological story of Belfast* (Dundonald, 2011)

O'Brien, Gerard (ed.), *Derry and Londonderry: history and society* (Dublin, 1999)

O'Day, Rosemary, *The family and family relationships, 1500–1900: England, France and the United States of America* (Basingstoke, 1994)

—, *The professions in early modern England, 1450–1800: servants of the commonweal* (Harlow, 2000)

O'Laverty, James, *An historical account of the Diocese of Down and Connor, ancient and modern* (5 vols, Dublin, 1878–95)

O'Regan, Philip, *Archbishop William King of Dublin (1650–1729) and the constitution in church and state* (Dublin, 2000)

Parker, E. L., *The history of Londonderry, comprising the towns of Derry and Londonderry, N. H.* (Boston, 1851)

Peacock, Edward, *Index to English speaking students who have graduated at Leyden University* (London, 1883)

Pollard, Mary, *A dictionary of members of the Dublin book trade 1550–1800: based on the records of the Guild of St Luke the Evangelist, Dublin* (London, 2000)

Porter, Classon, *The seven Bruces: Presbyterian ministers in Ireland in six successive generations* (Belfast, 1885)

—, *Witches, warlocks and ghosts* (Belfast, 1885)

—, *Congregational memoirs of the Old Presbyterian Congregation of Larne and Kilwaughter*, ed. and updated by R. H. McIlwrath and J. W. Nelson ([Larne, 1975])

Power, T. P., *Land, politics and society in eighteenth-century Tipperary* (Oxford, 1993)

Prest, Wilfrid (ed.), *The professions in early modern England* (London, 1987)

Purcell, Mark, *The big house library in Ireland: books in Ulster country houses* (Swindon, 2011)

Rankin, Kathleen, *The linen houses of the Lagan Valley: the story of their families* (Belfast, 2002)

Reid, C. I., *The past revisited: a history of Drumbo Presbyterian Church* (Banbridge, 1992)

Reid, H. M. B., *The divinity professors in the University of Glasgow 1640–1903* (Glasgow, 1923)

Reid, J. S., *History of the Presbyterian Church in Ireland ...*, ed. W. D. Killen (2nd ed., 3 vols, London, 1853)

Reilly, E. G. S., *Historical anecdotes of the families of the Boleynes, Careys, Mordaunts, Hamiltons, and Jocelyns, arranged as an elucidation of the genealogical chart at Tollymore Park* (rev. ed., Newry, 1839)

Richardson, E. M., *Long forgotten days (Leading to Waterloo)* (London, 1928)

Robinson, F. J. G. and Wallis, P. J., *Book subscription lists: a revised guide* (Newcastle-upon-Tyne, 1975)

Robinson, P. S., *The Plantation of Ulster: British settlement in an Irish landscape 1600–1670* (Belfast, 1994)

Robson, Robert, *The attorney in eighteenth-century England* (Cambridge, 1959)

Roebuck, Peter, *Yorkshire baronets 1640–1760: families, estates, and fortunes* (Oxford, 1980)

Rosenheim, J. M., *The emergence of a ruling order: English landed society 1650–1750* (London, 1998)

Roulston, W. J., *Researching Scots-Irish ancestors: the essential genealogical guide to early modern Ulster, 1600–1800* (Belfast, 2006)

—, *Restoration Strabane, 1660–1714: economy and society in provincial Ireland* (Dublin, 2007)

Scott, Hew, *Fasti Ecclesiae Scoticanae: the succession of ministers in the Church of Scotland from the Reformation* (new ed., 7 vols, Edinburgh, 1915–28)

Scott, W. R., *Francis Hutcheson: his life, teaching and position in the history of philosophy* (Cambridge, 1900)

Sharpe, J. A., *Early modern England: a social history 1550–1760* (2nd ed., London, 1997)

Simms, J. G., *The Williamite confiscation in Ireland 1690–1703* (London, [1956])

Skoczylas, Anne, *Mr Simson's knotty case: divinity, politics, and due process in early eighteenth-century Scotland* (London, 2001)

Smout, T. C., *Scottish trade on the eve of Union 1660–1707* (Edinburgh, 1963)

Smyth, Damian (ed.), *Francis Hutcheson: a special symposium on the thought, career and influence in Ireland, Scotland and America of the Ulster-Scots philosopher and Dissenter*: suppt. to *Fortnight*, no. 308 (1992)

Spring, Eileen, *Law, land and family: aristocratic inheritance in England, 1300 to 1800* (London, 1993)

Spurr, John, *English Puritanism 1603–1689* (Basingstoke, 1998)

Stevenson, John, *Two centuries of life in Down 1600–1800* (Belfast, 1920)

Stewart, A. T. Q., *A deeper silence: the hidden origins of the United Irishmen* (Belfast, 1993)

—, *The narrow ground: aspects of Ulster 1609–1969* (Belfast, 1999)

Stewart, David, *The history and principles of the Presbyterian Church in Ireland* (Belfast, 1907)

—, *The story of Kilmore Presbyterian Church* (Belfast, 1932)

Stone, Lawrence, *The family, sex and marriage in England 1500–1800* (London, 1977)

Stone, Lawrence and Stone, J. C. F., *An open elite? England 1540–1880* (Oxford, 1984)

Stuart, James, *Historical memoirs of the city of Armagh* ... (Newry, 1819)

Thomas, Avril, *Derry~Londonderry: Irish historic towns atlas* (Dublin, 2005)

Thompson, M. L., *'The meeting-house beside the big bush': a history of Pettigo Presbyterian Church* (Omagh, [2002])

Truxes, T. M., *Irish-American trade, 1660–1783* (Cambridge, 1988)

[Twiss, Richard], *A tour in Ireland in 1775* ... (London, 1776)

Underwood, E. A., *Boerhaave's men: at Leyden and after* (Edinburgh, 1977)

Upton, W. H., *Upton family records: being genealogical collections for an Upton family history* (London, 1893)

Widdess, J. D. H., *A history of the Royal College of Physicians of Ireland 1654–1963* (Edinburgh, 1963)

Wilson, D. A. and Spencer, M. G. (eds), *Ulster Presbyterians in the Atlantic world: religion, politics and identity* (Dublin, 2006)

Witherow, Thomas, *Historical and literary memorials of Presbyterianism in Ireland (1623–1800)* (2 vols, London, 1879–80)

Young, R. M., *Historical notices of old Belfast and its vicinity* (Belfast, 1896)

Young, W. R., *Fighters of Derry: their deeds and descendants* ... (London, 1932)

Articles

Barkley, J. M., 'The evidence of old Irish session-books on the sacrament of the Lord's Supper', *Church Service Society Annual*, no. 22 (May 1952), pp 24–34

—, 'Francis Hutcheson (1694–1746): professor of moral philosophy, University of Glasgow', *Bull. PHSI*, no. 14 (1985), pp 2–14

—, 'Marriage and the Presbyterian tradition', *Ulster Folklife*, xxxix (1993), pp 29–40

Barlow, R. B., 'The career of John Abernethy (1680–1740) father of nonsubscription in Ireland and defender of religious liberty', *Harvard Theological Review*, lxxviii (1985), pp 399–419

Barnard, T. C., 'Reforming Irish manners: the religious societies in Dublin during the 1690s', *Historical Journal*, xxxv (1992), pp 805–38

—, 'Lawyers and the law in later seventeenth-century Ireland', *IHS*, xxviii (1993), pp 256–82

Barnard, Toby, 'Art, architecture, artefacts and ascendancy', *Bullán*, i, no. 2 (1994), pp 17–34

—, 'Learning, the learned and literacy in Ireland, c.1660–1760' in idem, Ó Crónín, Dáibhí and Simms, Katharine (eds), *A miracle of learning: studies in manuscripts and Irish learning* (Aldershot, 1998), pp 209–35

Beckett, J. C., 'William King's administration of the Diocese of Derry, 1691–1703', *Irish Historical Studies*, iv (1944), pp 164–80

'Belfastiensis', 'David Manson', *UJA*, vii (1901), pp 158–9

Boyd, H. A., 'The parish of Finvoy: Diocese of Connor: beside the shining Bann', *Ballymena Observer*, 12 Oct., 19 Oct., 26 Oct., 2 Nov. 1945

Brown, A. G., 'John Abernethy: 1680–1740: scholar and ecclesiast' in O'Brien, Gerard and Roebuck, Peter (eds), *Nine Ulster lives* (Belfast, 1992), pp 126–47

Brown, A. W. G., 'Thomas Jackson: minister of Downpatrick 1700–1708', *Bull. PHSI*, no. 15 (1986), pp 2–13

Brown, K. D., 'Life after death? A preliminary survey of the Irish Presbyterian ministry in the nineteenth century', *Irish Economic and Social History*, xxii (1995), pp 49–63

Brown, Michael, 'Francis Hutcheson and the Molesworth connection', *Eighteenth-Century Ireland*, xiv (1999), pp 62–76

Bruce, William, 'The progress of nonsubscription to creeds', *Christian Moderator*, i (1826), pp 13–16, 33–7, 68–73, 127–32, 152–7, 192–6, 225–9, 271–4, 309–14, 353–61, 408–12, 427–33; ii (1827), pp 11–15, 49–53, 110–14, 145–8, 193–8, 283–8, 306–12, 348–54

Calwell, H. G., 'The kirk session of Broadisland (Ballycarry) Co. Antrim in the eighteenth century', *Non-Subscribing Presbyterian*, no. 866 (Jan. 1979), pp 3–7

Carson, J. T., 'John Howe: chaplain to Lord Masserene [sic] at Antrim Castle, 1671–1677', *Bull. PHSI*, no. 7 (1977), pp 11–16

—, 'From Thomas Cartwright to John Howe; some Puritans who came among us', *Bull. PHSI*, xix (1990), pp 3–28

Connolly, S. J., 'Ulster Presbyterians: religion, culture, and politics, 1660–1850' in Blethen, H. T. and Wood, C. W. (eds), *Ulster and North America: transatlantic perspectives on the Scotch-Irish* (Tuscaloosa, 1997), pp 24–40

Crawford, W. H., 'The origins of the linen industry in north Armagh and the Lagan Valley', *Ulster Folklife*, xvii (1971), pp 42–51

—, 'Economy and society in south Ulster in the eighteenth century', *Clogher Record*, viii (1975), pp 241–58

—, 'Landlord-tenant relations in Ulster, 1609–1820', *Irish Economic and Social History*, ii (1975), pp 5–21

—, 'The Ulster Irish in the eighteenth century', *Ulster Folklife*, xxviii (1982), pp 24–32

Crossle, Philip, 'Gordons in County Down', *Banbridge Chronicle*, 12 & 19 Mar. 1913

Cullen, K. J., Whatley, C. A. and Young, Mary, 'King William's ill years: new evidence on the impact of scarcity and harvest failure during the crisis of the 1690s on Tayside', *Scottish Historical Review*, lxxxv (2006), pp 250–76

Cullen, L. M., 'Population trends in eighteenth-century Ireland', *Economic and Social Review*, vi (1975), pp 149–65

Daultrey, Stuart, Dickson, David and Ó Gráda, Cormac, 'Eighteenth century Irish population: new perspectives from old sources', *Journal of Economic History*, xli (1981), pp 601–28

Dickson, David, 'In search of the old Irish poor law' in Mitchison, Rosalind and Roebuck, Peter (eds), *Economy and society in Scotland and Ireland, 1500–1939* (Edinburgh, 1988), pp 149–59

Dickson, David, Ó Gráda, Cormac and Daultry, Stuart, 'Hearth tax, household size and Irish population change 1672–1821', *Proceedings of the Royal Irish Academy*, lxxxii (1982), sect. C, pp 125–81

Drennan, A. S., 'On the identification of the first Belfast printed book', *The Library*, 7th ser., i (2000), pp 193–6

Dudley, Rowena, 'The Dublin parishes and the poor: 1660–1740', *Archivium Hibernicum*, liii (1999), pp 80–94

Durand, J. F., 'The history of forestry in Ireland' in Nelson, E. C. and Brady, Aidan, *Irish gardening and horticulture* (Dublin, 1979), pp 205–15

ffolliott, Rosemary, 'Irish social customs of genealogical importance', *Irish Ancestor*, x, no. 1 (1978), pp 18–23

Fleming, D. A., 'Diversions of the people: sociability among the orders of early eighteenth-century Ireland', *Eighteenth-Century Ireland*, xvii (2002), pp 99–111

Foley, Dermot, 'Presbyterianism in Drogheda, 1652–1827', *Journal of the County Louth Archaeological and Historical Society*, xxv (2002), pp 179–88

Gailey, Alan, 'The Scots element in north Irish popular culture', *Ethnologia Europaea*, viii (1975), pp 2–22

Gillespie, Raymond, 'The Presbyterian revolution in Ulster, 1660–1690' in Shiels, W. J. and Wood, Diana (eds), *The churches, Ireland and the Irish* ... (Oxford, 1989), pp 159–70

—, 'The social world of County Down in the seventeenth century' in Proudfoot, L. J. and Nolan, William (ed.), *Down: history and society* (Dublin, 1997), pp 141–58

—, 'Making Belfast, 1600–1750' in S. J. Connolly (ed.), *Belfast 400: people, place and history* (Liverpool, 2012), pp 123–59

[Gordon, Alexander], 'Congregational memoirs – Templepatrick', *Disciple*, i (1881), pp 42–5, 79–84, 110–14, 136–40, 171–5, 208–13, 236–40, 268–72, 302–4, 332–7, 363–8; ii (1882), pp 9–13, 44–8, 76–80, 108–12, 135–40, 170–5, 205–8, 234–9, 266–72, 299–304, 322–8, 359–64

—, 'Belfast list of ministers. First Presbyterian Church', *Disciple*, iii (1883), pp 82–4

—, 'Rademon congregation: Historical sketch', *Disciple*, iii (1883), pp 137–42

Greeves, J. R. R., 'Two Irish printing families', *Proceedings and Reports of the Belfast Natural History and Philosophical Society*, 2nd ser., iv (1950–5), pp 38–44

Griffin, Patrick, 'Defining the limits of Britishness: the "new" British history and the meaning of the Revolution Settlement in Ireland for Ulster's Presbyterians', *JBS*, xxxix (2000), pp 263–87

Hamilton, Bernice, 'The medical professions in the eighteenth century', *Economic History Review*, new ser., iv (1951), pp 141–69

Hayton, David, 'Moral reform and country politics in the late seventeenth-century House of Commons', *Past & Present*, no. 128 (1990), pp 48–91

Hayton, D. W., 'Presbyterians and the confessional state: the sacramental test as an issue in Irish politics, 1704–1780', *Bull. PHSI*, xxvi (1997), pp 11–31

Hill, George, 'Gleanings in family history from the Antrim coast', *UJA*, viii (1860), pp 27–44, 196–210; ix (1861/2), pp 1–16

Hincks, T. D., 'Notices of William Bruce, and of his contemporaries and friends, Hutcheson, Abernethy, Duchal, and others', *Christian Teacher*, new ser., v (1843), pp 72–92

Holmes, A. R., 'The Protestant clergies in the European world' in Brown, S. J. and Tackett, Timothy (eds), *The Cambridge history of Christianity*, vii: *Enlightenment, reawakening and revolution 1660–1815* (Cambridge, 2006), pp 109–27

Holmes, Geoffrey, 'The professions and social change in England, 1680–1730', *Proceedings of the British Academy*, lxv (1979), pp 313–54

Jevons, F. R. 'Boerhaave's biochemistry', *Medical History*, vi (1962), pp 343–62

Kelly, James, 'Harvests and hardship: famine and scarcity in Ireland in the late 1720s', *Studia Hibernica*, xxvi (1992), pp 65–105

Kernohan, J. W., 'Historic Ulster homes: castles and builders: Ballygally and the Shaws: Macartneys of Lissanoure', *Belfast Telegraph*, 27 Oct. 1919

—, 'Some Ulster castles: historic sketch of Upton', *Belfast Telegraph*, 29 Oct. 1919

Kirkham, Graeme, 'Literacy in north-west Ulster, 1680–1860' in Daly, Mary and Dickson, David (eds), *The origins of popular literacy in Ireland: language change and educational development 1700–1920* (Dublin, 1990), pp 73–96

—, 'The origins of mass emigration from Ireland' in Kearney, Richard (ed.), *Migrations: the Irish at home and abroad* (Dublin, 1990), pp 81–90

—, '"No more to be got off the cat but the skin": management, landholding and economic change on the Murray of Broughton estate, 1670–1755' in Nolan, William, Ronayne, Liam, and Dunlevy, Mairead (eds), *Donegal: history and society* (Dublin, 1995), pp 357–80

Kirkham, Graeme, 'Ulster emigration to North America, 1680–1720' in Blethen, H. T. and Wood, C. W. (ed.), *Ulster and North America: transatlantic perspectives on the Scotch-Irish* (Tuscaloosa, 1997), pp 76–117

Kirkpatrick, Laurence, 'The ideal and implementation of theological education', *Bull. PHSI*, xxxii (2008), pp 31–41

Latimer, W. T., 'The old session-book of Templepatrick Presbyterian Church', *JRSAI*, xxv (1895), pp 130–4; xxxi (1901), pp 162–75, 259–72

Lawlor, H. C., 'Historical sketch of old Glenarm', *Weekly Telegraph*, 11, 18, 25 Mar., 1, 8, 15 Apr. 1911

—, 'Rise of the linen merchants in the eighteenth century', *Irish and International Fibres and Fabrics Journal*, vii (1941), no. 7, pp 8–9, no. 8, pp 11, 28, no. 9, p. 6, no. 11, pp 8–9; viii (1942), no. 1, p. 16, no. 2, pp 44–5, no. 3, p. 68, no. 8, p. 196; ix (1942), p. 9

Lucas, Paul, 'A collective biography of students and barristers of Lincoln's Inn, 1680–1804: a study in the "aristocratic resurgence" of the eighteenth century', *Journal of Modern History*, xlvi (1974), pp 227–61

Macafee, W. A., 'The movement of British settlers into Ulster during the seventeenth century', *Familia*, ii, no. 8 (1992), pp 94–111

Macafee, William, 'The colonisation of the Maghera region of south Derry during the seventeenth and eighteenth centuries', *Ulster Folklife*, xxiii (1977), pp 70–91

Macafee, William and Morgan, Valerie, 'Population in Ulster, 1660–1760' in Roebuck, Peter (ed.), *Plantation to Partition: essays in Ulster history in honour of J. L. McCracken* (Belfast, 1981), pp 46–63

—, 'Mortality in Magherafelt, County Derry, in the early eighteenth century reappraised', *Irish Historical Studies*, xxiii (1982), pp 50–60

Magennis, Eoin, 'Belturbet, Cahans and two Presbyterian revolutions in south Ulster, 1660–1770', *Seanchas Ardmhacha: Journal of the Armagh Diocesan Historical Society*, xxi-xxii (2007/8), pp 129–48

Maguire, William, 'The Blackwoods of Ballyleidy' in Ulster Architectural Heritage Society, *Clandeboye* (Antrim, 1985), pp 35–43

Marshall, J. J., 'David Manson, schoolmaster in Belfast', *UJA*, xiv (1908), pp 59–72

McBride, Ian, 'Presbyterians in the penal era', *Bull. PHSI*, xxvii (1998–2000), pp 14–28

McCann, Wesley, 'Patrick Neill and the origins of Belfast printing' in Isaac, Peter (ed.), *Six centuries of the provincial book trade in Britain* (Winchester, 1990), pp 125–38

McLachlan, Herbert, 'The Irish academies', *Transactions of the Unitarian Historical Society*, vi (1936) pp 91–102

Meenan, James and Clarke, Desmond, 'The RDS 1731–1981' in idem (eds), *The Royal Dublin Society 1731–1981* (Dublin, 1981), pp 1–55

Mijers, Esther, 'Irish students in the Netherlands, 1650–1750', *Archivium Hibernicum*, lix (2005), pp 66–78

Mooney, Tighernan and White, Fiona, 'The gentry's winter season' in David Dickson (ed.), *The gorgeous mask: Dublin, 1700–1850* (Dublin, 1987), pp 1–16

Mor, The MacCarthy, 'The Fergusons of Belfast: a short account of the ancestry of H.R.H. the Duchess of York', *Familia*, ii, no. 2 (1986), pp 15–22

Mortimer, Ian, 'Diocesan licensing and medical practitioners in south-west England, 1660–1780', *Medical History*, xlviii (2004), pp 49–68

Mullin, T. H., 'Old customs and practices in the Irish Presbyterian church', *Bull. PHSI*, xxix (2004–5), pp 20–6

O'Dowd, Mary, 'Women and paid work in rural Ireland, c.1500–1800' in Bernadette Whelan (ed.), *Women and paid work in Ireland, 1500–1930* (Dublin, 2000), pp 13–29

Paterson, T. G. F., 'A County Armagh mendicant badge inscribed "Shankill poor 1699"', *UJA*, x (1947), pp 110–14

Pike, C. E., 'The origin of the regium donum', *Transactions of the Royal Historical Society*, 3rd ser., iii (1909), pp 255–69

Porter, Classon, 'Congregational memoirs: Ballycarry (or Broadisland) congregation', *Christian Unitarian*, ii (1864), pp 15–20, 49–55, 78–86, 121–30, 153–62, 188–95, 221–7

—, 'Congregational memoirs. No. IV.–Cairncastle', *Christian Unitarian*, iv (1866), pp 115–22, 150–5, 190–7, 223–30, 260–7, 294–300, 332–8, 366–76

Roberts, R. S., 'The personnel and practice of medicine in Tudor and Stuart England', *Medical History*, vi (1962), pp 363–82; viii (1964), pp 217–34

Roulston, William, 'The origins of the Reformed Presbyterian Church of Ireland with some comments on its records', *Familia*, no. 24 (2008), pp 86–109

Seaby, W. A. and Paterson, T. G. F., 'Ulster beggars' badges', *UJA*, 3rd ser., xxxiii (1970), pp 95–106

Simms, J. G., 'The making of a penal law (2 Anne, c. 6), 1703–4', *IHS*, xii (1960), pp 105–18

Smith, L. W., 'Reassessing the role of the family: women's medical care in eighteenth-century England', *Social History of Medicine*, xvi, no. 3 (2003), pp 327–42

Smith, W. S., 'Early register of the Old Presbyterian Congregation of Antrim', *UJA*, v (1899), pp 180–90

Smout, T. C., Landsman, N. C. and Devine, T. M., 'Scottish emigration in the seventeenth and eighteenth centuries' in Canny, Nicholas (ed.), *Europeans on the move: studies on European migration, 1500–1800* (Oxford, 1994), pp 76–112

Steers, A. D. G., 'Samuel Haliday (1685–1739): travelling scholar, court lobbyist, and non-subscribing divine' in Ruth Savage (ed.), *Philosophy and religion in Enlightenment Britain* (Oxford, 2012), pp 112–40

Steers, David, 'Samuel Haliday (1685–1739)', *Transactions of the Unitarian Historical Society*, xxii, no. 3 (2001), pp 275–89

—, '"The very life-blood of nonconformity of education": the Killyleagh Philosophy School, County Down', *Familia*, no. 28 (2012), pp 61–79

Stewart, David, 'Irish Presbyterian seminaries', *The Witness*, 1, 18 & 25 Mar., 1 Apr. 1910

Stewart, M. A., 'John Abernethy (1680–1740): a reappraisal', *Bull. PHSI*, xxxii (2008), pp 11–20

Stothers, James, 'Presbyterians and the Irish language', *Bull. PHSI*, xxxi (2007), pp 30–46

Swanzy, H. B., 'Notes and queries: the Eccles family', *UJA*, ix (1903), p. 144

Tenison, C. M., 'The old Dublin bankers', *Journal of the Cork Historical and Archaeological Society*, iii (1894), pp 120–1, 194–5, 221–2

Thomas, Roger, 'The Non-Subscription Controversy among Dissenters in 1719: the Salters' Hall debate', *Journal of Ecclesiastical History*, iv (1953), pp 162–86

Tosh, R. S., 'Presbyterian worship through the ages', *Bull. PHSI*, xxviii (2001–3), pp 1–19

Van Strien, Kees and De Withlaan, Witte, 'A medical student at Leiden and Paris: William Sinclair 1736–38', *Proceedings of the Royal College of Physicians of Edinburgh*, xxv (1995), pp 294–304, 487–94, 639–51

Vann, Barry, 'Presbyterian social ties and mobility in the Irish Sea culture area, 1610–1690', *Journal of Historical Sociology*, xviii (2005), pp 227–54

Whyte, Ian, 'Ministers and society in Scotland 1560–c1800' in MacLean, Colin and Veitch, Kenneth (eds), *Scottish life and society: religion* (Edinburgh, 2006), pp 433–51

Woodward, Donald, 'The Anglo-Irish livestock trade of the seventeenth century', *Irish Historical Studies*, xviii (1973), pp 489–523

Newspapers and Periodicals

Belfast Newsletter (1737–)

Irish Presbyterian (new ser.)

McComb's Presbyterian Almanack and Christian Remembrance (1840–89)

Presbyterian Historical Society of Ireland Annual Report (1907–56)

Electronic

'Dissenting academies online: database and encyclopedia', Dr Williams's Centre for Dissenting Studies (http://www.english.qmul.ac.uk/drwilliams/portal.html) (12 Jan. 2013)

'The Inner Temple admissions database' (http://www.innertemplearchives.org.uk/index.asp) (28 June 2013)

Innes-Smith, R. W., 'English-speaking students of medicine at continental universities', intro. Swan, H. T. (http://www.rcpe.ac.uk/library/read/people/english-students) (12 Jan. 2013)

Matthew, H. C. G. and Harrison, B. H. (eds), *Oxford dictionary of national biography: from the earliest times to the year 2000* (http://www.oxforddnb.com) (12 Jan. 2013).

McGuire, James and Quinn, James (eds), *Dictionary of Irish biography* (Cambridge, 2009) (http://dib.cambridge.org) (12 Jan. 2013)

Robinson, F. J. G. and Robinson, J. M., *Irish book subscription lists, 1700–1850* (CD-ROM, [Great Britain]: Romulus Press Ltd, 2004)

Theses

Allen, Robert, 'The principle of nonsubscription to creeds and confessions of faith as exemplified in Irish Presbyterian history' (2 vols, Ph.D. thesis, QUB, 1944)

Aubertin-Potter, N. A. R., 'Social mobility, marriage and kinship among some gentry and yeoman families of Wantage Hundred, c.1522–c.1670' (Ph.D. thesis, Oxford Brookes Univ., 1994)

Barbour, W. M., 'The ministry of the Presbyterian Church in Ireland' (Ph.D. thesis, QUB, 1965)

Barkley, J. M., 'A history of the ruling eldership in Irish Presbyterianism' (2 vols, M.A. thesis, QUB, 1952)

Beaumont, D. M., 'The gentry of The King's and Queen's Counties: Protestant landed society, 1690–1760' (2 vols, Ph.D. thesis, TCD, 1999)

Bishop, I. M., 'The education of Ulster students at Glasgow University during the eighteenth century' (M.A. thesis, QUB, 1987)

Brown, A. W. G., 'Irish Presbyterian theology in the early eighteenth century' (Ph.D. thesis, QUB, 1977)

Brown, L. T., 'The Presbyterians of Cavan and Monaghan: an immigrant community in south Ulster over three centuries' (2 vols, Ph.D. thesis, QUB, 1986)

Browne, R. M., 'Kirk and community: Ulster Presbyterian society, 1640–1740' (M.Phil. thesis, QUB, 1999)

Conway, K. P., 'The Presbyterian ministry of Ulster in the eighteenth and nineteenth centuries: a prosopographical study' (Ph.D. thesis, QUB, 1997)

Crawford, W. H., 'Economy and society in eighteenth century Ulster' (Ph.D. thesis, QUB, 1982)

Fitzgerald, P. D., 'Poverty and vagrancy in early modern Ireland 1540–1770' (Ph.D. thesis, QUB, 1994)

Hayton, D. W., 'Ireland and the English ministers, 1707–16. A study in the formulation and working of government policy in the early eighteenth century' (D.Phil. thesis, Oxford Univ., 1975)

Lockington, J. W., 'An analysis of the practice and procedure of Irish Presbyterianism' (Ph.D. thesis, QUB, 1980)

Maynard, Hazel, 'Irish membership of the English Inns of Court, 1660–1699: lawyers, litigation and the legal profession' (Ph.D. thesis, University College, Dublin, 2000)

McMillan, William, 'The Subscription Controversy in Irish Presbyterianism from the Plantation of Ulster to the present day; with reference to political implications in the late eighteenth century' (2 vols, M.A. thesis, Univ. of Manchester, 1959)

Middleton, K. M., 'Religious revolution and social crisis in southwest Scotland and Ulster, 1687–1714' (Ph.D. thesis, TCD, 2010)

Mijers, Esther, 'Scotland and the United Provinces, c.1680–1730: a study in intellectual and educational relations' (Ph.D. thesis, St. Andrews Univ., 2002)

Nelson, J. W., 'The Belfast Presbyterians 1670–1830: an analysis of their political and social interests' (Ph.D. thesis, QUB, 1985)

Richey, R. A., 'Landed society in mid-eighteenth century County Down' (Ph.D. thesis, QUB, 2000)

Sherry, John, 'Scottish commercial and political networks in Ulster during the reigns of King William III and Queen Anne, 1688–1714' (Ph.D. thesis, Univ. of Ulster, 2009)

Steers, A. D. G., ' "New Light" thinking and non-subscription amongst Protestant Dissenters in England and Ireland in the early 18th century and their relationship with Glasgow University and Scotland' (Ph.D. thesis, Glasgow Univ., 2006)

Vann, B. A., '"Space of time or distance of place": Presbyterian diffusion in south-western Scotland and Ulster, 1603–1690' (Ph.D. thesis, Glasgow Univ., 2006)

Warnock, S. S., 'Ulster emigration to Colonial America 1718–1730: the formative years' (M.A. thesis, National University of Ireland, Galway, 1997)

Whytock, J. C., 'The history and development of Scottish theological education and training, Kirk and Secession (c.1560–c.1850)' (Ph.D. thesis, University of Wales, Lampeter, 2001)

Unpublished or typescript material

Craig, Frances, 'The Adair family: proprietors of the estates of Ballymena from 1626 to 1988' ([Clough, 1991]) (typescript in N.E. Area Local Studies Collection, Ballymena Central Library)

Frazer, William, 'History of the General (Presbyterian) Fund for the south and west of Ireland, instituted in 1710' (1862) (typescript in PHS)

Hall, Thomas, 'The history of Presbyterianism in east Cavan: and a small portion of Meath and Monaghan' (typescript in Gamble Library, Union Theological College, Belfast)

Purcell, Mark, 'Springhill: County Londonderry' (2000)

Index